THE CLASH
OF VALUES

THE CLASH
OF VALUES

Islamic Fundamentalism
Versus Liberal Nationalism

MANSOOR MOADDEL

Columbia University Press
New York

Columbia University Press
Publishers Since 1893
New York   Chichester, West Sussex
cup.columbia.edu

Library of Congress Cataloging-in-Publication Data
Names: Moaddel, Mansoor, author.
Title: The clash of values : Islamic fundamentalism versus liberal
    nationalism / Mansoor Moaddel.
Description: New York : Columbia University Press, [2020] |
    Includes bibliographical references and index.
Identifiers: LCCN 2019026382 (print) | LCCN 2019026383 (ebook) |
    ISBN 9780231193825 (cloth)| 9780231193832 (paperback) |
    ISBN 9780231550529 (ebook)
Subjects: LCSH: Islam and politics. | Islamic fundamentalism. |
    Social values—Arab countries. | Nationalism—Arab countries. |
    Liberalism—Arab countries. | Arab countries—Social conditions—21st century.
Classification: LCC BP173.7 M62 2020 (print) | LCC BP173.7 (ebook) |
    DDC 303.3/72091767—dc23
LC record available at https://lccn.loc.gov/2019026382
LC ebook record available at https://lccn.loc.gov/2019026383

Columbia University Press books are printed
on permanent and durable acid-free paper.
Printed in the United States of America

Cover design: Martin Hinze

Dedicated to:
The Girls of Revolution Street, Tehran, Iran ✑

CONTENTS

ACKNOWLEDGMENTS

Between 1977 and 2018, a series of nonviolent mass movements for democratic change transpired in the Middle East and North Africa, each one appearing more powerful than the previous. Among the most remarkable were, first, the movement of Iranians for a more transparent, democratic, and peaceful government that brought about the reformists' success vis-à-vis the fundamentalists in the 1997 presidential elections and then the 2009 Green Movement, which was not only more massive but also quite daring in challenging the absolutist power of the ruling cleric in the country. Two years later the region experienced a sequence of upheavals in virtually every Arab country. Aptly labeled the Arab Spring, these movements managed to unseat entrenched dictators in Egypt, Libya, Tunisia, and Yemen in 2011. Finally, in 2018, Iran experienced the outbreak of nationwide demonstrations against both the emaciated reformist movement and political Islam, displaying favorable attitudes toward the formation of a secular liberal government.

Analyzing the data from full-scale cross-national and longitudinal surveys, this book assesses the extent to which these movements reflected, and are reinforced by, the profound changes in people's value orientations toward some of the most important principles of social organization and weather these changes signified the decline of Islamic fundamentalism and the rise of liberal nationalism in the Middle East and North Africa. To make this assessment possible, many individuals, organizations, and foundations contributed to the research projects that conceptualized the key constructs related to human values, measured these constructs through a series of survey questions, and collected data from nationally representative samples of respondents in seven countries: Egypt, Iraq, Lebanon, Pakistan, Saudi Arabia, Tunisia, and Turkey. I would like to begin by thanking the members of the research team, for which I was the principal investigator, at the Institute for Social Research (ISR), University of Michigan: Arland Thornton (co-principal investigator), Stuart Karabenick, Linda Young-Demarco (project manager), Julie de Jong (research associate), and Judy Baughn as well as by expressing gratitude to the ISR sampling experts Steven G. Heeringa and Zeina Mneimneh for their assistance and advice. Many thanks also to Gaye Bugenhagen, Karina Havrilla, Zinia Garcia, and other staff at the Sociology Department, University of Maryland, for their administrative support and hard work to ensure the department's smooth functioning; Kristine Ajrouch, Brian Anderson, Caryn Charter, Susan Campbell, and, with fond memories, the late Alethea Helbig from Eastern Michigan University; Matthias Koenig, University of Göttingen, Germany; and many individuals in the survey research firms in the Middle East and North Africa that were involved in the collection of empirical data: Abdul-Hamid Abdul Latif, director of the Egyptian Research and Training Center (ERTC), and Fatma El-Zanaty, president of El-Zanaty & Associates, Egypt; Munqith Dagher, chairman of the Independent Institute for Administration and Civil Society Studies (IIACSS), Iraq; Jean Kors, managing director of the International Center for Organizational Development (ICOD), Lebanon; Farooq Tanwir, University of Agriculture, Pakistan; Majid Jahangir and Tony Proudian, Pan Arab Research Center, Saudi Arabia; Mohamed Ikbal Elloumi, general manager of ELKA Consulting, Tunisia; and Caglayan Isik and Mert Teoman, Frekans Research, Turkey.

Foremost, I am grateful to the National Science Foundation for its continued support of my cross-national survey projects over the years in Egypt, Iran, Iraq, Jordan, Morocco, and Saudi Arabia and of the second wave of the panel survey in Egypt and Turkey (NSF Grant ID 1458953, 0748835, 0701376, 0522174, 0433773, 0338077, 0242861, 0139908); the Ford Foundation for contributing to the 2001 survey in Egypt; the World Values Survey Association and the Banks of Sweden Tercentenary Foundation; the Office of Naval Research (N00014-14-1-0579, N00014-09-1-0985) for its generous grant; the Air Force Office of Scientific Research (AFOSR); United States Africa Command (AFRICOM); the Jack Shand Research Grant and the Society for Scientific Study of Religion; the Max Planck Institute for the Study of Religious and Ethnic Diversity and University of Göttingen in Germany; and Economic Research Forum, Cairo, Egypt, which together provided funding for cross-national and longitudinal surveys in Egypt, Iraq, Lebanon, Pakistan, Saudi Arabia, Tunisia, and Turkey. I am also indebted to Gary Kollmorgen and Ivy Estabrook from the Office of Naval Research; Stacy Faulkenberry from AFRICOM; John Boiney and Barry Costa from MITRE Corp.; retired Captain Dylan Schmorrow, assistant director,

Human Systems, Office of the Secretary of Defense; and Major Lyle (Lucky) LaCroix, governance officer, CETCOM Iraq, for their support and advice.

Comments on the manuscript from Arland Thornton, Val Moghaddam, and Sohrab Behdad, as well as from anonymous reviewers for Columbia University Press, are gratefully acknowledged, and special thanks go to Erick I. Schwartz, editorial director, Lowell Frye, associate editor, and Marielle T. Poss, director of editing, design, and production, and Martin Hinze and Julia Kushnirsky for the cover design at Columbia University Press, and Ben Kolstad, editorial services manager, and Sherry Goldbecker copyeditor at Cenveo publisher services. Sherry Goldbecker's editorial work was thorough and effective; she left no stone unturned. I am grateful to Han Kleman, my research assistant, for helping in data analysis and to my students in classes on Researching the Middle East and Ideology and Social Conditions in the Making of Terrorism that I taught at the University of Maryland. Their questions and comments not only helped me improve and clarify the ideas presented in this book but also made my experience at the university truly enjoyable. I would like to thank Elizabeth (Izzy) Petty and Patricia (Trish) Petty for their hospitality at their house in Maine in the summer of 2018 and 2019; its relaxing atmosphere put mind at ease, and I was able to make substantial progress in completing this book. Finally, I am grateful to my wife, Marjan; my children, Armin, Nilufar, and Payvand; and my grandchildren, Oliver and Reza, for their love and support. Needless to say, none of these individuals or institutions bears responsibilities for the shortcomings, errors, and opinions expressed in this book.

This book is inspired by the people in the Middle East and North Africa who have courageously participated in the struggle for liberty, equality, inclusion, and economic prosperity and, in particular, by the bravery and resoluteness of the young Iranian women who stood up on a utility box on a sidewalk in Tehran, took off their headscarves, and turned that symbol of female oppression into the banner of liberation. It is to the Girls of Revolution Street in Tehran that I dedicate this book.

THE CLASH
OF VALUES

INTRODUCTION

People and Their Issues

The Puzzle of Politics

The political conditions of the contemporary Middle East and North Africa appear complicated and therefore hard to grasp. This book attempts to reduce this complexity by highlighting the opposition between Islamic fundamentalism and liberal nationalism as the key dimension of ideological warfare and political conflict currently transpiring in the region. This book brings empirical evidence on the depth and breadth of the clash of fundamentalist and liberal values among members of the ordinary public in seven countries—Egypt, Iraq, Lebanon, Pakistan, Saudi Arabia, Tunisia, and Turkey—and shows that the factors that weaken fundamentalism also strengthen liberal values among individuals and across these countries, and vice versa. In doing so, this book proposes that the future political development of the region lies in how this conflict is resolved. This future will be determined by whether such liberal values as expressive individualism, gender equality, secular politics, religious tolerance, and national identity are turned into permanent features of the social order or are undermined as a result of the fundamentalists' rigorous patronage of patriarchy, male supremacy, gender segregation, Islamic authoritarian government, religious intolerance, in-group or sectarian solidarity, and hostility toward outsiders—the West, in particular.

This conflict is all the more significant and intense under the current conditions of political transition set in motion by the Arab Spring, opposition to Turkish President Recep Tayyip Erdoğan's authoritarian rule, and the liberal-oriented nationalist movements of Iranians, especially Iranian women, against the country's religious absolutist regime. Alternative discourses signifying the third way were tried and found wanting. They are all gone. Pan-Arab nationalism, once mustering the loyalty of millions and used to justify military coups in Egypt, Syria, Iraq, and Libya from 1952 to 1969, now has little appeal to the Arab publics. Various forms of anti-American or anti-European state socialism, ethnic nationalism, Marxist-Leninist parties, and modernizing authoritarianism of the twentieth century are no longer the popular, galvanizing ideologies of the masses. Recent attempts at Islamic democracy in Egypt, Iran, and Turkey have reached a dead end. In Egypt, the Islamization efforts of President Mohamed Morsi (of the Muslim Brothers) prompted secular political parties to form the National Salvation Front and launch mass protests against what they perceived to be an impending religious dictatorship. The popular uprising was, alas, hijacked by an equally ineffectual and despotic military. What appears to have remained in the social arena of conflict is an intense collision between liberal nationalism and the idea of equality of all individuals, on the one hand, and Islamic fundamentalism and the idea of patriarchy, a disciplinarian God, religious exclusivity, and religious intolerance, on the other.

Among the various discourses that were produced in the Middle East and North Africa as alternatives to liberal nationalism, Islamic fundamentalism appears to have been the most resilient. While the social context varies from one country to the next, the shift in the dominant oppositional discourse toward radical Islamism began in the late 1960s. However, the episode of Islamic fundamentalism began in earnest with the nearly simultaneous occurrences in 1979 of three disparate events—the Iranian Revolution, the Soviet invasion of Afghanistan, and the Muslim militants' seizure of the Grand Mosque in Saudi Arabia—and has now been concluded in the decadent Shia fundamentalist regime in Iran and the Sunni extremism of the Islamic State in Iraq and Syria (ISIS) of late. This forty-year episode conjures up a complex picture of a region dense with despotic rulers, corruption in high places, economic inequality and poverty, reckless hatred and disregard for human life perpetrated by Muslim terrorists and sectarian warfare, maltreatment of women and religious minorities, and contemptuous and destructive foreign interventions. In some countries, the movements that managed to unseat the entrenched dictators in recent years failed to establish transparent and responsive governments. In Egypt, the Arab Spring ended in the resurrection of the structure of the previous regime and the reconstitution of military-backed authoritarian rule under President Abdel Fattah el-Sisi, a former general who overthrew the unpopular presidency of Mohamed Morsi (June 30, 2012–July 3, 2013). In Yemen, the removal of Ali Abdullah Saleh resulted in Shia-Sunni sectarian strife; in Libya, the overthrow and execution of Colonel Muammar Qaddafi turned the country into a theater of violence between armed militias vying for political power; and in Syria, peaceful protests degenerated into tragic sectarian conflicts reinforced by foreign interventions, in which over 500,000 perished and millions were displaced or turned into refugees in the neighboring countries or Europe. In Turkey, the hope for Islamic democracy was dashed as President Erdoğan turned increasingly authoritarian during his tenure as the prime minister (2003–2014). His election as the president of the republic in 2014 complicated the prospect for democracy in the country. In Pakistan, following the assassination of Prime Minister Liaquat Ali Khan in 1951, political power vacillated between military dictatorship and elected government. Since the 1977 coup by General Zia ul-Haq, an expanding Islamic fundamentalism has been vying for political and intellectual control of the country. In Tunisia, the Islamization policies of the ruling Ennahdha (Islamic Revival) Party and the killing of secular politicians by Muslim extremists resulted in the formation of the Nidaa Tounes (Voice of Tunisia)—a front that united secularists, trade unionists, liberals, and others. Unlike in Egypt, the conflict was resolved at the ballot box, where Nidaa Tounes won a plurality of seats in the 2014 parliamentary elections, paving the way for a peaceful transition to democracy.

What seems clear is that the incumbent authoritarian regimes have not been able to resolve their countries' economic difficulties and combat Muslim extremism without persistently resorting to repressive means, which have thus far proven ineffective. Nor is there a clear outlook as to how the ruling elite in the region—most notably, in Egypt, Iran, Iraq, Pakistan, Saudi Arabia, and Turkey—will be able to resolve the economic and political difficulties they face in terms of the intellectual categories they know. It is also clear that, despite considerable variation in the forms of government across the countries in the region, the structure of power in essence resembles that of a monarchy, where the head of the state and his cronies are in full control not only of all the instruments of power but of a substantial section of the national economy as well. If Foucault's assertion that Western political modernity is wanting because "we still have not cut off the head of the king" borders on hyperbole, it is literally true in the political context of the contemporary Middle East and North Africa. Iranians in 1979 overthrew the shah and jubilantly declared that they successfully had ended the monarchy, which they thought was the source of all evils, but in reality, the shah was replaced by a more despotic and ferocious totalitarian monarch-cum-ayatollah, who reconstituted the monarchical power in the divine. The failure of a stable, transparent, and democratic government in these countries may be a result of the confluence of such cross-nationally variable factors as a weak economy, political corruption, religious extremism and sectarian solidarity, outgroup hostility, the military desire for power, and foreign intervention that either shaped politics in an authoritarian direction or threw the country into a maelstrom of sectarian warfare.

More fundamentally, however, this failure may also be an outcome of the absence of a liberal democratic discourse as the dominant framework for political action. Discourse in fact matters—and matters a lot in bringing into relief a new pattern of historical growth. For example, the formation of secular states in Egypt, Iran, and Turkey between 1920 and 1925 was preceded by the decline of the traditional-cum-Islamic conception of government and the spread of liberal nationalist ideas in these countries in the nineteenth and early twentieth centuries; the formation of pan-Arab nationalist governments in Egypt, Iraq, Syria, and Libya between 1952 and 1969 was the political outcome of the ideology of pan-Arab nationalism—a belief system that rested on the singularity of the Arabs as a people and a single nation—which was formulated by Arab intellectual leaders Sati al-Husri and Darwish al-Miqdadi decades earlier; and the Islamic regimes in Afghanistan, Iran, and elsewhere came to be in 1979 and thereafter as a result of the effective onslaught on secular discourse and the propagation of political Islam by such Muslim ideologues–cum–political activists as Abu Ala Maududi, Hasan al-Banna, Sayyid Qutb, Ayatollah Ruhollah Khomeini, and Abdullah Azzam. These ideologues invoked a handful of key concepts like *jahiliyya* (age of ignorance in pre-Islamic Arabia), *taghut* (an infidel tyrant), *jihad* as *fard al-ayn* (acts that must be fulfilled by all individual Muslims), *kafir* (infidel), martyrdom, and the "Crusader-Zionist alliance" as the building blocks of religious extremist ideologies, providing justifications for despotic rule, the subjugation of women, in-group solidarity and sectarianism, and suppression of dissent. Thus, if discourse constituted the politics of the past, the current contesting discourses of Islamic fundamentalism and liberal nationalism will be a key factor in determining the future of the Middle East and North Africa.

Political discourse in the sense used in this book reflects a set of practical ideas that are uttered by intellectual leaders, political activists, and the public at large as they debate historically significant sociopolitical and cultural issues in order to construct a new political order. Because there is more than one way to resolve such issues, depending on the nature of the social context, the manner in which these issues are resolved decides the type of sociopolitical discourse that emerges and becomes popular in the society. The dominant discourse in turn frames collective action, shapes political order, decides the rules governing relations among individuals and groups, and forms the basis of identity. Thus, one way to manage the complexity of politics, reduce the haze created by unfolding unexpected events, enhance the visibility of the emerging pattern of human interactions on the social horizon, and comprehend the process of political transformation is to figure out what specific set of issues the social actors are debating and what the most likely outcomes are of their efforts to resolve these issues.

The significant issues are indicative of the scale and form of unfolding cultural cleavages and contestations in a society—whether the issue being debated is, for example, a woman's reproductive right, in one society, or her right to drive, in another. The extent of people's active involvement in taking positions on different sides of the issues signals the intensity of these contestations and how they may be resolved. The resolution of issues where more people favor one side of an issue than the other may yield an understanding of the rise of the dominant discursive framework and the emergence of the movement for change. The knowledge of the extant issues thus enables social investigators to speculate about the types of political modalities that are likely to come into relief in the future. The arrangement of social forces, however, decides whether these resolutions institutionalize liberal democracy, fundamentalism, state socialism, or xenophobic nationalism. Because issues reflect concrete problems and the resolutions of these issues mark either the reproduction or the transformation of social relations, the approach adopted in this book accounts for historical specificity.

Pertinent, historically significant issues in the social context of the contemporary Middle East and North Africa have revolved around such organizing principles of the social order as the utility and standing of individual autonomy versus obedience to parental authority or patrimonial norms, gender equality versus gender hierarchy and male supremacy, secular politics versus Islamic government, the nation or ethnicity as the primary basis of identity versus the primacy of religion, religious equality versus religious intolerance, religious modernism versus fundamentalism, the West as the exemplar of progress and civilization versus the West as the epitome of cultural decadence, and peaceful methods of political action versus violent revolutionary behavior (Moaddel 2005).

There is certainly more than one way to resolve these issues, and these resolutions produce diverse outcomes. In the contemporary Middle East and North Africa, these outcomes have resulted in the generation of such political discourses as liberal nationalism, territorial nationalism, authoritarian state-centered secularism, state socialism, ethnic (pan-Arab or pan-Turkish) nationalism, national chauvinism, and a combination of national chauvinism and Islamic fundamentalism. Under the current conditions of the seven countries, however, as it will be shown, the real conflict is the clash of values between liberal nationalism and Islamic fundamentalism. This book provides the information necessary to assess the segment of the population that is favorably oriented toward liberal issues—that is, those who support individual rights, gender equality, secular politics, and national identity—and the segment that supports religious fundamentalism and Islamic government.

An important implication of this study is that liberal nationalism is one possible future for the Middle East and North Africa. While this future is not inevitable, after analyzing the respondents' perceptions of the cultural causes and consequences of developmental change (chapter 6) and the trends in values (chapter 7) presented in this book and considering the types of ideological targets (obstacles) faced by intellectual leaders and the public at large, liberal nationalism may have a much better chance of coming to the fore and shaping a pattern of democratic politics in the present moment than it did in the last century.

Problems with Classification

It is an established axiom among scientists that stereotyping and categorizing peoples, events, and things are fundamental, indispensable, and inevitable to the process of cognition. Without categorization, comprehension of the empirical reality may not be possible. As Smith and Medin (1981, 1) suggest, "We do not perceive, remember, and talk about each object and event as unique, but rather as an instance of a class or object that we already know something about." At the same time, classification and stereotyping may distort empirical reality, lead to faulty generalizations and misleading scientific predictions, provide a frame of mind that generates cultural bias and ethnocentrism, and contribute to inequality in the distribution of power. Moreover, classification at one level of reality—that is, the macro (country) level—may not even be necessary for understanding empirical reality at another level—that is, the micro (individual) level. If one is interested in explaining how values and political discourses shape human behavior, for example, it may not be necessary to classify the society in which such micro phenomena transpire. In trying to figure out the causes and processes of social change, classification may become particularly problematic where social investigators presume that human behavior and values are, in the final analysis, derivative of a priori properties of the created societal categories.

For social scientists, historians, and social philosophers who were trying to make sense of the stark differences in the levels of technological development and economic prosperity between Western and other societies in the early part of the nineteenth century, the question was not simply whether categorizing nations was necessary or even inevitable in order to understand the complex world in which they lived. Rather, they speculated that the categories they created reflected different stages in the dynamic process of evolutionary change. For them, progress was the organizing principle of history and thus the standard of categorization. This exercise, however, results in a number of problems for the social scientific study of social change. First, the principle of classification they employed glosses over the historical specificities of the societies falling into each of the presumed historical categories, rather than accounting for such specificities. Second, because culture is viewed as a reflection of a more fundamental social structure that ostensibly propels change, the explanation of cultural change tends toward structural reductionism. Third, the method of organizing societies along an evolutionary line rests on what Thornton (2005) says is reading history sideways—that is, inferring history from cross-sectional differences between countries. Finally, the theory of historical progress is hard to test because the various economic, social, and cultural indicators used to assess the theory rest on the assumption that the theory is in fact correct. In other words, it is presumed that the categories that the practitioners created are real and that world societies represent different instances of a broader historical process of societal development and evolutionary change. For practitioners of this approach who wanted to empirically assess the theory, the challenge was to figure out what factors accounted for the differences among nations (e.g., level of economic development, technological innovation, type of religious beliefs, and conception of human nature or the individual). They then speculated that these factors were the cause of the evolutionary process. Certainly, social scientists have improved considerably the yardstick of classification, shifting from the Eurocentric scale of historical progress that was popular in the nineteenth century to a more sophisticated and empirically verifiable scale in various versions of the modernization theory. Yet the presumption that the yardstick represents an organizing principle of history that is governed by a (single) dynamic of economic development, social differentiation, or technological innovation has remained by and large the same.

The classificatory schemata presented in diverse literature on social change and comparative studies of societies may be divided into two broad categories: those that employ "objective" classification standards and those that rest on "subjective" criteria. The first group categorized societies in terms of factors that are in the realm of concrete existence—outside and independent of individuals' values and perceptions—such as the structure of economic production, the level of technological development, the form of the state, and the level of economic prosperity. The second group organized societies in terms of people's value structures, value priorities, and perceptions.

However, the social scientific explanations of change that rested on these classificatory schemata came under criticism from scholars with diverse methodological and theoretical approaches associated with comparative historical sociology and social history; the subaltern studies, discursive history, and postcolonial criticisms; and developmental idealism. The conclusion drawn from these criticisms is that it may not be possible to explain the process of change based on any of these classificatory schemata. Following their lead, this book attempts to do away with the need for any of the classificatory schemes. Instead, it focuses on people and their issues, proposing that social change is the outcome of people's attempts to resolve the specific issues they collectively encounter. The resolution of issues leads to a variety of political options, ranging from a democratic pattern of social organization that enables societies to evolve and make progress, at one extreme, to an authoritarian pattern that constrains individuals, subjugates women, undermines the principle of individual autonomy, and sustains an ineffective and corrupt government, at the other. Under the current conditions in the Middle East and North Africa, it appears that Islamic fundamentalism and liberal nationalism present two competing resolutions of the same set of issues.

This introduction first discusses and assesses the objective approaches and historically grounded methods of explanation. It then moves on to evaluate the subjective approaches. Next, it discusses and critically evaluates the subaltern studies and postcolonial criticism. Given the position that the subalterns must be understood and analyzed as they are and without a priori assumptions about their motivation and ideology, this introduction lays the groundwork needed to establish the utility of survey research in answering the key questions posed in the subaltern studies and postcolonial criticisms. It also acknowledges and critiques the attempt in postcolonial criticisms to do away with societal classification. It points, however, to the methodological fallacy of the classificatory schemata presented in evolutionary theories, rather than their alleged contributions to the reproduction of Western hegemony. Finally, it presents an issue-centered theoretical framework of change in order to navigate the empirical data and arrive at a better understanding of the political conditions of the Middle East and North Africa.

Objective Approaches

General Evolutionary Theories of Change
The involvement of the European states and commercial interests in the affairs of peoples and cultures far beyond their borders expanded considerably in the eighteenth and nineteenth centuries. Paralleling this expansion were the new efforts among European scholars to address and explain the vast differences in the levels of economic development, technological advancement, and scientific discoveries between Europe—Great Britain, in particular—and the rest of the world and to speculate about the conditions necessary for historical progress and civilizational change. What account for Europe's impressive advancement in science and technology? Why was the rest of the world unable to make similar progress and fell so conspicuously behind Europe? What is the dynamic underpinning European success and other nations' failure? For Europeans, answering these questions required the adoption of a global scientific perspective. For them, the romantic school of sympathetic understanding that was spearheaded by Sir William Jones in late eighteenth-century India was too parochial to allow historical generalization, although in hindsight it appears to have provided a far more effective tool to address the practical problem of colonial administration—that is, the proper way to rule peoples whose cultures were so vastly different from their own (Forbes 1951).

History of British India (Mill 1826), first published in 1817, represents one of the earliest efforts to take this global and purportedly scientific perspective. To account for European progress compared to that of the rest of the world and identify the organizing principle of the world's historical development, James Mill (1773–1836) offered an evolutionary theory of change with progress being its organizing principle. Ostensibly rationalist universal historiography, his perspective derived the criteria of civilization from a "conjectural" history, the Benthamite principles of utility, and the general intellectual heritage of the Enlightenment. The organizing principle of history was measured by the "scale of nations," which he used to assess the location of world societies on a civilizational continuum. He employed the utilitarian standards of "completeness" and "exactness" to judge the laws and customs of Indians and peoples from other less developed countries, and he applied the Enlightenment principle of the treatment of women as the test of civilization. In reality, however, his approach was speculative and Eurocentric, leading him to conjecture that the place of India on the scale was low and thus to condemn every single aspect of their way of life as barbarous—not only their science but their philosophy, art, and manners as well (Forbes 1951). In Forbes's assessment, "given the 'scale of nations' as the organizing principle of history, and the uniformitarianism of Rationalist historiography, the logical result is an extreme form of Europocentricism, 'scientifically' established" (31).

Later social evolutionary theorists from Comte to Spencer, Marx, Durkheim, Guizot, Tönnies, and Parsons and latter-day modernization theorists were less blatantly Western-centric and more methodologically sophisticated than was Mill in his *History of British India*. Nonetheless, in the theories they proposed, the standard of societal classification is also the organizing principle of history. In the modernization perspective, for example, societies are placed in three successive stages of economic development—traditional, transitional, and modern. The level of economic development is measured using a set of clear, specific, and cross-nationally comparable indicators of the conditions of the national economy. Driven by the dynamic of economic development, historical progress is thus perceived as a transition from the primitive or the traditional stage to the advanced or modern stage (Rostow 1960; Deutsch 1961; Apter 1965; Levy 1966; Huntington 1968). Marxism claims to have departed from these theories by pointing to its discovery of the irreconcilability of the conflict between social classes in the system of production relations, where the resolution of this conflict inevitably propels the locomotive of historical progress toward human emancipation and the realization of a truly egalitarian social order. Its view of change, however, also rests on a stage theory of history—an evolutionary succession of modes of production. Growing out of Marxism, world systems theory rejects the tripartite division of world societies in the modernization perspective and proposes an alternative classification scheme. Accordingly, world societies in the modern period are organized into, and dominated by, a global system of capitalism consisting of three different and functionally interdependent economic zones—the core, semiperiphery, and periphery. These zones are hierarchically organized, resting on an international system of asymmetrical exchange relations. This hierarchy is necessary for the functioning of an inegalitarian world political, economic, and social order, where the appropriation of surplus by interests located in the dominant core (developed) countries is facilitated at the expense of the subordinate peripheral (less developed) countries (Wallerstein 1979, 1984, 2000; Chase-Dunn and Rubinson 1977).

Although world systems theory is posed as an alternative to the modernization theory, in an important respect it is a defense of evolutionary theories. If the structure of the world economy stalls the transition of "traditional" societies to modernity, it is because the economic interests emanating from the core of the world capitalist system penetrate, exploit, and thus peripheralize the traditional societies, causing the reproduction of economic underdevelopment. This is done as the structure of domestic economic production in the traditional societies is recalibrated according to the dictates of these dominant core interests. The peripheralization of these societies thus destroys the "normal" line of evolutionary progress. The fault of the modernization perspective is thus a result of its misconception of the nature of the world economy and international relations, not its proposition concerning the relations of economic development to historical progress. It is, however, one thing to claim that, in the world economy, stronger societies tend to dominate the weaker ones and the conditions of this subjugation shape people's perceptions of themselves and others. It is quite another to propose that a country's level of economic development and its mode of social organization are governed by a single dynamic of the world economy, and that the social evolution of traditional societies is possible only through the breakdown of the world capitalist system and a worldwide transition to socialism.

Generally, however, these evolutionary theories of change do not explain the specifics of historical cases with similar levels of economic development. Neither do they explain how an objective process of change, such as economic development, technological invention, or social differentiation, is connected to changes in people's perceptions concerning the most important organizing principles of politics (democracy versus authoritarianism), gender relations (gender equality versus gender hierarchization), secular politics (the separation of religion and politics versus religious rule), the basis of identity, and in-group–out-group relations.

Historically Grounded Explanation of Change
The principle of classification in modernization, classical Marxism, and world systems theories rests on a general evolutionary conception of history that

is purportedly governed by a dynamic affecting all societies in the modern period. The conceptualization of the master historical process is different in different perspectives, depending on whether one adheres to Marxism or to an alternative. As a general theory of change, none, however, could account for the specifics of historical outcomes—that is, why certain societies exhibit radically different forms of political organization despite having similar levels of economic development or comparable locations in the world economy. Given this failure, the notion that the world's societies were embedded in a unilinear process of change or in the single dynamic of the hierarchically organized global system of capitalism lost its appeal for a large group of social scientists interested in identifying the historical contingencies that account for specific outcomes. Beginning with Barrington Moore's seminal work, *Social Origins of Dictatorship and Democracy* (1966), many scholars opted for grounded explanations of a set of known historical and comparative cases. As the pioneer of this approach, Moore (1966) selects such concrete forms of political organizations as parliamentary democracy, fascism, and communism and explains different historical trajectories of change from the agrarian economy to the modern industrial world that corresponded to these forms (i.e., the capitalist democratic, the capitalist reactionary, and the communist). Moore's pledge to universality is his use of general and abstract concepts like social class and the state as elements of any social structure (although some have argued whether the concept of *class* conveys the same meaning in Asiatic societies as it does in the West). His explanation, however, details the varied ways in which a specific set of historical preconditions—the class capacity of the peasantry, the strength of the bourgeoisie, the alliance (or lack thereof) between landed aristocracy and the bourgeoisie, the structure of the state, and a revolutionary break with the past—combine to produce the three varied types of political organizations. Other sociologists followed suit in explaining, for example, the causes, processes, and outcomes of diverse revolutions (Wolf 1969; Paige 1975; Skocpol 1979; Goldstone 1991; Tilly 1984; Parsa 2000) and ideological and religious movements (Fullbrook 1983; Zaret 1985; Wuthnow 1989; Collins 1998; Moaddel 2005).

The methodology of comparative historical analysis is better equipped to account for the specificities of historical cases and thus overcomes the explanatory difficulties associated with the notion of universal history advanced in modernization, classical Marxism, and other evolutionary perspectives. Nevertheless, because the classificatory principles in grounded theories rest on the characteristics of social structure, there has been a tendency to gloss over the role of human agency in shaping variations in historical outcomes—that is, the relationship of human perception and emotion to the events and social structures people encounter and how this relationship shapes their collective action that transforms or reproduces social structures.[1] In some cases, the explanation of human subjectivity is derived from the property of the structural categories, arguing that human actors subjectively internalize the objective requirements of the social structure.[2] This type of explanation cannot be taken seriously. But if one overlooks the structural deterministic mode of explanation employed by some of its practitioners (e.g., Moore 1966; Skocpol 1979) and considers those who took seriously the role of human agency in shaping historical outcomes, particularly in the area of ideological production (e.g., Wuthnow 1989; Collins 1998), it is still unclear how different forms and models of social organizations are produced and what dynamics are at work that explain the generation of this diversity. If one's explanation stops at the level of comparative analysis of the social structures in which human actors are embedded, it is still important to ask how they arrived at a democratic, fascist, communist, or religious fundamentalist modality of politics.

For the sake of elaboration, consider the rise of diverse, diametrically opposed ideologies in Iran and Saudi Arabia in the last decades despite the fact that both regimes are almost equally repressive and religiously sectarian and rely on the sale of oil as the principal source of revenue. If one starts with the premise that human subjectivity has its own autonomous dynamics, then social structure may be conceived of as a factor that shapes the options that are available to human agency. That is, in explaining the contrasting cases of Iran and Saudi Arabia, one begins by presuming that people's quest for freedom and spiritual fulfillment against the oppressive religious state in both countries is an autonomous process. Given this autonomy, the fact that the oppositional response to the religious regime among Iranians has been predominantly liberal and reformist, while among Saudis this opposition has taken a militant fundamentalist form, may be attributed to the fact that the *fragmented* structure of the regime of the Islamic Republic of Iran provided broader options than did the *unified* state structure of the Kingdom of Saudi Arabia. The fragmented structure expanded the discursive space that permits the growth of a variety of oppositional discourses, including liberal reformism, while the unified structure narrowed this space, directing political activists to fall back on religious fundamentalism in an attempt to revive the teachings and practices of pristine Islam (Moaddel 2016).

Subjective Approaches

The development of comparative historical sociology paralleled the expansion of cross-national studies of human values that used survey research methodology. Focusing on a detailed assessment of a small number of comparative cases, the former is better situated to produce evidentiary materials that spell out the significance of historical contingencies in order to advance causal explanations of such phenomena as, for example, revolutionary change, the formation of alternative forms of social organizations, and the production of diverse ideologies. It would be hard, however, to generalize its findings to other cases. Cross-national studies of human values, by contrast, analyze the data collected from a representative sample of a large population to explain the value structures and belief systems of that population. Making probabilistic empirical generalizations about that population is thus not a problem. Furthermore, these studies try to answer a set of key questions that center on the values, perceptions, and feelings of individual actors.

The subjective approaches, however, do not quite incorporate the role of human agency in explaining changes in values. These approaches are also informed by structural presuppositions. Researchers in this category have considered value structures as the principles by which to categorize human societies, and in the same way that objective structures of social relations are proposed to *constrain* individual options, people's subjective attitudes and behaviors are construed in terms of the extent to which they have *internalized* the societal values. Singelis et al. (1995), for example, suggest that societal value structures vary along an individualism-collectivism dimension within which vertical and horizontal cultural distinctions are nested. In vertical collectivism, the collectivity is hierarchically organized, where the individuals perceive themselves as unequal members of the collectivity. In horizontal collectivism, on the other hand, they perceive themselves as equal partners within the collectivity. Vertical individualism rests on the conception of autonomous but unequal individuals, while horizontal individualism rests on both the autonomy and the equality of individuals. Although collectivism and individualism are the properties of the social structure, these authors see them as ultimately reflected in individuals' conceptions of themselves. Value structures are thus imputed from responses to a series of survey items that revolve around such core questions as these: Who am I and what do I value? How should I present myself to others? How do I perceive the social environment? (Shavitt, Torelli, and Riemer 2010, 310).

As empirical support for the measures of these constructs in the world's diverse cultural contexts, it has been argued that in vertical-individualist societies like the United States, the United Kingdom, and France, people are concerned with improving their own individual status and stress their standing out. In horizontal-individualist societies—Sweden, Denmark, Norway, and Australia, by contrast—people prefer to view themselves as equal to others in status, and instead of trying to stand out, they focus on expressing their uniqueness and establishing self-reliance. In vertical-collectivist societies, including Korea, Japan, and India, people focus on complying with authorities and enhancing the cohesion and status of their in-groups, even at the expense of their own personal goals. In horizontal-collectivist societies, like the Israeli kibbutz, people tend to stress sociability and interdependence with others within an egalitarian framework (Shavitt et al. 2010).

Similarly, Inglehart divides human societies in terms of their value structures. For him, the key division is between the cultural values that are materialist and those that are expressive or postmaterialist. Materialist values are concerned with mundane and material aspects of life. Postmaterialist values are self-expressive, stressing freedom, governmental transparency, and the significance of ideas in one's life. Inglehart views the transformation of values from materialism to postmaterialism as a consequence of two processes. First, economic development brings about economic prosperity, and the latter in turn satisfies the needs for physical survival, enhancing the feeling of security. He calls this *a security hypothesis*. A further increase in economic prosperity provides only a diminishing marginal utility for security, but it also provides a context for a shift in values from materialist to self-expressive and esthetic values. Second, this shift occurs primarily among those who are in their impressionable years (those under age 25). Because people's basic values are largely fixed when they reach adulthood and change relatively little thereafter (Rokeach 1968, 1973; Inglehart 1977, 1997), the older generations, socialized in terms of materialistic values under the economic insecurity of the past, are too rigid to embrace modern self-expressive values even though they are currently living under prosperous economic conditions. However, as the younger generations grow older, overall societal values undergo a major shift toward postmaterialism. This Inglehart calls *a socialization hypothesis* (Inglehart 1971; Inglehart and Welzel 2005).

While the security hypothesis implies that prosperity is conducive to the spread of postmaterialist values, the socialization hypothesis indicates that fundamental value change takes place gradually. That is, there is a sizable time lag between economic changes and their political and cultural effects. Fifteen or twenty years after an era of prosperity began, the birth cohorts that had spent their formative years in prosperity would begin to enter the electorate. Because there are substantial differences between the value priorities of older and younger generations and because the latter's values were shaped by different experiences in their formative years, societal value change occurs as younger generations replace older ones in the adult population.

Young people, however, are not necessarily more postmaterialist than their elders: this happens only if they have grown up under substantially more secure living conditions than their elders. No intergenerational value difference exists in stagnant societies—and if future generations no longer grew up under more- or less-secure conditions than their elders, there would be no intergenerational value difference. On the other hand, intergenerational differences in values exist insofar as there are intergenerational differences in experiencing security or insecurity. The shift toward postmaterialist values is driven by changing existential conditions, reflecting the change from growing up with the feeling that survival is precarious to growing up with the feeling that survival can be taken for granted (Inglehart 2017).

Gelfand et al. suggest another approach to the cross-cultural classification of values. They classify cultures from the perspective of the degree to which societies enforce rules and severely punish deviance. On one end of the continuum are "tight" societies, where strongly enforced rules are many and intolerance for deviance is high. On the other end are "loose" societies, where there are only a few strongly enforced rules and intolerance for deviance is low. They then relate tightness-looseness to ecological and historical threats, including high population density, resource scarcity, a history of territorial conflict, disease and environmental threats, and autocratic societal institutions (Gelfand et al. 2011).[3] Finally, Schwartz (2006, 2012) advances a schema by developing an a priori proposition concerning the existence of three basic dimensions in all cultures: autonomy versus embeddedness, egalitarianism versus hierarchy, and harmony versus mastery. He then identifies seven cultural value orientations—affective autonomy, egalitarianism, embeddedness, harmony, hierarchy, intellectual autonomy, and mastery—and argues that these value orientations are different resolutions of the critical issues that the three dimensions reflect. He then relates these value orientations to gross domestic product per capita, democratization, and household size.

The Subaltern Studies

The historically grounded model of scientific explanation is an alternative to the teleological reading of history and the notion of a unilinear process of change that dominated the views on historical transition to modernity. It remains, however, fully committed to structuralism. The proponents of the subaltern studies, on the other hand, reject not only universal history and teleology but structuralism as well. These scholars question such bifurcation of human societies as traditional versus modern, primitive versus advanced, barbaric versus civilized, South versus North, and East versus West. They argue that these dichotomies are a legacy of the colonial past and provide little guidance for understanding the values, desires, identities, and behaviors of the people living in the non-Western world. The cerebral force of the subaltern studies has also been shaped, as it were, by their opposition to the teleological conceptions of history that have characterized various Marxist and nationalist accounts of the resistances, rebellions, assertions, and insubordinations of the subalterns—mainly involving the peasants in India, where this intellectual movement started in the late 1970s (Prakash 1994). The key social division in this paradigm is between the elite and the subalterns, those in society who are considered socioculturally inferior and economically downtrodden. "Accusing colonialist, nationalist, and Marxist interpretations of robbing the common people of their agency," says Prakash (1994, 1477), "it announced a new approach to restore history to the subordinated." The focus of these scholars is thus to understand the subjective orientations of the subalterns as they are, *without* an a priori assumption that such orientations reflect a broader desire for national emancipation that was shared by other social classes and groups or confirm an evolutionary pattern of historical change that was forecast by Marxism.

Subaltern scholars' historical analysis departs from structuralism and turns toward understanding the process of discursive formation. In writing history, they propose, researchers must focus on the consciousness and desire of the subaltern (Bhadra 1988; Cooper 1994; Mallon 1994; Prakash 1994). Following Foucault's notions of the knowledge-power relation and the irreducibility of discourse, they investigate the nature of the cultural exchange between European empires and colonial societies. In this exchange, they explore how European hegemony transformed the subjective conditions of the subjugated nations in such a way that inequality in the distribution of power between the (colonial) elite and the subaltern was maintained and reproduced (Larson 1997). Here, their view parallels world systems theory. The premise that the colonies were intellectually organized by European powers to ensure the latter's cultural hegemony corresponds to world systems theory's claim concerning the functioning of the hierarchy of the world capitalist system for the benefit of the imperialist core. Nonetheless, the proponents of the subaltern studies eschew the overgeneralizing and homogenizing claim of world systems theory. In their postcolonial criticisms, they question not only the history authored and authorized by colonialism but Marxist historiography as well. For them, it is problematic to thematize indigenous histories in terms of the development of capitalism because "making capitalism the foundational theme amounts to homogenizing the histories that remain heterogeneous with it" (Prakash 1992, 13).

As a pioneer of the subaltern studies, Guha criticizes colonial and nationalist historiographies as elitist, proposing to redirect the methodology of historical analysis toward understanding the subalterns: their consciousness and identities as well as the modality and logic of their rebellions. These topics, in his view, are all but absent in both colonial and postcolonial narratives. Fixing his gaze on the peasants who participated in various forms of agrarian disturbances and insurgencies in British India between 1783 and 1900, Guha attempts to uncover what he considers the elementary aspects of these insurgencies. He begins by noting that peasants developed their identity and sense of self-awareness not through insurgency alone but also in opposition to the ruling elite and landowners:

> It was they who made him aware of his place in society as a measure of his distance from themselves—a distance expressed in differential of wealth, status, and culture. His identity amounted to the sum of his subalternity. In other words, he learnt to recognize himself not by the properties and attributes of his own social being but by a diminution, if not negation, of those of his superior. (Guha 1999, 18)

Consistent with Marx, Guha attributes the notion of peasants' false consciousness to the force of the ruling ideologies, especially that of religion, that "imbued the peasant with this negative consciousness, so that he could be induced to look upon his subservience not only as tolerable but almost covetable" (Guha 1999, 19). The peasants, however, attained consciousness of their own situation and interests through participation in insurgency. This process started with a series of *negations*, when they identified the landed elite as the target of attack and destroyed or appropriated the signs of elite authority. At first, the act of insurgency appeared *ambiguous*, as it was difficult to discern whether it was an individualistic criminal act or a reflection of a rebellion against the authorities. Then the insurgency displayed the *modality* of publicity and a collective act of defiance. It was also *emulative*, wherein rebellion in the colonial perspective was contagious, being transmitted from locality to locality; it had a *solidarity* structure that was reinforced by ethnicity and expressed in violence against those who actively collaborated with the enemy; and it was *territorial*, being related to the locality where peasants lived (Guha 1999). These peasants as the subalterns were thus autonomous because of the internally located and self-generating sources of their rebellion. Without understanding this dynamic, one's understanding of history would remain insufficient.

Avoiding a priori theorizing about the motivation and desire of the subaltern and appreciating the significance of inductive history, Guha presents empirical evidence showing that peasant insurgency conformed neither to (post)colonial descriptions of the peasantry nor to various teleological readings of historical change in India (e.g., the peasants' action as an instance of the national liberation movement or the struggle for the transition to socialism). He tries to demonstrate that the peasants were autonomous actors and that this autonomy was realized through self-generating struggle against the ruling elite and for a better life.

Shortcomings and Contributions

The major challenge facing a Guha-style historical investigation is that the empirical data on the subalterns' perceptions of identity and values are not readily available. The subalterns would seldom leave traces of their thoughts, opinions, and discourses about problems and issues they encountered and their participation in upheavals against the members of the dominant classes, foreign power, or indigenous ruling elite. Investigating the subalterns in India between the late eighteenth century and the end of the nineteenth century, Guha had little choice but to rely on the available historical documents and other unobtrusive measures. In the present context, however, the use of digital communication technology and the availability of social media as a source of information have made it possible to observe through one's smartphone the subalterns' protest and resistance—to witness, for example, the courageous act of defiance of a group of Iranian women against mandatory veiling, standing on a utility box on a sidewalk, casting off their headscarves, and turning this symbol of oppression into a banner of liberation.[4] More systematically, however, the problem of investigating the subalterns may be overcome by the use of the methodology of intensive observations and (qualitative) interviews of a representative sample of respondents from a subaltern population. The extensive refinements of the basic tools of survey research—sampling, the survey instrument, and interviewing—in recent decades have made it possible to collect empirical data on a large section of the population in virtually every part of the world. Setting aside the antiestablishmentarianism of the subaltern studies, the mode of researching the subalterns—whether women, workers, minorities, the unemployed, or heavily indebted college students—without any presumption concerning their identities, values, missions, and desires is remarkably consistent with survey research methodology.

Like the subaltern studies, the social survey rests on the premise that explaining the values, political orientations, and long-term concerns of the ordinary people requires understanding what their organizations, solidarity structures, and resources are and how they process information and perceive the events and social structures they encounter. Acquiring this understanding requires drawing a representative sample, formulating an effective questionnaire that is meaningful to the respondents, and employing interviewers who are honest, objective, and skillful. The research activities of many social science survey researchers interested in the causes and consequences of human values are thus similar to the research strategies advocated by the scholars of the subaltern studies.

There are, however, two areas in which the subaltern studies display serious conceptual and theoretical shortcomings. One is the tendency toward homogenizing the subalterns—that is, treating them as if they are an undifferentiated mass that exhibits a uniform set of attitudes toward the dominant classes and the ruling elite. This tendency is rather surprising, considering that the proponents of the subaltern studies have been quite vociferous in rejecting the homogenizing characteristics of various colonial, nationalist, and Marxist historiographies. Certainly, from a broad historical perspective, the differences between the living conditions and the lifestyle of the colonial administrators and the indigenous elites, on the one hand, and those of the subalterns, on the other, are so vast that they may overshadow the differences within either group, and as a result, each side, in the eyes of the other, appears remarkably homogeneous. However, there is little reason to assume that, because the subalterns are uniformly downtrodden, they must also be culturally homogeneous. As will be discussed in this book, findings from comparative values surveys across the seven countries have shown that such subaltern groups as women vary considerably in their rejection or endorsement of polygamy and of obedience of a wife to her husband, that a segment of economically disfranchised respondents variably supports a political system controlled by a strongman, and that members of lower social classes display considerable variation in supporting attitudes that are intolerant and sectarian. The provisions of social justice that would ameliorate the social conditions of, and empower, the subalterns are certainly the sine qua non for the foundation of a civilized social order. There is, however, little to celebrate in such cultural attitudes as a woman endorsing the practice of polygamy or an unemployed white member of the working class embracing the politics of a xenophobic and anti-immigrant demagogue.

The second and more fundamental shortcoming of the subaltern studies is the absence of a mechanism that explains the process of discursive formation—that is, how the subaltern develops identity, awareness, and shared patterns of concerns and perspectives. Lacking this mechanism, the proponents of the subaltern studies appear to have fallen back, perhaps unwittingly, on the same explanatory logic used by those in the classical sociological tradition who have sought a correspondence between social conditions and the generation of discourse—that changes in people's conditions bring about changes in their subjectivity in a determinate manner. There are, of course, subtle differences in the methods used by different scholars to establish this connection. At one extreme is the Western-centric explanation, which posits that, with economic development and advancement in science and technology, the rest of the world will adopt Western values, sensibilities, and lifestyles. At the other extreme are the more credible, empirically based explanations of the sort advanced by Inglehart and others using subjectivist approaches or by the enthusiasts of the subaltern studies who have pointed to the significance of the subalterns' struggle against the colonialists and nationalist elites in developing identity and consciousness. The key explanatory logic in these approaches, however, is still governed by an attempt to use a series of steps—like the security and socialization hypotheses proposed by Inglehart or the phases in peasants' autonomous struggles evident in the subaltern studies—to connect the objective social conditions to the generation of subjectivity or discursive formation. The central theoretical problem, however, is explaining *how* economic prosperity in Inglehart's revision of the modernization theory, for example, prompts the rise of self-expressive values among the younger generations. What is the mechanism? Likewise, how do we substantiate that what the proponents of the subaltern studies claim to be the subaltern's subjectivity in fact reflects the *intrinsic* consciousness of the subaltern? Could not this consciousness be a reaction to the type of ideological discourses the subaltern had encountered and thus be subject to change as the content and orientation of the encountered discourses change? In other words, would it not be the case that the subaltern discourse is a function of, or shaped in opposition to, the type of discourse employed by the ruling elite?

By eschewing an a priori attribution of a revolutionary consciousness to the subaltern, proponents of the subaltern studies avoided a serious political problem that beset Marxism. Marxists tackled the question of the working-class revolutionary consciousness for a long time without being able to answer it once and for all. The problem began when Marx first predicted the development of the revolutionary consciousness as the proletariat's liberating potential. Recognizing that such a consciousness was not forthcoming from within the ranks of the proletariat, Lenin argued that this consciousness must be brought in from without; it was to be manufactured by the intellectual vanguards of the working people who are organized in the Communist Party. These intellectuals—being purportedly firmly committed to the cause of the working class, arguably in the same way the subaltern scholars are committed to the subaltern—are capable of understanding the course and dynamics of historical development. They can therefore lead the working class in the struggle against the bourgeoisie and toward the transition to socialism. However, in an effort to fix the Marxian emancipatory project in order to bring this historic transition to reality, Lenin upended Marxism by moving the site of the emancipatory agency from the dynamic context of the working-class struggle at the level of economic production to the "the ideological superstructure." Instead of creating an egalitarian society, as a result the Leninist solution furnished not only a justificatory account for an elitist hierarchical political order but also the intellectual foundation for totalitarianism. The failure of Leninism thus provides ample reasons to reject elitism, the teleological reading of history, and character attributions by outsiders to the values and behaviors of the working class qua the subalterns.

That the rise of consciousness among the subalterns is a self-generating process and that this process does not conform to any outsider's project, including Marx's presumption concerning the relations of consciousness with social class, certainly form a credible proposition. A systematic attempt to debunk any injection of attributes into the subalterns by outsiders constitutes the scholarly motto and the intellectual agenda of the subaltern studies. In his foreword to Guha and Spivak (1988, viii), Said uses Foucault's notion of "relentless erudition" to praise the historiography of the subaltern studies as "a deeply engaged search for new documents, a brilliantly resourceful re-deployment of old documents, so much so that what emerges . . . is a new knowledge, more precarious perhaps than its familiar competitors, but strikingly rigorous, intellectually demanding, forceful and novel." Although he was not a historian, his appreciation of what comprises a rigorous methodology is certainly praiseworthy. It nonetheless borders on the obvious; any graduate seminar on the social scientific method of historical investigation is prefaced with a similar scholarly attitude. Unfortunately, a trend in this scholarly genre under the rubric of postcolonial criticism does not appear to have remained faithful to such a rigorous standard of historical investigation.

The postcolonial broadsides advanced by some of the scholars connected to this trend are unconvincing. The practice of sati (a widow's self-immolation by surrendering to the burning funeral pyre of her deceased husband) among Hindus in nineteenth-century British India and the veil among Muslim women are pertinent examples. Between 1815 and 1828, there were 8,134 recorded cases of sati, and the debate on this horrific act culminated with its abolition by the British in 1829. Mani (1987) demonstrates the "specifically 'colonial'" nature of the debate between the British colonial administrators and indigenous liberal intellectuals, like Rammohun Roy, who favored the abolition of the practice, on the one hand, and those who defended it, on the other. At the outset, Mani states that her concern is not "so much with who was for or against the practice but, rather, with how these ideological positions were argued . . . what various sides assumed about sati, Indian society and the place of women in it, what they understood to be tradition, what counted as evidence, and so on" (121).

To abolish sati through legislation, the British tried to uncover injunctions against the practice based on authoritative exegeses solicited from the pundits of the Brahmanic scriptures. This strategy, which shaped the official discourse on sati, Mani (1987) argues, "rested on three interlocking assumptions: the hegemony of religious texts, a total indigenous submission to their dictates, and the religious basis of sati" (128). Their problematic nature notwithstanding, she posited that these assumptions shifted the discourse on sati away from concerns for women and centered on the scriptures and what constituted the authentic Brahmanic tradition. She apparently disagrees with the way the British handled the problem. Nonetheless, beyond stating that it was "primarily initiated by colonial officials," there is little in her argument that makes the debate specifically colonial in nature or clarifies what the adjective *colonial* is supposed to signify when one characterizes a debate like this as colonial. What is more, being all too willing to characterize any British attempt ostensibly to raise the status of women in India as colonial and therefore suspect, Mani takes a position on the widow that is hard to sustain. She says, "If the hegemony of religious texts and its corollary, an unthinking obedience to scripture, is problematized by regional variation in the incidence and mode of performing sati, *the representation of widows as perennial victims is similarly [sic] debatable*" (129, italics added). Here, she is referring to the apparent willingness of some widows to jump into the flames and to the widows' warnings to the "relatives seeking to restrain them [about] the so-called legendary curse of the women about to commit sati" (129). Nonetheless, it is hardly defensible to simply label as colonial the British view on the widow as the victim and therefore reject it. The act is immoral and repulsive; it matters little whether widows were coerced to self-immolate or willingly submitted to the flames. The belief in human dignity as a universal principle may be an outsider's injection; it is nonetheless morally justifiable to condemn sati, the subjugation of women, or any form of slavery, whether the victims agree or not.

This line of argument, or rather casuistry, serves Mani's claim that the arguably inadequate British strategy of using scriptural justifications to abolish sati foreclosed "any possiblity [sic] of women's agency, thus providing justification for 'civilizing' colonial interventions" (1987, 130). However, if one is serious about agency and remains faithful to the principle that the subjectivity, desire, and interest of women qua subalterns in British India must be taken seriously, then an alternative account of sati requires a better understanding of how women felt about the horrific act. It is not, however, reassuring that, as Mani confesses, "we have no independent access to the mental or subjective states of widows outside of these overdetermined colonial representations of them" (129).

To give another example, Ahmed (1992), following Said's critique of Orientalism, presented a disapproving portrayal of Qasim Amin's exposé on the maltreatment of women in Egypt, accusing him of expressing "not just a generalized contempt for Muslims but also contempt for specific groups, often in lavishly abusive details." In particular, "those for whom Amin reserved his most virulent contempt—were Egyptian women" (156). In her view, Amin's description of the condition of Egyptian women was suspect not simply because he had "exceedingly limited access to women other than members of his immediate family and their retinue, and perhaps prostitutes" (157) but also because "the ideas to which Cromer and the missionaries gave expression formed the basis of Amin's book" (155). On veiling, she says, "when one considers why the veil has this meaning in the late twentieth century, it becomes obvious that, ironically, it was the discourses of the West, and specifically the discourse of colonial domination, that in the first place determined the meaning of the veil in geopolitical discourses and thereby set the terms for its emergence as a symbol of resistance" (235).

It is self-evident that those who used the veil in the late twentieth century to attack the Western lifestyle were not the same people who experienced British domination. Rather, they were members or followers of the Muslim Brothers and other Islamic fundamentalist groups in the Middle East and North Africa, or they were influenced by the incessant anti-Western propaganda launched by these groups. Nor was there a colonial power in the region in the late twentieth century. It may thus be asked against whom the veil had become "a symbol of resistance." In fact, as Ahmed is certainly aware, the unveiling movement in the early twentieth century symbolized not only a rebellion against the constraining traditional culture but also the liberation movement against foreign domination. Female activists appeared unveiled while participating in the early twentieth-century nationalist movements in Egypt (Safran 1961; Reid 1975; Vatikiotis 1980; Shaarāwī 1987), Tunisia (Lazreg 1994; Charrad 2001, 2011;

Cavatorta and Haugbølle 2012; Kerrou 2010), and Turkey (Nashat and Tucker 1999). Besides, it is prejudicial to hold an a priori assumption about the disingenuousness of any purportedly prowomen discourse advanced by a colonial power.[5]

If the subalterns are to be the emancipators of, or to be emancipated from, their subjugations, the theoreticians of the subaltern studies have not demonstrated what that emancipation is going to look like and what type of egalitarian social order the subalterns are capable of constructing. The subaltern-based twentieth-century revolutionary movements in the Middle East and North Africa not only failed to create a more democratic and prosperous political order than the old regimes but also supported a political order that was far more oppressive. The military coups by pan-Arab nationalists in Egypt, Iraq, Libya, and Syria between 1952 and 1969, as well as the Iranian Revolution against the pro-Western Pahlavi monarchy, are prime examples.

Doing Away with Classification

One of the most significant contributions of postcolonial criticism is the rejection of the classification of human societies into traditional and modern, primitive and advanced, East and West, and so forth. The rationale for abandoning these dualities is the concern with the role of European cultural discourses in reproducing imperial power. Pointing to the capacity of ideas to transform human relationships, they try to explain and critique how "European powers discursively defined imperial subjects as governable others" (Larson 1997, 969). For Prakash (1992), the aim of postcolonial criticism is thus to compel "a radical rethinking and reformulation of forms of knowledge and social identities authored and authorized by colonialism and Western domination [and] to undo the Eurocentrism produced by the institution of the West's trajectory" (8). This rethinking, for them, is all the more significant and necessary because the prior challenges to colonialism posed by nationalism and Marxism rested on master narratives that put Europe at their center and therefore proved defective. Nationalism "staked a claim to the order of Reason and Progress instituted by colonialism" (Prakash 1992, 8), and the Marxists' denunciation of colonialism "was framed by a universalist mode-of-production narrative" (8). To liberate historiography from the burden of Western cultural hegemony and to recover, recognize, and document the agency of the subaltern is to engage in what Spivak terms catachresis or "reversing, displacing, and seizing the apparatus of value-coding" (cited in Prakash 1992, 8).

Hands held far apart dropped the catch. Postcolonial criticism is substantialist, rather than methodological. Its rejection of traditional versus modern and similar dualities emanates from an alarmist attitude toward what it presumes to be the substance of Western discourses underpinning these dualities and from the menace of the restoration of Western hegemony over postcolonial societies posed by that substance, which appears to be, although not always clearly stated, the belief in reason, progress, and Western-style liberal democracy. This view, however, is hard to defend. On the one hand, as Larson (1997, 969) has demonstrated in the case of the early history of Malagasy Christianity, postcolonial criticisms "have underestimated the intellectual resilience of 'colonized minds.' " Larson argues that "by filtering European discourses through their own orders of meaning, 'subalterns' limited the potential of those discourses to rule effectively in the service of colonial power." On the other hand, postcolonial critics have done very little to fully elaborate on and empirically verify what constitutes the substance of colonial discourse, clarify how this discourse corresponds to colonial power, or specify who makes, or what mechanism explains, the power-knowledge connection. It is not convincing to argue that, given the Western dominance in the Middle East and North Africa in the late nineteenth and the first part of the twentieth centuries, for example, the emergent liberal nationalist discourses were disingenuous because they displayed an affinity with the colonialists' "order of Reason and Progress" (Prakash 1992, 8). Far from relying on the colonial discourse, the indigenous intellectual leaders arrived at a liberal nationalist resolution of their political problem as a result of the distinctive constellation of the domestic sociopolitical forces they encountered. Egyptian intellectual leaders and political activists, for example, found liberal nationalism a most suitable model for the future of their country because they perceived that such other, and arguably realistic, alternatives as pan-Islamism, the restoration of the Ottoman suzerainty in the form of administrative decentralization, and khedivial rule were utterly unattractive. They certainly had recognized the otherness of British domination.

Moreover, the model of culture production that has informed postcolonial criticism presumes a determinate relationship between ideology and the structure of power relations, a theoretical presupposition that is abandoned in sociological theories of ideology (Wuthnow 1989; Alexander and Smith 1993; Collins 1998; Moaddel 2005). To be sure, it is true that the dominant (colonial) power or the ruling elite tries to inspire or impose its cultural hegemony on the subjugated people. It is also true that domination begets its own ideological nemesis. The history of cultural change in the contemporary Middle East and North Africa has demonstrated that the discourse of the domineering power forms an ideological target in opposition to which the discourse of the resistance is formulated, and as the dominant discourse-cum-target changes, so does the oppositional discourse.

Postcolonial criticism fails to realize that the fundamental methodological fallacy of the evolutionary binaries is what Thornton (2005) says is reading history sideways. This fallacy is a result of the effort to deduce a historical dynamic from cross-sectional (national) data, presuming that the so-called primitive societies represent an earlier stage in historical development toward Western modernity and that the contemporary Western societies are the future of the rest of the world. Thornton further argues that such an evolutionary paradigm, which dominated social science for centuries, contributed to the misinterpretation of Western trends in family structure, marriage, fertility, and parent-child relations. Through public policies, aid programs, and colonialism, it has reshaped families in both Western and non-Western societies as well (Thornton 2005).

The dualities of traditional versus modern, primitive versus advanced, East versus West, and the like were employed to convey value judgments and to have moral implications (Thornton 2005). Therefore, subaltern scholars are justified in rejecting these categories even if they are treated as strictly *nominal* categories used simply to distinguish one type of society from another. The core methodological problem, however, lies in presuming that these categories are *real* and giving them an ontological status in the sense that (1) they capture different realities, (2) these realities represent instances of a transnational evolutionary dynamic, (3) there are social forces underpinning this dynamism, and (4) the traces of these forces are observable and can be measured in terms of the variable features of the objective conditions of the historical cases that represent each category. It is thus not the reality or substance of Western domination or cultural superiority that makes evolutionary models of change inadequate. Rather, such models rest on a faulty methodology. The practice of arranging societies along an evolutionary continuum of traditional versus modern is not sound methodologically. Nor is it conducive to the production of testable and verifiable knowledge of the process of cultural change even if one abandons any pretense of Western cultural superiority and fully accepts the apparatus of value coding prescribed by the intellectual leaders of the subaltern studies.

To further elaborate, it has been shown cross-nationally that traditional, collectivist, materialist, or tight cultures are associated with a low level of economic development and prosperity, a high level of economic insecurity, and authoritarianism. Modern, individualistic, postmaterialist, or loose cultures, on the other hand, represent the opposite end of the developmental continuum. An economic developmental logic is claimed to tie the two types of societies together: economic development and prosperity are said to put people at ease about material things. When doing well economically, people may worry less about food, housing, health care, and their children's education. Generally, new and diverse occupational positions generated by the process of economic development increase social differentiation and loosen the grip of traditional social norms in shaping human behavior, and the feeling of economic security acquired as a result is associated with the rise of postmaterialist values, loose cultures, and expressive individualism.

There is no problem of categorizing societies in terms of people's cultural sensibilities on the aggregate level into materialist versus postmaterialist, tight versus loose, collectivist versus individualist, and so forth. The problem, however, is that certain countries, while appearing similar on the traditional, collectivist, materialist, or any other scale used for cross-national comparison, may still exhibit diverse value orientations toward similar, if not identical, historically significant issues. Certainly, the proclivity to homogenize otherwise diverse historical cases may be an inevitable outcome of any attempt at stereotyping and categorizing social phenomena for the sake of better comprehension. Nonetheless, a more fundamental problem lies in the very proposition that attributes a dynamic to such artificially created cultural dualities. Even if one empirically establishes that all the world societies fall on one or the other side of these binaries, it would be hard to substantiate that their differences are the outcome of the operation of a certain historical dynamic—that is, scientific breakthrough, inventions in modern technologies, technological innovation, economic development, and so forth. It appears that the only way one can claim the presence of a historical dynamic that explains variation in these constructed categories is by presuming that these categories are true and magically come to life in order to play their part in the historical trajectory of evolutionary change. At the end, this exercise may require accepting as true the very hypothesis on the causes and processes of historical cultural change that is supposed to be tested. Moreover, while one may establish an empirical association between the level of economic development and value structures, economic development may relate only tangentially to the mechanism that explains variation in a *specific* set of value structures.

The assumption that economic development is the prime determinant of evolutionary change in culture is problematic. The existing empirical data on the processes and outcomes of social change point only to the accumulation of anomalies. Countries attain impressive levels of economic development, but the corresponding cultural patterns forecast by evolutionary theories are not realized. What is more, the emergent cultural patterns appear to be just the reverse of those that were predicted in some cases. For example, while it is debatable whether Iranians during the Revolution of 1979 were intellectually and economically less resourceful than Americans in 1776 who wrote the Declaration of Independence and drafted a liberal democratic constitution, they were certainly more educated and economically more prosperous than their fellow Iranians who participated in the Constitutional Revolution of 1906. Then how does one explain in terms of an evolutionary model of historical progress that in 1979 Iranians endorsed a constitution that gave absolutist power to an ayatollah, while in 1906 (i.e., seventy-five years earlier) the participants in the Constitutional Revolution enthusiastically endorsed a constitution that did away with any form of absolutist rule? If evolutionary theories of change were correct, the Revolution of 1979 should have occurred in 1906 and the Constitutional Revolution in 1979. There were certainly other social forces at work that prompted the latter-day Iranians to support an admittedly reactionary constitution that did away with individual rights, endorsed the subjugation of women, and forsook secular politics.

Beyond Iran, the economic transformation of Middle Eastern and North African countries in the modern period, which started with Napoleon's invasion of Egypt in 1798 (Lewis 2007), failed to produce a consistent pattern of value structures anticipated by the macro social scientific theories of evolutionary change. Rather, the contemporary history of these countries displays an episodic or discontinuous trajectory of cultural change in which people's orientations toward some of the key principles of social organization in one episode were different from, if not diametrically opposed to, those in the preceding or the following episode and in which changes in cultural discourse bore little relationship to the (continuous) process of economic development. The emergent episodes differed from one another in terms of the type of ideological discourse that was dominant in the sociopolitical space, including Islamic modernism, liberal nationalism, secular authoritarian nationalism, pan-Arab or other forms of ethnic nationalism, and Islamic fundamentalism. These discourses shaped state policies, religious attitudes, gender relations, basis of identity, and attitudes toward outsiders.

Explaining Change: People and Their Issues

There is no need to categorize societies in order to explain how and why people in a society decide to adopt a certain form of politics. The alternative analytical model used here rests on the premise that the dominant modality of politics is an outcome of people's efforts to address and resolve issues. It is proposed that (1) people's value orientations toward the governing principles of social organizations—e.g., religion, social class, forms of government, and gender—change when these principles are turned into issues and then get resolved; (2) issues are resolved within the context of ideological debates, religious disputations, and political conflict; (3) debates and conflicts occur in the context of a cultural episode—a bounded historical process that has a beginning and an end; (4) an episode is characterized by the domination of either a single discourse or a plurality of discourses with varying relationships to the dominant political and cultural institutions; (5) the dominant discourse or discourses form the ideological targets in opposition to which intellectual leaders produce ideas as they attempt to resolve issues—that is, the production of ideas is an oppositional response to what is expressed by the proponents of the dominant discourse(s); (6) the existing targets shape the meaningfulness of the oppositional discourse and, one step removed, the options available to construct an alternative political order; and (7) the articulation of the oppositional discourse with the social environment produces a new pattern of historical development.

Issues are useful indicators of the state of cultural conflict in a society. Changes in values can be forecast by understanding the way in which issues are likely to get resolved. In any society, only a finite number of issues are debated at a given historical moment, only a quite limited number of resolution options are available, and only a very small number of political outcomes—no more than two or three, including the status quo—are possible. As the social actors resolve issues through opposition to the target or the dominant ideology, new ideological discourses are produced and brought into the limelight. The arrangement of the social forces at a particular historical juncture makes it possible for the new discourses to articulate with the social environment and shape the pattern of historical growth.

The Region's Contemporary History as a Succession of Cultural Episodes

These propositions are intended to provide the mental map for navigating through various historical events, different social actors, and traces of their behaviors and expressions in order to understand the generation of discourse and the emergence of meaningful options for the construction of a new sociopolitical order. Certainly, an option may not necessarily be sensible, practical, or effective in creating a more productive and empowering social order. Perhaps only one set of ideological resolutions is the product of a historically bounded liberated cognition, a truly transcendental discourse, and is thus conducive to evolutionary change and historical progress. In the modern period, for example, liberal democracy is a more effective way of organizing society, controlling and taming political power, reducing corruption in high places, promoting individual creativity, and efficiently allocating resources than any other of the existing models of social organization. However, cultural forces— or, more specifically, ideological targets—must be organized in such a manner that intellectual leaders and the members of the ordinary public come to realize the significance of liberal democracy in bringing about a more empowering and prosperous social order.

The history of the contemporary Middle East and North Africa is replete with examples that demonstrate the production of discourse in opposition to the dominant ideological targets, discontinuities in the process of discursive change and the episodic character of this change, and the articulation of the emergent discourse with the social environment in realizing a new

political order. Notable among these examples is the rise of liberal nationalism as a powerful emancipatory movement in early twentieth-century Egypt,
an outcome of a historical process that began with Napoleon's invasion of
the country in 1798–1801. In the early nineteenth century, Egyptians were
organized as a religious community and probably identified themselves in
terms of their locality, tribe, or clan. Their revolt in Cairo against Bonaparte
in 1798 and support for Muhammad Ali in 1805 were not conducted in the
name of Egypt.[6] But the invasion made Egyptians aware of Europe's scientific
and technological progress, and the work of 150 savants Napoleon brought
along to study the country's culture, history, and natural environment
contributed significantly to cultural change. By 1828, these scholars had
published twenty-three volumes of *Description de l'Egypte*, which included
materials on native animals and plants, minerals, local trade and industry,
and, most famously, ancient Egypt.[7] The knowledge of ancient Egypt might
have contributed to a growing conception of the country as an entity sep-
arate from the Ottomans, which had a historical presence far beyond the
Ottomans' grandeur and the Islamic period. Moreover, Muhammad Ali's
policy of sending young Egyptians to Europe to acquire knowledge of modern military technology created an educated class interested in sociopolitical
issues that were broader than those related to the military (Hourani 1983;
Vatikiotis 1980).

This process favored the rise of liberal nationalism. First, Muhammad Ali's
program to modernize Egypt and establish autonomy ran into conflict with
the *ulama* and the Ottomans and turned the latter into a target of ideological
attack. Then, late in the century, with the *ulama* and the Ottoman suzerainty
lurking in the background, the increasing awareness of the illegitimacy of khedivial arbitrary rule triggered interest in the idea of secular politics and liberal values. Finally, British colonial rule not only shaped Egyptian nationalism
but also fused this nationalism with Islamic modernism (Hourani 1983). The
nationalist revolution of 1919 and the formation of a liberal government created a new context for the production of oppositional discourse. On the one
hand, the government's secularist policies and the secularism of the country's
intellectual leaders weakened the nationalist-religious alliance of the prerevolutionary period and prompted the rise of Islamic fundamentalism. This process
contributed to the formation of the Society of the Muslim Brothers in 1928.
On the other hand, the domination of the liberal government by landowners
and merchants resulted in the identification of liberalism with the interests of
these classes and thus undermined its legitimacy among the members of the
dominated classes, expanding the popular base of the Muslim Brothers at the
expense of the liberal parties in the subsequent decades. The exclusionary policies of the nationalist government disaffected the Muslim Brothers, prompting their participation in the 1952 military coup that ended the constitutional

monarchy a year later (Mitchell 1969; Safran 1961; Gershoni and Jankowski 1986, 1995; Moaddel 2005).

Similarly, in late nineteenth-century Syria, Ottoman Sultan Abdülhamid's pan-Islamic despotism and then the Turkish nationalism of the Committee of Union and Progress constituted the system in opposition to which liberal Arabism was produced. That is, the sultan's religious despotism prompted the rise of liberal secular ideas, and then the shift in the Ottoman Empire's ideology from religion to Turkish nationalism in the early twentieth century provoked the rise of Arab identity among Syrian intellectual leaders. The breakdown of the Ottoman Empire and the colonial partitioning of Arab lands into disparate states generated yet another context for the production of meaning. In this context, the perceived collective mistreatment of the diverse Arab-speaking populations of the region by European powers overshadowed and homogenized this diversity and signified the idea that these populations constituted a people, a single nation, who were entitled to form a political community of their own. In opposition to the domination of Arab countries by continental Europe, the supranationalist ideology of pan-Arab nationalism was formed to unify the "continental" Arab into a single Arab nation (Antonius 1961; Haim 1962; Cleveland 1971; Zeine 1973; Dawn 1973, 1988; Hourani 1983; Moaddel 2005). Appropriated by the military in Egypt, Iraq, Syria, and Libya, pan-Arab nationalism was used as the ideology of power to justify the overthrow of the political order in these countries between 1952 (Egypt) and 1969 (Libya).

The military regimes of the postcoup period dramatically transformed the sociopolitical context. By dissolving all the existing political parties and nationalizing the properties of both foreign companies and members of the indigenous dominant classes, these regimes managed to reconstitute themselves as the dominant, if not the sole, political, economic, and cultural actors across the four Arab countries. The totalitarianism of the military regimes, however, was the context that triggered the generation of an equally totalitarian oppositional ideology of Islamic extremism and suicide terrorism. The defeat of the military regimes in the Six-Day War with Israel in 1967, as well as these regimes' inability to promote the economic prosperity and the Arab unity they promised and prescribed, resulted in the decline of pan-Arab nationalism, providing a favorable discursive context for the rise of Islamic fundamentalism (Rabinovich 1972; Ayubi 1980; Vatikiotis 1980; Hinnebusch 1982, 1990; Olson 1982; Roberts 1987; Holmström 1973; Moaddel 2005).

Iran experienced a similar historical pattern of diverse cultural episodes. In the nineteenth century, monarchical despotism and *ulama* obstructionism prompted the rise of constitutional ideas and anticlerical secularism. These ideas shaped, as it were, the political movements for the construction of the modern state, culminating in the Constitutional Revolution of 1906 (Bayat 1991; Afary 1996). While the revolution failed to produce a democratic government, it unleashed a secular trend that remained unabated well into the second half of the twentieth century. The administrative weakness of the Pahlavi state, an outcome of the Allies' forced abdication of Reza Shah in 1941, contributed to the revival of the liberal ideas that had shaped the 1906 Constitutional Revolution. However, the domination of the British over Iran's oil industry provoked the economic nationalism of the early 1950s (a similar historical process contributed to the rise of economic nationalism in Algeria and Egypt in the mid-twentieth century). However, similar to what occurred in Egypt and Syria, the military coup in 1953 and the secularist orientation of the Pahlavi monarchy and its interventionist authoritarian character, particularly following the reforms of the early 1960s, formed a new context in which the discourse of Shia fundamentalism was produced by lay intellectuals Jalal ale-Ahmad and Ali Shariati as well as clerics Ayatollah Khomeini and Ayatollah Taliqani. The state's authoritarian character also prompted a de facto alliance among fundamentalist, leftist, and liberal groups in the revolutionary movement that overthrew the monarchy in 1979 (Parsa 1989; Moaddel 1993, 2005).

Islamic Fundamentalism Versus Liberal Democracy

Islamic fundamentalism has primarily been a reaction to the secular change promoted and supported by the modern national state, which was first formed in Egypt, Iran, and Turkey in the early 1920s and later in other Middle Eastern and North African countries. In countries where the state turned overly secularist, exclusivist, authoritarian, and interventionist, the fundamentalist movement also turned extremist and exclusivist. There were also other historical patterns in the development of Islamic fundamentalism. In Saudi Arabia, for example, fundamentalism was a consequence of the kingdom's policy of proselytizing of Islam in order to fend off the challenges it faced from pan-Arab nationalism. The kingdom not only courted the fundamentalists who had fled Egypt or expelled from secular Arab countries, but also engaged in supporting Islamic movement worldwide, a policy that benefited the Wahhabi clerics and contributed to the rise of a strong fundamentalist movement in the kingdom (Okruhlik 2002; Prokop 2003; Dekmejian 1994; Moaddel 2006). In a different manner, the rise of fundamentalism in Pakistan is also a consequence of state policies. Facing the demand from powerful regional movements in East Bengal, Sindh, Baluchistan, and the North West Frontier Province for political inclusion, the Punjabi dominated elite decided to change conversation by invoking the Islamic identity of the nation as a way to transcend ethnic differences. Started with Prime Minister Liaqat Ali Khan (1947-1951), subsequent political leaders of the country increasingly resorted to Islam in order to legitimize their rule.

This process created a favorable political space for the rise of Islamic fundamentalism in Pakistan (Alavi 2009).

Before the late 1970s, however, Islamic fundamentalism was simply a religious trend. The Sunni fundamentalists of the Muslim Brothers in Arab countries, Jamaat-i Islami in Pakistan, and the Shia fundamentalist followers of Ayatollah Khomeini and Ali Shariati were hard at work, vociferously and unrelentingly attacking the expanding secular order. Their stated objectives were to repel what they considered onslaughts on Islam by secular intellectuals and politicians, who were perceived to be conspiring with Christians and other religious minorities to undermine the religion, targeting the Christians in Egypt, the Bahai's in Iran, and the Ahmadis in Pakistan. The fundamentalists questioned the validity of nationhood in Islam, rejected separation of religion and politics, promoted the idea of male supremacy and gender segregation, attacked Western culture as decadent, and inculcated rigorously among the public the importance of the strict application of the sharia law for the formation of a pure Islamic order (Ahmad 1967; Mitchell 1969; Banna 1978; Lia 1998; Abrahamian 1982; Kazemi 2012; Sadri 2012).

These and other separately determined and nationally specific fundamentalist movements came together and took the appearance of a homogeneous and worldwide Islamic revivalism as a result of a somewhat simultaneous outbreak of four major historical events. The first was the 1977 military coup by General Zia ul-Haq in Pakistan and the subsequent Islamization program launched by his regime. The second was the Iranian Revolution of 1979, which brought Shia fundamentalists to power. The formation of the Islamic Republic of Iran created euphoria among Muslim activists worldwide, particularly as a result of the Islamic regime's success at recasting the status of the United States from the seat of the world's most powerful and stable democracy, worthy of emulation, to that of the "Great Satan" and a decadent culture. Next, the 1979 Soviet invasion of Afghanistan brought strong reactions from a significant section of the Muslim world and Western democracies in an effort to push the Soviets out of the country. Both the pro-Islamic military coup in Pakistan and the Iranian Revolution in all likelihood boosted the morale of the Muslims who were fighting the Soviet forces in Afghanistan. Worldwide mobilization of Muslim activists against the invasion lent legitimacy to and promoted an Islamic extremist view of violent jihad as the *fard al-ayn* (the necessary duty). Finally, the fourth event was the 1979 seizure of the Grand Mosque in Mecca by several hundred armed Muslim militants led by Juhayman al-Otaybi. The militants were swiftly crushed, but their act demonstrated the vulnerability of the Saudi kingdom.

Taken together, these events created a remarkable historical conjuncture that made it possible for Islamic fundamentalism to get articulated with the social conditions and thus transformed fundamentalism from a religious extremist trend into a normal and acceptable feature of the social order. Ideologically, from the Islamic political lexicon, these events brought to the fore an extremist interpretation of a handful of concepts like *jahiliyya, jihad, fard al-ayn, kafir, taghut,* Pharaoh, martyrdom, and the "Crusader-Zionist alliance" in order to shape the discursive framework of Islamic extremism. If jahiliyya in histori-cal Islam characterized the decadent cultural order that purportedly existed in Arabia before the advent of Islam in the seventh century, the term now applies to the political order in the existing Muslim-majority countries, which were claimed to have bypassed the sharia law and were therefore no longer Islamic. If the term jihad referred to a defensive war, a war against the infidels, or simply the utmost efforts by Muslims to excel, it now means violence against the secular order-cum-jahiliyya. If fard al-ayn indicated such religious obliga-tions as prayer, fasting, payment of zakat, and similar duties that all Muslims must perform, its application is now expanded to include obligatory participa-tions in violent jihad against the secular regimes and suicide terrorism. If such terms as Pharaoh and taghut were used to mean infidel tyrants, they now refer to such secular Muslim rulers as the president of Egypt or the Shah of Iran. Finally, if the support of Western governments, the United States in particular, for the state of Israel vis-à-vis Palestinians was considered unfair by many in the region, this support is now interpreted as an indicator of Crusader-Zionist alliance against the Muslim world. Prior to 1979 these interpretations were at the fringe of Islamic political thought, but in the late twentieth and early twenty-first centuries, they constituted the building blocks of the guiding man-ifestos of Muslim extremism presented in Abdullah Azzam's *Join the Caravan,*[8] Abu Bakr Naji's *The Management of Savagery,*[9] and Abu Musab al-Suri's *Global Islamic Resistance Call.*[10]

The period between the formation of the Islamic Republic of Iran in 1979 and the degeneration of Islamic fundamentalism into the suicide terrorism of al-Qaeda and then the Islamic State in Iraq and Syria (ISIS) in the early twenty-first century is marked by the recurrence of religiously inspired violence and terrorism, religious intolerance and sectarianism, and the subjugation of women, perpetrated by Islamic regimes in Iran, Afghanistan, and Saudi Arabia; conscious attempts by Muslim extremists to generate the conditions of savagery and chaos in Egypt, Iraq, Pakistan, Nigeria, and Syria; and the dynamic of Iran- and Saudi-led sectarian warfare in Iraq, Lebanon, Syria, and Yemen. This interval in fact represents one of the darkest episodes in the mod-ern history of Islam in the Middle East and North Africa. The domination of social life by either the authoritarian religious regimes or the violence perpe-trated by Islamic extremism, however, begot a secular response. The rise of anticlerical secularism, religious reformism, and liberal values among Iranian intellectual leaders and the public at large in the past decades is a clear indica-tion that the installation of authoritarian religious regimes brings about liberal oppositional responses (Rajaee 2007; Kamrava 2008; Moaddel 2009; Mahdavi 2011). The people from other countries in the region have also displayed similar changes in values. As the data presented in this book will show, it appears that they have abandoned the ideas connected to political Islam and are oriented toward secular politics, gender equality, and religious tolerance. The Arab Spring in fact signifies the start of a new cultural episode in the Middle East and North Africa.

The Organization of This Book

One way to understand trends in sociopolitical thought and the transformation of values in a country is to assess the expressions of the intellectual leaders and opinion makers: to analyze the opposing positions among these thinkers, examine the way in which they have addressed and resolved issues, and presume that their views are the harbingers of the change that is yet to come. This book adopts a complementary approach. It focuses on the value orientations of the members of the ordinary public and tries to measure their orientations toward the issues that also concern the intellectual leaders. The individual members of the public, however, like the subalterns, hardly leave traces of their thoughts for social investigators to describe and analyze. Thus, survey research methodology is employed in an effort to gain access to and understand their value orientations.

These value orientations are analytically broken down into a series of survey questions. The survey instrument is widely pretested and then used to collect comparative cross-national survey data from randomly selected nationally representative samples of respondents in seven Middle Eastern and North African countries—Egypt, Iraq, Lebanon, Pakistan, Saudi Arabia, Tunisia, and Turkey. The surveys provide the data to assess micro (individual) and macro (country) variations in the support for Islamic fundamentalism and liberal nationalism across these seven countries. Evidentiary materials obtained through survey research are clearly different from historical documents. However, the survey instrument used is informed by the history and cultures of these countries. It includes multiple measures of the same set of historically significant issues that have been addressed, discussed, and debated by secular and religious intellectual leaders in the modern period.

These multiple measures are used to create various components of liberal values and religious fundamentalism. The constructs constituting liberal values are the belief in expressive individualism, gender equality, secular politics, and national identity; the components of religious fundamentalism are the belief in a disciplinarian deity, literalism or inerrancy of the scriptures, religious exclusivity, and religious intolerance. Comparative cross-national, longitudinal, and panel data are used to analyze (1) the extent of social support for liberal values and religious fundamentalism and the variation in this support across the seven countries and by age, gender, and education; (2) the correlates of the measures of liberal values and religious fundamentalism at the micro (individual) and macro (country) levels; (3) the laypersons' perceptions of what makes a country more developed, the liberal and religious causes and consequences of development, and the factors that make the differences between development and Westernization; and (4) trends in values across some of these countries in recent years in order to show that the Arab Spring heralded the coming of a new cultural episode in the region. The term *Arab Spring* is used in this book in a sense broader than it is commonly used; it refers to movements not just in specific Arab countries but a general trend toward liberal nationalism in the region as a whole, including Iran, Pakistan, and Turkey.

Chapters 1 through 3 discuss and measure the concepts of expressive individualism, gender equality, secular politics, liberal values, and national identity across the seven countries. Chapter 4 focuses on describing, conceptualizing, and measuring religious fundamentalism. It considers the construct to be multidimensional, consisting of four components: the belief in a disciplinarian deity, literalism, religious exclusivity, and religious intolerance. Each chapter begins with a discussion on the status of these concepts in the culture of the region and historical Islam. Chapter 4 also reports that on the micro (individual) level, the variables that strengthen religious fundamentalism weaken liberal values, and vice versa, consistently across the seven countries. In all four chapters, variation in liberal values and religious fundamentalism is presented and assessed cross-nationally and by age, gender, and education. These chapters take a micro (individual) perspective. Chapter 5 discusses variation in religious fundamentalism and liberal values on the macro (country) level. Here again the data show that the attributes of the national context that are positively linked to aggregate religious fundamentalism are negatively connected to aggregate liberal values, and vice versa.

Chapter 6 discusses the question of development and what makes a country more developed from the respondents' perspectives. It evaluates how they related liberal values and religious fundamentalism to the causes and consequences of development. It also discusses the differences between Westernization and development in bringing about changes in values. Chapter 7 discusses trends in values in Egypt, Iraq, Saudi Arabia, Tunisia, and Turkey (countries for which longitudinal data are available) toward secular politics, national identity, gender equality, and religious tolerance. Based on these trends, it argues that the Arab Spring marks a new cultural episode in the region. The conclusion discusses the implications of the analysis advanced in this book for a better understanding of the people and cultures of the Middle East and North Africa and why liberal nationalism is a most viable option in these countries.

Comparative Cross-National, Longitudinal, and Panel Survey Data

The analysis advanced in this book is based on several datasets. The first dataset, which includes the bulk of the data (discussed in chapters 1 through 6), is from seven-country cross-national comparative surveys carried out in Egypt, Iraq, Lebanon, Pakistan, Saudi Arabia, Tunisia, and Turkey in 2011 and 2013. These surveys employed a multistage stratified probability sampling design to gather information from a nationally representative sample of adult respondents (aged 18 and older) from all walks of life.[11] The sample included 3,496 respondents from Egypt; 3,000 from Iraq; 3,034 from Lebanon; 3,523 from Pakistan; 2,005 from Saudi Arabia; 3,070 from Tunisia, and 3,019 from Turkey—a total of well over 21,000 completed face-to-face interviews. In order to make a more effective comparison between religious groups, Christians in Egypt and Shias in Saudi Arabia were oversampled. The questionnaire used in these surveys consisted of more than 250 items that required approximately one hour on average to complete. It explored the respondents' views on a wide range of religious, gender, political, and other cultural issues as well as demographics. Items were translated from English into the languages used in these countries, including Arabic, Kurdish, Pashto, Urdu, and Turkish; back translated into English by someone who had not seen the original English version; and then compared with the original English items to ensure consistency of meaning across the seven countries. Some of the items, but not too many, were not asked in some of the countries. Questions related to child qualities (chapter 1) and development (chapter 6) were not used in Tunisia, two questions on secular politics were not allowed in Saudi Arabia, and three items on religious fundamentalism, out of sixteen items used, were excluded in Egypt. These will be discussed in the relevant chapters. A copy of the questionnaire appears in the appendix. Table I.1 shows the sample sizes, fieldwork dates, response rates, oversampling information, if applicable, and the organization that carried out the survey in each country, and table I.2 provides demographic characteristics of the respondents.

The second dataset is from two waves of a panel survey carried out in Egypt, Tunisia, and Turkey. The first wave occurred in 2011 and 2013, as noted in tables I.1 and I.2, and the second wave was carried out in the three countries in 2015 and 2016. The characteristics of the two waves are reported in table I.3.

TABLE I.1 Data Collection Overview

	n	Oversample	Survey Dates	Response. Rate (%)	Data Collection Agency
Egypt	3,496	Christians	June–August 2011	93	ERTC, Cairo, Egypt
Iraq	3,000	None	January–February 2011	88	IIACSS, Baghdad, Iraq
Lebanon	3,034	None	March–July 2011	61	ICOD, Beirut, Lebanon
Pakistan	3,523	None	May–September 2011	83	University of Agriculture, Faisalabad, Pakistan
Saudi Arabia	2,005	Shias	January–February 2011	73	PARC Jeddah, Saudi Arabia
Tunisia	3,070	None	March–May 2013	78	ELKA Consulting, Tunis, Tunisia
Turkey	3,019	None	April–June 2013	62	Frekans, Istanbul, Turkey

TABLE I.2 Respondents' Demographic Characteristics

Characteristic	Pakistan	Egypt	Saudi Arabia	Iraq	Lebanon	Tunisia	Turkey
Mean age	35	39	34	36	35	44	41
Male	51%	49%	50%	53%	59%	45%	44%
University education	4%	15%	17%	13%	28%	17%	13%
Religion:							
Sunni	82%	0%	75%	40%	23%	99%	86%
Shia	7%	0%	25%	31%	33%	0%	2%
Allawi	—	—	—	—	—	—	4%
Muslim (sect unknown)	8%	86%	0%	29%	3%	0%	7%
Druze	—	—	—	—	6%	0%	0%
Christian	1%	14%	0%	<1%	27%	0%	0%

TABLE I.3 Panel Survey Characteristics: Multistage Area Probability Sampling Frame

Egypt	Tunisia	Turkey
Sample: Census data from CAPMAS	Sample: Census data from the Institute for National Statistics	Sample: Voter registry
Wave 1: 6/12–8/7/2011	Wave 1: 3/5–6/1/2013	Wave 1: 3/16–6/26/2013
Wave 2: 8/19–12/7/2016	Wave 2: 5/4–8/21/2015	Wave 2: 2/9–7/1/2016
n, wave 1: 3,496	n, wave 1: 3,070	n, wave 1: 3,019
n, wave 2: 3,858 (2,430 panel respondents, 1,428 replenishment respondents)	n, wave 2: 2,391	n, wave 2: 2,759 (1,682 panel respondents; 1,077 replenishment respondents)
Response rate, wave 1: 93%	Response rate, wave 1: 78%	Response rate, wave 1: 62%
Response rate, wave 2: 70%	Response rate, wave 2: 78%	Response rate, wave 2: 56% (among panel respondents)
Firm, wave 1: ERTC, Cairo, Egypt	Firm, waves 1 and 2: ELKA Consulting, Tunis, Tunisia	Firm, waves 1 and 2: Frekans, Istanbul, Turkey
Firm, wave 2: El-Zanaty & Associates, 6th of October, Egypt		

Finally, the third dataset is from several longitudinal surveys carried out in Egypt, Iraq, Saudi Arabia, and Turkey before 2011. To construct trends in values, the data gathered in the surveys referenced in tables I.1 and I.3 were combined with data collected from nationally representative samples of respondents as follows: in Egypt, 3,000 respondents in 2001, 1,036 in 2007, 1,677 in fall 2007, and 1,384 in 2014; in Iraq, 2,325 respondents in 2004, 2,701 in 2006, 6,692 in 2006, 7,994 in March 2007, 7,839 in July 2007, 1,500 in 2008, and 1,729 in 2010; in Saudi Arabia, 1,000 respondents in 2003; and in Turkey, 3,000 respondents in 2001. The second and third datasets were used to construct trends or changes in values in Egypt, Iraq, Saudi Arabia, Tunisia, and Turkey. Considering all the cross-national, longitudinal, and panel data, the analysis advanced in this book uses more than 60,000 completed face-to-face interviews.

CHAPTER 1

EXPRESSIVE INDIVIDUALISM

Expressive individualism is the first component of liberal values to be considered. It rests on the recognition, exaltation, and celebration of individuals' private judgment about and ability to decide matters related to their lives, giving precedence to their choices and preferences over parental authority, patrimonial domination, and religious instructions. Although the exigencies of the communal or nationalist liberation struggle against foreign domination may complicate or even limit individual choices, the ultimate objective of the struggle for democratic change is the recognition and institutionalization of individual sovereignty.

The concept of expressive individualism has been the subject of considerable philosophical and political debate, and the varied operational meanings assigned to it have generated enormous controversies in different social contexts, including the contemporary Middle East and North Africa. This chapter, while discussing these debates, is concerned with measuring and analyzing expressive individualism, using a survey of people's preferences concerning the basis for marriage, a woman's right to dress as she wishes, and the most favorable qualities for children. A more liberal democratic order is predicated on the extent to which individual choices in these domains of social life are confirmed, promoted, strengthened, and institutionalized. A society may change in an individualistic or a collectivist direction, depending on how social actors resolve these practical issues and how their resolutions are institutionalized and become a part of the permanent features of the social order. In this book, I discuss the predictors of liberal values, of which expressive individualism is a component, on the macro (country) and micro (individual) level. In this chapter, I limit the discussion to analyzing cross-national variation in expressive individualism. I also analyze this variation by age, gender, and education.

The realization of the ideal of individual equality is also a matter of degree and a function of social arrangements. In modern democratic societies, this autonomy is the quintessential component of equality of opportunity and of political voice. It is formally sanctioned by law and practiced most of the time, though violations of individual rights do happen. In the patriarchal cultures of the Middle East and North Africa, on the other hand, priority is often given to the patriarch or the dominant male member of the family, religious authorities, or the ruling regime. The cultures of these countries tend to emphasize obedience to authority in family, politics, and other forms of social hierarchy. They, however, vary in terms of their support for individualistic values. Although one may arrive at the utility of the idea of individual equality through moral and rational reasoning, its wide social acceptance is an outcome of the operation of social forces, some of which are addressed in this book.

This chapter first discusses the concept of expressive individualism. It then suggests three indicators as measures of the construct: basis for marriage, a woman's freedom to dress as she wishes, and favorable qualities for children. Next, it assesses variation in these measures across the seven countries and by age, gender, and education.

Liberal Democracy

Expressive individualism is one of the key dimensions of liberal democracy, along with gender equality, secular politics, and national identity. From a philosophical viewpoint, however, individualism may be construed as the foundation or the essence of liberal democracy, not just one constitutive element. Liberal democracy is the exaltation of individual freedom and the right of private judgment. A liberal democratic order recognizes and institutionalizes the principle of the individual as an autonomous actor in every domain of social life. This recognition is reflected in the emergence of the institution of free labor—that is, free peasantry—and the recognition of property rights in economic relationships following the breakdown of the precapitalist social order. More directly, liberal democracy rests on the acceptance of the principle of equal voice in politics and on the belief that individual rights are not defined by gender and are equally applicable to men and women in social relations. Finally, it is rooted in the tenet that knowledge about the world resides in the faculties of the individual—that is, rational thought and the experience of the senses and intuition, which are the foundation of modern science. The basis of this knowledge neither emanates from God, nor is it extracted from religious texts. Without the presence of the autonomous individual whose rights are protected in all these domains of social life—the family, economic, political, educational, and scientific—a fully developed liberal democratic order would not be possible.

From a sociological perspective, individualism in one domain of social life may not be readily transferrable to another domain, and the process of the rise and recognition of individual rights in the scientific, educational, political, economic, and gender domains has been subject to different societal and historical dynamics. Concerning the relationship of gender and democracy, for example, until the first half of the twentieth century, the existing democratic orders were male democracies in western Europe and a white male democracy in the United States. Thus, some societies may apply the principle of equality in politics only to men and rigorously defend gender hierarchy and male supremacy. They may also variably accept the authority of scientific knowledge over religious beliefs. A liberal democratic order is thus possible at the point of convergence of the diverse dynamics that promote equality in all the domains of social life. The empirical data from the seven countries presented in this book show that on the micro (individual) and macro (country) levels, three components of liberal values—expressive individualism, gender equality, and secular politics—are all positively correlated (see chapters 3 and 5).

Territorial nationalism or adherence to national identity, on the other hand, cannot always be considered a component of liberal values or liberal democracy. More often than not, nationalism has also been linked to authoritarian or even chauvinistic and xenophobic political movements. To account for such opposing tendencies in people's perceptions of their collective sovereignty, historians and political scientists have made a distinction between nationalism and patriotism. The former is connected to national pride, defined in differential or sometimes oppositional relationships to other nations, and based on in-group solidarity and insistence on the superiority of one's nation over others. Nationalism thus tends to capture primarily relational and synchronic interactions among nations. Patriotism, on the other hand, is not relational. Instead, it is self-referential, unrelated to other nations. It rests on the feeling of love for one's country—its natural beauty, peoples, and contributions to human development, historical progress, and civilization (Viroli 1995; de Figueiredo and Elkins 2003; Moaddel 2017a). Nonetheless, considering the context of the contemporary Middle East and North Africa, where territorial nationalism is defined in contrast to religious nationalism, those who identify with the territorial nation, rather than Islam, tend to more strongly favor liberal values than do those who consider Islam to be the primary basis of their identity (Moaddel 2017a). From this specific (and narrow) historical perspective, national identity is considered here to be one of the dimensions of liberal values and liberal democracy.

Liberal democracy is possible when the arrangement of objective social forces prevents the rise and functioning of an authoritarian system and includes, for example, the institutionalization of property rights, limited state control over the economy, industrialization, a strong bourgeoisie, a weak landed aristocracy, an organized working class, an organized women's movement, a heterogeneous and contentious ruling elite, the separation of powers and the presence of a system of checks and balances, organized professional associations, and an educated elite. In the final analysis, however, liberal democracy works insofar as citizens predominantly support liberal democratic values and are fully prepared to defend liberal democracy when it faces the menace of xenophobic political demagogues. The key message of this book, however, concerns neither the basis for democracy nor the combat readiness of the public to defend it. Rather, it proposes that liberal democratic ideas as an alternative to the existing polity have gained more popularity today than at any time since the decline of the liberal age in Arab countries in the late 1930s.

What Is Individualism?

Among the components of liberalism, individualism appears to be the most controversial, and its operational definitions have been subject to varied and even contradictory interpretations. Individualism as a moral philosophy rests on the principle of the equality of all individuals. From this perspective, individuals are viewed as an autonomous beings—preordained, for some, by God—with the inalienable right to control and manage their own life. Individualism rests on the premise that the individuals are the most knowledgeable about their own interests. Therefore, it is immoral for other individuals to impose their will on the individual. The recognition of individual rights is fundamental to the formation of a civilized and democratic social order. It provides for a peaceful coexistence among people and is conducive to individual empowerment.

In practice and from a historical perspective, however, individualism is not an easy concept to operationalize. The expression, according to Weber, "includes the most heterogeneous things imaginable" (Weber 1992, 178n22). Lukes (1971, 45) concurred, adding that the term is "used in a great many ways, in many different contexts with an exceptional lack of precision . . . [and that] it has played a major role in the history of ideas, and of ideologies, in modern Europe and America." Individualism, he said, carries "a pejorative connotation, a strong suggestion that to concentrate on the individual is to harm the superior interests of society" (48), a view that has been commonly shared by factions across the political spectrum. The theocratic Catholic reactionaries in nineteenth-century France, for example, cried out that "the social order had been 'shattered to its foundations because there was too much liberty in Europe and not enough Religion'; everywhere authority was weakening and there was a frightening growth of 'individual opinion . . .'" (46). Saint-Simonians, on the political left and the first to use individualism systematically, referred to "the pernicious and 'negative' ideas underlying the evils of the modern critical epoch, whose 'disorder, atheism, individualism, and egoism' they contrasted with the prospect of 'order, religion, association, and devotion'" (48).

In Germany, on the other hand, a romantic conception of individualism—referring to the notion of individual uniqueness, originality, and self-realization—became prevalent in the nineteenth century (Lukes 1971, 54). This latter conception is consistent with the idea of expressive individualism, stressing the uniqueness of each individual in terms of the role, feeling, and intuition that need to be expressed for this individuality to be realized and to flourish (Bellah et al. 1985). This conception has gained widespread popularity in the United States, where expressive individualism is believed to be associated with and promoted by laissez-faire capitalism, liberal democracy, limited government, equal opportunity, and individual rights. Walls (2015), however, presented a different take on the history and the role of individualism in the country. For her, individualism has changed since the formation of the republic in the late eighteenth century, and its operational meaning today is quite different from what was intended two centuries ago. She distinguishes among three types of individualism: political individualism, economic individualism, and social individualism. For her, social individualism is based on the assumption that individuals are unable to understand and respond to the needs of society. They are not necessarily selfish. Rather, they are more qualified to speak to what is good for themselves. This assumption justifies their decision to focus on matters that are of utmost importance to them and to resist attempts by others to decide these matters on their behalf. Political individualism, by contrast, rests on the idea of positive liberty. The idea that a strong national government is necessary to protect individual rights and ensure societal stability presumes that one person can know what is best for someone else. Political individualism "involves trusting the government to identify and protect activities and choices that will promote individual interests and the public good. For this to work, one certainly must be able to know what these interests are. Social individualism is based on the idea that this is not possible" (Walls 2015, 116).

In contrast to these conceptions, for Lukes (2006, 3), individualism is "an *ideological* construct, in the double sense that it embodies and conveys illusions and that these illusions serve partisan interests." From this viewpoint, individualism constitutes "a protective bulwark against the dangers of ideological thinking, from both right and left" (3). From a Marxist perspective, individuals may not be free and autonomous in a class-divided society because of the constraints of the forces emanating from unequally distributed economic and political power. Any claim to the existence of a free individual masks the reality that such forces limit individual autonomy and options in the pursuit of happiness. Only after the constraints of class structures are eliminated in a socialist society are individuals able to freely pursue their interests, truly experience happiness, and engage in productive activities as they please. As Marx (1976, 47) said in *German Ideology* in 1845:

> For as soon as the distribution of labour comes into being, each man has a particular, exclusive sphere of activity, which is forced upon him and from which he cannot escape. He is a hunter, a fisherman, a herdsman, or a critical critic, and must remain so if he does not want to lose his means of livelihood; while in communist society, where nobody has one exclusive sphere of activity but each can become accomplished in any branch he wishes, society regulates the general production and thus makes it possible for me to do one thing today and another tomorrow, to hunt in the morning, fish in the afternoon, rear cattle in the evening, criticise after dinner, just as I have a mind, without ever becoming hunter, fisherman, herdsman or critic.

Individualism in the Islamic Cultural Tradition

There have been lively debates among historians and Islamicists as to whether the institutional development of individualism followed varying historical trajectories in Western and Islamic cultural traditions. One train of thought has maintained that the Islamic cultural tradition, in contrast to that of the West, exhibits conceptual inadequacy in the area of individual rights and that this inadequacy explains the failure of liberal democracy in the Muslim world. A prominent representative of this view is Lewis (1993), who argued that Western democracy is rooted in Roman law of the legal person, defined as a corporate entity with certain rights and obligations. This principle provided a legal scaffolding that contributed to the emergence of a form of council or assembly in which qualified individuals were able to participate in the formation, conduct, and, on occasion, replacement of the government. Over the centuries, such bodies in the West gained increasing legislative power. This development was made possible because Christianity "was forced to recognize the authority of Roman law" (Gibb 1947, 85). In the Islamic tradition, by contrast, there was no recognition of corporate persons and, hence, no legislative function. And without legislative function, there was no need for legislative institutions and the principle of representation (Lewis 1993).

The existence of cultural categories that provided a basis for the formulation of sociopolitical discourses constituting patriarchy and institutional practices is claimed to have further undermined societal recognition of individual autonomy in Muslim-majority countries. It is said that such concepts as *zaim* (leader) and *zaama* (leadership), as well as the associated norms, dissolve individuality in the institution of patriarchy. The term *zaim* in Arabic refers to a charismatic political leader. In the modern period, however, it has been used by the leaders of the military who seized power in many Arab countries, including Algeria, Egypt, Iraq, Libya, and Syria, to give credence to their authoritarian rule (Sharabi 1963; Vatikiotis 1973; Lewis 1988). For Lapidus (1992), on the other hand, modern authoritarianism is rooted in the second golden age of historical Islam, in which power, far from being an expression of the total society, became the prerogative of certain individuals or groups. Because "the exercise of power is organized through networks of clients and retainers" (17), little room is left for free individual expressions.

It is also argued that if individualism is understood not in the narrow sense of protecting individual liberty against the coercive state powers but as a general "cluster of ideas and social practices that collectively characterized Euro-American modernity, then one can find elements of individualistic thinking in premodern intellectual traditions" of historical Islam (Karamustafa 2012, 253). In Islamic jurisprudence, for example, there are rules to protect civil rights, mostly those of private individuals against each other rather than against the state, and in Sufism, the preoccupation with the self, scrutiny of inner motivations, and "personal experiential verification of religious truths" is said to parallel the modernist notions of subjectivity and self-consciousness in the context of individualism (253). Moreover, the Quran considers individuals responsible for their actions, which will be assessed on Judgment Day, and this implies that they are rational and autonomous actors. Other commentators have pointed out that "individualism has never been annulled in Islam, nor has the sense of belonging, clanism, been repealed. The reassurance of private ownership in Islam and the special regard given to protecting it is a demonstrable proof of the recognition of individualism" (El-Ashker and Wilson 2006, 25). Another states that "individualism from Islamic perspective consists of salient traits of which self-building is one and accountability before Allah (God) is the other" (Musah 2011, 71).

Finally, where Islam appears to be clearly leaning toward individualism, and even displaying a celebratory attitude toward it, is in the economic (commercial) domain. A system of individualistic instrumental rationality that is derived from and driven by commerce governs God's principles of rewards and punishments on Judgment Day. Torrey's (1892) content analysis of the Quran reveals how the theology of the scripture is expressed in and informed by the language of trade. He observes that the Quran "manifests everywhere a lively interest in matters of trade" (2) and that "words elsewhere used to express some familiar commercial idea, here transferred to the relations between God and man" (3). Such commercial terms as "reckoning," "weights," "measures," "payments," "loss," "gain," "fraud," "buying," "selling," "profits," "wages," "loans," and "security" occur about 370 times in the Quran (3, 8) and thus "impart a certain commercial tone to the whole" (4). In addition, the Islamic tradition glorifies commerce. There are numerous statements on the preeminence of commerce as a vocation and the esteem of merchants in the sayings of the Prophet. He is reported to have said that "the merchant who is sincere and trustworthy will (at the Judgment Day) be among the prophets, the just and the martyrs . . ., will sit in the shade of God's throne at the Day of Judgment . . . [and] are the messengers of this world and God's faithful trustees on Earth" (cited in Rodinson 2007, 44). According to holy tradition, trade is a superior way of earning one's livelihood: "If thou profit by doing what is permitted, thy deed is djihad" (cited in Rodinson 2007, 44). The taste for business that was the characteristic of the Prophet and the caliphs, his first successors, was reported with tenderness. Omar, the second caliph, is alleged to have said, "Death can come upon me nowhere more pleasantly than where I am engaged in business in the market, buying and selling on behalf of my family" (cited in Rodinson 2007, 44). It is recorded, says an eighteenth-century commentator on Ghazali, that Ibrahim an-Nakhai, a pious authority of the first century AH, was asked which he preferred: an honest merchant or a man who has given up all forms of work so as to devote himself wholly to the service of God. He is said to have replied, "The honest merchant is dearer to me, for he is in the position of one waging a holy war" (cited in Rodinson 2007, 151).

Individualism in Different Domains of Social Life

The concept of individualism in both Western and Islamic cultural traditions has been the subject of philosophical debates and political disputes, generating opposing interpretations and complicating the operationalization of the construct. These debates and disputes over the role and significance of individual rights and responsibilities are important because they affect social processes in two crucial respects. First, they shape public opinion and thus contribute to the rise or decline of the virtue of individualism in society. Second, they may contribute to a change in the moral foundation of the social order—for example, from a social order perceived as desirable because people are tied together via the bonds of religion to one in which people are free to choose and pursue different paths to happiness as they see fit, from a society based on the commonality of creed to one that rests on and recognizes the variety of individual tastes. Nonetheless, the apparently simple principle that the recognition of individual rights and autonomy contributes significantly to individual happiness and social harmony is more complex than it first appears. Even if one tries to manage this complexity by viewing the construct as a distinctive social practice in a specifically pertinent domain of social life and assessing its moral adequacy, political effectiveness, and relevance within that domain, one may still be unable to eschew controversy.

In the economic domain, for example, individualism is expressed in terms of the freedom to engage in unconstrained labor markets, commerce, and other forms of economic activities (i.e., laissez-faire capitalism). Within this domain, debates and contentions may arise, depending on the sociohistorical context. On the one hand, individualism may be morally justified as an inalienable right in the context of a people's struggle to liberate themselves from the bonds of servitude. On the other hand, applying this right to the case of a factory owner who would lay off workers on the grounds that he is not making enough profit makes economic individualism synonymous with capitalist greed. In politics, individualism is conveyed in the concept of "one person, one vote." People celebrate when they enjoy the freedom to vote for their political representatives—and are morally justified in doing so. There is, however, nothing celebratory in exercising one's political freedom in order to elect a xenophobic politician who could potentially or practically trample the rights and liberties of religious or ethnic minorities. In the family, individualism is reflected in the parental style that encourages the child to be independent and imaginative. But it is considered immoral for an individualistic child to refuse to take care of his elderly parents. In marriage, the selection of one's spouse is an individual choice, and a young adult may be justified in rebelling if his parents select his mate, but he will be universally censured if he, as a married man, were to abandon his wife and children on the grounds that he wanted to be free (or to freely pursue his own interests). The invocation of individualism in the latter case implies utter social irresponsibility.

A valid measure of expressive individualism in a specific domain of social life must therefore be selected in such a way that it clearly captures whether a person favors or is against individual autonomy in that domain. Such a measure must not have the potential to be used to indicate, as shown in the preceding examples, individual greed, xenophobia, or social irresponsibility.

Measures of Expressive Individualism

An individual's right of choice has different operational definitions in different social domains. Although equality of political voice, gender equality, equality of opportunity in the labor market, freedom to choose one's religious faith, and individual autonomy in lifestyle all reflect various aspects of individualism, this chapter narrows the focus to aspects that are outside politics, gender relations, the labor market, and religious domains but that are within the realm of how people express their individuality—their *expressive individualism*.

Here expressive individualism is measured in terms of respondents' views on the following three issues:

1. Preference for love as a more important basis for marriage than parental approval,
2. Endorsement of a woman's right to dress as she wishes, and
3. Recognition of imagination and independence, not obedience and religious faith, as favorable qualities for children.

Basis for marriage: The recognition of the individual's freedom to select one's mate is viewed as a historical civic rebellion against the aristocratic norms of obedience to parental authority and patrimonial domination. The rationale justifying this rebellion is rooted in the humanist tradition that stressed not only individual freedom to choose whom to marry but also equality between spouses. Social scientists have coined the phrase "the Romeo and Juliet revolution" (Deutsch 1981; Huntington 1996a) to describe the phenomenon in which the young rebel against parental authority and pursue marriages based primarily on love. In the cultural context of the Middle East and North Africa, there have also been didactic parables that celebrate love as an important part of a happy marriage. A prime example is the poetry of Nizami Ganjavi (1141–1209), a prominent Iranian literary figure. In *Layli and Majnun*, he versifies the tragic consequence of a love forbidden by tradition, as Layli's authoritarian father forces Layli to forgo her love for Majnun and marry an older man (Talattof 2000).

Love is also believed to transcend aristocratic, tribal, ethnic, and national divisions. The recognition of the individual's right to choose is in fact considered a cornerstone of Western liberal democracy. To assess the extent of support for love as the basis for marriage across the seven countries, respondents were asked, "Which of the following is the more important basis for marriage: (1) parental approval, or (2) love?" Those who responded that love is more important are considered to have more individualistic values than do those who placed greater importance on parental approval.

A woman dresses as she wishes: Considerable empirical evidence and historical documents indicate that a woman's sartorial practices serve as a historical marker of Muslim orientation toward Western modernity. Ideological warfare on the social status of women in Muslim-majority countries, waged uninterrupted for well over a century among intellectual leaders, produced three major cultural episodes. These episodes reflected a succession of opposing orientations toward gender equality, and each began with a rupture in the cultural directives on the right way for a woman to appear outside her home. The first cultural episode was Islamic modernism, encompassing the late nineteenth and early twentieth centuries, where Muslim reformers advanced a new exegesis of the Quran in order to uplift the social status of women. Their Islamic feminist exposé rejected polygamy, defended women's right to participate in the social affairs, relaxed some of the restrictions on their dress such as covering the face, and lessened the limitations on their activities outside the home. Beginning with the rise of nationalism and a cultural shift toward secularism in the first quarter of the twentieth century, the second cultural episode promoted a new sartorial regime, in which the public presence of an unveiled woman gained an emancipatory significance. The third episode started with the decline of the secular state and the rise of Islamic fundamentalism in the second half of the twentieth century. For the fundamentalists, the veil constituted the essential protective shield of a woman's sanctity and sexual purity and therefore was a condition for her public appearance (Amin [1899] 1992; Ahmad 1967; Motahhari 1969; Minault 1990; Taraki 1996; Moaddel 2005).

Drawing on this debate, the recognition of a woman's right to dress as she wishes is considered a reasonable indicator of the concept of expressive individualism. It is a measure of the extent to which respondents disapprove of the social constraints on a woman's options in clothing and support her choice to dress as she wishes. Furthermore, because this measure assesses the degree of support for the freedom of sartorial expression for women, who have been the prime target of social constraints in the region, it is a reasonable yardstick of support for expressive individualism among men as well. Thus, it is argued that people who support a woman's prerogative to dress as she wishes in public are more supportive of expressive individualism than are those who do not.

To measure this construct, respondents were asked whether they (1) strongly agree, (2) agree, (3) disagree, or (4) strongly disagree that "it is up to a woman to dress whichever way she wants." The coding for this variable is reversed, so that a higher value indicates a stronger support for a women's right to dress.

Child qualities: People who adhere to individualistic values may promote and support similar values among their children, preferring to raise them to be more independent and imaginative and less obedient and religious (presuming that religiosity promotes blind obedience to authority). To measure this construct, respondents were given a list of ten qualities children can have: independence, hard work, feeling of responsibility, imagination, tolerance and respect for other people, thrift, determination and perseverance, religious faith, unselfishness, and obedience. They were then asked to choose the five qualities they considered more favorable. Based on their responses, an individualistic child qualities index was constructed as the sum of four dummy variables: (i) independence (1 = those who selected independence, 0 = otherwise), (ii) imagination (1 = those who selected imagination, 0 = otherwise), (iii) nonreligious faith (0 = those who selected religious faith, 1 = otherwise), and (iv) nonobedience (0 = those who selected obedience, 1 = otherwise), resulting in a variable with a possible range from 0 to 4. It is argued that people who more strongly favor expressive individualism are more likely to prefer a child to be independent and imaginative and less likely to prefer a child to be obedient and religious.

Attitudes in favor of marriage based on romantic love, a woman's freedom to dress as she wishes, and independent and imaginative children reflect different aspects of expressive individualism. To create a more robust measure, a composite measure of expressive individualism was constructed. First, the variables for the basis for marriage and child qualities were adjusted to range between 1 and 4, and then an expressive individualism index was constructed by averaging these three measures.[1] People who score higher values on this index are more strongly oriented toward expressive individualism. Table 1.1 shows responses to these measures across the seven countries and the value and range of the expressive individualism index for each country.

Cross-National Variation

The measures of expressive individualism varied considerably across the seven countries. According to table 1.1, preference for love as the basis for marriage was highest among Lebanese, with 69 percent of respondents endorsing love, and lowest among Pakistanis, with just 6 percent favoring love. The other countries fell in between: 54 percent of Turkish respondents, 47 percent of Saudis, 31 percent of Iraqis, 29 percent of Egyptians, and 26 percent of Tunisians considered love to be a more important basis for marriage than parental approval.

Respondents from the seven countries also expressed varying levels of support for a woman being free to dress as she wishes, with the largest endorsements coming from Tunisia (56 percent), Turkey (52 percent), Lebanon (49 percent), and Saudi Arabia (47 percent) and the smallest endorsements coming from Iraq (27 percent), Pakistan (22 percent), and Egypt (14 percent).

Finally, this table shows how the seven countries differed on the child qualities index. Lebanese, with a mean index of 2.50, were the most individualistic, while Egyptians and Pakistanis, each with a mean index of 1.71, were the least individualistic. In between were Turkey (mean = 2.25), Saudi Arabia (mean = 2.11), and Iraq (mean = 1.79). According to an analysis of variance, the differences in the child qualities index across the countries were significant ($F = 554.26$, $p < .001$). Post hoc analyses using Scheffé's test for significance indicated statistically significant differences among all countries, except between Pakistan and Egypt, which were nearly identical.

Lastly, these three indicators were combined to construct an expressive individualism index by country.[2] The analysis of variance of the expressive individualism index showed significant differences among the seven countries

TABLE 1.1 Measures of Expressive Individualism

	Iraq	Lebanon	Pakistan	Saudi Arabia	Tunisia	Egypt	Turkey
Basis for marriage[a]							
Love	31%	69%	6%[a]	47%	26%	29%	54%
Parental approval	69%	31%	90%[a]	53%	74%	71%	46%
Woman dresses as she wishes							
Strongly agree	5%	17%	4%	18%	29%	5%	12%
Agree	22%	32%	18%	29%	27%	9%	40%
Disagree	38%	34%	39%	28%	26%	36%	36%
Strongly disagree	35%	17%	39%	25%	18%	50%	12%
Favorable qualities for children							
Independence (% selected)	41%	63%	22%	55%	N/A	38%	37%
Imagination (% selected)	16%	19%	7%	38%	N/A	9%	24%
Obedience (% not selected)	31%	57%	49%	37%	N/A	35%	79%
Religion (% not selected)	23%	62%	16%	29%	N/A	13%	28%
Child qualities index (mean)	1.79	2.50	1.71	2.11	N/A	1.71	2.25
Expressive individualism index (mean)	1.89	2.68	1.61	2.31	2.24	1.76	2.46
Range (min–max)	1–4	1–4	1–4	1–4	1–4	1–3.7	1–4
Median	1.75	2.83	1.58	2.25	2.00	1.58	2.50

[a] If respondents reported that both parental approval and love were important, interviewers were instructed to probe further, asking respondents to choose just one. If respondents were still unable to choose, interviewers recorded the response as "don't know," and the respondent's data for this measure was considered missing. However, in the case of Pakistan, interviewers separately recorded all responses where respondents reported the two as equally important: 4 percent of the cases were recorded as such and are not shown.

($F = 840.91$, $p < .001$), and post hoc analyses using Scheffé's test indicated statistically significant differences among all the countries. With an index value of 2.68, Lebanon was the most individualistic country, followed by Turkey (2.46), Saudi Arabia (2.31), Tunisia (2.24), Iraq (1.89), Egypt (1.76), and Pakistan (1.61).[3] While it was expected that respondents from relatively more democratic and

open countries such as Lebanon, Turkey, and Tunisia would be more supportive of expressive individualism than those from the less democratic countries,
the Saudis' comparatively high support for individualism is paradoxical. The
Saudis have been quite conservative in their attitudes toward gender equality
and in their support for religious fundamentalism (Moaddel and Karabenick
2013), yet their score on the expressive individualism index was much higher
than the scores of Egyptians, Iraqis, and Pakistanis. Their score was similar to
that of Tunisians, who are considerably less conservative than Saudis.

There are two plausible explanations for this paradox. One rests on the
view that relates expressive individualism to the level of economic development. It has been argued that in a prosperous economy, secure employment
and income stability enhance people's ability to make independent financial
decisions. Economic security in turn contributes to a more favorable subjective condition in which people think and reflect about such expressive
values as individual autonomy and choice in marriage, family, and dress style
(Inglehart and Welzel 2005; Inglehart, Moaddel, and Tessler 2006). Expressing individualism in Saudi Arabia may thus reflect the high level of economic
development the country has experienced in the past decades (as will be
shown in chapter 6, the country's GDP per capita is much higher than those
of the other six countries).

Another interpretation considers the view that the greater support for
expressive individualism among the Saudi respondents is a reaction to the
patriarchal values promoted by the dominant religious and political institutions. These values include the priority of parental authority over the children,
obedience to religion, and religious injunction concerning the veil for women.
Thus, this context turned patriarchy into a clear target of ideological attack,
particularly by the youth, signifying the desirability of expressive individualistic values. Living in a relatively more prosperous economy, the Saudis have in
fact been able to afford the lifestyle that is associated with expressive individualism. As shown later in table 1.2, Saudi youth, in particular, were far more
individualistic than the older age group.

To more effectively assess the status of individualism in a country, the
median value of the expressive individualism index for each country was constructed. Given 1 to 4 as the range of the index, the median value of 2.50 means
that there are as many people who are generally individualistic as there are
those who are not—that is, the society is individualistically neutral. Lebanon,
with the median index value of 2.83, was the only country among the seven that
may be considered individualistic, and Turkey, with the median index value of
2.50, is an individualistically neutral country; the rest, with median index values ranging between 2.25 for Saudi Arabia and 1.58 for Egypt and Pakistan, were
generally nonindividualistic countries.

Variation by Age, Gender, and Education

Age

A country's rapid population expansion, resulting in an excess of youth, which Fuller (1995) defines as a "youth bulge," has considerable consequences in terms of the social stability, unrest, and political violence in that country (Goldstone 1991; Urdal 2006). This phenomenon is evident in many countries in the Middle East and North Africa, where the youth segment of the populations has considerably expanded recently. Since the 1960s, structural changes in service provision, especially in health care, have created the conditions for a population explosion, resulting in a dramatic increase in the proportion of younger people. In 2010, around 65 percent of the regional population was estimated to be under the age of 30 (Pew Research Center 2011). Additionally, the youth unemployment rate was higher in this region than in any other region of the world, with 29 percent of people aged 15 to 24 being unemployed; the second-highest rate of 19.5 percent was found in Europe and Central Asia (UNDP 2015). This phenomenon prompted observers to claim that these youth played a major role in the protest movements known as the Arab Spring that toppled the ruling regimes in Egypt, Tunisia, Libya, and Yemen (Chaaban 2009; Hvistendahl 2011; LaGraffe 2012; Campante and Chor 2012; Hoffman and Jamal 2012).

To assess whether the youth are significantly different in value orientations from the rest of the population, the sample was divided into two categories: (1) those aged 18 to 29, generally considered the youth bulge, and (2) those aged 30 and older, designated the older age group. Variation in the expressive individualism index by age group and country is reported in table 1.2. This table also reports the median age for each country. As shown in column 5 of this table, the size of the youth bulge varied considerably across the seven countries. The higher the median age, the smaller the size of the youth bulge. The median ages for Tunisia, Lebanon, and Turkey were above the upper limit of the youth bulge: 31, 29.8, and 29.2, respectively. This means that more than 50 percent of the population in these three countries was over the age of 29. Iraq and Pakistan, where the median ages were 20.9 and 21.6, respectively, had the youngest populations, and Egypt and Saudi Arabia, with median ages of 24.3 and 25.3, respectively, were in between.

It is suggested that this variation in median age is linked to variation in support for expressive individualistic values. That is, cross-national variation in expressive individualism is positively linked to median age (or inversely linked to the size of the youth bulge). An explanation for this hypothesis would be that people in countries with stronger individualistic values prefer having fewer children, resulting in a smaller youth bulge. In other words, there is an inverse

TABLE 1.2 Age Differences in Expressive Individualism and Median Age by Country

	1	2	3	4	5
	Mean Index: 18–29	Mean Index: 30+	$Col_1 - Col_2$	Mean Index: Total	Median Age[a]
Tunisia	2.34	2.18	0.16	2.22	31.0
Lebanon	2.81	2.59	0.22	2.68	29.8
Egypt	1.89	1.71	0.18	1.76	24.3
Turkey	2.65	2.39	0.26	2.46	29.2
Iraq	2.01	1.81	0.20	1.89	20.9
Saudi Arabia	2.48	2.16	0.32	2.31	25.3[b]
Pakistan	1.87	1.47	0.40	1.61	21.6
$r_{ol4Col5}$	.80[c]				

[a] The median ages for Tunisia and Turkey are from 2013; the median ages for all other countries are from 2011 (CIA 2011, 2013).
[b] The population figure used to compute the median age for Saudi Arabia includes about 25 percent nonnationals.
[c] $p < .05$.

or negative association between the size of the youth bulge and expressive individualism and a corresponding direct or positive relationship between median age and mean aggregate individualism. As shown in table 1.2, the correlation coefficient between the mean aggregate expressive individualism index and the median age is 0.80, which is statistically significant ($p < .05$).

Table 1.2 also shows that there were consistent differences in support for individualistic values between the youth bulge and the older age group in these countries. That is, younger individuals were significantly more individualistic than were people aged 30 and older. The difference between the two age groups was greatest among Pakistani respondents (0.40), followed by Saudi (0.32), Turkish (0.26), Lebanese (0.22), Iraqi (0.20), Egyptian (0.18), and Tunisian (0.16) respondents (table 1.2, column 3). Independent samples t-tests showed that the differences between the two groups across all countries are statistically significant ($p < .01$). Young Lebanese were the most individualistic, and older Pakistanis were the least individualistic.

The data also show that what is true on the individual level is just the opposite on the country level. While younger individuals are more individualistic than older ones, countries with younger populations are less individualistic on the aggregate level.

Gender

In terms of gender, the fact that men have more power in Middle Eastern and North African countries led to an assessment of whether this power differential causes men to be more individualistic than women. To assess the connection between gender and expressive individualism, figure 1.1 illustrates the distribution of the expressive individualism index by gender across the seven countries. Surprisingly, however, the data presented in this figure reveal that there were no significant differences on this measure between men and women across these countries, with the exception of Tunisia and Pakistan, where women appeared to be significantly more supportive of expressive individualistic values than men. This difference by gender is 0.15 in Tunisia and 0.07 in Pakistan (both are statistically significant at $p < .001$).

Thus, it is concluded that, although men may be more individualistic in other domains, in terms of expressive individualism there is little gender difference, except for two cases in which women scored higher than men.

Education

It is suggested that education removes the cognitive barriers to enlightenment, as educated individuals are more skilled in understanding events, stay focused longer, and are more capable of analyzing issues autonomously than are those who are less educated (Krueger and Malečková 2003; Schussman and Soule 2005). Therefore, they may be more readily drawn to the values of expressive individualism than are people with less education. To assess this statement, respondents were grouped into two categories, those without university

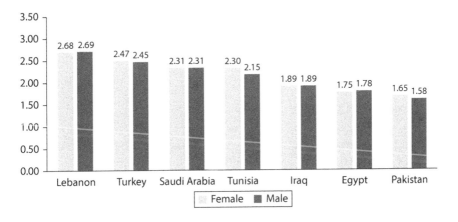

Figure 1.1 Expressive Individualism Index by Gender.

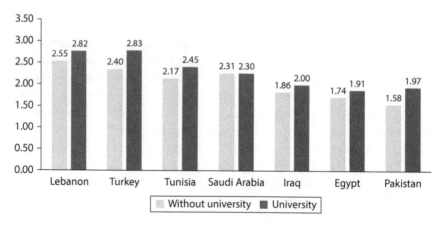

Figure 1.2 Expressive Individualism Index by Education.

education and those with university education. The results are reported in figure 1.2. University education resulted in a significant difference in individualistic values among respondents: those with university education were more supportive of expressive individualism than were those without university education, except in Saudi Arabia, where there was no significant difference between the two educational groups. Independent samples t-tests showed that the differences between the two groups across all countries are statistically significant ($p < .001$).

As figure 1.2 shows, university education made a larger difference in expressive individualism in the more liberal countries of Lebanon, Tunisia, and Turkey, compared to the other countries. The differences for the liberal countries were between 0.27 for Lebanon and 0.43 for Turkey, while the differences for the other countries were between −0.01 for Saudi Arabia and 0.17 for Egypt. The only departure from this pattern was in Pakistan, where the difference in the index of expressive individualism between those with and without university education was 0.39.

Age and Education

Because there were no significant gender differences in the index of expressive individualism in five of the seven countries, only the differences between respondents with and without university education within each of the two age groups were assessed across the seven countries. As shown in table 1.3, among those in the youth bulge across all countries, university education had inconsistent effects on the expressive individualism index. Only in Lebanon, Tunisia, and Turkey,

TABLE 1.3 Expressive Individualism Index by Age and Education (Mean/ Standard Deviation; *n*)

	Youth Bulge (Aged 18–29)			Older Age Group (Aged 30+)		
	Without University	University	Difference	Without University	University	Difference
Iraq	2.00/.67; 942	2.05/.73; 197	0.05	1.77/.62; 1,461	1.98/.67; 369	0.21[a]
Lebanon	2.73/.68; 373	2.86/.65; 781	0.13[b]	2.47/.72; 1,075	2.76/.74; 673	0.29[a]
Pakistan	1.82/.58; 1,116	2.06/.68; 147	0.24[a]	1.44/.43; 2,112	1.87/.62; 139	0.41[a]
Saudi Arabia	2.52/.74; 417	2.41/.77; 231	−0.11[b]	2.15/.68; 665	2.15/66; 194	0.00
Tunisia	2.27/.91; 410	2.46/.94; 289	0.19[a]	2.15/.86; 1,878	2.45/.97; 393	0.30[a]
Egypt	1.88/.64; 764	1.93/.60; 223	0.05	1.67/.58; 1,846	1.89/.67; 309	0.22[a]
Turkey	2.59/.68; 652	2.89/.68; 193	0.30[a]	2.34/.68; 1,923	2.77/.73; 236	0.43[a]

Significance of independent samples *t*-tests for differences in the gender equality index by age:
[a] $p < .001$.
[b] $p < .05$.

which were the more liberal countries, did respondents with university education score significantly higher on this index than those without university education, except for Saudi respondents, where this effect was just the opposite. The Saudi youth with university education were *less* individualistic than their peers with no university education. In other countries, there was no significant difference. Among the older age group, respondents with university education scored significantly higher on the expressive individualism index than did those without university education, except for Saudi Arabia, where university education did not make any difference in respondents' level of expressive individualism.

Summary

Expressive individualism is one of the dimensions of liberal democracy. This chapter discussed and measured this construct in terms of three indicators:

(1) preference for love versus parental approval as the basis for marriage, (2) attitude toward a woman's freedom to dress as she wishes, and (3) preference for independence and imagination versus obedience and religiosity as favorable qualities in children. These three measures were then averaged to create an expressive individualism index. Based on this measure, only Lebanese and young or university-educated Turkish respondents were predominantly individualistic. However, respondents from all seven countries vary considerably in terms of this measure.

Comparison by age groups showed consistent differences in support for individualistic values between the youth bulge and the older age group in the seven countries. Individuals in the youth bulge were significantly more individualistic than were people aged 30 and older. The difference between the two age groups was largest among respondents in Pakistan and then in Saudi Arabia. It was smallest among Tunisian respondents. Level of education also resulted in a significant difference in individualistic values among the respondents: those with university education were more supportive of expressive individualism than were those without university education, except in Saudi Arabia, where this relationship was not significant. This may indicate the weakness of liberal education in the institutions of higher learning in Saudi Arabia. In terms of gender, there were no significant differences between men and women across the countries, except in Tunisia and Pakistan, where women appeared to be significantly more supportive of expressive individualistic values than were men.

Among respondents in the youth bulge, those with university education were more individualistic than were those without university education only in Lebanon, Tunisia, and Turkey; it was just the opposite in Saudi Arabia, and there were no differences in expressive individualism between the two educational groups in the other three countries. Among the older are group, those with university education were consistently more individualistic across the countries, except in Saudi Arabia, where university education had no effect on expressing individualism.

In short, this analysis showed that members of the youth bulge and those with university education were more strongly oriented toward the values of expressive individualism than were those in other categories. However, countries with younger populations (i.e., larger youth bulges) were less individualistic. As a whole, Lebanon is the only country that can be considered individualistic, Turkey is individualistically neutral, and the rest of the countries are nonindividualistic.

CHAPTER 2

THE SOCIAL STATUS OF WOMEN AND GENDER EQUALITY

Maltreatment of women has been one of the most serious obstacles to the provision of social justice, equality, and liberal democracy in contemporary Middle Eastern and North African societies. In the modern period, many liberal, secular, and Muslim reformist intellectual leaders and political activists recognized this problem. More significantly, this period showed the rise of women's movement for a better treatment and inclusion into sociopolitical affairs and equality. In fact, women's rights in educational institutions, politics, the job market, and the family have become one of the most hotly contested issues in the cultural warfare that has transpired between these intellectuals and activists, on the one hand, and those attached to the patriarchal culture, traditional Islam, Islamic orthodoxy, and fundamentalism, on the other. While serious attempts were made and policies enacted in order to uplift the social status of women in the twentieth century, the decline of the secular states and the rise of Islamic fundamentalism in the 1970s slowed or even, in some countries, reversed this process, further contributing to the deterioration of the social conditions for women in the region. The ruling Islamic regimes in Iran and Saudi Arabia, in particular, have officially lowered the status of women to that of a second-class citizen.

This chapter measures attitudes toward gender equality and female sartorial practices. It assesses variation in these attitudes across the seven countries and by age, gender, and education. Its first key finding is that there is substantial support among women for the existing structure of gender inequality, even though this support is considerably lower than that among men. Its second key finding is that young educated women are the most important group favoring gender equality and perhaps the most likely participants in the movements for a more egalitarian relationship between men and women and for liberal democracy in the region. Also more favorable toward gender equality are among those in the youth bulge (those aged 18 to 29) and those with university education.

Gender Equality

It is not an overstatement to argue that the social status of women and the idea of gender equality constitute the main point of ideological contestations among intellectual leaders, ruling elites, political activists, and the public at large virtually everywhere in the world in the contemporary period. This issue, which even in the West has not been fully resolved, is multifaceted, and the struggles for gender equality have been waged in different domains of social life, including women's rights to education, political leadership, employment outside the home, engagement in commerce, equal treatment compared to their male counterparts in the family, equal access to health care compared to men, and control over their own body as well as their right to appear in public places, travel alone, and dress as they wish. Given its significance in shaping political outcomes, the social status of women is one of the most important organizing principles of the social order. A liberal democratic order may not be possible without equality between the sexes.

Social philosophers and activists have long recognized the civilizational significance of women's social status. As an early proponent of women's rights, Millar (1781) believed that the test of civilizations is provided by the status of women. Echoing this view, James Mill, in *History of British India* (1826, 384–85), stated:

> The condition of the women is one of the most remarkable circumstances in the manners of nations. Among rude people, the women are generally degraded; among civilized people they are exalted. In the barbarian, the passion of sex is a brutal impulse, which infuses no tenderness; and his undisciplined nature leads him to abuse his power over every creature that is weaker than himself. The history of uncultivated nations uniformly represents the women as in a state of abject slavery, from which they slowly emerge, as civilization advances.

Nonetheless, despite efforts by the harbingers of the eighteenth-century Enlightenment to defend individual equality, as well as the institutionalization of this equality in politics, many of the male thinkers of the Enlightenment did not endorse equality between the sexes. Mill mercilessly criticized the conditions of women in British India and considered the institution of *pardah* (literally "curtain," referring to the institutionalized seclusion of women in India) a sign of barbarism (Forbes 1951). Yet in his *Essays on Government*, he failed to give women the right to vote. In 1820, he wrote, "one thing is pretty clear, that all those individuals whose interests are indisputably included in those of other individuals, may be struck off without inconvenience. In this light may be viewed all children, up to a certain age, whose interests are involved in those of their parents. In this light, also, women may be regarded, the interest of almost all of whom is involved either in that of their fathers or in that of their husbands" (cited in Ball 2014).

In fact, after the victory of male suffrage in the West, women carried on a long and hard-fought struggle to win the right to vote. They were enfranchised mainly in the twentieth century and in some cases well over a century after their male counterparts gained universal suffrage. "In New Zealand," for example, "women were enfranchised in 1893, in Switzerland not until 1971; in the American south, White women gained the right to vote fifty years before black men, but in Finland the two sexes achieved suffrage simultaneously in 1906. In France 150 years, and in Switzerland over 120 years separated the first adoption of universal male suffrage from the effective enfranchisement of women, whereas in other countries the gap was much shorter" (Thernborn 1971, 37).

In Western societies, the recognition of the significance of gender equality for building a civilized order shaped, and was reinforced by, women's movements in the nineteenth and twentieth centuries, culminating in the formulation of laws that banned discrimination against them and established equal treatment of men and women before the law. In practice, however, women still face systematic biases, discriminatory practices, and sexual harassment at workplaces. Their reproductive rights, control over their bodies, and right to end unwanted pregnancy are still contested, fervently debated, and among the most significant political issues in Western societies today.

The Status of Women in the Middle East and North Africa

Western attitudes toward gender equality, women's rights, and the treatment of women differ substantially from those of Muslim-majority countries. This difference indicates a fundamental dimension separating the two cultural traditions in the contemporary period. Inglehart and Norris (2003, 62) argue that "the cultural fault line that divides the West and the Muslim world is not about democracy but sex . . . Muslims and their Western counterparts want democracy, yet they are worlds apart when it comes to attitudes toward divorce, abortion, gender equality, and gay rights—which may not bode well for democracy's future in the Middle East." Consistent with their assertion is the fact that gender inequality in diverse domains of social life, including politics, the labor market, education, and the family, is not only tolerated and practiced but also sanctioned by the state. In many Middle Eastern and North African countries, women are de facto or de jure second-class citizens.

One central factor underpinning the existing differences in social status and political power between men and women is the gender disparity in employment outside the home. Findings from the cross-national comparative surveys show that, among the representative samples of 21,150 respondents interviewed between 2011 and 2013 across the seven countries, 70 percent of male respondents reported that they were employed, compared to only 18 percent of female respondents. These percentages, however, varied substantially across the seven countries. The percentages of males versus females employed were 77 percent versus 15 percent among Egyptians, 64 percent versus 19 percent among Iraqis, 75 percent versus 38 percent among Lebanese, 84 percent versus 9 percent among Pakistanis, 68 percent versus 6 percent among Saudis, 56 percent versus 24 percent among Tunisians, and 58 percent versus 16 percent among Turkish respondents. While these figures may be different than the actual employment data, the reported gender difference in employment is striking. There is, however, much less gender disparity in education. The percentages of male and female respondents who reported having university education, respectively, were 23 percent versus 14 percent among Egyptians, 24 percent versus 14 percent among Iraqis, 50 percent versus 50 percent among Lebanese, 10 percent versus 6 percent among Pakistanis, 28 percent versus 23 percent among Saudis, 25 percent versus 22 percent among Tunisians, and 18 percent versus 11 percent among Turkish respondents.

The institutional and cultural discriminations against women have been stubbornly persistent. The acrimonious debates over female social status and gender equality have continued unabated since the Middle East's and North Africa's systematic encounters with Western modernity in the nineteenth century. at that time, the institution of male supremacy and such practices as female infanticide, gender segregation, early marriage, and polygamy became the most visible targets of polemics against Islam and Muslim communities advanced by the followers of the Enlightenment among indigenous intellectual leaders, Christian missionaries, Westernizers (those interested in emulating Western culture), and think tanks connected to European colonial administrations. Trusting that the orthodox *ulama* (Muslim theologians, who interpreted Islamic law) were ill-equipped to respond effectively to these criticisms, Muslim reformers formulated a rationalist exegesis of the scriptures in order to defend not only their faith but also women's rights against the onslaughts of the critics. Their exposé on gender relations, known as Islamic feminism, intended to uplift the social status of women (Minault 1990; Amin [1899] 1992; Ahmad 1967; Moaddel 2005).

In the early twentieth century, women in the Middle East and North Africa participated in the rising tide of nationalism and anticolonial movements in increasing numbers and with heightened enthusiasm. The formation of modern states in Egypt, Iran, and Turkey in the 1920s and the cultural shift toward secularism in the region in the same period created a favorable context for female activism and the ruling elites to implement a series of gendered policies known as feminism from above. The Iranian and Turkish elite, in particular, not only encouraged female participation in societal affairs but also made veiling in public places illegal, as it was considered inconsistent with the official developmental ideology. "In Turkey, where modernism, secularism and Westernization comprised the national ideals of the new post-Ottoman state, the state's efforts to create women-citizens went hand in hand with the denunciation of veiling as a 'backward' and 'uncivilized' practice, a tradition to be overthrown in the same manner as the Islamic Caliphate had been abolished by Turkish revolutionaries" (Secor 2002, 5–6).

The unveiled woman in Western vestimentary style thus turned into a sartorial symbol of her emancipation. In 1919, for example, Turkish nationalist Halide Edip unveiled in public while rallying her fellow Turkish citizens to resist the Greek invasion (Nashat and Tucker 1999). In 1923, Egyptian Huda Shaarāwī publicly removed her face veil upon returning from an international meeting of feminists abroad. Many other women soon followed suit. Beginning in the late 1920s, these women slowly forced their way into the Egyptian university system (Safran 1961; Reid 1975; Vatikiotis 1980; Shaarāwī 1987). This push for equality culminated in the acceptance of the new sartorial practices and more revealing forms of dress illustrated by organized marches of unveiled women in the streets of Cairo, which continued unabated well into the 1970s. In 1969 Cairo, says Abu-Lughod (1971, 239), "almost no women are veiled." Similar movements emerged in Tunisia and Algeria. Habiba al-Mansari led the movement in Tunisia in 1929 when she unveiled and urged other Tunisian women to do the same as part of the nationalist struggle (Charrad 2001). Unveiling in Algeria was promoted by female anticolonial fighters, although reveiling gained new political significance in 1958 when French women pressed Algerian women to unveil, and among Tunisian women, Bourguiba and Ben Ali likewise opposed the role of Islam in public life (Lazreg 1994; Charrad 2011; Cavatorta and Haugbølle 2012; Haugbølle and Cavatorta 2012; Kerrou 2010). In places such as the Balkans, Russia, and Yugoslavia, where Muslims were in the minority, encouraging or forcing women to unveil was also considered a component of building a modern nation-state (Neuburger 1997; Huisman and Hondagneu-Sotelo 2005).

The rise of Islamic fundamentalism in the second half of the twentieth century paralleled a significant decline in favorable attitudes toward gender equality and an increase in restrictions on women's sartorial practices. In a marked contrast to secularism, the Islamic fundamentalist movements favored the unity of religion and politics in Islamic government, considered Islam rather than the nation as the basis of identity, rejected Western culture as decadent, and promoted the institution of male supremacy and gender segregation.

The veil was presented as the essential protective shield of a woman's sanctity and sexual purity as well as a condition for her presence in public places. As one of the chief spokespersons of Iranian Shia fundamentalism, Ayatollah Morteza Motahhari linked clothing to religious morality and denounced the sartorial practices of an unveiled woman as the contemporary "epidemic" (Motahhari 1969, xii). For him, an unveiled woman was engaged in free distribution of sex. "The debate," he said, "is not over whether it is good for a woman to appear covered or nude in public. The heart of the debate is whether a man's desires for a woman should be free. Should or should not a man have the right to enjoy any woman in any gathering to the highest degree save actual intercourse?" (Motahhari 1969, 66–67).

Sunni fundamentalists advanced a similar rationale on veiling, a conservative gender role, and gender segregation. According to Taraki's (1996, 145) description of Jordanian fundamentalists, the mixing of the sexes (*ikhtilat*) and going bareheaded and exposed (*sufur*) were condemned because they would give away women's principal asset:

> Despite the intelligence of the gentle sex, its members have not woken to the fact that beautiful women are in the minority. So how did the majority prefer *al-sufur*, since inasmuch as it makes the beautiful few more attractive it detracts from the desirability of the ordinary many. . . . How do the less beautiful accept *al-sufur*, since it does nothing but rob them of the capital in the hearts of men, a capital generated by the *hijab* [veiling]? How do they accept that the more beautiful add this capital to their already large wealth? (145)

Taraki further observes that

> The young Muslim woman could not resist [the Western cultural assault]. She began to imitate the Western woman, and went out of her home dressed but naked . . . under the pretext of liberation. She insisted on competing with men in all fields of life, claiming equality with them. But what was the result of all this? The woman was the one to lose. She lost the protective shadow of her home; she gained materially but lost her dignity. . . . But then came this sweeping tide, a call for a return to the pure spring, to Islam. A call for the return of the Muslim woman to her kingdom at home!" (145)

Gender Inequality in the Familial, Political, Economic, and Educational Domains

Patriarchy variably persists and is exercised in a variety of social institutions. In the family, the husband (or father or elder brother) exercises formal custodial power over the wife, and in such other domains of social life as economic, political, educational, religious, and other cultural institutions, men enjoy a privileged position vis-à-vis women. The exercise and reproduction of male domination is a complex process, however. It rests on a set of beliefs about gender differences that justify this domination. These beliefs are grounded in a variety of organizations, informing organizational norms on gender relations; are objectified into symbols and various sartorial styles for women; are enacted in the rituals of courtship, reinforced by the desire (and necessity) of shielding one's mother, wife, or daughter from harm; shape political discourses and daily conversations on gender relations; and specify the normative behaviors that are sanctioned by state and nonstate actors. Gendered socialization of children, in which the mother also plays an active role, is another factor that contributes to the regeneration of patriarchal institutions.

People's attitudes toward gender equality may reflect these beliefs. Such attitudes, however, may change as a result of changes in gender socialization, changes in social conditions, and unfolding debates on the social status of women. Several survey questions tap into these attitudes in different domains of social life, including the family, politics, economics, and education. One survey question explores the respondents' veiling preferences by showing them photographs of women and probing their views on the most appropriate vestimentary form for a woman to adopt in public. The following sections analyze attitudes toward gender equality across the seven nations and assess variation in the respondents' sartorial preferences for women.

Measures of Attitudes Toward Gender Inequality

Assuming that women's rights are variably contested in different institutional settings, gender equality is conceptualized here as a multidimensional construct that is differentially exercised in various domains of social life, including politics, the job market, education, and the family. Respondents' attitudes toward women compared to men in these domains are measured using several survey questions in the Likert-scale response format:

Do you (1) strongly agree, (2) agree, (3) disagree, or (4) strongly disagree that

a. On the whole, men make better political leaders than women do (*political leadership*)?
b. When jobs are scarce, men should have more right to a job than women (*job market*)?

   c. A university education is more important for a boy than for a girl (*university education*)?

   d. A wife must always obey her husband (*obedience*)?

   e. It is acceptable for a man to have more than one wife (*polygamy*)?

Questions a through c have appeared in multiple waves of the World Values Survey, while questions d and e were specifically designed for the Middle Eastern and North African countries. Both questions are drawn from the Quran and address the necessity for a wife to obey her husband and the right of a man to marry more than one wife. Verse 34 of the Quran chapter on women speaks to the concept of obedience:

> Men are in charge of women by [right of] what Allah has given one over the other and what they spend [for maintenance] from their wealth. So righteous women are devoutly obedient, guarding in [the husband's] absence what Allah would have them guard. But those [wives] from whom you fear arrogance— [first] advise them; [then if they persist], forsake them in bed; and [finally], strike them. But if they obey you [once more], seek no means against them. Indeed, Allah is ever Exalted and Grand.[1]

Regarding polygamy, verse 3 of the Quran chapter on women commands men as follows:

> And if you fear that you will not deal justly with the orphan girls, then marry those that please you of [other] women, two or three or four. But if you fear that you will not be just, then [marry only] one or those your right hand possesses. That is more suitable that you may not incline [to injustice].

The Islamic modernists of the late nineteenth century abandoned the literal reading of the text. In their view, the Quran endorsed neither wife obedience nor polygamy. On the issue of polygamy, for example, they reexamined the Quranic injunction on polygamy from a rationalist perspective and concluded that the practice was illegal according to the religion. The pertinent verse in the Quran stated that polygamy was conditional on the husband treating his wives equitably and with justice, and for Islamic modernists, justice in marriage was synonymous only with love. And because a man was emotionally incapable of loving two or more women equally at the same time, polygamy was therefore prohibited (Cheragh [Chiragh] Ali 1883; Ahmad 1967; Amin (1899) 1992; Minault 1990; Moaddel 2005). In the Islamic orthodoxy, on the other hand, the notion of justice was interpreted as economic justice, meaning that a polygamous husband was obligated to treat his wives

equally in economic terms. The survey questions on polygamy and wife obedience are intended to assess whether respondents agreed with the literal
meanings of the Quran's injunctions on these issues or conformed to the
modernist interpretations.

To create a more stable and comprehensive measure of attitudes toward
gender equality, a gender equality index is constructed by averaging the
responses to all the five questions. Then, the variation in this index is assessed
across the seven countries and by age, gender, and education. The gender
equality index ranges from 1 to 4, with a higher value indicating stronger support for gender equality.

Cross-National Variation

Table 2.1 shows that attitudes toward gender equality vary in different domains
of social life and across the seven countries. First, considering attitudes
toward a wife's obedience to her husband, 89 percent of Iraqis, 62 percent of
Lebanese, 92 percent of Pakistanis, 79 percent of Saudis, 77 percent of Tunisians, 94 percent of Egyptians, and 70 percent of Turkish respondents either
strongly agreed or agreed with the statement that "a wife must always obey her
husband." On this measure, the majority of the respondents from the seven
countries—even those from Lebanon, which is considered the most liberal
country in the region—supported male supremacy in the family, conforming to
the literal reading of the scripture. On the other hand, the majority of respondents did not support polygamy, with the level of disapproval ranging from 50
percent among Saudis to 92 percent among Turkish respondents, indicating
that the majority of respondents from the seven countries disagreed with the
literal reading of the Quran.

On political leadership, respondents across the seven countries were less
uniform, but a majority of these respondents considered that men make better political leaders than women do; those who strongly agreed or agreed
ranged between 54 percent of Turkish respondents and 83 percent of Egyptians.
Respondents also gave priority to men over women in a tight job market. Those
who strongly agreed or agreed with the statement that "when jobs are scarce,
men have more right to a job than women" ranged between 56 percent among
Turkish respondents and 86 percent among Egyptians. Lebanese, Tunisians,
and Turkish respondents, however, favored male primacy in the job market less
strongly than did respondents from the other countries. Further, the majority
of respondents disagreed with the idea of gender inequality in university education. That is, fully 72 percent of Iraqis, 74 percent of Lebanese, 65 percent
of Egyptians, 80 percent of Tunisians, and 71 percent of Turkish respondents

TABLE 2.1 Measures of Gender Equality

	Iraq	Lebanon	Pakistan	Saudi Arabia	Tunisia	Egypt	Turkey
A wife must always obey her husband							
Strongly agree	42%	17%	39%	48%	44%	68%	19%
Agree	47%	44%	53%	31%	33%	26%	51%
Disagree	10%	28%	7%	16%	19%	5%	20%
Strongly disagree	1%	11%	1%	5%	4%	0%	10%
On the whole, men make better political leaders than women do							
Strongly agree	33%	20%	29%	49%	33%	59%	11%
Agree	43%	36%	42%	30%	22%	24%	43%
Disagree	21%	30%	23%	13%	28%	10%	33%
Strongly disagree	3%	14%	6%	8%	17%	7%	13%
When jobs are scarce, men have more right to a job than women							
Strongly agree	27%	26%	41%	39%	53%	63%	16%
Agree	52%	40%	44%	39%	22%	23%	40%
Disagree	17%	23%	13%	17%	15%	8%	31%
Strongly disagree	4%	11%	3%	5%	10%	6%	13%
A university education is more important for a boy than for a girl							
Strongly agree	8%	8%	15%	32%	11%	21%	7%
Agree	21%	18%	34%	25%	10%	14%	22%
Disagree	49%	39%	33%	28%	35%	34%	45%
Strongly disagree	23%	35%	17%	15%	45%	31%	26%
It is acceptable for a man to have more than one wife							
Strongly agree	11%	7%	6%	23%	7%	8%	3%
Agree	37%	22%	19%	27%	12%	22%	5%
Disagree	35%	33%	44%	24%	16%	32%	24%
Strongly disagree	17%	38%	31%	27%	65%	38%	69%
Gender equality index (mean)	2.22	2.58	2.22	2.06	2.50	2.07	2.73
Range (min–max)	1–4	1–4	1–4	1–3.8	1–4	1–3.8	1–4
Median	2.20	2.60	2.20	2.00	2.50	2.00	2.75

strongly disagreed or disagreed with the statement that "a university education is more important for a boy than for a girl." However, Pakistanis were evenly divided and only 43 percent of Saudis strongly disagreed or disagreed that a university education is more important for a boy than for a girl. Thus, out of the five different domains of social life where male supremacy is exercised, support for the practice of polygamy is the lowest and support for female education is the highest in virtually all seven countries. It is important to note that the disparities in attitudes toward education for men and women and toward their right to a job correspond to the reported gender disparities in education and employment that were noted earlier.

Finally, as shown in table 2.1, the seven countries varied on the gender equality index: Turkish respondents, with a mean index value of 2.73, more strongly favored gender equality than did respondents from the other six countries; they were followed by Lebanese and Tunisians, with aggregate index values of 2.58 and 2.50 respectively, while Iraqis and Pakistanis, both at 2.22, were less favorable, and Egyptians and Saudis were least favorable, having index values of 2.07 and 2.06, respectively. The analysis of variance of the gender equality index across the seven countries shows strong country effect ($F = 635/372$, $p < .001$). Post hoc analyses using Scheffé's test for significance indicated that Saudis and Egyptians were nearly identical to each other, as were Pakistanis and Iraqis, and that these two sets were statistically different both from each other and from the other three countries, where each differed significantly from the others.

Inegalitarian attitudes toward women may also be linked to gender discrimination in society. For example, Saudi Arabia harbors the least favorable attitude toward gender equality across the seven countries. This attitude is linked to strong discriminatory practices against women. Even though 58 percent of university students in the kingdom were women, they made up only 5 percent of the labor force (Cordesman 2003). Women were not even allowed to drive in the kingdom until very recently—the ban was lifted in 2018.[2] The marked differential participation in the labor market by gender corresponds to a strong bias against women, as 78 percent of Saudi respondents gave more rights to men over women in a tight job market. The least favorable attitudes toward gender equality among Saudis thus correspond to the high level of gender discrimination in the country.

However, given the variation in support for the institution of patriarchy by domain, the process of change toward gender equality may be uneven. As shown in table 2.1, the respondents from the seven countries were more willing to support gender equality in education and much less willing to do so in the family. It is thus possible to speculate that an increase in the level of female education will have a positive effect on gender equality in other domains in the coming years. A woman with a higher level of education would be able not only to analyze events, resolve issues, and articulate interests more effectively than her less educated sister but also to find a better-paying job and attain financial independence. When educated and gainfully employed, women have more resources and are in a much better position to resist patriarchal institutions and challenge male supremacy in other domains of social life. Financial independence, which is associated with outside employment, and a more effective articulation of interests, which is often linked to a higher level of education, will certainly contribute to the decline of the stereotypical perspective of women as the weaker of the two sexes. This change would in turn contribute to the rise of more favorable attitudes toward gender equality among men.

The median values for the gender equality index were used to assess which countries favored gender equality and which gender hierarchization. Any value above 2.5 indicates that the respondents were more in favor of gender equality than against it; the opposite is true if the index falls below 2.5. As shown in table 2.1, Lebanon and Turkey, with median index values of 2.60 and 2.75, respectively, were generally favorable to women; Tunisia, with a median index value of 2.50, fell in between; and the rest were favorable toward gender inequality, with median index values ranging from 2.00 for Saudi Arabia and Egypt to 2.20 for Pakistan and Iraq. Being a conservative country that officially sanctions gender hierarchy and segregation, the low value for Saudi Arabia was expected. The equally low support for gender equality or the high support for inequality among Egyptians, whose country experienced the rise of Islamic feminism and a fairly strong women's movement in the early twentieth century, might have been the consequence of the antifeminist ideology propagated for decades by political Islam and the followers of the Muslim Brothers.

Variation by Age, Gender, and Education

Age

Table 2.2 shows the differences in the gender equality index values between the youth bulge (aged 18–29) and the older age group (aged 30 and older) across the seven countries. According to this table, there are consistent differences in support for gender equality between age groups across these countries. Those in the youth bulge were significantly more likely to support gender equality than were those in the older age group, with the difference between the two groups being greatest among Pakistanis (0.31). In other countries, the differences ranged from 0.05 among Egyptians and Turkish respondents to 0.11 among Iraqis. Independent samples t-tests indicated that the differences between the two groups are statistically significant ($p < .05$) in all seven countries. Young Turkish respondents held the most egalitarian attitudes toward women, and older Saudis held the least egalitarian attitudes.

As shown in table 2.2, cross-nationally the mean for the gender equality index is positively related to the size of the median age or negatively related to the size of the youth bulge. In other words, people in countries

TABLE 2.2 Age Differences in Gender Equality and Median Age by Country

	1	2	3	4	5
	Mean Index: 18–29	Mean Index: 30+	$Col_1 - Col_2$	Mean Index: Total	Median Age[a]
Saudi Arabia	2.11	2.02	0.10[c]	2.06	25.3[b]
Egypt	2.11	2.05	0.05[c]	2.07	24.3
Iraq	2.29	2.18	0.11[c]	2.22	20.9
Pakistan	2.42	2.11	0.31[c]	2.22	21.6
Tunisia	2.55	2.48	0.06[c]	2.50	31.0
Lebanon	2.63	2.55	0.08[c]	2.58	29.8
Turkey	2.76	2.71	0.05[c]	2.73	29.2
$r_{Col4Col5}$	.80[c]				

[a] The median ages for Tunisia and Turkey are from 2013; the median ages for all other countries are from 2011 (CIA 2011, 2013).
[b] The population figure used to compute the median age for Saudi Arabia includes about 25 percent nonnationals.
[c] $p < .05$.

with stronger egalitarian attitudes toward women preferred having fewer children. Alternatively, countries with smaller families provided a more favorable context for the development of egalitarian attitudes toward women. Larger families would increase the amount and intensity of household tasks for women, restricting their access to higher education and employment outside the home and thus reinforcing traditional inegalitarian attitudes toward women. According to this table, the correlation coefficient between the aggregate mean for the gender equality index and the median age is 0.80 (statistically significant at $p < 0.05$). This means that the higher the median age, or the smaller the size of youth bulge, the higher the aggregate mean for the gender equality index.

Gender
Figure 2.1 shows the differences in men's and women's attitudes toward gender equality across the seven countries. In all these countries, without exception, women expressed greater support for gender equality than did men, with the greatest difference among Lebanese (0.48), followed by Pakistanis (0.31), Iraqis (0.27), Turkish respondents (0.22), Saudis (0.20), and Egyptians (0.17).

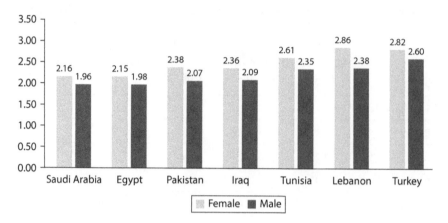

Figure 2.1 Gender Equality Index by Gender.

All these differences are statistically significant (the mean difference for every country is significant at $p < .001$). Naturally, it is to be expected that women are more supportive of gender equality than men. It may be speculated that the larger this difference, the sharper the cultural division in the country by gender.

Of significance in the study of gender equality is knowing why men hold inegalitarian attitudes toward women and support discriminatory practices against women. However, it is also important to understand why women themselves hold inegalitarian attitudes toward women. Figure 2.1 shows the mean value of the gender equality index for men and women across the seven countries. Accordingly, women held inegalitarian attitudes variably across these countries, and only in Lebanon, Tunisia, and Turkey is the mean for women for the gender equality index significantly above the 2.5 threshold—2.86, 2.61, and 2.82, respectively—indicating that the majority of women in these three countries favored gender equality (there was no significant statistical difference between the mean and median values for either men or women in these countries). Despite women being significantly less supportive of gender inequality than men, they still displayed submissive attitudes toward gender hiearachy. A significant decline in such attitudes may be necessary for a more effective challenge of the institutions of male domination and for the development of liberal democracy in these countries. As the data show, men, on the other hand, appeared as a male supremacist bunch. Across the seven countries, only in Turkey is the mean for men for the gender equality index above the 2.5 threshold. In all other countries, this index value for men is far below 2.5, indicating men fairly strongly support the ideology of male domination.

Age and Gender

Table 2.3 shows variation in the gender equality index by age among females and males across the seven countries. As this table shows, among women, the differences in support for gender equality between the youth bulge and the older age group are significant, and women aged 18–29 consistently scored higher on the gender equality index than did those aged 30 and older across the seven countries. The age differences on the index values among female respondents are also greater than the differences among male respondents. Among men, these differences are inconsistent. In Iraq, Pakistan, and Saudi Arabia, male youth were more strongly in favor of gender equality than were older males, but among male respondents from Lebanon, Egypt, and Turkey, there were no significant differences in the gender equality index values between the two age groups. However, in Tunisia, male youth were significantly less supportive of gender equality than were older males. Given the consistently favorable view toward gender equality among young women across the seven countries, in contrast to young men, it is reasonable to speculate that these young women may form a solid basis of support against the existing system of patriarchy and for change.

TABLE 2.3 Gender Equality Index by Gender and Age (Mean/Standard Deviation; n)

	Female			Male		
	Aged 18–29	Aged 30+	Mean Difference	Aged 18–29	Aged 30+	Mean Difference
Iraq	2.46/0.51; 540	2.31/0.47; 866	0.15[a]	2.14/0.48; 614	2.06/0.46; 974	0.08[b]
Lebanon	2.93/0.56; 490	2.81/0.58; 729	0.12[a]	2.41/0.63; 683	2.37/0.62; 1,038	0.04
Pakistan	2.56/0.51; 681	2.26/0.56; 1,025	0.30[a]	2.25/0.57; 582	1.98/0.53; 1,226	0.27[a]
Saudi Arabia	2.22/0.53; 404	2.11/0.53; 526	0.11[b]	2.01/0.58; 411	1.92/0.56; 519	0.09[c]
Tunisia	2.73/0.58; 394	2.56/0.55; 1,325	0.17[a]	2.31/0.62; 326	2.37/0.58; 1,025	−0.06[a]
Egypt	2.22/0.51; 546	2.12/0.51; 1,081	0.10[a]	1.96/0.51; 441	1.99/0.52; 1,075	−0.03
Turkey	2.90/0.56; 456	2.79/0.54; 1,233	0.11[a]	2.61/0.62; 394	2.60/0.57; 929	0.01

Significance of independent samples t-tests for differences in the gender equality index by age:
[a] $p < .001$.
[b] $p < .01$.
[c] $p < .05$.

Education

Figure 2.2 shows attitudes toward gender equality by the respondents' level of education in the seven countries. Except among the respondents in Saudi Arabia, people with university education were significantly more supportive of gender equality than were those without university education. University education had the greatest effect among Pakistanis, where there is a 0.47 mean difference between the two educational groups, followed by respondents from Tunisia (0.29), Lebanon (0.22), Turkey (0.19), Egypt (0.16), and Iraq (0.11). Independent samples *t*-tests showed that the differences between the two groups across all countries, except Saudi Arabia, are statistically significant ($p < .01$). This finding indicates that university education had a greater effect on liberal attitudes toward women in countries that supported a more liberal environment (i.e., Tunisia, Lebanon, and Turkey). An exception to this pattern is Pakistan, not a liberal country, where university education made the largest difference in attitudes toward gender equality. One may speculate that, despite the rise of religious extremism, the institutions of higher learning in Pakistan have managed to maintain commitments to secularism and liberal values. The case of Saudi Arabia, where university education had no significant effect on attitudes toward gender equality, is a result of the failure of such institutions to foster liberal values, and that this failure is an outcome of the influence of the conservative religious institutions on the content of the curricula of the system of higher education. More crucially, it may also be a result of the gender-segregated and curriculum-differentiated model of education that was intentionally instituted to reproduce gender divisions and support women's domestic functions in the country. While female education considerably expanded in Saudi Arabia, thus increasing women's social and occupational options, this expansion did not

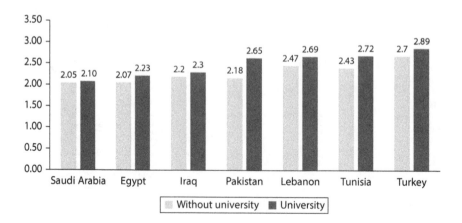

Figure 2.2 Gender Equality Index by Education.

alter attitudes toward gender inequality and the relationship between gender and power in the country (el-Sanabary 1994; Baki 2004; Moaddel 2016).

Education and Age

Table 2.4 shows the distribution of the gender equality index in the two educational groups for respondents in the youth bulge and the older age group across the seven countries. Among respondents in the youth bulge, the difference between those with and without university education was significant in Lebanon, Pakistan, Tunisia, Egypt, and Turkey, showing that young respondents with university education were more supportive of gender equality than were those without university education. For Iraq and Saudi Arabia, this difference was not statistically significant. Among older respondents, those with university education scored significantly higher on the gender equality index across six of the seven countries. In Saudi Arabia, there was no difference in the gender equality index values between the two educational groups.

University education made the greatest difference in attitudes toward gender equality among Pakistanis in both age groups (0.39 among the youth bulge and 0.53 among the older age group) and the least difference among Iraqis (0.05, which was not significant, among the youth bulge and 0.10 among the older age group), after the Saudis. Again, as was the case for expressive individualism, university education appeared to have little effect on attitudes toward gender equality among Saudis.

TABLE 2.4 Gender Equality Index by Age and Education (Mean/Standard Deviation; n)

	Youth Bulge (Aged 18–29)			Older Age Group (Aged 30+)		
	Without University	University	Difference	Without University	University	Difference
Iraq	2.28/0.51; 1,031	2.33/0.60; 112	0.05	2.16/0.48; 1,567	2.26/0.50; 266	0.10[b]
Lebanon	2.56/0.64; 749	2.77/0.65; 404	0.21[a]	2.48/0.64; 1,322	2.76/0.61; 430	0.28[a]
Pakistan	2.40/0.56; 1,203	2.79/0.57; 60	0.39[a]	2.09/0.55; 2,160	2.62/0.62; 91	0.53[a]
Saudi Arabia	2.09/0.56; 713	2.15/0.59; 100	0.06	2.01/0.55; 880	2.01/0.58; 165	0.00
Tunisia	2.50/0.63; 538	2.65/0.63; 181	0.15[b]	2.43/0.55; 2,019	2.78/0.61; 326	0.35[a]
Egypt	2.08/0.53; 834	2.23/0.53; 153	0.15[b]	2.03/0.51; 1,881	2.19/0.56; 275	0.16[a]
Turkey	2.74/0.59; 670	2.86/0.68; 179	0.12[b]	2.69/0.55; 1,948	2.93/0.62; 214	0.24[a]

Significance of independent samples t-tests for differences in the gender equality index by education:
[a] $p < .001$.
[b] $p < .01$.

Cross-National Variation in Veiling Preference

Beginning in the 1970s, the number of women appearing in the Islamic hijab in public increased considerably, first in Egypt and Iran and in the subsequent years in other Muslim-majority countries, reflecting a major shift in female sartorial practices from nonveiled dress, as an increasingly fashionable practice after World War I, to the hijab, which has remained a mark of distinction for Muslim women ever since. The female vestimentary form, however, has remained a contentious arena. If wearing the veil, even for a segment of secular women, was a fashionable way to express dismay with the shah's cultural policies during the 1979 Iranian Revolution (Moaddel 1993), the imposition of the hijab by the Islamic regime in postrevolutionary Iran incited rebellion among female activists, for whom appearing unveiled in public was not only fashionable but a sign of emancipation as well (Osborne 2018). A key dimension of the sartorial contention relates to the amount of female body that is revealed or concealed by the dress. This variability may be represented along a veiling-unveiling or conservative-liberal continuum. On one extreme, some prefer ultraconservative vestimentary forms for women who appear in public, such as the black garment that covers the body from head to toe (burqa, niqab, or chador). On the other extreme, some opt for a liberal form that imitates Western style. The rest choose a form that falls in between. Generally, Islamic fundamentalists preferred a more conservative veiling, and the secular citizens preferred a more liberal style of clothing.

Conducting a comparative cross-national survey of female vestimentary forms, however, is hampered by the near impossibility of writing a survey question about veiling preferences that adequately captures all the nuances and variations in the types of covering worn by women in the seven countries. The term veil or Islamic hijab has different operational meanings in different countries and among the followers of diverse sects in Islam. As a result, six caricaturized photographs of women wearing different styles of veiling were used. They varied from the most conservative to the most liberal. A showcard was created that contained all six photographs, labeling each with a number from 1, most conservative, to 6, most liberal, and the interviewers were instructed to show the card to the respondents and ask, "Which one of these women is dressed most appropriately for public places?" Figure 2.3 represents the showcard used in the interviews. It also shows the distribution of the responses from each of the seven countries.

For Shia fundamentalists, the truly Islamic hijab is the *chador* (veil), an outer garment or open black cloak that covers the woman from head to toe, except for the face and hands (photo 3). For less conservative or moderate

Woman	1	2	3	4	5	6
Egypt (n = 3,014)	1.5%	8.9%	20.4%	52.3%	12.5%	4.4%
Iraq (n = 2,934)	3.9%	7.6%	31.9%	44.2%	9.9%	2.6%
Lebanon (n = 2,906)	2.2%	0.8%	3.0%	32.4%	12.3%	49.3%
Pakistan (n = 3,523)	3.2%	32.2%	30.8%	24.4%	8.0%	1.5%
Saudi Arabia[a] (n = 1,631)	10.5%	63.4%	8.2%	9.7%	5.4%	2.7%
Tunisia (n = 3,033)	1.1%	1.9%	2.9%	56.6%	22.7%	14.8%
Turkey (n = 2,917)	0.4%	1.7%	2.2%	46.0%	17.3%	32.4%

[a]Weighted frequency distribution reported.

Figure 2.3 Preferred Vestimentary Style.

Muslims, a headscarf showing no hair is considered the appropriate dress (photo 4), and for more casual yet conservative women, it is photo 5. For secular Muslims, photo 6 indicates the style most preferred. For Sunni fundamentalists in Afghanistan and Pakistan, the proper dress is the *burqa*, an enveloping outer garment (photo 1). In Saudi Arabia and other Persian Gulf Arab countries, the proper clothing for women is the *niqab*, or mask, a piece of cloth that covers the face, in addition to the black cloak that covers the entire body (photo 2).

According to figure 2.3, the seven countries vary considerably in veiling preferences. The burqa (photo 1) is the least favorite style of dress in Egypt, Tunisia, and Turkey, and second least favorite in Iraq and Pakistan after the unveiled woman portrayed in photo 6. Conversely, a less conservative, more moderate style of dress (photo 4) was preferred by the plurality in these same countries—Egypt, Iraq, Tunisia, and Turkey. In Pakistan and Saudi Arabia, the woman in the niqab (photo 2) was most preferred and the unveiled woman least preferred, while in Lebanon, the opposite was true, with the woman in the niqab least preferred and the secular woman most preferred.

The photographs are ranked from the most conservative (photo 1) to the most liberal (photo 6). Based on this ranking, a single veiling preference score was computed by averaging the responses to the question for each country. These averages were also computed for each of the age, gender, and education groups, and the results are reported in table 2.5. A higher score indicates a more liberal sartorial preference. Lebanon, with a score of 5, was the most liberal in veiling preference, and Saudi Arabia, with a score of 2.43, was the most conservative. In between were Turkey (4.75), Tunisia (4.42), Iraq (3.56), Egypt (3.96), and Pakistan (3.06). This table also shows that the youth bulge (those aged 18–29) consistently scored higher than the older age group (aged 30 and older). The difference between the two age groups was greatest among Pakistanis (0.54), followed by Lebanese (0.16), Iraqis (0.13), Saudis (0.12), Tunisians (0.10), Turkish respondents (0.09), and Egyptians (0.08). Likewise, respondents with university education on average consistently preferred a more liberal dress style for women than did those without university education. The difference between the two educational groups was greatest among Pakistanis (0.93), followed by respondents from Turkey (0.53), Saudi Arabia (0.45), Tunisia (0.32), Lebanon (0.28), Egypt (0.17), and Iraq (0.16). As this table shows, these differences were much larger than the age differences in sartorial preference across the seven countries. The differences between the two age groups and educational groups are statistically significant ($p < .01$).

In terms of gender, there were statistically significant differences in veiling preference between men and women in Egypt, Lebanon, Tunisia, Pakistan, and Saudi Arabia. But this difference did not present a consistent pattern across the countries. In Egypt, Lebanon, and Tunisia, male respondents scored higher— that is, they preferred a more liberal fashion for women, with differences of 0.18, 0.08, and 0.07, respectively. The difference of 0.03 for Turkey is not statistically significant. In Saudi Arabia and Pakistan, by contrast, female respondents scored higher and thus displayed a more liberal preference, with the male-female differences being −0.36 and −0.17, respectively. In Iraq, there was no difference between men and women.

While variation in dress style may relate to individual taste, this variation is also significantly linked to variation in expressive individualism and gender equality. As shown in figure 2.4, the correlation coefficients of veiling preference with the indices of gender equality and expressive individualism are negative and statistically significant across all the seven countries ($p < .001$). The strength of these relationships, however, varies, with Pakistan displaying the strongest relationships between veiling preference and the indices of gender equality and expressive individualism (−0.54 and −0.46, respectively) and with Iraq showing the weakest relationships (−0.11 and −0.11, respectively). Thus, the more conservative veiling preference is linked to less favorable attitudes toward gender equality and expressive individualism across the countries.

TABLE 2.5 Veiling Preference (Higher Values Indicate More Liberal Preferences)

	Age		Difference	Gender		Difference	Education		Difference	Country Total
	Youth (Y; 18–29)	Older (O; 30+)	Y–O	Male (M)	Female (F)	M–F	Without University (W/o U)	University (U)	U–W/o U	
Egypt	4.01	3.93	0.08	4.05	3.87	0.18	3.93	4.1	0.17	3.96
Iraq	3.64	3.51	0.13	3.56	3.57	−0.01	3.53	3.69	0.16	3.56
Lebanon	5.09	4.93	0.16	5.03	4.95	0.08	4.86	5.14	0.28	5.00
Pakistan	3.41	2.87	0.54	2.89	3.25	−0.36	2.99	3.92	0.93	3.06
Saudi Arabia	2.44	2.32	0.12	2.34	2.51	−0.17	2.31	2.76	0.45	2.43
Tunisia	4.5	4.4	0.10	4.46	4.39	0.07	4.35	4.67	0.32	4.42
Turkey	4.82	4.73	0.09	4.77	4.74	0.03	4.68	5.21	0.53	4.75

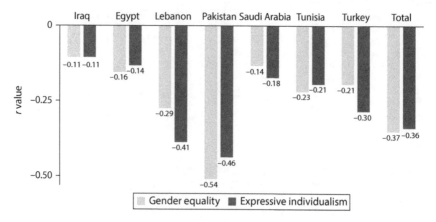

Figure 2.4 Correlation Coefficients of Conservative Veiling Preference with the Indices of Gender Equality and Expressive Individualism.

Note: *r* or correlation coefficient varies between +1 (perfect positive relationship) and –1 (perfect negative relationship). 0 indicates no relationship.

Summary

The social status of women has been one of the most controversial and persistent issues in the cultural warfare among intellectual leaders, political activists, and the public at large in the Middle East, North Africa, and Pakistan in the modern period. The vestimentary forms that women were allowed to wear in public places have also been a subject of debates and controversies among the secularists and the supporters of Islamic fundamentalism and conservative Islam in the region. The resolution of these issues in a manner favorable to women will certainly contribute to the transformation of the current structures of patriarchy and male domination in the family and in political, economic, and educational institutions.

To assess cross-national variation in attitudes toward gender equality in such domains of social life as the family, the labor market, politics, and education, this chapter measured and analyzed these attitudes among the samples of respondents from the seven countries. It also constructed a gender equality index as a summary measure of these attitudes across the different domains. The findings indicated that attitudes toward gender equality varied considerably cross-nationally. Turkish respondents, with an aggregate gender equality index of 2.73, were more supportive of gender equality, followed by Lebanese and Tunisians, with index values of 2.58 and 2.50, respectively. Iraqis and Pakistanis, having index values of 2.22 and 2.22, respectively, were less supportive of gender equality, and Egyptians and Saudis, with index values of 2.07 and

2.06, respectively, were least favorable toward gender equality. However, only among the Lebanese and Turkish respondents did a majority score significantly above the 2.5 median of the gender equality index, which indicated these two countries as a whole were more favorable toward gender equality than gender inequality. The low support for gender equality in Saudi Arabia is a reflection of its patriarchal culture, but in Egypt, it may be an outcome of the influence of the Islamic fundamentalist movement in the past decades.

Findings from this analysis also showed that the youth bulge was significantly more favorable toward gender equality than was the older age group, with the differences between the two age groups being largest among Pakistanis (0.31) and smallest among Egyptians (0.05). Young Turkish respondents were the most egalitarian in their attitudes toward women, and older Saudis were the least egalitarian.

The assessment of attitudes toward gender equality by gender showed that, without exception, women reported greater support for gender equality than men across the seven countries, with the largest difference among Lebanese and the smallest among Egyptians. Furthermore, among women, differences in favor of gender equality based on age were significant; those in the youth bulge consistently scored higher on the gender equality index than did those in the older age group across the seven countries. Mean age differences on this index were also larger among female respondents than among male respondents. Among men, there were inconsistent but significant age differences across the seven countries. In Iraq, Pakistan, and Saudi Arabia, male youth were more strongly in favor of gender equality than were older males, but in Tunisia, they were less supportive. However, among male respondents from Lebanon, Egypt, and Turkey, there was no significant difference in the gender equality index values between the two age groups.

In terms of the effects of education on attitudes toward women, respondents with university education were consistently more favorable toward gender equality, with the exception of Saudis, whose attitudes on gender equality were not differentiated by education. This may be both an outcome of the influence of the conservative religious institutions on the content of the curricula of the system of higher education and a result of the gender-segregated and curriculum-differentiated model of education that was intentionally instituted to reproduce gender hierarchy and support women's domestic functions in the country.

Assessment of the effects of education within the two age groups showed that among respondents in the youth bulge, the difference between those with and without university education was significant in Lebanon, Pakistan, Tunisia, Egypt, and Turkey, indicating that young respondents with university education were more supportive of gender equality than were those without university education. For Iraq and Saudi Arabia, this difference is not statistically significant. Among respondents in the older age group, those with university education scored significantly higher on the gender equality index across six of the seven countries. In Saudi Arabia, there was no difference in the gender equality index values between the two educational groups.

University education made the greatest difference in attitudes toward gender equality among Pakistanis in both age groups (0.39 among the youth bulge and 0.53 among the older age group) and the smallest difference among Iraqis (0.05, which is not significant, among the youth bulge and 0.10 among the older age group), after the Saudis. Again, as was the case with expressive individualism, university education appeared to have little effect on attitudes toward gender equality among Saudis.

On veiling preference, there was considerable variation across the seven countries, with Lebanese, Tunisian, and Turkish respondents favoring a more liberal vestimentary form for women and Pakistani and Saudi respondents preferring a more conservative form. The youth bulge and people with university education opted for a more liberal veiling style than did the older age group and those without university education. There was no consistent pattern of gender difference in veiling preference. Finally, the analysis of the data showed that people who favored a more conservative veiling style for women were also less supportive of gender equality and expressive individualism.

The analyses advanced in this chapter showed that females, particularly young educated females, and generally younger people and people with university education were more supportive of gender equality. For them, a more liberal sartorial practice was a more appropriate style for women. They are thus more likely to join movements for change in favor of more egalitarian gender relations. However, countries with larger youth populations provide weaker support of gender equality.

CHAPTER 3

SECULAR POLITICS, LIBERAL VALUES, AND NATIONAL IDENTITY

Secular politics is a third component of liberal values and the most contentious issue in the cultural warfare between liberal activists and the followers of political Islam in the contemporary period. In places like Iran, it is currently at the center of a serious ideological struggle over the future of the country. This conflict, however, is not an outcome of the belief in the unity of religion and politics in Islam (or, more precisely, the religious constitution of politics). Rather, the subject turned into a fiercely contested issue in Muslim-majority countries only during the heyday of Islamic fundamentalism from the 1970s on, an outcome of the crisis caused by authoritarian secular ideological states, the shift in orientations among a significant segment of the intellectual leaders from secular to religious subjects, and the fundamentalists' unrelenting onslaughts on secularism in the second half of the twentieth century.

In historical Islam, secular politics was recognized de facto. In their systematic efforts to reconcile the Islamic theory of government with the changing political realities of the post-Rashidun caliphate, which did not conform to the early Islamic theory of the caliphate, Muslim theologians gradually and progressively arrived at a resolution that admitted the reality of secular politics. This admission was reflected in the development of a bifurcated perspective on legitimate leadership of the Muslim community, with the sultan in charge of the government and the *ulama* in charge of religion. This differentiation of the legitimate political authority, however, carried an important element that aided the development of political modernity in Islam in the late nineteenth century. This element was a discursive space in Islamic political thought that allowed Muslim intellectual leaders to detect, recognize, and debate the sultan's discretionary power (or monarchical absolutism) as the problematic element in this thought and thus abandon the notion that the monarch was the shadow of God on Earth, rejecting the legitimacy of his rule, particularly after realizing that the sultan or the shah was too incompetent to protect the Islamic community.[1] They did so, however, in light of the eighteenth-century political Enlightenment coming to the region from Europe in the nineteenth century, which shaped the belief that a constitutional government was not only superior to an absolutist monarchy but also necessary for their countries' economic development and prosperity. This latter belief may explain why Muslim leaders expressed no disagreement with political modernity during the days when nationalist movements were blossoming and seeking the construction of modern constitutional states in the early twentieth century. These leaders were in fact actively involved and in some countries played leading roles in such movements. They did not see any contradiction between Islam and the principles of a constitutional government, which, for them, was a far superior alternative to the existing despotic rule of the monarch, the Ottomans' pan-Islamism, or colonial rule, depending on the country. The conservatives and traditionalists who thought otherwise were either badly defeated or pushed to the sidelines. An exemplary case is the 1906 Iranian Constitutional Revolution, in which two prominent ayatollahs (high-ranking religious scholars in Shia Islam) played leading roles. A more astonishing aspect of the revolution was its pro-Western orientation and predisposition to emulate the Western political model (Adamiyat 1976). Sheikh Fazlullah Nuri, a prominent cleric who rose up against the constitution and in defense of the absolutist monarch, was arrested, tried, and executed. Egyptians were even more successful in creating a modern constitutional order in their country following the nationalist revolution of 1919 (Safran 1961; Marsot 1977).

The rise of political Islam in the 1970s—reinforced by the 1977 pro-Islamic fundamentalist military coup by General Zia al-Haq in Pakistan, the 1979 Iranian Revolution, and the worldwide Muslim mobilizations against the 1979 Soviet invasion of Afghanistan—turned secularism into a serious political issue in the Middle East and North Africa. This chapter measures attitudes toward secularism, constructs a secular politics index, and assesses variation in support for secular politics across the seven countries and by age, gender, and education. It also combines the indices of expressive individualism, gender equality, and secular politics to create an index of liberal values. Finally, it discusses the issue of identity and the extent to which this identity, in the perspectives of the respondents from the seven countries, rests on the idea of territorial nation, ethnicity, or religion. A cross-national analysis of support for liberal values in conjunction with national identity provides a basis for assessing the extent of support for liberal nationalism and the variation in this support by age, gender, education, religion, and religious sect.

The Modern State, Secular Politics, and Historical Islam

The historical debate on the modern state among the region's intellectual leaders and political activists revolved around the idea of the separation of religion and politics as the foundation of political modernity. This debate, however, was obscured by two factors: the use of a *narrow* conceptualization of the modern state and the failure to consider the status of the *secular* in the Islamic theory of government.

The Modern State as Ideologically Neutral

The narrow conceptualization of the modern state considers it a political community that is separated from religion. This is an insufficient, and even misleading, description of the modern state. In liberal democratic theory, the modern state is considered legitimate insofar as it represents the common interests of the individuals living within the national borders. For modern political philosophers, including Jeremy Bentham (1748–1832), John Austin (1790–1859), James Mill (1773–1836), and John Stuart Mill (1806–1873), the modern state is, and must be, a utility maximizer, functioning to boost overall aggregate individual benefits. It serves as the guarantor of the free-market economy and the provider of political utility—the security of rights, the security of property, and the individual freedom of movement. Furthermore, the state's legitimacy, and therefore its effectiveness, in supplying these common goods is predicated on the principles of the consent of the governed, responsiveness to the governed, and adherence to the law. The consent of the governed is not forthcoming because the state claims to be executing, say, the Islamic laws of the sharia, the creed of pan-Arab nationalism, or the communist code of working-class interests. The state's purported representation of the interests of Muslims, Arabs, or members of the working class, respectively, does not automatically make the state legitimate. Rather, the consent of the governed is realized through equal entitlement to a political voice, or the concept of one person, one vote, in the selection of the government (Macpherson 1965; Brink 2014).

For the equality of the political voice to work, the state must be free from interventions by weighty social forces that represent special interests, including the landed aristocracy, the royal power, the military, and, of course, the religious institutions. This conception of the modern state resonated with Marx, who approved of the French Revolution for freeing the state from all manner of medieval rubbish, seigniorial rights, local privileges, and municipal and guild monopolies of provincial constitutions (Marx 1977, 274–313). His misgiving about the liberal democratic project was that, given that the modern state is inserted into a class-divided society, the state transforms into an instrument of class rule or its actions are constrained by the structure of unequally distributed economic resources. As a result, the state begins to function in the interest of economically powerful members of the upper classes. From Marx's perspective, it was nearly impossible for the state to remain a neutral political institution—a sine qua non for representing the universal interests of the society. Thus, beyond the separation of religion and politics, the formation and effective functioning of the modern state are contingent on its neutrality from both ideological and institutional standpoints. The modern state must be ideologically neutral or nonideological. It must also be separated from and independent of not simply religious institutions but also any institutions connected to special interests, including the military, whose control of the government and intervention in the economy has been a fundamental political problem in the region in the contemporary period. If the laws sanctioned by the modern state are to be *made* by the people's representatives, rather than being *discovered* from a religious text, then, in order to maintain the state's ideological neutrality, it is important to replace this text with the social context, where individuals freely engage in debates over issues and support the political representative who is closer to their perspective. Here it is argued that the twentieth-century modern states formed in the Middle East and North Africa, however, were not built on the axiom of neutrality. Rather, they were ideological states, where the religious text was replaced with such other texts as those drawn on evolutionary theories of change or developmental idealism, pan-Arab or ethnic nationalism, Marxism or Marxism-Leninism, functioning as a "secular religion" (Moaddel 2002).

The Status of Secular Politics in Historical Islam

The second factor obscuring the debate on the modern state is a misreading of the status of secular politics in historical Islam. This misreading resulted from a text-based reading of Islamic politics and from an overgeneralization of the political experience of the Islamic movement under the Prophet and the Rashidun caliphate (632–661) to the entire history of Islam. Islamicists have long claimed that Islam rejected secular politics and that legitimate rule rested on the unity of religion and politics (Gibb 1947; Lewis 1993). Countering this interpretation are profound changes in the Islamic conception of political authority that gradually transpired after the death of Prophet Muhammad. While Sunni theologians have been unanimous in their belief in the legitimacy of the political power of the first four caliphs or the prophet's successors (Abu Bakr,

Omar, Othman, and Ali), who were bestowed with the honorific title of the Rashidun (rightly guided), the rise of dynastic rule after the assassination of the fourth caliph in AD 661 posed serious problems for Muslim jurists: How could the Islamic conception of sovereignty be reconciled with the claims of self-made caliphs among the emerging military leaders and tribal chiefs in different parts of the Muslim world? To reconcile the Islamic theory of government and the existing political reality, Muslim scholars steadily turned away from the notion of the unity of religious and political leadership in the original theory of caliphate and took positions that progressively amounted to the admission of the reality of secular politics. First, Abu al-Hasan Ali al-Mawardi (972–1058) bound rulers who had effective power within their own territories in different parts of the Islamic empire to the centralized spiritual authority of the Abbasid caliphate (750–1258), which in turn gave them delegated legal authority in their own territories and a claim to the loyalty of their subjects (Gibb 1947; Rosenthal 1958). Later developments, however, undermined this formula, as effective power fell into the hands of Kurdish, Turkish, or Caucasian military chiefs, whose actions were dictated by political exigencies, not by the sharia. Thus, "to maintain that the sultan derived his power from the caliph was increasingly difficult as it became clear that in fact the caliph was set up and deposed by the sultan" (Hourani 1983, 14). As a further concession to reality, Imam Muhammad al-Ghazali (1058–1111) argued that, as long as the sultan recognized the authority of the caliph, the sultan should be treated as lawful. To unseat the sultan by declaring his power illegal would result in lawlessness and chaos, a condition more detrimental to the welfare of Muslims than having a tyrant in power (Rosenthal 1958).

Clearly, in al-Ghazali's thinking, there was a shift "from the origin of political power to its use" (Hourani 1983, 2), but later scholars as diverse as Taqi al-Din Ahmad Ibn Taymiyya (1263–1328) and Abd al-Rahman Ibn Khaldun (1333–1406) conceded that the caliphate had ceased to exist after the fourth caliph and that the sovereignty exercised by the Umayyads and the Abbasids had never been more than a form of royalty (Ibn Khaldun 1967). Nonetheless, rather than suggesting the overthrow of the existing ruler, these thinkers, like their predecessors, worked out a formula that bestowed Islamic legitimacy on the ruler. Ibn Taymiyya expanded the concept of the sharia to bring within its scope the ruler's "discretionary power without which he could neither maintain himself nor provide for the welfare of the community" (Hourani 1983, 20). He did so by applying the principle of *maslaha*; because God's purpose in giving laws was human welfare, the ruler's discretionary power was necessary not just to protect himself but also to provide for the welfare (*maslaha*) of the community. His doctrine contained the precept that a good government depended on an alliance between the amirs, political and military leaders, and the *ulama*, interpreters of the law. In a similar fashion, Ibn Khaldun offered a way to incorporate Islam into the natural life span of dynasties such that a more stable and universalistic regime would be created (Hourani 1983).

Shia Islam rejects the legitimacy of the rule of the first three caliphs, Abu Bakr, Omar, and Othman. Its doctrine of *imamat* states that the political authority of the Prophet devolves on Ali—the Prophet's son-in-law and the fourth caliph in Sunni Islam—and his male descendants. Ali is considered the first rightful imam, followed by eleven imams in twelver Shiism. As long as the Shia lived as a minority in a hostile Sunni environment, they took the practical course of renouncing the legitimacy of the existing order while abstaining from any rebellious action (Watt 1960; Algar 1969). The elevation of Shia Islam to the state religion under the Safavids (1501–1722) paralleled a significant shift in the sect's political theory in a direction that was remarkably similar to that of Sunni Islam. In this new development, the doctrine of *imamat*, which initially embodied the twin functions of religion and politics in the twelfth imam, was replaced by one of divided authority: the *ulama* assumed religious authority and the shah political leadership. Mutual assistance and cooperation between the ruler and the *ulama* was considered necessary for the betterment of the country and religion (Adamiyat 1976; Arjomand 1984).

Secular Politics in the Contemporary Period

Political developments in historical Islam prompted Muslim theologians–cum–political theorists to resolve that the sultan's discretionary power was necessary not only for his own protection but for the security and political stability of the Muslim community as well. After all, rebellion against him, they thought, would cause sedition (*fitneh*), a deteriorated social condition that was believed to be far worse than having an illegitimate ruler in power. Because these Muslim theologians neither provided a clear Islamic justification for the utility of the separation of religion and politics in preserving the welfare of the Islamic community nor acknowledged that the caliphate failed because its theoretical underpinning was defective (Cragg 1957; Kerr 1966), it is possible to conclude that they recognized the reality of secular politics pragmatically, not through intellectual speculation. However, the incorporation of the sultan's discretionary power as a principle in the Islamic theory of government gave this theory a flexible character, which enabled it to adapt to the conditions of modernity (Moaddel and Karabenick 2013).

When facing the challenges of political modernity in the nineteenth century, Muslim theologians and political activists were able to use this flexibility to take favorable positions toward a secular constitutional government. Believing that the West made progress because of its constitutional government and realizing the glaring contrast between constitutional government and the existing ineffective and corrupt monarchy in Muslim countries (Adamiyat 1976), these theologians developed an Islamic rationale that supported establishing a constitutional system and parliamentary democracy. This rationale was quite simple: their political system would be even closer to the spirit of true Islam if a constitutional government was substituted for monarchical absolutism, a point clearly stated and argued for by Iranian Ayatollah Naini (Hairi 1977). Likewise, Muhammad Abduh, mufti of Egypt and a harbinger of Islamic modernism in the late nineteenth century, expressed little desire for the reestablishment of Ottoman authority in his country. For him, British rule, while in principle unacceptable, provided the only viable opportunity for the gradual education of his fellow Egyptians. What is more, the British would be easier to get rid of than the khedivial autocracy. To give yet another example, a leading Sunni political theorist from Syria, Abdul Rahman al-Kawakibi (1849–1903), categorically rejected political despotism, arguing, in a scarcely veiled reference to Ottoman Sultan Abdülhamid (r. 1876–1909), that a tyrannical regime would not only distort individual character but undermine religion as well.

Islamic Fundamentalism as a Reaction to the Twentieth-Century Secular State

The formation of modern states in Egypt, Iran, and Turkey in the 1920s was the political outcome of the nationalist movement that started in the late nineteenth century. These states in turn provided further support for the creation and maintenance of a new cultural environment, in which secularism was the dominant discourse, shaped the view of the intellectual leaders, and informed state policies. Connected to these developments were (1) the rise of a powerful critical attitude toward Islam, Islamic institutions, and traditional culture; and (2) the implementation of a series of policies purportedly to modernize and standardize the court system, establish and foster secular education and the institutions of higher learning, reform the rule concerning the property of Islamic charitable endowments (*waqf*), and promote the participation of women in social affairs.

These changes, however, begot fundamentalist reactions from religious activists. The state-initiated and -sponsored cultural programs to promote secular institutions, endorse national identity in contradistinction to religious identity, and institute laws that ran contrary to the sharia appear to have contributed to the perception among the faithful that their religion was under siege, their core values were offended, and their freedom to engage in religious rituals was frustrated. Such a perception of *besieged spirituality* activated religious awareness, prompting some to use religious categories to frame issues, analyze events, and make claims—all of which culminated in the adoption of alarmist attitudes and conspiratorial perspectives that their religion was under attack by "the Crusaders-Zionists alliance." An extremist trend within the fundamentalist movements gained momentum as Egypt, Iran, Turkey, and other countries in the region turned increasingly authoritarian and interventionist in the second half of the twentieth century. On the one hand, the authoritarianism of the state weakened and undermined collectivities within the civil societies. As a result, oppositional politics was channeled through religion, expanding the resources and influences of Islamic fundamentalism in the society. On the other hand, the totalitarianism of the state prompted and reinforced a disciplinarian conception of God, whose forces must be mobilized against the all-encompassing power of the ruling dictator (Moaddel and Karabenick 2013, 2018).

Moreover, while the fundamentalist discourse was produced in opposition to the secularism of the state in many parts of the Middle East and North Africa—most notably, in Algeria, Egypt, Iran, Tunisia, and Turkey—in other places the specific national context also played a significant role in bringing political Islam into the limelight. Saudi fundamentalism, for example, was promoted by the state in order to combat the challenges, first, of pan-Arab nationalism in the fifties and sixties and then of the Iranian Revolution and Shia sectarianism. In Pakistan, the Punjabi ruling elite, who were facing political challenges from the excluded ethnic minorities, invoked Islam as a unifying ideology, a policy that enhanced the political influences of the *mollas* and fundamentalist groups. In Lebanon, Shia fundamentalism was sponsored by the Iranian Islamic regime and Sunni fundamentalism by the Saudis (Moaddel 1993, 2002, 2005, 2006; Alavi 2009).

Measures of Secular Politics

This historical background has examined the changes in the Islamic theory of government from the belief in the caliphate as unifying the religious and politically authority to the acceptance of the institutional separation of religious and political leadership (which had become the modus operandi of Muslim politics in the premodern period), to the embrace of constitutionalism and parliamentary democracy by Muslim theologians in the early twentieth century, and, finally, to the religious absolutism espoused by Islamic fundamentalists in the late twentieth and early twenty-first centuries—all are indicative of significant historical changes in the Islamic conception of political authority, changes that came as a result of changes in social conditions. More crucially, this background is also instructive for measuring and understanding public opinion on forms of government and on secular politics.

This historical background provides four different conceptions of politics and form of government, whose significance among the respondents across the seven countries may indicate the extent to which the historical debates have shaped their perception of secular politics: (1) Islamic absolutist rule, (2) the importance of having a secular government that observes and implements the sharia, (3) the separation of religion and politics, and (4) the importance of having a Western-style government to ensure the country's level of economic development and mass prosperity. Four survey questions were developed that corresponded to these four varied conceptions of the desirable political system. By analyzing data related to these questions, this chapter measures and assesses variation in public attitudes toward secular politics:[2]

1. Would it be (1) very good, (2) fairly good, (3) fairly bad, or (4) very bad to have an Islamic government [a Christian government (for Christian respondents)] where religious authorities have absolute power? (*religious government*, not asked in Saudi Arabia)
2. Is it (1) very important, (2) important, (3) somewhat important, (4) least important, or (5) not important for a good government to implement only the laws of the sharia [only the laws inspired by Christian values (for Christian respondents)]? (*sharia/Christian values*)[3]
3. Do you (1) strongly agree, (2) agree, (3) disagree, or (4) strongly disagree that [name of the country] will be a better society if religion and politics are separated? (*separation of religion and politics*, not asked in Saudi Arabia)
4. Do you (1) strongly agree, (2) agree, (3) disagree, or (4) strongly disagree that [name of the country] will be a better society if its government was similar to Western governments? (*Western-type government*, not asked in Saudi Arabia)

The first question measures the significance of Islamic government where religious authorities enjoy absolute power, a form of religious rule that is supported by the theory of the caliphate, and the second measures the religious function of a secular government, which has been the key element in Islamic political theory as revised by theologians like Ibn Taymiyya (1263–1328). The third addresses the orientation of respondents toward the separation of religion and politics, and, finally, the fourth gauges the desirability of Western-type government, which was the view of the region's many leading intellectuals and political activists in the early twentieth century.

The responses to the last two questions were recoded so that higher values indicate stronger agreement with the separation of religion and politics and the implementation of Western-type government. A secular politics index was then created by averaging the responses to these four questions in order to provide an overall measure of the support for secular politics. This index ranges between 1 and 4, with higher values indicating stronger support for secular politics or weaker support for a religious government. In Saudi Arabia, three of the four questions used to construct this index were excluded from the survey (they were not allowed to be asked). Only the question on implementing the sharia as the characteristic of a good government was allowed to be included in the survey. To construct a secular politics index for Saudi Arabia, respondents were asked two substitute questions. One measured confidence in religious institutions: Do you have (1) a great deal of confidence, (2) quite a lot of confidence, (3) not very much confidence, or (4) none at all in religious institutions?

To be sure, strictly speaking, confidence in religious institutions is not an indicator of secular politics. Nonetheless, within the context of Saudi Arabia, where the institutions of the Wahhabi establishment have played a significant role in politics, varied confidence in the religious institutions could be considered a proxy measure for variation in support for secular politics. A lower confidence in such institutions may indicate a more favorable attitude toward secular politics. The other question, which is arguably a reasonable substitute for attitudes toward the separation of religion and politics, probes respondents on whether an increase in the influence of religion on politics would affect the level of development in their country: "Would your country be (1) a lot more developed, (2) more developed, (3) less developed, or (4) a lot less developed, if the influence of religion on politics increases?" Presumably, the respondents who said that this increase would make their country less or a lot less developed were more likely to favor secular politics than were those who said otherwise. The responses to these three questions were averaged to create a secular politics index for Saudi Arabia.

Variation in attitudes toward secular politics is assessed across the seven countries and by age, gender, and education. How these attitudes vary by religion (Christians versus Muslims) and religious sect (Shia versus Sunni) is also evaluated in countries where such divisions exist.

Cross-National Variation

Table 3.1 shows cross-national variation in attitudes toward Islamic government and the sharia (Christian government and values for Christian respondents, respectively), separation of religion and politics, and Western-type government. It also shows the distribution of Saudis' confidence in their religious institutions and perception of whether their country would be more or less developed if the influence of religion on politics increases (as substitutes for two of the three questions excluded from the Saudi survey). Finally, the table reports the secular politics index for the seven countries. First, those

TABLE 3.1 Measures of Secular Politics

	Iraq	Lebanon	Pakistan	Saudi Arabia	Tunisia	Egypt	Turkey
Religious government with absolute power/for Saudi Arabia: Confidence in religious institutions							
Very good/A great deal	15%	8%	14%	40%	16%	26%	8%
Fairly good/Quite a lot	34%	23%	19%	35%	21%	33%	26%
Fairly bad/Not very much	34%	34%	46%	14%	20%	24%	35%
Very bad/None at all	17%	36%	21%	2.0%	43%	18%	31%
Implement only the sharia							
Very important	14%	9%	37%	35%	14%	29%	6%
Important	34%	15%	37%	33%	14%	27%	14%
Somewhat important	26%	25%	23%	21%	19%	23%	13%
Least important	19%	24%	2%	7%	21%	11%	21%
Not important	7%	27%	1%	3%	33%	10%	46%
Religion and politics separated/for Saudi Arabia: More or less developed if religion shapes politics							
Strongly disagree/A lot more developed	7%	4%	65%	33%	13%	18%	7%
Disagree/More developed	24%	15%	27%	35%	15%	32%	17%
Agree/Less developed	39%	32%	5%	23%	23%	19%	36%
Strongly agree/A lot less developed	30%	48%	4%	9%	49%	32%	40%
Western-type government							
Strongly disagree	19%	11%	33%	NA	25%	35%	18%
Disagree	36%	26%	41%	NA	28%	32%	39%
Agree	33%	36%	21%	NA	24%	18%	33%
Strongly agree	12%	27%	5%	NA	23%	15%	11%
Secular politics index (mean)	2.53	2.96	1.97	1.86	2.81	2.29	2.86
Median	2.56	3.00	1.94	1.83	2.88	2.25	3.00
Range (min–max)	1–4	1–4	1–4	1–4	1–4	1–4	1–4

who considered a religious government to be fairly bad or very bad were a majority in Lebanon, Pakistan, Tunisia, and Turkey—70 percent, 67 percent, 63 percent, and 66 percent, respectively; a slim majority in Iraq, 51 percent: and a sizable minority in Egypt, 42 percent. Second, on the sharia, 24 percent of

Lebanese, 28 percent of Tunisians, and 20 percent of Turkish respondents; a sizable minority of Iraqis, 48 percent: and a majority of Pakistanis, Saudis, and Egyptians—74 percent, 68 percent, and 56 percent, respectively—considered it very important or important for a good government to implement only the sharia. Third, higher percentages of Lebanese and Turkish respondents either strongly agreed or agreed that their country would be a better society if religion and politics were separated (80 percent and 76 percent, respectively), followed by Tunisians (72 percent) and Iraqis (69 percent). However, about half of the respondents from Egypt (51 percent) and only 9 percent of those from Pakistan shared similar views. Finally, the percentages of those who strongly agreed or agreed with the desirability of Western-type government were 45 percent of Iraqis, 63 percent of Lebanese, 26 percent of Pakistanis, 47 percent of Tunisians, 33 percent of Egyptians, and 44 percent of Turkish respondents. In response to the substitute questions for secular politics in Saudi Arabia, only 16 percent said they had not very much confidence or none at all in the religious institutions, and 32 percent believed that their country would be either less developed or a lot less developed if the influence of religion on politics increases.

Finally, the aggregate secular politics index scores for Lebanon, Tunisia, and Turkey were 2.96, 2.81, and 2.86, respectively. For Pakistan and Saudi Arabia, the scores were 1.97, and 1.86, respectively. In between were Iraq and Egypt, with secular politics index scores of 2.53 and 2.29, respectively. The analysis of variance showed that the differences in the secular politics index across countries are significant ($F = 1343.56$, $p < .001$). Post hoc analyses using Scheffé's test indicated statistically significant differences among all countries, except for Tunisia and Turkey, where the differences are not statistically significant. The median values for the secular politics index were significantly higher than 2.5 for Iraq, Lebanon, Tunisia, and Turkey, a threshold value indicating that the majority of the respondents favored secular politics; the reverse was true for Egypt, Pakistan, and Saudi Arabia.

Variation by Age, Gender, and Education

The index of secular politics was used to assess cross-national variation in people's orientations toward secular politics by age, gender, and education.

Age

Table 3.2 shows the differences in the secular politics index between the youth bulge (aged 18–29) and the older age group (aged 30 and older) across the seven countries. Respondents in the youth bulge were significantly more supportive

TABLE 3.2 Age Differences in Secular Politics and Median Age by Country

	Mean Index: 18–29	Mean Index: 30+	$Col_1 - Col_2$	Mean Index: Total	Median Age[a]
Egypt	2.36	2.36	0.00	2.36	24.3
Iraq	2.55	2.52	0.03	2.53	20.9
Lebanon	3.06	2.88	0.18[c]	2.96	29.8
Pakistan	2.17	1.85	0.32[c]	1.97	21.6
Saudi Arabia	1.89	1.79	0.10[d]	1.86	25.3[b]
Tunisia	2.90	2.79	0.11[d]	2.81	31.0
Turkey	2.85	2.86	−0.01	2.86	29.2
$r_{Col4Col6}$	.82[d]				

[a] The median ages for Tunisia and Turkey are from 2013; the median ages for all other countries are from 2011 (CIA, 2011, 2013).
[b] The population figure used to compute the median age for Saudi Arabia includes about 25 percent nonnationals. Also note that the secular-politics index for Saudi Arabia is based on different indicators.
[c] $p < .001$.
[d] $p < .05$.

of secular politics in four of the seven countries: Saudi Arabia, Pakistan, Tunisia, and Lebanon. Independent samples t-tests of the youth bulge and the older age group are statistically significant across these four countries ($p < .01$). In the other countries, there were no significant differences between the two age groups.

The difference in secular politics between the youth bulge and the older age group was greatest among Pakistani respondents (0.32), while the differences for all other countries ranged from negligible to 0.18 for Lebanon (table 3.2, column 3). The analysis shows that cross-national variation in attitude toward secular politics was directly related to the country's median age (or inversely related to the size of the youth bulge). That is, as shown in table 3.2, the correlation coefficient between the secular politics index and the median age is 0.82 (statistically significant at $p < .05$). This means that the higher the median age of a country's population (i.e., the smaller the size of its youth bulge), the greater the endorsement of secular politics in that country. That is, while the youth bulge tended to support secular politics in four countries and exhibited no difference with the older age group in the other three, on the macro (country) level the younger the population of a country, the less that population favored secular politics.

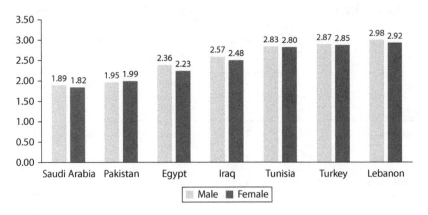

Figure 3.1 Secular Politics Index by Gender.

Gender

Figure 3.1 shows the differences in attitudes toward secular politics by gender across the seven countries. In Lebanon, Iraq, Egypt, and Saudi Arabia, men were significantly more supportive of secular politics than were women, while in Pakistan, women were more favorable ($p < .05$, based on independent samples t-tests). In Tunisia and Turkey this difference is not statistically significant. Thus, the connection between gender and secular politics remains inconsistent across these countries.

Gender and Age

Table 3.3 shows cross-national variation in attitudes toward secular politics by gender and age groups. This variation is inconsistent across the seven countries. Among female respondents, the youth bulge scored statistically significantly higher on secular politics than the older age group only in Lebanon, Pakistan, and Tunisia; while among the male respondents, this was also true only in Saudi Arabia, Lebanon, and Pakistan. There were no significant differences between the two age groups for either sex in the other countries. Again, the difference between the age groups was greatest among Pakistani respondents.

Education

Considering the education–secular politics nexus, respondents with university education were more supportive of secular politics than were those without university education across the countries, except for Saudi Arabia, where university education made no significant difference (figure 3.2). University education had the greatest effect in Pakistan; there was a 0.35 difference in the mean values of the secular politics index between the two educational groups.

TABLE 3.3 Secular Politics Index by Gender and Age (Mean/Standard Deviation; *n*)

	Female			Male		
	Aged 18–29	**Aged 30+**	**Difference**	**Aged 18–29**	**Aged 30+**	**Difference**
Egypt	2.23/0.60; 535	2.22/0.60; 1,034	0.01	2.35/0.63; 439	2.37/0.63; 1,064	−0.02
Iraq	2.50/0.60; 521	2.47/0.59; 849	0.03	2.59/0.59; 607	2.56/0.62; 957	0.03
Saudi Arabia[a]	1.81/0.62; 324	1.78/0.60; 431	0.03	1.98/0.58; 327	1.80/0.55; 430	0.18[c]
Lebanon	3.02/0.57; 480	2.85/0.72; 721	0.17[b]	3.09/0.63; 676	2.91/0.65; 1,030	0.18[b]
Pakistan	2.19/0.49; 681	1.86/0.53; 1,025	0.33[b]	2.15/0.56; 582	1.85/0.59; 1,226	0.30[b]
Tunisia[a]	2.92/0.72; 388	2.76/0.72; 1,280	0.16[b]	2.88/0.80; 324	2.82/0.79; 1,015	0.06
Turkey	2.83/0.66; 435	2.86/0.65; 1,148	−0.03	2.87/0.72; 389	2.87/0.65; 916	0.00

[a] Sample sizes are reported without the use of weights for Tunisia and Saudi Arabia. Significance of independent samples *t*-tests for differences in the secular politics index by age (equal variances not assumed):
[b] $p < .001$.
[c] $p < .01$.

Independent samples *t*-tests showed that the differences between the two groups across the six countries are statistically significant ($p < .01$). It should, however, be noted that the value of this index for Saudi Arabia was based on different indicators (see table 3.1).

Education and Age
Table 3.4 shows variation in support for secular politics by age and education groups. In Iraq, Lebanon, Pakistan, and Turkey, those with university education

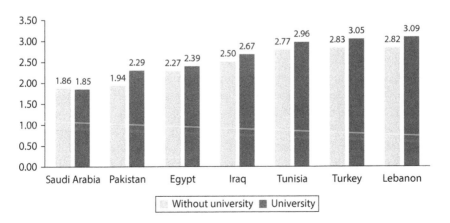

Figure 3.2 Secular Politics Index by Education.

TABLE 3.4 Secular Politics Index by Age and Education (Mean/Standard Deviation; n)

	Youth Bulge (Aged 18–29)			Older Age Group (Age 30+)		
	Without University	University	Difference	Without University	University	Difference
Iraq	2.53/0.60; 921	2.64/0.61; 194	0.11[d]	2.47/0.60; 1,414	2.69/0.58; 362	0.22[b]
Lebanon	2.97/0.59; 362	3.11/0.60; 776	0.14[c]	2.77/0.69; 1,068	3.07/0.63; 668	0.30[b]
Pakistan	2.15/0.51; 1,116	2.35/0.60; 147	0.20[b]	1.83/0.55; 2,111	2.24/0.58; 139	0.41[b]
Saudi Arabia[a]	1.91/0.60; 418	1.88/0.62; 231	−0.03	1.81/0.56; 666	1.74/0.60; 195	−0.07
Tunisia[a]	2.89/0.72; 415	2.92/0.79; 296	0.03	2.74/0.74; 1,882	2.98/0.78; 410	0.24[b]
Egypt	2.28/0.62; 752	2.29/0.62; 222	0.01	2.27/0.60; 1,791	2.46/0.68; 307	0.19[b]
Turkey	2.81/0.65; 632	2.98/0.66; 191	0.17[c]	2.83/0.65; 1,832	3.11/0.58; 232	0.28[b]

[a] Sample sizes are reported without the use of weights for Tunisia and Saudi Arabia.
Significance of independent samples t-tests for differences in the secular politics index by age (equal variances not assumed):
[b] $p < .001$.
[c] $p < .01$.
[d] $p < .05$.

were significantly more supportive of secular politics than those without university education in both age groups. In other countries, the results were inconsistent. In Egypt and Tunisia, the difference between the two education groups was significant among the older age group, and in Saudi Arabia, university education had no significant effect on secular politics for either age group.

Liberal Values

Expressive individualism, gender equality, and secular politics are components of liberal values. The indices of these constructs are positively correlated, and using pooled data from all seven countries, exploratory factor analysis showed that these three indices made one factor with an eigenvalue of 1.71 and a Cronbach's alpha of 0.62. These three indices were averaged in order to create a liberal values index, and the results by country are reported in table 3.5. Post hoc analysis of variance ($F = 1631.459$, $p < .001$) confirms significant differences in the index of liberal values by country, with Scheffé's test showing that Pakistan was the least liberal country, with a mean index value of 1.93. Less conservative than Pakistan were Egypt, Saudi Arabia, and Iraq, with index values of 2.04, 2.08, and 2.21, respectively. Tunisia, Turkey, and Lebanon, with index values of 2.52, 2.68, and 2.74, respectively, were the most liberal countries. All these differences

TABLE 3.5 Age Differences in Liberal Values and Median Age by Country

	1	2	3	4	5
	Mean Index: 18–29	Mean Index: 30+	Col_1–Col_2	Mean Index: Total	Median Age[a]
Pakistan	2.15	1.81	0.34	1.93	21.6
Egypt	2.09	2.01	0.08	2.04	24.3
Saudi Arabia	2.16	1.98	0.18	2.08	25.3
Iraq	2.28	2.16	0.12	2.21	20.9
Tunisia	2.60	2.49	0.11	2.52	31.0
Turkey	2.76	2.65	0.11	2.68	29.2
Lebanon	2.83	2.67	0.16	2.74	29.8
$r_{Col4Col5}$	.84[b]				

[a] The median ages for Tunisia and Turkey are from 2013; the median ages for in all other countries are from 2011 (CIA 2011, 2013).
[b] $p < .05$.

are statistically significant ($p < 0.01$). Given that the median values of the liberal values index were significantly higher than 2.5 for Lebanon (2.76) and Turkey (2.67) (not reported in the table), the respondents from these countries on average were more liberal than illiberal. For Tunisia, it is 2.50 (not reported in the table), which means that the respondents were evenly divided between those who favored secular politics and those who preferred otherwise. The reverse is true in the other four countries.

Variation by Age, Gender, and Education

Age

As was true for other components of liberal values, respondents in youth bulge across the seven countries were consistently more liberal than were respondents in the older age group, as shown in table 3.5. Independent samples t-tests of the differences between age groups showed that these differences are statistically significant ($p < .001$) across all countries (equal variances not assumed). This age difference in the index of liberal values was greatest among Pakistanis, with a mean difference of 0.34, and smallest among Egyptians, with a mean difference of 0.08.

On the other hand, the data showed that variation in support for liberal values was inversely related to the youthfulness of the population or the size of the youth bulge. The correlation coefficient between the liberal values index and the median age is 0.84 (significant at $p < .05$). The higher the median age of the population of a country, the higher the average liberal values index for that country (table 3.5). Thus, the relationship between age and liberal values depends on the level of analysis. On the micro (individual) level, respondents in the youth bulge were on average more supportive of liberal values than were those in the older age group; however, countries that had younger populations were less supportive of such values.

Gender

Figure 3.3 shows the differences in the liberal values index by gender across the seven countries. With the exception of Egypt, female respondents were more supportive of liberal values than were males. In Egypt, there was no significant difference between men and women. Independent samples *t*-tests showed that the differences in liberal values between males and females are statistically significant in Pakistan, Iraq, Tunisia, Turkey, and Lebanon (at $p < .01$) and in Saudi Arabia (at $p < .05$).

Gender and Age

Table 3.6 shows the distribution of the liberal values index by gender and age: among both male and female respondents, those in the youth bulge were significantly more liberal than those in the older age group across the seven

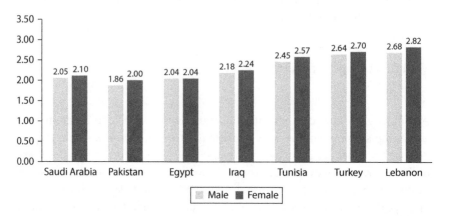

Figure 3.3 Liberal Values Index by Gender.

TABLE 3.6 Liberal Values Index by Gender and Age (Mean/Standard Deviation; n)

	Female			Male		
	Aged 18–29	Age 30+	Mean Difference	Aged 18–29	Age 30+	Mean Difference
Egypt	2.10/0.37; 546	2.01/0.37; 1,081	0.09[c]	2.09/0.40; 441	2.02/0.38; 1,074	0.07[c]
Iraq	2.32/0.41; 542	2.19/0.39; 866	0.13[c]	2.25/0.41; 613	2.14/0.40; 974	0.11[c]
Saudi Arabia[a]	2.18/0.39; 324	2.01/0.40; 431	0.19[b]	2.15/0.44; 327	1.97/0.40; 430	0.18[b]
Lebanon	2.92/0.44; 490	2.74/0.51; 728	0.18[b]	2.77/0.45; 685	2.62/0.50; 1,040	0.15[b]
Pakistan	2.21/0.38; 681	1.87/0.41; 1,025	0.34[b]	2.08/0.46; 582	1.76/0.41; 1,226	0.32[b]
Tunisia[a]	2.70/0.51; 394	2.53/0.50; 1,322	0.17[b]	2.48/0.57; 325	2.45/0.55; 1,023	0.03
Turkey	2.79/0.46; 457	2.67/0.44; 1,232	0.12[c]	2.71/0.48; 393	2.61/0.45; 929	0.10[c]

[a] Sample sizes are reported without the use of weights for Tunisia and Saudi Arabia.
Significance of independent samples t-tests for differences in the liberal values index by age (equal variances not assumed):
[b] $p < .001$.
[c] $p < .01$.

countries, except among Tunisian males, where there was no significant difference between the two age groups. This table also shows that females in the youth bulge were the most liberal and males in the older age group were the least liberal across the countries (however, this difference is not statistically significant between Egyptian male and female respondents in the older age group). Young males and females in Lebanon and Turkey and young females in Tunisia, with liberal values index scores ranging between 2.92 and 2.70, were the most liberal groups, and older males and females in Pakistan, Saudi Arabia, and Egypt, with liberal values index scores ranging between 1.76 and 2.02, were the least liberal groups.

Education

Figure 3.4 shows the differences in the liberal values index between the two education groups by country. With the exception of Saudi Arabia, respondents with university education were more favorable toward liberal values. Independent samples t-tests of the differences between those with and without university education are statistically significant ($p < .001$) in

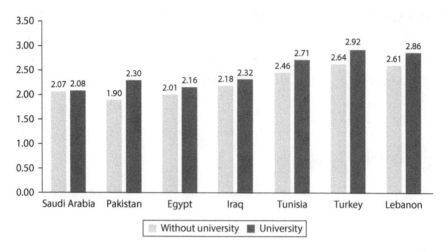

Figure 3.4 Liberal Values Index by Education.

the six remaining countries (equal variances not assumed). Among Saudi respondents, there was no significant difference between the two educational groups, indicating the influence of religious institutions on the country's education system, an overemphasis on religious subjects, and a lack of adequate attention to the liberal arts and humanities in the university curriculum (Prokop 2003; Moaddel 2006). The greatest differences in support for liberal values between the two education groups were seen among Pakistani and Turkish respondents, with mean differences of 0.40 and 0.28 respectively.

Education and Age

The distribution of the liberal values index by age and education, presented in table 3.7, shows that across both age categories, the respondents with university education were more supportive of liberal values than were those without university education in all the countries, except Saudi Arabia. The magnitude of this difference was again largest for Pakistani respondents in both age groups. Comparing the columns showing the differences between those with and without university education across the two age groups, university education appeared to have a greater impact on liberal values among the older age group than it did among the youth bulge. Among Saudis, there was no difference between the two educational groups for either the youth bulge or the older age group.

TABLE 3.7 Liberal Values Index by Age and Education (Mean/Standard Deviation; *n*)

	Youth Bulge (Aged 18–29)			Older Age Group (Aged 30+)		
	Without University	University	Difference	Without University	University	Difference
Iraq	2.26/0.40; 947	2.34/0.45; 197	0.08[c]	2.13/0.39; 1,462	2.31/0.38; 371	0.18[b]
Lebanon	2.72/0.40; 374	2.89/0.45; 781	0.17[b]	2.57/0.49; 1,079	2.84/0.49; 674	0.27[b]
Pakistan	2.12/0.41; 1,116	2.37/0.46; 147	0.25[b]	1.78/0.39; 2,112	2.23/0.42; 139	0.45[b]
Saudi Arabia[a]	2.17/0.39; 418	2.15/0.44; 231	−0.02	1.99/0.39; 666	1.97/0.42; 195	−0.02
Tunisia[a]	2.55/0.53; 420	2.68/0.57; 298	0.13[c]	2.43/0.50; 1,928	2.74/0.54; 412	0.31[b]
Egypt	2.08/0.38; 764	2.13/0.38; 223	0.05[d]	1.98/0.36; 1,846	2.18/0.42; 309	0.20[b]
Turkey	2.71/0.46; 654	2.90/0.51; 195	0.19[b]	2.61/0.43; 1,925	2.93/0.48; 236	0.32[b]

Significance of independent samples *t*-tests for differences in the liberal values index by age (equal variances not assumed):
[a] Sample sizes are reported without the use of weights for Tunisia and Saudi Arabia.
[b] *p* < .001.
[c] *p* < .01.
[d] *p* < .05.

Religion, Religious Sect, and Liberal Values

Egypt and Lebanon have substantial Christian populations: about 10 percent of Egyptians and 40 percent of Lebanese are Christians. There are also sizable Shia populations in Iraq, Lebanon, and Saudi Arabia. In Turkey, the Alavis, an offshoot of the Shia sect, are a noticeable religious minority. In Pakistan and Tunisia, religious minorities are very small. Variation in liberal values among these religious groups was assessed across the countries. According to table 3.8, in the pool sample, atheist/other/NR were the most liberal, having an overall index value of 2.99, followed by Christians, 2.81; Druze, 2.61; Shias, 2.34; Sunnis, 2.25; and Muslims (sect unidentified), 2.23, who were the least liberal. The national context, however, shapes these groups' value orientations. Iraqi Sunnis were more liberal than Iraqi Shias, with index values of 2.24 versus 2.19, but in all other countries, Sunnis were significantly less liberal than Shias. Muslims whose sects were unidentified were more liberal than Shias or Sunnis in Iraq and Lebanon but not in Turkey. Finally, Lebanese Christians were significantly more liberal than Egyptian Christians. All these differences are significant at *p* < .01. The Christian samples in the other countries and the distributions of the atheist/other/NR in all countries were too small to allow reasonable generalizations.

TABLE 3.8 Liberal Values Index by Religion (Mean/Standard Deviation; *n*)

	Sunni	Shia/Alavi	Muslims (Sect Unidentified)	Druze (Shia Offshoot)	Christian	Atheist/Others/ NR	Total
Iraq	2.24/0.39; 1,331	2.19/0.41; 1,249	2.41/0.41; 402	—	2.84/0.34; 13	—	2,995
Lebanon	2.55/0.49; 708	2.62/0.46; 994	2.72/0.43; 80	2.61/0.50; 190	3.00/0.40; 813	3.00/0.45; 248	3,033
Pakistan	1.90/0.43; 2,902	2.09/0.44; 278	1.98/0.45; 297	—	2.87/0.31; 26	2.63/0.26; 20	3,523
Saudi Arabia[a]	2.05/0.41; 1,506	2.38/0.35; 497	—	—	—	—	2,003
Egypt	2.02/0.37; 3,010		—	—	2.47/0.36; 486	—	3,496
Tunisia	2.51/0.53; 3,031	2.70/0.46; 3	2.72/0.91; 4	—	—	2.83/0.70; 28	3,066
Turkey	2.67/0.45; 2,590	2.95/0.47; 184	2.55/0.43; 199	—	2.63; 1	2.83/0.50; 43	3,017
Total	2.25/0.53; 15,078 71%	2.34/0.48; 3,205 15%	2.23/0.50; 982 5%	2.61/0.50; 190 1%	2.81/0.46; 1,339 6%	2.99/0.50; 339 2%	2.32/0.55; 21,133 100%

[a] Sample sizes are reported without the use of weights for Saudi Arabia.

These findings support several conclusions. First, the relation of religion with liberal values is shaped by the national context and whether the religion in question has a minority status. Christians, being a minority in Egypt and Lebanon, were more liberal than Muslims in both countries. Second, Christians in Egypt, a more conservative country than Lebanon, were significantly less supportive of liberal values than were Lebanese Christians. Third, similar results are found among religious sects. Lebanese Sunnis and Shias were significantly more liberal than their counterparts in Egypt, Iraq, Pakistan, and Saudi Arabia, where the social context was more conservative than that in Lebanon. The respondents from the sects that were not politically dominant—Sunnis in Iraq, Shias in Pakistan, Shias in Saudi Arabia, and Alavis in Turkey—were more supportive of liberal values than were the respondents from the majority sect that controls the political power in each of these countries. In Lebanon, although the Shias have wielded considerable political power through Hezbollah, the Sunnis have historically been much more powerful economically and politically than the Shias.

Identity: National Versus Religious

Identification with the territorial nation, the political community of a people defined in terms of the territory on which they live, has historically been associated with liberalism. The term *liberal nationalism* thus implies a nationalist movement that is committed to liberal values. In such a case, people define themselves primarily as, for example, Egyptians, Iraqis, Iranians, or Tunisians. A political community may also be defined in terms of ethnicity or language, identifying this community as primarily Arabic, Kurdish, or Turkish—hence, Arab, Kurdish, or Turkish nationalism—or in terms of religion, like Christianity or Islam—hence, Christian or Islamic nationalism. Ethnic or religious nationalism is often categorized as supranationalism.

Which of these cultural differentiae—territory, ethnicity, or religion—becomes predominant in a country depends on the historical circumstances that activate these varying identities. A historical circumstance provides the ideological target in opposition to which people's identity takes shape. For example, national territorial identity is triggered in opposition to foreign occupation (e.g., the rise of Algerian or Egyptian nationalism in opposition to the French or British occupation, respectively, in the early twentieth century) or to religious domination (e.g., Iran in the post-1979 revolutionary period); ethnic identity is triggered in opposition to domination by another ethnic group (e.g., Kurdish nationalism in opposition to Arab, Turk, or Persian domination, and pan-Arab nationalism in opposition to European domination of Arabic-speaking countries in the post–World War I period); and religious identity is triggered in opposition to the secular authoritarian state (e.g., the rise of Islamic fundamentalism in twentieth-century Egypt and Iran).

In the Middle East and North Africa, the shift from one dominant basis of identity to the next has been associated with changes in cultural episodes. Between the early twentieth and early twenty-first centuries, the region experienced a succession of such cultural episodes: territorial nationalism in the first half of the twentieth century, pan-Arab nationalism in Arab countries and secular illiberal nationalism in Iran and Turkey in the fifties through the sixties, Islamic fundamentalism-cum-nationalism from the seventies on, and the post–Arab Spring (post-2011) period, which has been characterized by the decline of political Islam, the rise of territorial nationalism, and a shift toward liberal values (see chapter 6). These episodes began and ended with a revolution, a military coup, or a major social upheaval.

Liberalism has historically been associated with national identity, where a territorial nation is considered the primary basis of identity for the people living on that territory. The people may belong to different ethnic groups or have diverse religious affiliations, but they are defined as a single nation (i.e., a people) insofar as their identity is defined (or they predominantly describe themselves) in terms of the national territory or the land on which they reside. Currently, territorial nationalism and Islamic nationalism are two dominant competing discourses in the Middle East and North Africa (generalizing from the seven-country comparative survey data). Those who adhered to national identity tended to be more liberal than those who adhered to religious identity (Moaddel 2017a). Ethnic nationalism, on the other hand, had little support among the subject populations, except among the Kurds, where Kurdish identity was popular among a segment of the Kurdish population.

Measures of the Basis of Identity

Actually, individuals may carry multiple identities simultaneously. A person may define him or herself as an Egyptian Arab Muslim, an Iraqi Arab, or a Lebanese Christian, for example. Nonetheless, it is argued here that at any given point in time, one of these identities tends to predominate, particularly under the condition of a major revolutionary movement or cultural transformation. The identity that predominates—national, ethnic, or religious—may indicate the domination of the corresponding discourse; territorial, ethnic, or religious nationalism. Two survey questions on identity were used. The first measures whether the respondents identify primarily with the territorial nation, ethnicity, religion, or something else. The second measures the identity of the community to which respondents primarily considered themselves belonging. Respondents were instructed to select the identity they considered to be primary to them when answering the following:

1. Which of the following best describes you: (a) above all, I am an Egyptian/ Iraqi/Lebanese/Pakistani/Saudi/Turkish citizen; (b) above all, I am a Muslim [Christian (for Christian respondents)]; (c) above all, I am an Arab, a Kurd, a Punjabi . . .; or (d) other____?
2. Which of these statements comes closest to the way you feel: (a) I see myself as a citizen of the world; (b) I see myself as a citizen of [country]; (c) I see myself as a citizen of the Islamic *umma* [worldwide Christian community (for Christian respondents)]; or (d) I see myself as a citizen of the Arab, Kurd- ish, Turkish, Punjabi . . . community?

Using these two items, a national identity index was constructed, first, by coding those who identified with the territorial nation, ethnicity, or other as 1 and those who identified with religion as 0 for both variables. Then the two variables were averaged so that a higher value indicates a stronger adherence to national identity. This index provides a clearer picture of the extent to which respondents were divided between those who identified with religion and those who identified with the national territory or ethnicity. The higher the value on this index, the higher the percentage of the respondents who identified with their nation or ethnicity. As will be shown, the percentage of the respon- dents who identified with their ethnicity is relatively small. This index therefore mostly reflects an orientation toward religious or national identity.

Cross-National Variation

Table 3.9 shows cross-national variation in identity. The percentages of respon- dents who defined themselves primarily in nationalist terms range from 28 and 30 percent, or a minority of respondents, in Pakistan and Tunisia, respectively, to 44 percent in Turkey, 48 percent in Saudi Arabia, 52 percent in Egypt, 57 percent in Iraq, and 60 percent in Lebanon. While 59 percent of Tunisians and 70 percent of Pakistanis defined themselves above all as Muslims, only a minority from the other five countries defined themselves as such—ranging between 29 percent of Lebanese and 47 percent of Egyptians. However, much higher percentages of the respondents said that they considered themselves as citizens of their respective countries—ranging from 47 percent of Tunisians to 70 percent of Iraqis. And much smaller percentages expressed an affinity to broader religious communities—ranging between 15 percent of Iraqis and 42 percent of Tunisians. It is also noteworthy that in Lebanon and Saudi Arabia, the percentages of respondents who identified themselves as citizens of the

TABLE 3.9 Measures of Identity

	Iraq	Lebanon	Pakistan	Saudi Arabia	Tunisia	Egypt	Turkey
Above all, I am a/an...							
Egyptian/Iraqi/Lebanese/ Pakistani/Saudi/Turkish citizen	57%	60%	28%	48%	30%	52%	44%
Muslim/Christian/Hindu	36%	29%	70%	46%	59%	47%	39%
Arab (Arab countries)/ Turk (Turkey)	3%	11%	0%	6%	7%	2%	11%
Kurd (Iraq)/Berber (Tunisia)/Kurd (Turkey)	4%	—	—	—	1%	—	3%
Other	—	—	2%	—	3%	—	2%
I see myself as a citizen of ...							
The world	5%	15%	2%	24%	4%	1%	5%
My country	70%	59%	65%	49%	47%	61%	62%
The Islamic umma/ Christian community	15%	19%	24%	21%	42%	36%	23%
Ethnic community: Arab/ Berber/Kurdish, Turkish/ Turkmen/Other in Pakistan	2.9%	7%	9%	7%	7%	1%	5.3%
National identity index (mean)	0.75	0.76	0.53	0.66	0.49	0.59	0.69

world were much higher than in the other five countries, with 15 percent of Lebanese and 24 percent of Saudis so identifying. However, only 5 percent of Iraqi and Turkish respondents and less than 5 percent of respondents from other three countries identified themselves as citizens of the world.

A small percentage of the respondents considered their ethnicity as the primary basis of their identity. In the Arab countries, only small minorities in Lebanon, Tunisia, and Saudi Arabia—between 6 percent in Saudi Arabia and 11 percent in Lebanon—defined themselves above all as Arabs. In Egypt, which is officially called the Arab Republic of Egypt and which formed the first pan-Arab state after the 1952 military coup, and in Iraq, which was the bastion of pan-Arab nationalism in the post–World War I period, less than 3 percent defined themselves as such in 2011, when the survey was conducted.

Combining the two items on identity to create a national identity index (ranging between 0 and 1), Lebanon and Iraq have the highest average national identity index values (0.75 and 0.76, respectively), and Tunisia has the lowest (0.49). In other words, Lebanese and Iraqis are the most likely to self-identify with nation and Tunisians are the least likely.

Ethnic identity has at best minority support even among the ethnic groups in Iraq, Turkey, Tunisia, and Pakistan. The Kurds, who have been collectively yearning and even fighting for independence in the contemporary period, surprisingly did not predominantly define themselves above all as Kurds. Table 3.10 shows what Kurds from Iraq and Turkey, Turks from Turkey, and Berbers from Tunisia consider to be the basis of their identity. Among Iraqi Kurds, only 27 percent reported that they described themselves above all as Kurds, compared to 13 percent who defined themselves as Iraqis and 59 percent who defined themselves above all as Muslims. Among Kurdish respondents from Turkey, only 20 percent defined themselves above all as Kurds, while 11 percent defined themselves as Turkish citizens and 66 percent defined themselves above all as Muslims. Among Turks in Turkey, only 14 percent defined themselves above all as Turks, compared to 51 percent who defined themselves as Turkish citizens and 34 percent who defined themselves above all as Muslims. Finally, 7 percent of the Tunisian respondents were Berbers, but only 3 percent of these respondents defined themselves above all as Berbers, while 38 percent defined themselves as Tunisians and 52 percent defined themselves above all as Muslims.

Ethnic identity was even weaker among Pakistan respondents. Table 3.11 shows self-definition of the basis of identity by respondents from major ethnic groups in Pakistan. The majority of these respondents, ranging from 58 percent

TABLE 3.10 Ethnicity and Identity in Iraq, Turkey, and Tunisia

	Iraqi Kurd	Turkish Kurd	Turkish Turk	Tunisia Berber
Above all, Iraqi/Turkish/Tunisian	13%	11%	51%	38%
Above all, Muslim	59%	66%	34%	52%
Above all, Kurd/Turk/Berber	27%	20%	14%	3%
Other	0%	2%	1%	7%
Total	466	477	2,343	210

TABLE 3.11 **Ethnicity and Identity among Major Ethnic Groups in Pakistan**

	Baluchi	Punjabi	Sindhi	Pathan	Sariaki	Kashmiri	Hindko	Biltistani
Above all, Pakistani	36%	21%	24%	36%	18%	32%	22%	42%
Above all, Muslim	60%	78%	71%	60%	82%	66%	77%	58%
Above all, my ethnicity	2%	0%	4%	3%	0%	2%	0%	0%
Other	1%	0%	0%	1%	0%	0%	1%	0%
Total	88	1,188	414	428	255	364	121	115

among Biltistanis to 82 percent among Sariakis, defined themselves above all as Muslims, while those defining themselves as Pakistanis ranged from 18 percent among Sariakis to 42 percent among Biltistanis. The percentages of those who defined themselves in ethnic terms range from 0 percent among Punjabis, Sariakis, Hindkos, and Biltistanis to 4 percent among Sindhis.

Variation by Age, Religion, and Sect

Age

Figure 3.5 shows the percentages of the respondents who identified with their respective nations (those who responded that they were above all Egyptians, Iraqis, or Saudis, for example, rather than identifying with Muslims, excluding other categories) by the two age groups across the seven countries. Among Iraqi, Saudi, and Egyptian respondents, the differences between the youth bulge and the older age group are between 1 and 2 percent and were not statistically significant. However, among the respondents from Lebanon, Pakistan, Tunisia, and Turkey, there were significant differences between the two age groups, but these differences were in opposite directions; among Lebanese and Pakistanis, a higher percentage of younger respondents, 8 percent and 18 percent, respectively, identified with their nations than the older age group. Among Tunisian and Turkish respondents, on the other hand, it was just the opposite; a higher percentage of the older respondents identified with their nations than the younger age group, 9 percent and 6 percent, respectively (these differences are statistically significant at $p < .05$). Again, as was the case with adherence to liberal values or religious fundamentalism, the gap between the two age groups among Pakistani respondents was much larger than it was among respondents from the other six countries.

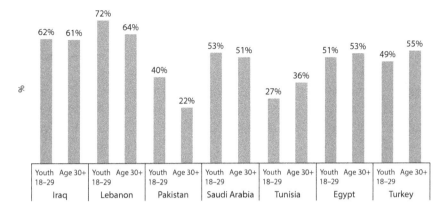

Figure 3.5 Percentages of Respondents Who Define Themselves in Nationalist Terms.

Religion and Sect

Table 3.12 is a cross-tabulation of the national identity index by religious sect (Sunni versus Shia) and by religion (Shia Muslim or Sunni Muslim versus Christian) across the six countries where such divisions exist. In five countries—Iraq, Lebanon, Pakistan, Saudi Arabia, and Turkey—the population is divided along sectarian lines. In these countries, Shias scored much higher than Sunnis on the national identity index, indicating that proportionally more Shias than Sunnis identified with the nation, except in Saudi Arabia, where this difference is not statically significant. On religion and identity, Christians scored much higher than either Sunnis in Egypt and Lebanon or Shias in

TABLE 3.12 National Identity Index by Religion (Mean/Standard Deviation; n)

	Sunni	Shia	Christian
Iraq	0.70/0.35; 1,204	0.76/0.33; 917	—
Lebanon	0.65/0.42; 705	0.75/0.38; 986	0.80/0.34; 810
Pakistan	0.52/0.35; 2,902	0.69/0.31; 230	—
Saudi Arabia[a]	0.66/0.36; 1,497	0.68/0.36; 497	—
Egypt	0.58/0.43; 3,010		0.81/0.37; 133
Turkey	0.68/0.40; 2,572	0.82/0.30; 183[b]	—

Note: Tunisia is not included because there is no variation by religion.
[a] Sample sizes are reported without the use of weights for Saudi Arabia.
[b] In Turkey, the Shia column includes both Shias and Alavis.

Lebanon. The independent samples t-tests for the differences in the national identity index by religion are significant for Iraq between Shias and Sunnis at $p < .001$; for Lebanon between Sunnis and Shias at $p < .001$; for Lebanon between Sunnis and Christians at $p < .001$; for Lebanon between Shias and Christians at $p < .01$; for Pakistan between Sunnis and Shias at $p < .001$; for Egypt between Sunnis and Christians at $p < .001$; and for Turkey between Sunnis and Alavis at $p < .00$. For Saudi Arabia, the difference between Shias and Sunnis is not statistically significant.

Summary

This chapter began with an argument that changes in the political conditions brought about by the rise of dynastic rules in historical Islam prompted Muslim theologians (1) to accept the reality of secular politics (i.e., to recognize the sultan's discretionary power) and (2) to consider the differentiation of legitimate authority between the sultan, who was in charge of political affairs, and the *ulama*, who were in control of religion, as an appropriate form of Muslim politics and state-religion relationships. This development in political authority was arguably superior to the conception in early Islam that united religious and political leadership in the person of the caliph for two principal reasons. First, the unity of religious and political leadership is an unworkable political formula. A person with superb religious credentials may not be interested in politics (Iran's postrevolutionary political development supports this view). Second, having a differentiated political authority provides a better context for checking arbitrary power than where this authority is undifferentiated from religious authority.

However, a factor that appears to have played a crucial role in facilitating the development of political modernity in Islam, as was argued here, is the degree of flexibility provided in the Islamic theory of government in use in the nineteenth century by this differentiation. Here flexibility refers to the presence of a favorable discursive space in the existing Islamic political theory that enabled Muslim theologians to recognize, debate, and remove the problematic element in this theory without questioning the basic principles of their belief system. For them, the sultan's discretionary power was recognized as the problematic element as their faith encountered the challenges of modernity. However, no damage would be done to Islam if they were to substitute parliamentary democracy for the sultan's discretionary power. They thus predominantly supported the construction of a modern constitutional political order, which was the principal goal of the nationalist movements of the late nineteenth and early twentieth centuries. Secularism therefore was not the exclusive domain of Western thought, as historical Islam recognized the reality, and implicitly the utility and inevitability, of secular politics. The rise of secular ideological interventionist states in the twentieth century, on the other hand, delegitimize secularism and prompted Muslim activists to abandon secular politics and call for the establishment of Islamic government. Thus, secular politics became a gravely contested issue between the liberals and Muslim fundamentalists only in the closing decades of the twentieth century.

This chapter assessed the extent to which the controversy between Muslim fundamentalists and their nemeses have shaped public attitudes toward secular politics across the seven countries. It developed indices of secular politics, liberal values, and national identity and analyzed variation in these indices across the seven countries and by age, gender, education, religion, and religious sect. The analysis of the data showed that attitudes toward secular politics varied across the seven countries and that Lebanese, Turkish, and Tunisian respondents were predominantly supportive of secular politics, followed by Iraqis and Egyptians, who were moderately supportive, and Pakistanis and Saudis, who were least supportive.

In terms of variation by age, gender, and education, the analysis of the data produced several results. (1) The youth bulge was more favorable toward secular politics than was the older age group in Lebanon, Pakistan, Saudi Arabia, and Tunisia. In other countries, there were no significant differences between the two age groups. On the macro (country) level, the smaller the size of the youth bulge or the higher the median age, the stronger the support for secular politics. (2) There was no consistent pattern concerning the effect of gender on secular politics across the seven countries. (3) Except for Saudis, respondents with university education were more supportive of secular politics than were those without university education.

A liberal values index was constructed by averaging the indices of expressive individualism, gender equality, and secular politics. The analysis of this index showed considerable variation across countries, with Pakistan as the least liberal country, followed by Saudi Arabia, Egypt, and Iraq; Tunisia, Turkey, and Lebanon were the most liberal countries. Across the seven countries, those in the youth bulge were consistently more liberal than those is the older age group. However, the youthfulness of the population, as indicated by a larger youth bulge, was negatively linked to liberal values. Concerning gender and liberal values, female respondents across the countries reported having stronger liberal attitudes overall than male respondents, except in Egypt, where males and females were similar in liberal attitudes. Moreover, female youth were significantly more liberal than older females across the seven countries. Male youth were also more liberal than those from the older age group, except in Tunisia, where there was no significant difference between the two age groups. Finally, with the exception of Saudi Arabia, there was a significant and positive association between university education and support for liberal values among respondents. Among Saudi respondents, there was no significant difference between those with and without university education. The distribution of the liberal values index by age and education showed that people with university education were more liberal within each of the two age groups, except among Saudis, who did not differ on liberal values by education.

The data also showed considerable variation in respondents' adherence to national and religious identity. In Pakistan and Tunisia, the majority of the respondents identified primarily with religion rather than nationality, while in the other five countries, respondents identified primarily with their nation. At the communal level, a much higher percentage of the respondents identified with their national community rather than their religious community. Between the two age groups, among Egyptian, Iraqi, and Saudi respondents, there were no significance differences in self-definition of identity. In Lebanon and Pakistan, on the other hand, the percentages of the youth bulge that identified with their nationality were higher than those of the older age group, while in Tunisia, and Turkey, it was just the opposite; higher percentages of the older age group identified with the nation than did the younger age group. In Pakistan, the gap in the percentages of those who adhered to national identity between the two age groups was larger than it was in the other six countries.

Ethnic identity did not have much traction among the respondents. The Kurds, who have been yearning and even fighting for independence for a long time, surprisingly did not predominantly define themselves above all as Kurds. Likewise, among the Arab-majority countries, only small minorities in Lebanon, Tunisia, and Saudi Arabia—between 6 percent (Saudi Arabia) and 11 percent (Lebanon)—defined themselves above all as Arabs. In Egypt and Iraq, where pan-Arab nationalism was strong in the mid-twentieth century, less than 3 percent defined themselves above all as Arabs. Likewise, only 2 percent of Pakistanis identified with their ethnicity. This was also true among Tunisians; only 3 percent of Berbers defined themselves above all as Berbers. Further, in Turkey, while the highest percentage of the respondents defined themselves as Turkish citizens, only 14 percent of the respondents defined themselves above all as Turks. Finally, it is noteworthy that 14 percent of Lebanese and 24 percent of Saudis considered themselves to be citizens of the world; these percentages were much higher than those for the other five countries, where 5 percent of Iraqi and Turkish respondents, 4 percent of Tunisian respondents, and 3 percent or less of Pakistani and Egyptian respondents considered themselves citizens of the world.

When the two measures of identity were combined to make a national identity index (ranging between 0 and 1), Lebanon and Iraq had the highest average national identity index values (0.75 and 0.76, respectively), and Tunisia had the lowest (0.49). In other words, Lebanese and Iraqis were the most likely to self-identify with nation, and Tunisians were the least likely.

In terms of religion and religious sect, a much higher percentage of Christians than Muslims (either Shias or Sunnis) defined themselves in nationalist terms and favored liberal values in Egypt and Lebanon, where there were substantial Christian populations. Likewise, a higher percentage of Shias than Sunnis defined themselves in nationalist terms in Iraq, Lebanon, Pakistan, and Turkey. However, there was no significant difference in self-definition of national identity between Shias and Sunnis in Saudi Arabia. The Shias were less liberal in Iraq but more so in Lebanon, Pakistan, Saudi Arabia, and Turkey.

These findings support several conclusions. First, the relationship of religion with liberal values is shaped by the national context and whether the religion in question has a minority status. Christians, being a minority in Egypt and Lebanon, were more liberal and more often adhered to national identity than did Muslims in both countries. Second, Christians in Egypt, which was culturally a more conservative country than Lebanon, were significantly less supportive of liberal values than were their counterparts in Lebanon. Third, similar results are found among religious sects. Lebanese Sunnis and Shias were significantly more liberal and more often defined themselves in nationalist terms than was the case with their counterparts in Egypt, Iraq, Pakistan, and Saudi Arabia, where the social context was more conservative than in Lebanon. The respondents from sects that were not politically dominant—Sunnis in Iraq, Shias in Pakistan, Shias in Saudi Arabia, and Alavis in Turkey—were more supportive of liberal values and preferred national identity over religious identity, compared to respondents from the respective majority sects in these countries.

CHAPTER 4

RELIGIOUS FUNDAMENTALISM AS DISCIPLINARIAN DEITY, LITERALISM, RELIGIOUS EXCLUSIVITY, AND RELIGIOUS INTOLERANCE

One of the central objectives of this book is to demonstrate that liberalism and religious fundamentalism are the two major ideological movements in the Middle East and North Africa. As alternative discourses, they have displayed opposing political and cultural orientations as they contend for intellectual control of the social order. There is little support for other competing ideologies, such as pan-Arab nationalism (in Arab countries), ethnic nationalism (except among the Kurds), communism or state socialism, and secular authoritarian nationalism.

The conflict between the two movements in the historical context of the contemporary Middle East and North Africa is reflected in the fight over issues. The Islamic fundamentalists have taken positions on important sociopolitical and cultural issues that were often diametrically opposed to the positions taken by liberal intellectual leaders and activists on the same issues. Contrary to those taking the liberal perspective, the advocates of Islamic fundamentalism have predominantly rejected secular politics in favor of the unity of religion and politics in an Islamic government; defended the institution of male supremacy and patriarchy; portrayed Western culture as decadent; considered religion as the principal, if not the only, source of social norms and legislation; and forcefully delineated religion, rather than the territorial nation, as the basis of identity, claiming that the political community to which the diverse peoples of the region belong is an Islamic nation (*ummat*), rather than one bounded by and identified with their territories. Symptomatic of the depth and breadth of this conflict is the existence of active ideological debates and political disputes over these issues in many Middle Eastern and North African countries—in Iran, in particular. The relative numbers of individuals or the sizes of the groups associated with the opposing positions on these issues are an indicator of the extent of support for each of the two opposing cultural movements, providing useful data on whether the society is oriented toward religious fundamentalism or liberal values (Moaddel 2005).

What makes a religious movement fundamentalist is not simply the position of its leaders on issues, however. Except for the rejection of secular politics in favor of the unity of religion and politics and adherence to religious identity, there is nothing specifically religiously fundamentalist in the view that espouses patriarchy and male supremacy, chastises expressive individualism, and rejects Western culture as decadent. Therefore, a more effective measure of religious fundamentalism is one that captures its distinctive religious character and is defined in religious terms.[1] Adhering to this stipulation, religious fundamentalism is defined here as a set of beliefs about and attitudes toward one's and others' religions that is based on a disciplinarian conception of the deity, literalism, religious exclusivity, and religious intolerance. This conceptualization allows for comparing fundamentalism across religions and religious sects. Fundamentalists in Christianity and Islam and in Shia and Sunni share these core orientations despite the fact that, in their concrete and specific historical context, Christian fundamentalists have irreconcilable differences with their Muslim counterparts, as do Shias with Sunnis. Moreover, as this chapter shows, individuals who have fundamentalist orientations, based on this religious definition of the term, are more likely to reject secular politics, recognize religion as the basis of identity, defend the institution of male supremacy and patriarchy, and consider Western culture decadent. Individuals with stronger fundamentalist orientations would thus be less favorable toward the liberal values of expressive individualism, gender equality, and secular politics. Positions on issues are, however, the predictors of fundamentalist beliefs and attitudes, not measures of such beliefs and attitudes.

This chapter first advances a multidimensional conception of religious fundamentalism and measures its different components. It then shows that (1) the measures of the constructs are negatively correlated with the measures of liberal values—expressive individualism, gender equality, secular politics, and national identity—and (2) on the micro (individual) level, the factors that are positively linked to religious fundamentalism are negatively connected to liberal values, and vice versa. Chapter 5 will show that on the macro (country) level, the variables that are positively linked to religious fundamentalism have negative relationships with the measures of the liberal values as well.

Religious fundamentalism is conceptualized as a distinctive set of beliefs about and attitudes toward whatever religious beliefs one has. It is a multidimensional construct consisting of four components: (1) a disciplinarian conception of the deity, (2) literalism or inerrancy, (3) religious exclusivity, and (4) religious intolerance. Using this conceptualization, religious fundamentalism is first measured in terms of a series of survey questions. Then cross-national variation in religious fundamentalism, its relationship with liberal values, and variation by age, gender, education, religion, and religious sect are analyzed. Finally, the predictors of religious fundamentalism on the micro (individual) level are examined across the seven countries.

Historical and Cross-National Diversity of Islamic Fundamentalism

An important characteristic of religious fundamentalist movements is that they vary greatly in different historical periods, across nations, and by religious faiths. In the modern period, Islamic fundamentalism emerged as a potent oppositional force in two distinctive cultural episodes. The first consisted of the militant fundamentalism of Muhammad Ibn Abd al-Wahhab (1703–1787) in Arabia and the reformist fundamentalism of Shah Waliallah (1703–1762) in India in the eighteenth century. These two movements arose in the context of the decline of Muslim politics—the gradual falling of the Ottomans in Asia Minor and the Mughals in India—and were aided by the political vacuum that this decline generated.[2] The objective of the two Muslim thinkers, their associates, and their disciples was to purify the faith by rejecting what they considered to be the un-Islamic beliefs and practices that had crept into the Islamic way of life. They questioned the static formalism of the orthodox Islamic jurisprudence, rejected the interpretive functions of the *ulama*, and claimed the scriptures should be accessible to ordinary individual Muslims. They wanted to transform the state of affairs currently existing in their political communities to align with the political order that had existed under the first generation of Muslim leaders. Their efforts favored strengthening the literalist reading of the Quran and the *hadith* (the dicta attributed to Prophet Muhammad) and promoting a religion-centric and exclusivist conception of the Islamic community. The Wahhabis, in particular, exhibited an intolerant view of all sects in Islam other than the Sunni.

These teachings shaped the rise of militant movements that sought to rehabilitate Islam in Arabia and India. The Wahhabi militants gained control of central Arabia, occupied the Hijaz, sacked the Iraqi city of Karbala, and massacred thousands of Shias living in the area. They were, however, defeated by the forces of Muhammad Ali, the khedive (viceroy) of Egypt, who at the request of the Ottoman sultan destroyed the Wahhabi power in the early nineteenth century. The Indian militants faced the same fate as their Wahhabi counterparts. The Indian movement, labeled *Wahhabi* by the British and *mujahidin* by its followers, was led by Sayyid Ahmad Barelvi (1786–1831), a disciple of Shah Waliallah's son and successor, Abdul Aziz, whose circle he joined in 1807. Two learned scions of the family of Shah Waliallah, Shah Ismail and Abdul Hayy, joined him as his disciples, marking the progress of Shah Waliallah's program "from theory to practice, from life contemplative to life active, from instruction of the elite to the emancipation of the masses, and from individual salvation to social organization" (Ahmad 1964, 210; Lapidus 1988). Barelvi declared as *dar ul-harb* (the abode of war) the Indian territories that were occupied by the British and other non-Muslim forces, and he called on the regional Muslims to join him in a holy war against the infidels. The movement, however, was crushed by the British in 1858, suffered another defeat in 1863, and was persecuted throughout India in the same period (Ahmad 1964, 1967; Hardy 1972).

The second Islamic fundamentalist episode is separated from the first by more than a century in the Arab world—from the Wahhabi defeat in 1818 to the formation of the Society of the Muslim Brothers in 1928 and the establishment of the Wahhabi-inspired and supported Kingdom of Saudi Arabia in 1932—and by about three-quarters of a century in Asia—from the defeat of the Indian *mujahedin* around 1863 to the formation of Jamaati Islami in India in 1941 and in Pakistan in 1947. The interregnum is characterized by the decline of sacred spirituality, the Islamic orthodoxy and the *ulama*, and religion as an organizing principle of social order, on the one hand, and by the rise of secular spirituality, science, and evolutionary ideologies, on the other (Moaddel and Karabenick 2013). Muslim intellectual leaders, influenced by the nineteenth century's seminal ideas of evolutionary progress and civilizational change and impressed by remarkable scientific discoveries and technological innovation during this period, launched widespread efforts to reexamine Islamic worldviews in light of these changes and the intellectual standard of the eighteenth-century Enlightenment. Their efforts resulted in Islamic modernism, a new set of religious ideas and treatises generated in the late nineteenth and early twentieth centuries.

The Islamic modernist movement was stronger in places like late nineteenth-century Egypt and India, where the cultural context was diversified, and where the encounter with Western culture contributed in turning some of the taken-for-granted principles of social organization and deeply held beliefs into issues, including revelation versus reason, religion versus nationhood as the basis of identity, monarchical absolutism versus constitutional government, gender hierarchization and male supremacy versus gender equality, and the West as culturally inferior or decadent versus the West as the civilized order. Islamic modernism was an outcome of the religious disputations and ideological debates that transpired over these issues among such cultural or religious groups as the followers of the eighteenth-century Enlightenment, modern indigenous intellectual leaders, Christian missionaries, and the think tanks connected to colonial administrations. The criticisms leveled against the Islamic faith by evangelical Christianity, on the one hand, and by the followers of the Enlightenment, on the other, prompted a significant number of Muslim intellectual leaders–cum–theologians to reexamine the traditional sources of Islamic jurisprudence in light of the Enlightenment's intellectual standards. The principal issues that engaged these Muslim thinkers revolved around whether the knowledge derived from the sources external to Islam was valid and whether the four traditional sources of jurisprudence were methodologically adequate to effectively address the challenges posed to their faith. Considering these traditional sources—the Quran, the dicta attributed to Prophet Muhammad (*hadith*), the consensus of the theologians (*ijma*), and juristic reasoning by analogy (*qiyas*)—they resolved to advance a modernist exegesis of the first two sources and to transform the last two in order to formulate a reformist project in light of the prevailing standards of scientific rationality. Such prominent intellectuals and theologians as Sayyid Jamal ud-Din al-Afghani, Sir Sayyid Ahmad Khan, Chiragh Ali, Muhammad Abduh, Amir Ali, Shibli Nu'mani, and Mirza Muhammad Hussein Gharavi Naini presented Islamic theology in a manner consistent with modern rationalist ideas. Some of these thinkers claimed that Islam was compatible with deistic and natural religion. They applauded the achievements of the West in science and technology as well as its constitutional form of government. They all argued that Islam, as a world religion, was thoroughly capable of adapting itself to the changing conditions of every age, the hallmarks of the perfect Muslim community being law and reason (Ahmad 1967; Hourani 1983; Moaddel 2005).

The liberal nationalist movements, of which Islamic modernism was an integral part, resulted in the formation of secular states from the early 1920s on. Although the lifespan of liberal government in the Middle East and North Africa was short, the secular trend unleashed by the revolutionary or national liberation movements in the early twentieth century continued unabated until the seventies. In certain countries like Egypt, Iran, and Turkey, secularism turned overly critical of the religious establishment, which in turn begot a fundamentalist response. The major fundamentalist challenges to the secular order were launched by the Society of the Muslim Brothers in Egypt in 1928 and in other Arab countries in the subsequent decades; by Jamaati Islami (Islamic Congregation) in India in 1941, in Pakistan in 1947, and in Kashmir and Bangladesh in the subsequent decades; and by a terrorist organization named Fedaiyane Islam (Self-Sacrificers of Islam) in Iran in 1946. As was discussed in the introductory chapter, the transformation of Islamic fundamentalism into a worldwide influential religious nationalist movement was a result of four historical events that occurred almost simultaneously: (1) The military coup by General Zia ul-Haq in Pakistan in 1977, which expanded the fundamentalists' influence in the country; (2) the Iranian Revolution of 1979, which brought

Shia fundamentalists to power; (3) the 1979 Soviet invasion of Afghanistan, which gave legitimacy to the fundamentalists' call for jihad as *fadr al-ayn* (the necessary duty incumbent upon all Muslims) against the invaders; and (4) the 1979 seizure of the Great Mosque in Mecca by Muslim militants, which demonstrated the vulnerability of the Saudi kingdom. Although each of these events was the outcome of nationally specific historical dynamics and social conditions (Moaddel 1993, 2006; Okruhlik 2002; Alavi 2009), the concurrence of the four events gave the impression of a worldwide unitary Islamic resurgence, often referred to as "Islamic awakening," and contributed to the popularization of fundamentalist ideas and practices among a significant number of Muslim political activists the world over.

The outcome of the Iranian Revolution demonstrated the degeneration of Islamic fundamentalism into the repressive totalitarian ideology of the Islamic Republic of Iran. In the early twenty-first century, Islamic fundamentalism further degenerated into militant Shia and Sunni sectarianism, political violence, and suicide terrorism. These movements, however, have been widely differentiated, as they are represented by numerous diverse religious organizations: Sunni Islam by the Society of the Muslim Brothers in Egypt and its affiliated organizations in other Arab countries, Jamaati Islami in Pakistan, Front Islamique du Salut (FIS) in Algeria, the Taliban in Afghanistan, the National Islamic Front in Sudan, Hamas in the Gaza Strip, al-Shabaab in Somalia, and Boko Haram in Nigeria; and Shia Islam by the Iranian Fedaiyan-e Islam and the followers of Ayatollah Khomeini, the Lebanese Hezbollah, and the Yemeni Houthis. Also included are myriad Islamic extremist and suicide terrorist groups such as al-Qaeda and more recently the Islamic State in Iraq and Syria that have emerged in the region, primarily since the terrorist attacks on the World Trade Center in New York on September 11, 2001 (Ahmad 1964; Mitchell 1969; Sivan 1985; Kepel 1985; Roy 1994; Almond, Appleby, and Sivan 2002; Moaddel and Karabenick 2013).

Conceptual Development

Despite their diversity, these fundamentalist movements, as well as their Christian counterparts, share a set of core orientations toward their own and other religions. The first is a preoccupation with God's discipline and retributive character—God's rewards in heaven, the fear of punishment in hell, and Satan's scheme. The second is the tendency toward literalism, the belief that the scriptures are inerrant and literally true. The third is an orientation toward religious centrism or an exclusivist view of their religious community. The fourth is a degree of religious intolerance; fundamentalists tend to exhibit an intolerant view not only of other religions but also of religious sects other than their own.

Drawing on these shared features, religious fundamentalism is conceptualized as a set of distinctive beliefs about and attitudes toward whatever religion one has (Altemeyer 2003; Altemeyer and Hunsberger 2004; Schwartz and Lindley 2005; Summers 2006; Moaddel and Karabenick 2008, 2013, 2018). The belief in God, for example, is a religious belief; the belief in the oneness of God is specifically Islamic; and the belief in the Trinity of the Father, the Son, and the Holy Spirit is specifically Christian. But the beliefs that one's own religion is closer to God than other religions, that only the followers of one's religion will go to heaven, that one's religious community should have more rights than other communities, and that God severely punishes people even though they have engaged in only a minor infraction of religious laws are all conceptualized as fundamentalist beliefs, for they display distinctive orientations toward one's religion rather than being the beliefs or principles adhered to by the followers of a specific religion.

Fundamentalism is thus a multidimensional concept consisting of four components: (1) a *disciplinarian deity*, the belief in an almighty God who is fearful and severely punishes in hell those who fail to follow his instructions; (2) *the literal nature of the scriptures*, the belief that the scriptures are a comprehensive system of universal truth, having historical accuracy; (3) *religious exclusivity and religious centrism*, the belief that one's faith is superior to other faiths and that one's religious community must have more rights than other religious communities; and (4) *religious intolerance*, the belief that the followers of other faiths must be restricted in practicing their religions and that no one should be allowed to criticize one's faith or the religious authorities. As will be shown, these components are conterminous with one another and form a single fundamentalism construct.

Measurement of Religious Fundamentalism

The four components of religious fundamentalism were operationalized in terms of sixteen survey questions that were intended to grasp the multiple meanings linked to each of the components. These questions had a Likert-scale response format (coded as strongly agree = 1, agree = 2, disagree = 3, and strongly disagree = 4). Muslim respondents were asked about the Quran, Islam, and Muslims, while Christian respondents were asked about the Bible, Christianity, and Christians. Although some of the questions were not allowed in Egypt, no more than one question was excluded from each component, identified by * in the following list, so the remaining questions were deemed sufficient to provide stable estimates of each component. Four survey questions measured each of the four components of religious fundamentalism, designated as *disciplinarian deity*, *literalism*, *religious exclusivity*, and *religious intolerance*. The response categories for these questions were recoded (strongly agree = 4, agree = 3, disagree = 2, and strongly disagree = 1) so that those who scored higher on the scale indicated having stronger fundamentalism orientations. Principal components analysis (PCA) of the question responses across all countries combined resulted in a single-factor solution (i.e., only one factor with an eigenvalue > 1) for each of the components: disciplinarian deity = 2.06, literalism = 2.05, religious exclusivity = 2.25, and religious intolerance = 1.84. The question responses in each component were then averaged, yielding a single score for each of the four components. A second PCA of these four means yielded a single factor with an eigenvalue of 2.41 that explained 60 percent of the variance. The four means were then averaged to create a single fundamentalism index that balanced the four components of fundamentalism. Using the sixteen questions, internal consistency estimates (Cronbach's α) were well within the 0.70 to 0.90 range, which is considered satisfactory, for all the countries separately, except for Egypt, where the estimate was slightly lower but still acceptable: Turkey = 0.88, Lebanon = 0.88, Iraq = 0.84, Tunisia = 0.80, Saudi Arabia = 0.80, Pakistan = 0.72, and Egypt = 0.65. Reliability (α) was 0.84 when all countries but Egypt were combined and 0.80 when Egypt was included (but with the excluded items).

The distribution of the sixteen questions in the four components is as follows:

Please tell me if you (1) strongly agree, (2) agree, (3) disagree, or (4) strongly disagree with the following statements:

Disciplinarian Deity: Reward and Punishment from, and Fear of, God

- Any infraction of religious instruction will bring about Allah's severe punishment.
- Only the fear of Allah keeps people on the right path.*
- Satan is behind any attempt to undermine the belief in Allah.
- People stay on the right path only because they expect to be rewarded in heaven.

Literalism: The Literal Truth, Accuracy, and Comprehensiveness of the Scriptures

- The Quran [Bible] is true from beginning to end.
- The Quran [Bible] has correctly predicted all the major events that have occurred in human history.*
- In the presence of the Quran [Bible], there is no need for man-made laws.
- Whenever there is a conflict between religion and science, religion is always right.

Religious Exclusivity: The Uniqueness and Superiority of One's Religion

- Only Islam [Christianity] provides comprehensive truth about Allah.
- Only Islam [Christianity] gives a complete and unfailing guide to human salvation.
- Only Muslims [Christians] are going to heaven.
- Islam [Christianity] is the only true religion.*

Religious Intolerance: Nonrecognition of the Rights of Others' Religions and Criticism of Religion

- Our children should not be allowed to learn about other religions.
- The followers of other religions should not have the same rights as mine.
- Criticism of Islam [Christianity] should not be tolerated.
- Criticism of Muslim [Christian] religious leaders should not be tolerated.

Cross-National Variation

Table 4.1 provides the distribution of the responses to the sixteen questions organized into the four components of religious fundamentalism, an index for each component, and an overall religious fundamentalism index across the seven countries. The index for each of the four components is the average of the numerical responses to the four questions that measure that component, and the overall religious fundamentalism index is the average of all sixteen responses (or the average of the four component indices). All indices range between 1 and 4. A score of 1 indicates strong disagreement with the beliefs and attitudes expressed in the fundamentalism items; thus, it denotes a religious orientation that is counter to religious fundamentalism. A score of 4 indicates strong agreement with or support for the beliefs and attitudes expressed in the fundamentalism items; it is religious fundamentalism proper. A median value of 2.5 for the religious fundamentalism index indicates neither disagreement nor agreement with religious fundamentalism. An aggregate median index of 2.5 for a country means that there are as many respondents in that country who adhere to fundamentalist beliefs as there are who believe otherwise. Any value that is significantly above or below this median value indicates that the respondents on average are predominantly oriented either toward or against religious fundamentalism, respectively.

The percentages of those who strongly agree or agree with each of the fundamentalism questions were combined, and the results are reported in table 4.1. It is clear that support for religious fundamentalism is fairly strong in these countries. Respondents who strongly agreed or agreed with the disciplinarian deity items range between 98 percent among Egyptians and 64 percent among Lebanese, with literalism between 100 percent among Pakistanis and Saudis and 47 percent among Turkish respondents, with religious exclusivity between 98 percent among Pakistanis and 47 percent among Lebanese, and with religious intolerance between 9 percent among Pakistanis and 86 percent among Pakistanis and Saudis. The index values for three of the indices—disciplinarian deity, literalism, and religious exclusivity—are significantly higher than 2.5 across the seven countries. That is, the disciplinarian deity index varies between 2.98 for Lebanese and 3.77 for Egyptians, the literalism index between 3.02 for Lebanese and 3.69 for Egyptians and Pakistanis, and the religious exclusivity index between 2.85 for Lebanese and 3.69 for Pakistanis. Based on these three measures, the respondents from the seven countries display fairly strong fundamentalist orientations, although this strength varies among these countries. The values of the religious intolerance index, however, are much lower than 2.5 across the countries, ranging between 2.26 among Tunisians and 3.09 among Saudis.

The questions measuring religious intolerance provide a more varied picture of religious fundamentalism across the seven countries. These questions can be divided into two subcategories. One, which can be labeled *interfaith intolerance*, included these two questions: (1) "Our children should not be allowed to learn about other religions," and (2) "The followers of other religions should not have the same rights as mine." These questions measure the extent to which one is tolerant of other religion. Findings indicate that the respondents were significantly more tolerant than intolerant, except among Saudi and Pakistani respondents: 63 percent of Pakistanis and 66 percent Saudis strongly agreed or agreed that "Our children should not be allowed to learn about other religions" and 73 percent of Saudis strongly agreed or agreed that "The followers of other religions should not have the same rights as mine." In the other countries, only a minority of respondents conformed to these intolerant beliefs, ranging from 45 percent of Egyptians to 9 percent of Pakistanis. The other subcategory, which can be defined as *antiauthoritarian intolerance*, included these two questions: (3) "Criticism of Islam [Christianity (for Christian respondents)] should not be tolerated," and (4) "Criticism of Muslim religious leaders [Christian religious leaders (for Christian respondents)] should not be tolerated." These questions measured the extent to which the respondents were intolerant of expressions that are critical of one's religion or religious authorities. The strongly agree and agree responses to the third question vary between 65 percent among Lebanese and 86 percent among Pakistanis and Saudis; these responses to the fourth question vary between 30 percent among Tunisians and 76 percent among Saudis. Much higher percentages of respondents strongly agreed or agreed

TABLE 4.1 Measures of Religious Fundamentalism (Strongly Agree/Agree)

	Iraq	Lebanon	Pakistan	Saudi Arabia	Tunisia	Egypt	Turkey
Disciplinarian deity							
Any infraction of religious instruction will bring about Allah's severe punishment	91%	76%	83%	91%	89%	98%	73%
Only the fear of Allah keeps people on the right path	90%	67%	98%	86%	88%	96%	84%
Satan is behind any attempt to undermine belief in Allah	95%	79%	95%	83%	89%	97%	81%
People stay on the right path only because they expect to be rewarded in heaven	86%	64%	95%	81%	75%	94%	76%
Disciplinarian deity index (mean)	**3.48**	**2.98**	**3.57**	**3.35**	**3.48**	**3.77**	**3.06**
Literalism							
The Quran [Bible] is true from beginning to end	98%	89%	100%	100%	99%	99%	93%
The Quran [Bible] has correctly predicted all the major events that have occurred in human history	98%	83%	99%	86%	95%	N/A	89%
In the presence of the Quran [Bible], there is no need for man-made laws	72%	54%	85%	75%	56%	80%	47%
Whenever there is a conflict between religion and science, religion is always right	90%	67%	97%	89%	89%	98%	72%
Literalism index (mean)	**3.50**	**3.02**	**3.69**	**3.44**	**3.49**	**3.69**	**3.08**

Religious exclusivity

Only Islam [Christianity] provides comprehensive truth about Allah [God]	88%	95%	86%	88%	96%	68%	92%
Only Islam [Christianity] gives a complete and unfailing guide to human salvation	89%	N/A	92%	88%	97%	71%	93%
Only Muslims [Christians] are going to heaven	57%	78%	57%	82%	86%	47%	74%
Islam [Christianity] is the only true religion	89%	N/A	90%	89%	98%	68%	90%
Religious exclusivity index (mean)	3.19	3.54	3.45	3.43	3.69	2.85	3.44

Religious intolerance

Our children should not be allowed to learn about other religions	42%	45%	32%	66%	63%	28%	35%
The followers of other religions should not have the same rights as mine	37%	30%	22%	73%	9%	25%	32%
Criticism of Islam [Christianity] should not be tolerated	69%	77%	67%	86%	86%	65%	82%
Criticism of Muslim [Christian] religious leaders should not be tolerated	57%	66%	30%	76%	69%	54%	68%
Religious intolerance index (mean)	2.57	2.75	2.26	3.09	2.72	2.37	2.67
Religious fundamentalism index (mean)	2.98	3.44	3.18	3.33	3.42	2.80	3.28
Range (min–max)	1–4	2.1–4	1–4	1.3–4	1.4–4	1–4	1.4–4
Median	3.0	3.5	3.3	3.4	3.5	2.8	3.3

with questions 3 and 4 than strongly agreed or agreed with questions 1 and 2. These differences thus show that, while respondents displayed a willingness to tolerate the followers of other faiths, they were quite intolerant of criticisms of their religion and religious leaders.

Only respondents from Lebanon and Tunisia, with religious intolerance index values of 2.37 and 2.26, respectively, can be considered as tolerant, while those from the other countries cannot be considered so at the time the surveys were completed, assuming that the survey items were adequate. Nonetheless, the level of support for religious intolerance among the respondents was much lower than support for the other three components of religious fundamentalism across the seven countries. The difference between those three indices and the religious intolerance index may suggest that any significant change in religious attitudes across these countries toward religious modernity and tolerance may begin with further decline in the level of intolerance. (This hypothesis is in fact supported by findings from two waves of panel surveys carried out in Egypt, Tunisia, and Turkey, as will be shown in chapter 6.)

The overall religious fundamentalism index, which is based on the average of all sixteen items (or the average of the four component indices), shows strong support for fundamentalist beliefs and attitudes among the respondents across the seven countries. The measure also displays cross-national variation. Post hoc analysis of variance ($F = 822.53$, $p < .001$) confirms significant differences in the religious fundamentalism index by country, with Scheffé's test showing that Egyptians and Pakistanis reported the highest levels of fundamentalism, with mean index values of 3.44 and 3.42, respectively, which were statistically nearly identical. They are followed by respondents from Saudi Arabia, with a religious fundamentalism index of 3.33; Iraq, with 3.28; Tunisia, with 3.18; Turkey, with 2.98; and Lebanon, with 2.80. Between-country differences in religious fundamentalism across these last five countries are statistically significant.

Variation by Age, Gender, and Education

Age

Table 4.2 shows that the age differences in the religious fundamentalism index are statistically significant for all the countries, except Egypt. It indicates that individuals in the youth bulge (aged 18–29) were less strongly fundamentalist than were those in the older age group (aged 30 and older). The table also shows that countries that have a smaller youth bulge (i.e., those that have a higher median age) were significantly less fundamentalist than were those with a large youth bulge ($r = -.73$). Thus, while it is true that the younger individuals had weaker fundamentalist beliefs and attitudes, the opposite is true of countries with younger populations. That is, countries with younger populations exhibited on average stronger support for religious fundamentalism.

TABLE 4.2 Age Differences in Religious Fundamentalism Index and Median Age by Country

	1	2	3	4	5	6
	Mean Index: 18–29	Mean Index: 30+	Col_1–Col_2	Mean Index: Total	Col_3/Col_4	Median Age[a]
Egypt	3.42	3.43	−0.01	3.43	−0.0%	24.3
Pakistan	3.36	3.45	−0.09[c]	3.42	−2.6%	21.6
Saudi Arabia	3.31	3.38	−0.07[c]	3.33	−2.1%	25.3[b]
Iraq	3.23	3.29	−0.06[c]	3.27	−1.8%	20.9
Tunisia	3.05	3.21	−0.16[c]	3.18	−5.0%	31.0
Turkey	2.91	3.00	−0.09[c]	2.97	−3.0%	29.2
Lebanon	2.76	2.83	−0.07[c]	2.80	−2.5%	29.8
$r_{ol4Col6}$	−.73[d]					

[a] The median ages for Tunisia and Turkey are from 2013; the median ages for all other countries are from 2011 (CIA 2011, 2013).
[b] The population figure used to compute the median age for Saudi Arabia includes about 25 percent nonnationals.
[c] $p < .01$.
[d] $p < .05$.

Gender

Figure 4.1 shows the values of the religious fundamentalism index for men and women. Lebanese, Tunisian, and Saudi women were significantly more fundamentalist than were their male counterparts. Using independent samples t-tests for differences in the religious fundamentalism index by gender, the

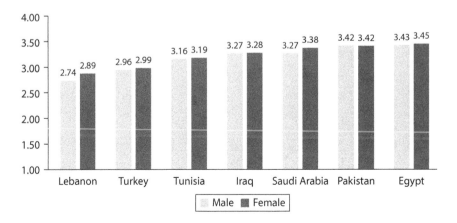

Figure 4.1 Religious Fundamentalism Index by Gender.

difference in Lebanon was significant at $p < .001$, in Saudi Arabia at $p < .001$, and in Tunisia at $p < .05$. (Although the difference in fundamentalism in Turkey is about the same as it is in Tunisia, this difference is not statistically significant in Turkey). In the other countries, however, there were no significant gender differences in fundamentalism.

There were significance differences in the religious fundamentalism index by age but not by gender, except among Lebanese, Saudi, and Tunisian respondents. Thus, there is no need to break down the religious fundamentalism index by gender and age.

Education

Figure 4.2 shows the variation in religious fundamentalism by education across the seven countries. People with university education had significantly weaker fundamentalist beliefs and attitudes than did people without university education across all countries, except for Saudi Arabia, where this difference was not statistically significant. The magnitude of this difference was greatest in Turkey (0.37), followed by Tunisia (0.32), Lebanon (0.18), Egypt (0.13), Pakistan (0.12), Iraq (0.08), and Saudi Arabia (0.06). It appears that university education had a greater effect in weakening fundamentalism in the more liberal countries of Turkey, Tunisia, and Lebanon (similar to its effect on liberal values, except among Pakistanis, noted in chapter 3) than in the more conservative countries of Egypt, Pakistan, Iraq, and Saudi Arabia. This finding thus suggests that the effect of education on fundamentalism is mediated by the cultural-cum-authoritarian context; that is, education has stronger negative effects on fundamentalism in more open and less authoritarian environments. Independent samples t-tests for differences in the religious fundamentalism index

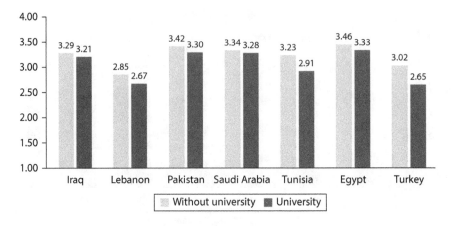

Figure 4.2 Religious Fundamentalism Index by Education.

TABLE 4.3 Religious Fundamentalism Index by Age and Education (Mean/Standard Deviation; *n*)

	Youth Bulge (Aged 18–29)			Older Age group (Aged 30+)		
	Without University	University	Difference	Without University	University	Difference
Iraq	3.24/0.41; 946	3.19/0.42; 195	−0.05	3.31/0.41; 1,459	3.21/0.44; 371	−0.10[a]
Lebanon	2.87/0.56; 372	2.70/0.59; 776	−0.17[a]	2.93/0.58; 1,076	2.67/0.58; 673	−0.26[a]
Pakistan	3.37/0.33; 1,116	3.28/0.34; 147	−0.09[b]	3.46/0.31; 2,112	3.27/0.34; 139	−0.19[a]
Saudi Arabia	3.30/0.52; 418	3.31/0.42; 231	0.01	3.39/0.47; 666	3.34/0.42; 195	−0.05
Tunisia	3.14/0.41; 419	2.94/0.48; 298	−0.20[a]	3.29/0.41; 1,929	2.88/0.52; 411	−0.41[a]
Egypt	3.45/0.32; 764	3.33/0.32; 223	−0.12[a]	3.45/0.33; 1,845	3.32/0.35; 309	−0.13[a]
Turkey	2.96/0.55; 650	2.71/0.58; 186	−0.25[a]	3.04/0.51; 1,918	2.63/0.58; 232	−0.41[a]

Significance of independent samples *t*-tests for differences in the fundamentalism index by age (equal variances not assumed);
[a] $p < .001$.
[b] $p < .01$.

by education show significance for Iraq at $p < .01$ and for Lebanon, Pakistan, Tunisia, Egypt, and Turkey at $p < .001$.

Education and Age

Table 4.3 shows variation in the religious fundamentalism index by age and education across the seven countries. People with university education were significantly less fundamentalist across both age categories among respondents from Egypt, Lebanon, Pakistan, Tunisia, and Turkey. Among Iraqis, university education significantly reduced fundamentalist beliefs and attitudes only among the older age group, and among Saudis, it had no significant effect on religious fundamentalism among respondents from either age group.

Variation by Religion

Table 4.4 compares the indices of disciplinarian deity, literalism, religious exclusivity, religious intolerance, and religious fundamentalism by religion and religious sects—Christians, Shia Muslims, and Sunni Muslims—across six countries: Egypt, Lebanon, Iraq, Pakistan, Saudi Arabia, and Turkey. Tunisia is excluded from this table because over 99 percent of its population was Sunni Muslims and the

TABLE 4.4 Indices of Religious Fundamentalism and its Components by Religion (Mean/Standard Deviation)

Religion/sect (n)	Egypt		Lebanon			Iraq		Pakistan		Saudi Arabia		Turkey	
	Christian (473)[a]	Sunni (2,995)[a]	Christian (789)	Sunni (670)	Shia (968)	Sunni (1,247)	Shia (1,193)	Sunni (2,901)	Shia (278)	Sunni (1,499)[a]	Shia (491)	Sunni (2,488)[a]	Shia[b] (169)
Disciplinarian deity index	3.63/0.40	3.77/0.34	2.89/0.63	3.19/0.65	2.99/0.61	3.56/0.47	3.43/0.52	3.61/0.41	3.33/0.55	3.41/0.55	2.66/0.76	3.06/0.61	2.80/0.77
Literalism index	3.49/0.47	3.69/0.40	2.71/0.68	3.38/0.61	3.17/0.64	3.51/0.50	3.52/0.48	3.71/0.33	3.57/0.40	3.49/0.47	2.82/0.64	3.08/0.60	2.72/0.69
Religious exclusivity index	3.02/0.83	3.56/0.60	2.61/0.76	3.17/0.77	3.00/0.69	3.50/0.56	3.44/0.49	3.71/0.36	3.55/0.51	3.51/0.56	2.45/0.81	3.20/0.62	2.81/0.80
Religious intolerance index	2.68/0.70	2.76/0.63	2.28/0.63	2.74/0.66	2.51/0.68	2.72/0.66	2.63/0.52	2.75/0.53	2.69/0.54	3.15/0.61	2.41/0.79	2.57/0.72	2.25/0.80
Fundamentalism index	3.21/0.40	3.44/0.33	2.62/0.53	3.05/0.56	2.91/0.53	3.32/0.41	3.25/0.39	3.44/0.29	3.29/0.35	3.39/0.41	2.59/0.64	2.98/0.52	2.64/0.65

Note: Values ranges from 1 to 4; a higher value indicates stronger fundamentalism. Independent samples t-tests for differences in the fundamentalism index by religion (equal variances not assumed) are significant for Iraq at $p < .001$; for Lebanon between Sunnis and Shias at $p < .001$, between Sunnis and Christians at $p < .001$, and between Shias and Christians at $p < .001$; for Saudi Arabia at $p < .001$; for Egypt between Sunnis and Christians at $p < .001$; for Pakistan at $p < .001$; and for Turkey at $p < .001$.

[a] Sample sizes are reported without the use of weights for Saudi Arabia and Egypt.

[b] In Turkey, the Shia column includes both Shias and Alavis.

numbers of religious minorities in the Tunisian sample were thus negligible. As this table shows, in Egypt and Lebanon, Christians scored lower than Sunnis and Shias on each of the four indices of the components of religious fundamentalism, and in Lebanon, Iraq, Pakistan, Saudi Arabia, and Turkey, Shias scored lower than Sunnis, except that Iraqi Shias and Sunnis scored almost the same on the index of literalism. Lebanese Christians and Turkish Shias (mainly Alavis) had religious intolerance index scores of 2.28 and 2.25, respectively, making them the least intolerant (or the most tolerant), and Saudi Sunnis had a religious intolerance index score of 3.15, making them the most intolerant (or the least tolerant) group in the samples.

Considering the religious fundamentalism index, Christians were also less fundamentalist than Sunnis and Shias in Lebanon and Sunnis in Egypt. Lebanese Christians were considerably less fundamentalist than Egyptian Christians, indicating the effect of the liberal and pluralistic context of Lebanon on fundamentalism. Shias were significantly less fundamentalist than Sunnis across the samples from Iraq, Lebanon, Pakistan, Saudi Arabia, and Turkey. The magnitude of the Sunni-Shia difference on fundamentalism was 0.80 among Saudi respondents. This difference was 0.34 for Turkey, 0.15 for Pakistan, 0.14 for Lebanon, and 0.07 for Iraq. One of the most remarkable findings of this study is that, with a religious fundamentalism index score of 2.59, Saudi Shias were the least fundamentalist group across both the religions and the religious sects reported in this table (the difference in religious fundamentalism between Saudi Shias and Lebanese Christians, who had a score of 2.62, however, is not statistically significant), and Egyptian and Pakistani Sunnis, who scored 3.44 on this index, were the most fundamentalist.

These differences in fundamentalism between the members of the religious minorities and the religious majority may indicate that the minorities, in trying to accommodate the religious majority and reduce tension, have espoused a more moderate approach to religion and thus have developed a weaker fundamentalist orientation. The stronger fundamentalism among members of the majority religion, on the other hand, may reflect their claim to a greater ownership of religion and the perception that the religious minorities have deviated from the true path and are therefore posing a threat to their religion.

Variation by Religion and Gender

Although not reported in the tables, the analysis showed that across religions and religious sects, respondents in the youth bulge were either less fundamentalist than or displayed no difference from those in the older age group. Also university education generally had negative effects on fundamentalism across Christianity and Shia and Sunni Islam.

Table 4.5 reports differences in religious fundamentalism by religion and gender. Both Shia and Sunni women were more strongly fundamentalist than

TABLE 4.5 Religious Fundamentalism Index by Religion and Gender (Mean/Standard Deviation; n)

	Sunni			Shia			Christian		
	Female	Male	Difference	Female	Male	Difference	Female	Male	Difference
Iraq	3.37/0.38; 552	3.37/0.39; 648	0.00	3.27/0.35; 447	3.26/0.38; 473	-0.01	—	—	—
Lebanon	3.12/0.47; 281	3.00/0.61; 422	-0.12[c]	3.00/0.48; 476	2.84/0.56; 517	-0.16[b]	2.63/0.53; 330	2.61/0.53; 479	-0.02
Pakistan	3.44/0.29; 1,443	3.45/0.30; 1,459	0.01	3.35/0.29; 105	3.29/0.35; 125	-0.06	—	—	—
Saudi Arabia[a]	3.41/0.43; 760	3.37/0.39; 746	-0.04[d]	3.00/0.59; 251	2.16/0.34; 246	-0.84[b]	—	—	—
Egypt[a]	3.46/0.32; 1,568	3.43/0.34; 1,441	-0.03	—	—	—	3.24/0.40; 200	3.19/0.40; 286	-0.05
Turkey	2.99/0.52; 1,431	2.97/0.52; 1,142	-0.02	2.63/0.72; 99	2.67/0.57; 75	0.04	—	—	—

[a]Sample sizes are reported without the use of weights for Egypt and Saudi Arabia.
Significance of independent samples t-tests for differences in the fundamentalism index by gender (equal variances not assumed):
[b] $p < .001$.
[c] $p < .01$.
[d] $p < .05$.

men in Lebanon and Saudi Arabia, but there were no gender differences across these two sects in Iraq, Pakistan, Egypt, and Turkey. Among Christian respondents in Egypt and Lebanon, there were no significant differences in fundamentalism between male and female respondents. Again, Tunisia is excluded from this analysis because more than 99 percent of its population adhered to the Sunni sect.

Religious Fundamentalism Versus Liberal Values

Consistent with the argument that, in the context of the contemporary Middle East and North Africa, supporters of Islamic fundamentalism and liberal activists stand on opposite sides of significant sociopolitical and cultural issues, the analysis of the pooled survey data showed that the indices of religious fundamentalism and its components are inversely related to the indices of liberal values and its components. That is, the indices of fundamentalism, disciplinarian deity, literalism, religious exclusivity, and religious intolerance are all inversely linked to the indices of liberal values, expressive individualism, gender equality, secular politics, and national identity. The data reported in table 4.6 confirm the inverse relationships between the measures of both constructs.

The strongest correlation is between the indices of religious fundamentalism and liberal values ($r = -.56$), indicating the superiority of either of these composite indices over any of the measures of the four components. Among the components of liberal values, religious fundamentalism has strongest inverse correlation with secular politics ($r = -.46$), followed by gender equality

TABLE 4.6 Correlation Coefficients Between Components of Liberal Values and Religious Fundamentalism in the Pooled Data

	Liberal values components				
	Expressive Individualism	Gender Equality	Secular Politics	National Identity	Liberal Values
Religious fundamentalism components					
Disciplinarian deity	−.34	−.35	−.36	−.23	−.48
Literalism	−.35	−.35	−.42	−.24	−.52
Religious exclusivity	−.33	−.30	−.38	−.24	−.46
Religious intolerance	−.16	−.27	−.29	−.10	−.33
Religious fundamentalism	−.37	−.40	−.46	−.26	−.56

Note: All values are significant at $p < .001$, listwise deletion.

($r = -.40$), then expressive individualism ($r = -.37$), and finally national identity ($r = -.26$), which has the weakest correlation. The strength of these correlation coefficients may reflect the intensity of the clash between fundamentalism and these components of liberal values. These varying relationships imply that respondents may have a clearer idea about their stance on secular politics and gender equality than they do on expressive individualism. On identity, while the respondents who identify with the nation rather than religion, tend to be more liberal and less fundamentalist, national identity is not as clear mark of distinction between the two conflicting values than other measures. In some cases nationalism and fundamentalism may merge into a single authoritarian religious nationalist movement. This fact explains why the correlation coefficient between fundamentalism and national identity is weakest ($r = -.26$). In fact, among the components of liberal values, the national identity index had the weakest relationships with the components of fundamentalism (with correlation coefficients ranging between $-.10$ and $-.24$).

Finally, compared to other components of fundamentalism, the religious intolerance index had the weakest relationships with the components of liberal values, including national identity (with correlation coefficients ranging between $-.10$ and $-.29$). Again, while fundamentalists appeared to have a strong and clear view on the disciplinarian conception of the deity, literalism, and exclusivity, they are not consistently intolerant. All these correlation coefficients are, however, statistically significant ($p < .001$).

Cross-National Variation in the Fundamentalism-Liberalism Relationship

Conceptually, religious fundamentalism and liberalism are opposing discourses. Empirically, however, the inverse relationship between the indices of religious fundamentalism and liberal values is far from perfect. This is not simply because individuals vary in terms of their orientations toward liberalism or fundamentalism. Rather, an individual may not be fundamentalist or liberal on all the issues. As shown in table 4.6, respondents expressed much stronger fundamentalist beliefs and attitudes on items related to the disciplinarian deity, literalism, and religious exclusivity than they did on items related to religious intolerance. Likewise, a respondent may be strongly supportive of secular politics but not as strongly supportive of gender equality. Finally, as demonstrated by public opinion research, individuals may simultaneously hold values that clash (Sniderman, Tetlock, and Carmines 1993). They may be strongly fundamentalist on one index but liberal on another.

The strength of the correlations between the indices of religious fundamentalism and liberal values also varies by country. According to table 4.7, across

TABLE 4.7 Covariances, Standard Deviations, and Correlation Coefficients for the Indices of Religious Fundamentalism and Liberal Values

	n	Religious Fundamentalism & Liberal Values Covariance	Religious Fundamentalism Standard Deviation	Liberal Values Standard Deviation	Correlation Coefficient
Iraq	2,986	−0.05	0.41	0.40	−0.30
Lebanon	3,018	−0.13	0.59	0.49	−0.46
Pakistan	3,523	−0.08	0.32	0.45	−0.53
Saudi Arabia	1,635[a]	−0.10	0.47	0.49	−0.31
Tunisia	3,061	−0.12	0.46	0.53	−0.39
Egypt	3,142[a]	−0.04	0.33	0.38	−0.31
Turkey	2,992	−0.12	0.55	0.46	−0.48

[a]Sample sizes are reported with the use of weights for Egypt and Saudi Arabia.

the seven countries, this coefficient is highest among Pakistani respondents ($r = -.53$), followed by Turkish, Lebanese, Tunisian, Saudi, Egyptian, and Iraqi respondents ($r = -.48, -.46, -.39 -.31, -.31,$ and $-.30$, respectively). Researchers have pointed to six factors that affect the size of a correlation coefficient: (1) the amount of variability in the data, (2) differences in the shapes of the two distributions, (3) lack of linearity, (4) the presence of outliers, (5) the characteristics of the sample, and (6) measurement error (Goodwin and Leech 2006). Here the same measures were used across the seven countries, the religious fundamentalism items were extensively pretested before being used in the surveys, and almost all the items measuring liberal values were used in the previous surveys in the region and in the World Values Surveys. Efforts were also made to keep the samples comparable, although the quality of the sample data was better in some countries than in others. The research design attempted to address factors 5 and 6. Also a lack of linearity and the presence of outliers (factors 3 and 4) were ruled out as factors explaining cross-national variation in the size of the correlation coefficients.

However, substantively, the characteristics of the national context may affect the variability in the data and the shape of the distribution of the variables of interests (factors 1 and 2). It was proposed that the inverse relationship between the two indices would be larger in countries where people more readily witnessed or experienced fundamentalism-liberalism debates. Probably, respondents in relatively more open and liberal countries like Lebanon, Turkey, and Tunisia were often exposed to such debates and, as a result, might be able to develop a clearer stance on one side or the other of the issues being debated, but each side might not necessarily adopt a more homogeneous set of attitudes (probably because open debates and discussions tend to direct individuals toward compromise and thus toward taking more moderate positions on issues, increasing the variability of the indices). Empirically, given the formula for the Pearson correlation coefficient,

$$r = \frac{Sxy}{\sqrt{Sx} * Sy}$$

a clear stance might produce a higher covariance between the indices of the two constructs, and homogeneous or heterogeneous attitudes toward issues might be translated into smaller or larger standard deviations for the indices. Table 4.7 shows that the covariances between the indices of religious fundamentalism and liberal values are higher for Lebanon (−0.13), Turkey (−0.12), and Tunisia (−0.12) than they are for the more conservative countries of Egypt (−0.04), Iraq (−0.05), and Pakistan (−0.08). As a result, the correlation coefficients for Lebanon, Turkey, and Tunisia remain higher than those for Egypt and Iraq. Saudi Arabia is an intrusive religious regime. Nonetheless, Saudis appeared to have developed keen awareness of the difference between religious fundamentalism and liberal values. This may explain a relatively higher value for the covariance between the two indices for Saudi Arabia (−0.10), resulting in a high correlation coefficient. The covariance value for Pakistan is low (−0.08), but for the index of religious fundamentalism, it has the lowest standard deviation (0.32), and for the index of liberal values, it has the third-smallest standard deviation (0.45); only Egypt (0.38) and Iraq (0.40) have smaller standard deviations for the liberal values index. As a result, the size of the denominator is reduced for Pakistan, indicating a higher correlation between the indices of religious fundamentalism and liberal values for Pakistan than for the other six countries. This may suggest that in Pakistan, a highly homogenous fundamentalism faces a moderately homogeneous liberalism.

Societal Support for Religious Fundamentalism and Liberal Values

Conceptually, fundamentalism and liberalism are incompatible discourses. Empirically, however, the fundamentalism-liberalism division is rarely reflected in the formation of two organized and culturally distinct groups. An ambiguous, cross-nationally variable intersection blurs the line of conceptual demarcation, making it hard to recognize the point where fundamentalism ends and liberalism begins. Some individuals tend to display both liberal and fundamentalist characteristics or are partly liberal and partly fundamentalist. Such individuals simultaneously adhere to values that clash, and their presence in society thus modifies the severity and intensity of the conflict between the two antagonistic ideological camps. Where the overlap is narrower or the gap wider, there is a higher likelihood of intense ideological conflict between the two groups.

To further clarify the relationship between religious fundamentalism and liberal values and to estimate the varying degrees to which individuals in the seven countries support either value orientation, the two indices were recoded into five categories. Those scored between 1 and 1.69 are labeled "strongly oppose" religious fundamentalism or liberal values, those between 1.70 and 2.39 "oppose," those between 2.40 and 2.59 "neither oppose nor support," those between 2.60 and 3.29 "support," and those between 3.30 and 4 "strongly support." The results for the two distributions are reported in tables 4.8 and 4.9.

The distribution of religious fundamentalism in the five categories in table 4.8 indicates that there were not very many respondents from Egypt, Iraq, Pakistan, or Saudi Arabia who opposed fundamentalism. There were no Egyptians and only 1 percent of Pakistanis, 4 percent of Iraqis, and 5 percent of Saudis who either strongly opposed or opposed fundamentalism. For the other three countries, these figures were higher; 23 percent of Lebanese, 6 percent of Tunisians, and 13 percent of Turkish respondents either strongly opposed or opposed fundamentalism. On the other hand, the percentages of those who strongly supported or supported fundamentalism were quite high, ranging

TABLE 4.8 Distribution of Religious Fundamentalism Index

	Iraq	Lebanon	Pakistan	Saudi Arabia	Tunisia	Egypt	Turkey	Total
Strongly oppose	0%	5%	0%	0%	1%	0%	2%	1%
Oppose	4%	18%	1%	5%	5%	0%	11%	7%
Neither oppose nor support	3%	11%	1%	5%	4%	1%	8%	5%
Support	39%	43%	26%	26%	45%	30%	47%	37%
Strongly support	54%	22%	72%	64%	44%	69%	30%	50%
n	2,969	3,000	3,520	1,633[a]	3,050	3,138[a]	2,962	20,990

[a]Sample sizes are reported with the use of weights for Egypt and Saudi Arabia.

TABLE 4.9 Distribution of Liberal Values Index

	Iraq	Lebanon	Pakistan	Saudi Arabia	Tunisia	Egypt	Turkey	Total
Strongly oppose	8%	3%	27%	13%	6%	19%	2%	11%
Oppose	51%	19%	56%	58%	33%	58%	24%	42%
Neither oppose nor support	19%	12%	8%	14%	14%	13%	15%	14%
Support	21%	54%	8%	15%	39%	10%	48%	29%
Strongly support	1%	13%	1%	0%	7%	0%	11%	5%
n	2,921	3,002	3,497	1,629[a]	3,029	3,101[a]	2,983	20,880

[a]Sample sizes are reported with the use of weights for Egypt and Saudi Arabia.

between 65 percent among Lebanese and 99 percent among Egyptians. In the pooled sample, only 8 percent strongly opposed or opposed fundamentalism, while 87 percent strongly supported or supported it and 5 percent neither opposed nor supported it.

The distribution of the index of liberal values in table 4.9 shows much less support for liberal values across the seven countries. Those who strongly opposed or opposed liberal values ranged between 22 percent among Lebanese and 83 percent among Pakistanis. On the other hand, those who strongly supported or supported such values varied between 9 percent among Pakistanis and 67 percent among Lebanese.

The above comparison is useful in order to assess where these countries stood on religious fundamentalism and liberal values. Nonetheless, considering the distributions in tables 4.8 and 4.9, it is premature to conclude that, because there was a low level of support for liberal values and a high level of support for religious fundamentalism among the respondents, the future of liberalism in these countries is doomed and that, as Huntington (1996a) speculated, the chance that liberal democracy will rise in the Muslim world is nil. For a better understanding of the transformation of values toward liberal democracy, the measures of both constructs need to be modified. First, it should be noted that the high values for religious fundamentalism are a result of the high levels of support for a disciplinarian deity, literalism, and religious exclusivity. In comparison, support for religious intolerance (the fourth component of religious fundamentalism) was much lower across all seven countries. Also, it is known that an increase in the level of tolerance is necessary (but not necessarily sufficient) for liberal politics to become institutionalized and function effectively. Thus, a decline in the level of religious intolerance may be a better indicator of a change toward liberal democracy than an overall decline in religious fundamentalism. Low support for liberal values, on the other hand, is mainly due to low support for the component of expressive individualism. To make a more balanced comparison between the support for religious fundamentalism and that for liberal values, expressive individualism must be excluded from the measure and liberal values recalculated as an average of the indices of secular politics and gender equality. Then the distribution of this recalculated index of liberal values can be compared with the distribution of the index of religious intolerance. The results are reported in table 4.10.

The distribution in table 4.10 portrays a more balanced picture of the status of liberal values versus religious fundamentalism. In the entire sample, 36 percent of respondents strongly opposed or opposed religious intolerance, while 49 percent strongly supported or supported it and 15 percent neither opposed not supported it. On the other hand, 49 percent strongly opposed or opposed liberal values, while 38 percent strongly supported or supported them and 13 percent neither opposed nor supported them. Comparing the relative support for religious intolerance versus that for liberal values, higher

TABLE 4.10 Distribution of Indices of Religious Intolerance and Liberal Values (%)

	Iraq		Lebanon		Pakistan		Saudi Arabia		Tunisia		Egypt		Turkey		Total	
	Rel Int[a]	Lib[b]	Rel Int	Lib	Rel Int	Lib	Rel Int	Lib	Rel Int	Lib	Rel Int	Lib	Rel Int	Lib	Rel Int	Lib
Strongly oppose	4	5	15	3	3	22	3	26	19	5	4	14	10	1	9	10
Oppose	27	48	33	20	23	53	13	60	37	25	22	56	30	17	27	39
Neither oppose nor support	18	20	17	13	15	10	6	7	16	13	14	12	15	13	15	13
Support	38	25	28	49	50	13	37	7	21	46	44	18	30	54	35	31
Strongly support	13	2	7	16	10	1	41	0	8	12	16	1	15	15	14	7

[a] Rel int = Religious intolerance index.
[b] Lib = Liberal values index (based on gender equality and secular politics).

percentages of respondents were more strongly supportive or supportive of religious intolerance than they were of liberal values among Iraqis, 51 percent versus 27 percent; Pakistanis, 60 percent versus 14 percent; Saudis, 78 percent versus 7 percent; and Egyptians, 60 percent versus 19 percent. But the opposite was the case among Lebanese, 35 percent versus 65 percent; Tunisians, 29 percent versus 58 percent; and Turkish respondents, 45 percent versus 69 percent.

Comparing the support for religious intolerance and that for liberal values (measured as the average of the indices of secular politics and gender equality) is useful because changes in values are more likely to occur first in the religious intolerance component of religious fundamentalism and in the secular politics component of liberal values. The final chapter of this book shows that the trends in values in Egypt, Tunisia, and Turkey indicate a significant decline in religious intolerance and an increase in support for secular politics and, to a limited degree, for gender equality.

Correlates of Religious Fundamentalism and Liberal Values: Opposing Relationships

To more fully understand the relationship between religious fundamentalism and liberal values, one must consider that these two diverse value orientations are subject to the opposing effects of the same set of social forces on individuals. It is argued that the factors that reinforce religious fundamentalist orientations among individuals tend to weaken their support for liberal values, and vice versa. To assess this hypothesis, the linkages of such factors as demographics (SES [socioeconomic status], gender [male =1, female=0], youth bulge, and area of residence), religion (religiosity, religious modernity, confidence in religious institutions), mixing of the sexes, pre-marital sex, and morality (mixing of the sexes corrupts, and premarital sex immoral), attitudes toward outgroups (ethnic sectarianism, conspiracy, and xenophobia), sources of information (internet use), and fate versus free will (fatalism) are evaluated,

First, with *demographics*, the focus is on social class, gender, the youth bulge, and urban-rural residence and their relationships with religious fundamentalism and liberal values. Here it is argued that more education and higher income are likely to weaken religious fundamentalism and strengthen liberal values. Education is said to lower cognitive barriers to enlightenment, and as a result, the educated are more skilled in analyzing issues, assessing alternative perspectives, and making sense of the world autonomously than are those who are less educated (Schussman and Soule 2005; Krueger and Malečková 2003). They are thus less likely to espouse a literalist, exclusivist, and intolerant view of religion, compared to those with lower levels of education. Also, individuals with higher incomes are less likely to harbor fundamentalist beliefs because they have greater access to more diverse cultural perspectives and networks. Lower-income individuals, on the other hand, are more likely to support religious fundamentalism. They experience a higher level of status insecurity (Weber 1964; Caudill 1963; Weller 1965; Shapiro 1978; Coreno 2002), and they are more likely to support the communitarianism of religious fundamentalism (Davis and Robinson 2006). People living in rural areas, with limited access to a more diversified religious environment, may display stronger religious fundamentalism than those in urban areas. Finally, the possible effects of gender and age on religious fundamentalism and liberal values are assessed.

Second, it is evident that without *religion*, religious fundamentalism may not exist. Higher religiosity may thus be linked to stronger religious fundamentalism. Moreover, people with greater confidence in religious institutions are more likely to self-restrict to such institutions for information and guidance, to develop a stronger monolithic view of religion, and thus to become more strongly fundamentalist. Finally, individuals who more strongly support the idea that religious beliefs foster development—espousing religious modernity—may develop a stronger attitude against secular change, a more holistic view of religion, and a stronger fundamentalist orientation. Being secular, the adherent of liberal values, on the other hand, exhibits weaker religiosity, lower confidence in religious institutions, and a less favorable attitude toward religious modernity.

Third, fundamentalists' *attitudes toward sex and morality* include censure of premarital sex and admonition against the mixing of the sexes in public places (Motahhari 1969; Taraki 1996). The linkages of people's conceptions of the immorality of premarital sex and their attitudes toward the mixing of the sexes with religious fundamentalism and liberal values are assessed.

Fourth is the factor of *in-group solidarity and out-group hostility*. Social science research has shown that hostility toward outsiders, or xenophobia, and the belief in conspiracies are linked to right-wing solidarity and religious fundamentalism (Pipes 1996; Euben 1999; Zeidan 2001; Maehr and Karabenick 2005; Inglehart, Moaddel, and Tessler 2006; Choueiri 2010; Bermanis et al. 2010; Koopmans 2014).

The fifth factor is that of *fatalism*. The belief that one must obey a disciplinarian God and surrender unconditionally to his will may be stronger among fatalistic individuals, who consider that their fate has been firmly established and there is little one can do to change it (Ford 1962; Quinney 1964; Booth 1991; Mercier 1995; Ellerbe 1995; Cohen-Mor 2001; Brink and Mencher 2014).

Finally, the use of the *internet* as a source of information among ordinary individuals may be linked to religious fundamentalism and liberal values in different ways. The internet enhances individuals' access to more diverse sources of information and a variety of perspectives on religion. Such sources of information enable individuals to develop a general awareness of a plurality of belief systems and alternative venues for spiritual satisfaction, and as a result, they tend to develop a weaker fundamentalist orientation and stronger adherence to liberal values.

Measurement of the Predictors of Religious Fundamentalism and Liberal Values

Demographics: Socioeconomic status was measured in terms of education and income. Education was coded in nine categories, ranging from 1 for no formal education to 9 for a university-level education with degree. Household income before taxes, counting all wages, salaries, pensions, and other income, was coded in approximate deciles by the local investigators in each country, with 1 as the lowest decile and 10 as the highest. Because education and household income were significantly correlated across the seven countries, a single index of socioeconomic status was constructed by averaging the two measures. Rural was a dummy variable, where areas with populations of 10,000 were coded 1 and areas with populations of more than 10,000 were coded 0. Gender and youth bulge were also dummy variables, where male was coded 1 and female was coded 0 and where youth bulge was coded 1 and otherwise 0.

Religion: A religiosity index was constructed by averaging three variables (coding on all three are reversed so that higher values indicate greater religiosity): (a) frequency of prayer—ranging from 1, never, to 6, five times daily; (b) self-description as religious—ranging from 1, not at all religious, to 10, very religious; and (c) the importance of God in life, ranging from 1, not at all important, to 10, very important. Confidence in religious institutions was measured by one survey question: "Please tell me whether you have (1) a great deal of confidence in religious institutions, (2) quite a lot of confidence, (3) not very much confidence, or (4) none at all." A religious modernity index was constructed by averaging the responses to three questions about the belief that religion fosters development (the coding for these variables are reversed for the higher values to indicate more developed): "Would it make your country (1) a lot more developed, (2) more developed, (3) less developed, and (4) a lot less developed, if (a) faith in Allah increases, (b) the influence of religion on politics increases, and (c) belief in the truth of the Quran [Bible (for Christian respondents)] increases?"

Attitudes toward sex and morality: One question asked respondents to rank the morality of premarital sex on a scale of 1 to 10, with 1 being moral and 10 being immoral. Another question dealt with the mixing of the sexes in public places: "How often does allowing men and women to work together in public places lead to moral decay: (1) always, (2) most of the time, (3) occasionally, or (4) never?" The coding for both variables are reversed.

In-group solidarity and out-group hostility: The belief in conspiracy was measured by whether respondents "(1) strongly agree, (2) agree, (3) disagree, or (4) strongly disagree that there are conspiracies against Muslims [Christians (for Christian respondents)]." This variable is recoded from the original so that a higher value indicates a stronger belief in conspiracy. An index of xenophobia was made by averaging the responses to a series of questions on whether respondents would like to have various groups as neighbors, including French, British, Americans, Iranians [for Pakistanis in Iran], Kuwaitis [for Iraq]/Indians [for Pakistan]/Iraqis [for all other countries], Turkish [for Iraq, Saudi Arabia, and Iran]/Saudis [for all other countries], and Jordanians [for Iraq]/Saudis [for Iran]/Afghanis [for Pakistan]/Pakistanis [for Saudi Arabia]/Syrians [for all other countries]. The responses were recoded as 2 for those who would not like to have them as neighbors and 1 for those who would like to have them as neighbors. Finally, sectarianism was measured in terms of intra- and intergroup trust differentials. Respondents were asked how much trust they have in the members of their own and other groups: (1) a great deal, (2) some, (3) not very much, or (4) none at all. Coding for this variable is reversed so that a higher value indicates a greater trust. It was calculated using this formula:

Ethnic sectarianism as trust differential for individual i in ethnicity e_1 = Trust in his/her ethnicity$_1$ – Mean (trust in ethnicity$_2$ + enthnicity$_3$ + . . .+ ethnicity$_n$)

Internet use: Internet use was measured by the extent to which respondents relied on it as a source of information: (1) a great deal, (2) some, (3) not very much, and (4) not at all. Coding for this variable is reversed so that a greater value indicates more reliance on the internet as the sources of information.

Fatalism: Respondents were asked to choose a number between 1 and 10, where 1 = "everything in life is determined by fate" and 10 = "people shape their fate themselves." Coding on this variable is reversed so that a greater number indicates stronger fatalism.

Findings: Correlates of Religious Fundamentalism and Liberal Values

Table 4.11 shows the correlation coefficients of the measures of demographics, religion, attitudes toward sex and morality, in-group solidarity and out-group hostility, internet use, and fatalism with the indices of religious fundamentalism and liberal values. There is a consistent pattern of opposing relationships between these predictors and the indices of religious fundamentalism and liberal values across the countries, except for gender and some minor deviations for some of the other measures. A higher socioeconomic status is negatively linked to religious fundamentalism and positively linked to liberal values across all the seven countries, except among Saudi respondents, where

TABLE 4.11 Correlation Coefficients for Religious Fundamentalism and Liberal Values at the Micro (Individual) Level

	Iraq		Lebanon		Pakistan		Saudi Arabia		Tunisia		Egypt		Turkey	
	Rel Fund[a]	Lib[b]	Rel Fund	Lib	Rel Fund	Lib	Rel Fund	Lib	Rel Fund	Lib	Rel Fund	Lib	Rel Fund	Lib
Demographics														
Socioeconomic status	-.146[c]	.184[c]	-.199[c]	.266[c]	-.246[c]	.372[c]	-.039	-.037	-.270[c]	.194[c]	-.179[c]	.189[c]	-.334[c]	.327[c]
Male	-.008	-.006	-.121[c]	-.065[c]	.005	-.114[c]	-.203[c]	.006	-.043[d]	-.086[c]	-.031	.075[c]	-.027	-.041[d]
Youth bulge	-.064[c]	.082[c]	-.062[c]	.139[c]	-.149[c]	.339[c]	-.078[c]	.135[c]	-.149[c]	.089[c]	-.023	.030	-.075[c]	.058[d]
Rural/Saudi Arabia: Smaller town	-.024	-.155[c]	.148[c]	-.094[c]	.137[c]	-.240[c]	-.205	.205	.007	-.001	.131[c]	-.077[c]	.182[c]	-.152[c]
Religion														
Religiosity	.230[c]	-.149[c]	.529[c]	-.426[c]	.361[c]	-.397[c]	.486[c]	-.266[c]	.209[c]	-.208[c]	.065[c]	-.125[c]	.329[c]	-.322[c]
Religious modernity	.386[c]	-.372[c]	.542[c]	-.432[c]	.392[c]	-.448[c]	.507[c]	-.367[c]	—	—	.180[c]	-.301[c]	.370[c]	-.348[c]
Confidence in religious institutions	.265[c]	-.395[c]	.338[c]	-.405[c]	.295[c]	-.460[c]	.211[c]	-.266[c]	.286[c]	-.273[c]	.103[c]	-.079[c]	.365[c]	-.397[c]
Attitudes toward sex and morality														
Mixing of the sexes corrupts	.133[c]	-.098[c]	.177[c]	-.256[c]	.247[c]	-.376[c]	-.024	-.101[c]	.200[c]	-.291[c]	.019	-.140[c]	.214[c]	-.345[c]
Premarital sex is immoral	.279[c]	-.149[c]	.405[c]	-.324[c]	.201[c]	-.215[c]	.231[c]	-.143[c]	.183[c]	-.159[c]	.051[d]	-.033	.157[c]	-.122[c]
In-group solidarity and out-group hostility														
Ethnic sectarianism	.181[c]	-.116[c]	.226[c]	-.222[c]	.248[c]	-.280[c]	—	—	—	—	—	—	.125[c]	-.146[c]
Conspiracy	.173[c]	-.016	.342[c]	-.374[c]	.300[c]	-.332[c]	.280[c]	-.258[c]	.082[c]	-.139[c]	.118[c]	-.089[c]	.200[c]	-.197[c]
Xenophobia	.082[c]	-.131[c]	.256[c]	-.272[c]	.241[c]	-.279[c]	—	—	.133[c]	-.030	.090[c]	-.061[c]	.147[c]	-.164[c]
Internet use														
Internet use	-.157[c]	.176[c]	-.179[c]	.276[c]	-.275[c]	.375[c]	-.129[c]	.065[c]	-.238[c]	.142[c]	-.141[c]	.122[c]	-.133[c]	.112[c]
Fatalism														
Fatalism	.251[c]	-.153[c]	.220[c]	-.227[c]	.233[c]	-.251[c]	-.050[d]	-.067[d]	.284[c]	-.169[c]	.101[c]	-.204[c]	.204[c]	-.231[c]

[a] Rel fund = Religious fundamentalism.
[b] Lib = Liberal values.
[c] $p < .001$.
[d] $p < .05$.

these relationships were not statistically significant. Those in the youth bulge were also less fundamentalist and more liberal, except in Egypt, where these relationships were not significant. Finally, respondents residing in rural areas, or smaller towns in the case of Saudi Arabia, were more strongly fundamentalist and less supportive of liberal values across the countries, except that rural residence had no significant relationship with religious fundamentalism among Iraqis and no significant relationship with either index among Tunisians. All religion-related variables—religiosity, religious modernity, and trust in religious institutions—are positively linked to fundamentalism and negatively linked to liberal values. The same was true concerning the mixing of the sexes and premarital sex, except that attitudes toward the mixing of the sexes had no significant link with religious fundamentalism among Saudis and Egyptians. All the variables related to in-group solidarity and out-group hostility were linked positively to religious fundamentalism and negatively to liberal values, except that liberal values and conspiracy among Iraqis and liberal values and xenophobia among Tunisians were not significantly linked. Internet use was consistently negatively linked to religious fundamentalism and positively linked to liberal values, but the opposite was the case with fatalism, except that Saudi fundamentalists were less fatalistic.

These findings thus support the hypothesis that the sociological factors that support religious fundamentalism weaken liberal values, and vice versa. Chapter 5 will show that the same is true on the macro (country) level; that is, pertinent features of the macro (country) context that strengthen aggregate religious fundamentalism on the national level weaken liberal values, and vice versa.

Summary

This chapter offered a distinctly religious definition of religious fundamentalism, without that definition resting on the specific beliefs of any religion. It conceptualized fundamentalism as a religious orientation or a set of beliefs about and attitudes toward whatever religious beliefs one has. It considered religious fundamentalism as a multidimensional construct, having four components: a disciplinarian conception of the deity, literalism, religious exclusivity, and religious intolerance. Four sets of survey items measured these components, and the average of these four components or sixteen items produced a religious fundamentalism index. The analysis showed that there is considerable variation in fundamentalism across the seven countries. However, the majority of the respondents from the seven countries tended to have fundamentalist orientations. Among the four components of religious fundamentalism, however, the religious intolerance component was much weaker than the other three—a disciplinarian deity, literalism, and religious exclusivity.

The findings also indicated that members of the youth bulge were less fundamentalist than the older age group, except among Egyptians. There were no gender differences in fundamentalism except among Lebanese, Saudi, and Tunisian respondents, where women were more fundamentalist than men. Also people with university education had significantly weaker fundamentalist beliefs and attitudes than did people without university education across all the countries, except Saudi Arabia, where there was no significant difference between the two educational groups. In terms of age and education, university education made a significant difference in religious fundamentalism among Egyptian, Lebanese, Pakistani, Tunisian, and Turkish respondents across both age groups and among Iraqis in the older age group and no difference among Saudi respondents across both age groups.

In terms of religions and religious sects, the pooled data showed that Christians were less fundamentalist than Shia or Sunni Muslims and that Shias were less fundamentalist than Sunnis. This finding was also true at the national context, with one exception concerning the Saudi Shias. Shias were consistently and significantly less fundamentalist than Sunnis across the samples from Iraq, Lebanon, Pakistan, Saudi Arabia, and Turkey; Christians in Egypt and Lebanon were less fundamentalist than their Muslim counterparts; and Lebanese Christians were significantly less fundamentalist than Egyptian Christians. The exception was that Saudi Shias scored the lowest on the religious fundamentalism index across religions and religious sects. The difference in religious fundamentalism between Saudi Shias and Lebanese Christians, however, is not statistically significant.

The analysis showed that religious fundamentalism and its four components were negatively correlated with three components of liberal values—expressive individualism, gender equality, and secular politics—across all seven countries. A comparative analysis of the respondents' orientations showed that the percentages of these respondents who favored religious fundamentalism were much higher than the percentages of those who favored liberal values across the seven countries, except among Lebanese, where support for the two opposing movements was about the same.

This analysis indicated the relative stand of the respondents on religious fundamentalism vis-à-vis liberal values, but to better understand how values might change toward liberalism, a more effective comparison was needed—that between support for religious intolerance and a measure of liberal values that was based on the average of the indices of gender equality and secular politics. The rationale was that the decline in religious fundamentalism is more likely to start with a decrease in support for religious intolerance and the shift toward liberal values is more likely to start with an increase in support for secular politics and gender equality. Adhering to this stipulation, these measures were recalculated, and variation in religious intolerance and liberal values (as the average of the indices of secular politics and gender equality) was assessed across the seven countries. The results showed that in Lebanon, Tunisia, and Turkey, there was significantly more support for liberal values than there was for religious intolerance. In the other four countries, those who favored liberal values varied between 7 percent among Saudis and 27 percent among Iraqis, while those who were religiously intolerant varied between 78 percent among Saudis and 51 percent among Iraqis.

Finally, this chapter showed that the individual attitudes and attributes that were positively linked to religious fundamentalism were negatively connected to liberal values, and vice versa. Religious fundamentalism was weaker and liberal values stronger among individuals who (1) had a higher socioeconomic status, (2) were younger, (3) lived in urban areas, (4) were less religious, (5) had weaker trust in religious institutions, (6) believed less strongly in religious modernity, (7) gave lower ratings to the immorality of premarital sex, (8) disagreed more strongly that the mixing of the sexes in the workplace would cause corruption, (9) believed less strongly in conspiracy theory, (10) were less xenophobic, (11) had weaker sectarian solidarity, (12) were less fatalistic, and (13) relied more strongly on the internet as the source of information.

CHAPTER 5

MACRO-CONTEXTUAL (COUNTRY) VARIATION IN RELIGIOUS FUNDAMENTALISM AND LIBERAL VALUES

I have argued in the preceding chapters that the ideological warfare for the cultural control of society in the Middle East and North Africa has been persistently focused on a set of historically significant issues. These issues, which have remained remarkably invariant in the contemporary period, are the autonomy of the individual, social status of women, role and function of religion in society, relationship between religion and politics, form of government, basis of the identity of one's community, and nature of the outside world (other countries or religions). Under the current conditions, only two dominant and opposing ideological movements are competing to resolve these issues in the region. One is supported by the enthusiasts of religious fundamentalism and the other by the advocates of liberal values. In each of the seven countries, orientations toward fundamentalism and liberal values were shown to be inversely linked. Individuals who were more strongly fundamentalist were less liberal.

As discussed in chapter 4, variation in religious fundamentalism and liberal values among individuals was linked to variation in the social attributes, attitudes, and perceptions of these individuals, and the individual characteristics that were positively associated with fundamentalism were negatively connected to liberal values. This chapter shows that these relationships are also true on the macro (country) level; that is, cross-national variation in aggregate Islamic fundamentalism is inversely related to variation in aggregate support for liberal values, variation in both Islamic fundamentalism and liberal values is connected to differences in the characteristics of the national contexts of the seven countries, and the characteristics of the national context that strengthen fundamentalism weaken liberal values. To demonstrate these relationships, this chapter first draws on the extant scholarly literature on the relationship between the national context and human values. Then it specifies and measures the pertinent characteristics of the national context. Finally, it proposes and empirically assesses several hypotheses on the relationships of these characteristics with Islamic fundamentalism and liberal values.

Religious Fundamentalism and Liberal Values on the Country Level

The indices of religious fundamentalism and the components of liberal values were discussed in chapters 1 through 4 and were shown to vary considerably across the seven countries. The aggregate values of these variables for each of the seven countries are reproduced in table 5.1.

As shown in table 5.1, the values of the index of religious fundamentalism are significantly higher than those of the index of liberal values across the seven countries, indicating that the respondents expressed stronger support for religious fundamentalism than for liberal values. The magnitudes of the differences between the two indices, however, vary cross-nationally: 3.42 for fundamentalism versus 1.93 for liberal values for Pakistan, 3.44 versus 2.04 for Egypt, 3.33 versus 2.08 for Saudi Arabia, 3.28 versus 2.21 for Iraq, 3.18 versus 2.52 for Tunisia, 2.98 versus 2.68 for Turkey, and 2.80 versus 2.74 for Lebanon.

TABLE 5.1 Means of Indices of Religious Fundamentalism and Liberal Values and its Components

	Pakistan	Egypt	Saudi Arabia	Iraq	Tunisia	Turkey	Lebanon
Religious fundamentalism	3.42	3.44	3.33	3.28	3.18	2.98	2.80
Expressive individualism	1.61	1.76	2.31	1.89	2.24	2.46	2.68
Gender equality	2.22	2.07	2.06	2.22	2.49	2.73	2.58
Secular politics	1.97	2.29	1.86	2.53	2.81	2.86	2.96
Liberal values	1.93	2.04	2.08	2.21	2.52	2.68	2.74
Difference between religious fundamentalism and liberal values	1.49	1.40	1.25	1.07	0.66	0.30	0.06

TABLE 5.2 Correlation Coefficients for Indices of Religious Fundamentalism and Liberal Values and its Components

	Religious Fundamentalism	Expressive Individualism	Gender Equality	Secular Politics	Liberal Values
Religious fundamentalism	1.00	—	—	—	—
Expressive individualism	-.89[d]	1.00	—	—	—
Gender equality	-.87[d]	.68[b]	1.00	—	—
Secular politics	-.82[c]	.62[a]	.86[d]	1.00	—
Liberal values	-.95[d]	.86[c]	.92[d]	.92[d]	1.00

[a] $p < .1$.
[b] $p < .05$.
[c] $p < .01$.
[d] $p < .001$.

The differences between religious fundamentalism and liberal values are much smaller for Lebanon (0.06), Turkey (0.30), and Tunisia (0.66) than for Iraq (1.07), Saudi Arabia (1.25), Egypt (1.40), and Pakistan (1.49).

The correlation coefficients for the aggregate religious fundamentalism index and the aggregate indices of expressive individualism, gender equality, secular politics, and liberal values at the macro (country) level are significant and negative, as shown in table 5.2. The religious fundamentalism index is negatively linked to the indices of expressive individualism ($r = -.89$), gender equality ($r = -.87$), secular politics ($r = -.82$), and liberal values ($r = -.95$). These inverse relationships on the aggregate level indicate that, where religious fundamentalism is stronger, there is weaker support for liberal values. Evidently, as these and the findings reported in chapter 4 indicate, in the same way that individuals with stronger fundamentalist beliefs and attitudes tend to express weaker support for liberal values, countries that on average scored higher on religious fundamentalism also scored lower on liberal values.

Explaining Macro Variation

Chapter 4 showed that the micro (individual) variations in religious fundamentalism and liberal values had opposing relationships with demographics (socioeconomic status, age, and urban-rural residence), religion (religiosity, confidence in religious institutions, and religious modernity), in-group solidarity and out-group hostility (sectarianism, conspiracy, and xenophobia), internet use, and fatalism. The previous chapters also showed that religious fundamentalism and liberal values varied on the macro (country) level and that the countries with younger populations scored higher on the aggregate religious fundamentalism index and lower on the aggregate liberal values index. This chapter further assesses the significance of the factors that are linked to macro- or country-level variation in people's fundamentalist and liberal orientations, in an effort to explain the variation in both indices in terms of such variable features of the national context as the structure of the religious environment, state structures and interventions, economic development, globalization, and the situation of women. Finally, it is argued that, similar to the micro factors, these macro factors have opposing relationships with aggregate religious fundamentalism and aggregate liberal values; that is, cross-nationally, the factors that strengthen religious fundamentalism weaken liberal values, and vice versa.

Structure of the Religious Environment

The structure of religious environment—whether it is monolithic or pluralistic and whether it supports religious authoritarianism or religious liberty—shapes conditions in ways that are more favorable either to the rise of Islamic fundamentalism or, alternatively, to that of religious modernism and liberal values. A pluralistic context that includes both secular and religious options for seekers of spirituality weakens religious fundamentalism but strengthens religious modernism and liberal values. Such a context is likely to offer a richer menu of options to satisfy a wider range of spiritual needs than a monolithic context (Montgomery 2003). As a result, fewer "spiritual shoppers" (Wuthnow 2005) would be willing to develop a monolithic view of religion and adopt religious fundamentalism. Furthermore, a pluralistic context exposes the public to a greater number of perspectives on life, security, and happiness, reinforcing views concerning the varied ways that metaphysical entities, supernatural beings, or gods may be worshipped (Berger and Luckman 1969). People are thus less likely to follow a disciplinarian deity, accept a literal reading of the scriptures, and adopt an exclusivist and intolerant view of religion and are more likely to support religious modernism and liberal values. Religious monopolies, on the other hand, contribute to religious fundamentalism through mobilizing resources, sanctioning religious behavior, punishing religious nonobservance, and exploiting sectarian rivalries (Handy 1991; Breault 1989; Blau, Land, and Redding 1992; Blau, Redding, and Land 1993; Ellison and Sherkat 1995). In certain contexts, like postrevolutionary Iran, religious monopolies may prompt the rise of liberal oppositional discourse.

The contrast between the historical conditions that promoted the rise of Islamic modernism and those that promoted the rise of religious fundamentalism supports this proposition—namely, Islamic modernism emerged under a condition of religious pluralism, while religious fundamentalism emerged under a monolithic cultural-cum-religious condition. Modernism and fundamentalism constituted two opposing responses to the intellectual problems Islam faced in the modern period. Muslim intellectual leaders produced a modernist discourse in Islam—most notably, in Egypt and India—in the second half of the nineteenth century because they encountered a plurality of discourses advanced by the followers of the Enlightenment, Westernizers, think tanks connected to the colonial administrations, missionaries, and the *ulama* (Muslim theologians). All these groups were competing for intellectual control of the society, while state intervention in culture was limited. Encountering a multitude of diverse challenges to their faith, these intellectuals tried to formulate a moderate transcendental discourse that bridged Islam with the ideology of the Enlightenment. Their twentieth-century counterparts turned fundamentalist in Algeria, Egypt, Iran, and Syria because they chiefly faced a monolithic discourse imposed from above by the authoritarian secular ideological state (Moaddel 2005).

An important mechanism that may explain the development of Islamic modernism is the presence of a discursive space in the Islamic orthodoxy that enabled Muslim reformers to recognize and pinpoint the location of the problematic elements in Islamic religious and political perspectives. These problematic elements in the Islamic orthodoxy consisted of (1) the constraint placed on reason (the closing of the gate of independent reasoning) and (2) the recognition of the sultan's discretionary power. The modernists had to reject both elements in order to be able to bring Islam closer to the sociopolitical perspective of the eighteenth-century Enlightenment and advance their rationalist exegesis of the scriptures. The rise of Islamic fundamentalism, on the other hand, was a result of the narrowing of the discursive space in the Islamic system of thought. The secular authoritarian state was thought to be the problematic element that had to be overthrown. Such a political context favored those Muslim activists who were advancing the notion of a religious despot—the *faqih* or caliph in Shia or Sunni fundamentalism, respectively—to combat the secular state and unconditionally execute God's instructions on Earth. These activists found that Islam was a perfect system of universal truth and glossed over the religion's theoretical inadequacies underpinning the remarkable failures of the caliphates in historical Islam to establish a transparent and effective system of rules. This chapter thus proposes that, across the seven countries, higher levels of support for liberal values or a lower level of support for religious fundamentalism is connected to higher levels of religious pluralism and religious freedom or weaker levels of religious monopolies.

State Structures and Interventions

The premise that state structures shape religious outcomes has a long pedigree in the sociology of religion. For example, Swanson (1967) links the success of Protestantism in sixteenth-century Europe to variations in the structures of political sovereignty, relating the varying conceptions of immanence in Protestantism and Catholicism to the manner in which political sovereignty was experienced in various parts of Europe. Wuthnow (1985), as an alternative, relates the victory of the Reformation movement in England and its failure in France in the sixteenth century to the British state's autonomy from the country's landed aristocracy and the French state's lack of such autonomy in this period.

Consistent with these arguments, this chapter relates variable features of the state to variations in people's orientations toward religious fundamentalism and liberal values. The pertinent features specified in this chapter, however, are different from those mentioned by Swanson (1967) and Wuthnow (1985). Two features are proposed here for a better understanding of the relationships between regimes and religious fundamentalism, on the one hand, and liberal values, on the other. One is the state's intervention in religious affairs, the extent to which it attempts to regulate religious institutions and their activities. Religious fundamentalism may arise as a reaction to such interventions. This may occur in several ways. First, by launching cultural programs to promote secular institutions, fostering national identity as a substitute for religious identity, and instituting laws that run contrary to religious beliefs, the secular authoritarian state may contribute to the perception among the faithful that their religion is under siege, their core values are offended, and their religious liberty is obstructed. This perception of *besieged spirituality* may activate religious awareness that prompts individuals to grow "hypersensitive even to the slightest hint of theological corruption within their own ranks" (Smith 1998, 8), use religious categories to frame issues, and adopt alarmist attitudes and conspiratorial perspectives (Moaddel and Karabenick 2013). At the same time, the authoritarian nature of the secular state may weaken liberal values as its policies of disorganizing and disrupting collectivities in civil society may channel oppositional politics through the medium of religion (Stepan 1985; Moaddel 1993). Finally, a religious authoritarian state by courting religious activists and groups in order to fend off challenges from secular and liberal currents may inadvertently contribute to the resources and societal influences of religious fundamentalist movements.

The other pertinent feature is the structure of the authoritarian state. It is argued here that the structure of power relations *within* the state is consequential for the formation of oppositional politics. Insofar as this power structure is unified, pluralism would decline and fundamentalism would be strengthened. Under a unified elite, an authoritarian state would be more effective in imposing a monolithic religion or culture on the subject population. Therefore, a limited number of secular or alternative religious options would be available for the seekers of spirituality. An authoritarian state that is controlled by a fragmented elite, on the other hand, tends to experience inter-elite rivalries and acrimonious debates. Such internal disputes would not only diminish the state's ability to impose religious uniformity on society but also generate a political–cum–discursive space that permits the growth of alternative religious and/or secular liberal groups (Moaddel and Karabenick 2013).

An authoritarian state with a unified structure would strengthen fundamentalism, while a fragmented authoritarian state would tend to strengthen liberalism. The Islamic Republic of Iran and the Kingdom of Saudi Arabia provide contrasting examples. While both regimes are remarkably similar in religious sectarianism, repressiveness, and rentierism (i.e., oil is the major source of revenue), the ruling elite is fragmented in Iran but unified in Saudi Arabia. The rise of liberalism and religious reformism in postrevolutionary Iran (Rajaee 2007; Kamrava 2008; Moaddel 2009) and fundamentalism in Saudi Arabia (Dekmejian 1994; Okruhlik 2002; Moaddel 2006, Moaddel 2016) appears to correspond to the difference in the structure of power relations between the two repressive religious regimes.

Economic Development

The modernization theory relates cross-national variation in values to the level of economic development (Rostow 1960; Deutsch 1961; Parsons 1964; Levy 1966; Apter 1965; Huntington 1968). It is, however, hard to establish a determinate relationship between a specific type of economic development (e.g., the development of capitalism) and changes in values in a particular direction (e.g., the rise of liberal democracy). Inglehart has tried to further elaborate the relationship between economic development and changes in values by suggesting specific links or mechanisms that mediate this relationship. He posits, first, that economic development brings about economic prosperity and the latter in turn satisfies the needs for physical survival, enhancing the feeling of security. The enhanced feeling of security in turn contributes to the subjective context necessary for a shift from materialist values to self-expressive and esthetic values. Second, this shift occurs primarily among those who are in their impressionable years (those under age 25). Therefore, as the younger generations grow older, a major shift toward postmaterialism occurs in the overall societal value structure (Inglehart 1971; Inglehart and Welzel 2005).

A fuller assessment of the modernization theory requires longitudinal data. Here, nonetheless, cross-national data are used in order to assess whether variation in the level of economic development across the seven countries is linked to variation in the aggregate indices of religious fundamentalism and liberal values.

Globalization

Two diverse hypotheses may be advanced to test the relationship between globalization and cultural change in the direction of religious fundamentalism or liberal values in the Middle East and North Africa. The first relates globalization to diversification of culture, which weakens religious fundamentalism and strengthens liberal values. Accordingly, the development of digital communication technology and the expansion of the means of mass transportation reduce the constraints of geography on social interactions (Waters 1995), intensifying "worldwide social relations" (Giddens 1990, 64) and widening intercontinental networks of economic, political, and cultural interdependence among nations (Keohane and Nye 2000; Frankel 2000; Sassen 2001). These developments help globalize economic activities and enhance diffusion and absorption of cultures. Globalization in turn facilitates access to diverse information sources, undermines cultural control by the ruling elite, weakens religious monopolies, and thus narrows the social basis of religious fundamentalism and strengthens liberal values.

The alternative hypothesis posits that globalization, by reducing the constraints of geography and enhancing intercultural contact, intensifies the clash of civilizations (Huntington 1996a). At the same time, globalization heightens efforts to eliminate barriers to the expansion of the world markets, to facilitate the employment of similar organizational structures (Stohl 2005), and to enforce a homogeneous cultural pattern popularly known as the McDonaldization of society (Ritzer 1993). Such policies in turn tend to cause the breakdown of the protective shields of small traditional communities, generating feelings of alienation and insecurity (Giddens 1991; Kinnvall 2004). Finally, globalization is said to expand inequality through the peripheralization of less developed countries as a result of the incorporation of their indigenous economies into the global capitalist system with its hierarchy of asymmetrical exchange relations (Wallerstein 2000). The increased economic inequality intensifies social tensions and class conflict, generating a basis for the rise of alternative cultural movements to resist worldwide capitalist expansion. Reflecting this process is the increase in support for Islamic fundamentalism and the concomitant weakening of support for liberal values.

Situation of Women

Finally, an important feature of the pertinent social conditions that may shape fundamentalism and liberal values is related to the situation of women in society. This section proposes that the strength of religious fundamentalism is inversely linked to female empowerment. In a national context where women are free to pursue their interests in various domains of social life, liberal values are stronger and fundamentalist attitudes weaker. A crucial factor that may have a strong effect on women's empowerment is their labor force participation. Female employment outside the home is associated with, but not necessarily reducible to, the level of economic development. Through labor force participation, women earn an income and thus gain financial autonomy, contributing to their overall ability to articulate interests. This ability enables them to overcome more effectively the limitations that are imposed on them by patriarchal institutions. Furthermore, increased female participation in the labor force entails more frequent interaction with men, which may lead to the formation of a more flexible outlook on gender equality. Thus, it is proposed that liberal values are stronger and support for religious fundamentalism weaker in countries where a larger proportion of women participate in the labor force outside the home.

It has also been suggested that sex ratio (the number of males per one hundred females in a society) is another macro structural factor that shapes gender relations and attitudes toward gender equality. According to Guttentag and Secord (1983), imbalanced sex ratios have consequences for gender relations: when men are in short supply, more opportunities are available to them to form dyadic relationships with women, resulting in men having more power over women. The social consequence of this imbalance may cause men to be promiscuous, weakly committed to monogamy, and less dependable as partners. At the same time, the traditional gender role for women is less valued; women have greater freedom to engage in nontraditional types of activities and have fewer restrictions imposed on their movements, so they are able to travel and to dress in public as they wish. Where women are in short supply, on the other hand, they have dyadic power over men. Yet in this case, their ability to use this power is constrained by the fact that men have structural power through control of "the political, economic and legal structures of the society" (Guttentag and Secord 1983, 26; see also South and Trent 1988). Men use their structural power to shape the social norms and practices in their favor, thereby effectively blocking women from using their dyadic power to promote their interests. In this situation, although women are valued greatly and protected, their traditional gender role is strengthened to the point where extrafamilial social functions become quite limited. Because women are in short supply, as the theory implies, they are expected to stay away from the gaze of other men. Forcing women to stay home, imposing gender segregation at work and other social gatherings, and implementing conservative public dress codes for women thus serve to discourage such male behavior.

Therefore, the higher the sex ratio in a country, the stronger the support for religious fundamentalism and the weaker the support for liberal values.

Measurement

To summarize, on the macro (country) level, religious fundamentalism and liberal values are shaped by the structure of the religious environment, state structures and interventions, economic development, globalization, and the situation of women. These constructs are measured in order to assess the strength of their relationships with the aggregate indices of religious fundamentalism and liberal values across the seven countries.

Structure of the Religious Environment

Two indicators are used to measure whether the structure of the religious environment is pluralistic or monolithic. One is a *religious liberty index*. It is constructed as the average of the indices of religious freedom (varies between 1 = high and 7 = low) and religious persecution (varies between 1 = religious freedom and no religious persecution and 10 = no religious freedom and high levels of religious persecution), which are reported by the Association of Religious Data Archives. The religious freedom index has been recoded so that higher values indicate greater religious freedom and less religious persecution.[1] The other indicator is a measure of *religious fractionalization* constructed from the sample data reported in table 5.3. This measure uses the religious fractionalization formula:

$$Religious\ fractionalization\ index = 1 - \sum p_i^2$$

In this formula, pi is the proportion of a religion or religious sect i (i = 1, 2, 3 . . ., n) in the sample (see table 5.3). Using the data in table 5.3, the religious fractionalization index for Saudi Arabia is equal to $1 - (0.92^2 + 0.08^2) = 0.15$. A higher value indicates a higher level of religious diversity.[2]

State Structures and Interventions

Three features of the state are measured. The first is the authoritarian structure of the state, which is measured by *political exclusion*. It indicates the degree

TABLE 5.3 Respondents' Religious Affiliations

	Pakistan	Egypt	Saudi Arabia	Iraq	Lebanon	Tunisia	Turkey
Sunni	82%	96%	92%	44%	23%	99%	82%
Shia	7%	—	8%	42%	33%	—	2%
Alavi	—	—	—	—	—	—	4%
Muslim (no sect specified)[a]	8%	—	—	13%	3%	—	7%
Druze	—	—	—	—	6%	—	—
Christian	1%	4%	—	0.4%	1%	—	—
Roman Catholic	—	—	—	—	6%	—	—
Maronite	—	—	—	—	13%	—	—
Greek Orthodox	—	—	—	—	7%	—	—
Other/none	—	—	—	—	2.4%	—	5%
Religious fractionalization index	0.18	0.08	0.15	0.50	0.79	0.02	0.20

[a]This row was excluded and the percentages were recalculated before computing the religious fractionalization index.

of openness of the political system and political freedom by averaging the extent of political rights and civil liberties in a country, ranging from 1 (free) to 7 (unfree).[3] Political exclusion is measured in 2010 for Egypt, Iraq, Lebanon, Pakistan, and Saudi Arabia—with a one-year lag of the dependent variable or the data collection in these countries in 2011—and in 2012 for Tunisian and Turkey—again with a one-year lag of data collection in these countries in 2013. GRRI was available for 2003 and ranges between 0 (no regulation) and 10 (high regulation). The second is state intervention in religious affairs. This construct is measured by the *Government Regulation of Religion Index* (GRRI), which is reported by the Association of Religion Data Archives.[4]

The third is the degree of fragmentation of the state's power structures. It is measured by a *fragmentation ratio*, which is the square root of a measure of the fractionalized elite[5] divided by the political and civil liberties index.[6]

$$Fragmentation\ Ratio = \frac{\sqrt{Fractionalized\ Elite}}{Political\ Rights\ \&\ Civil\ Liberties\ Index}$$

Economic Development and Situation of Women

Economic development is measured as *GDP per capita*. The situation of women involves two factors. The first, *female labor force participation*, is measured as the number of females in the labor force divided by the female population aged 15 and older, indicated as a percentage. Second, *sex ratio* is measured as the percentage of the population that is male.

Globalization

Two measures of globalization are used. One is *economic globalization*,[7] which is a linear combination of two standardized indicators: (1) international trade, the sum of imports and exports as a percentage of GDP, and (2) foreign capital penetration (FCP), which is measured as

$$FCP = \frac{Foreign\ Direct\ Investment}{\sqrt{(Domestic\ Capital\ Sock * Size\ of\ Labor\ Force)}}$$

Foreign direct investment is the net inflow of investment to acquire a lasting management interest (10 percent or more of voting stock) in an enterprise operating in an economy other than that of the investor. It is the sum of equity capital, reinvestment of earnings, and other long-term and short-term capital as shown in the balance of payments. The other measure, which may be called *cultural globalization*, measures internet penetration by determining the percentage of the population that has access to the internet.

To make the two measures more stable, three-year averages of the data on trade, foreign capital penetration, and internet access were calculated where such data were available for 2009–2011 and 2010–2012, depending on whether data collection for the country was completed in 2011 or 2013, respectively.

Hypotheses

Based on the analytical framework and these measures, support for religious fundamentalism would be stronger and support for liberal values weaker in countries characterized by

1. Weaker religious liberty and lower fractionalization;
2. Lower state fragmentation ratio, higher political exclusion, and higher government regulation of religion;
3. Lower level of economic development;
4. Weaker economic and cultural globalization; and
5. Lower female labor force participation and higher sex ratio.

Analysis and Findings

Table 5.4 reports measures of the five categories of variables used in the analysis: religious environment (religious liberty and religious fractionalization), state structures and interventions (political exclusion, fractionalization ratio, and government regulation of religion), economic development (GDP per capita), globalization (economic globalization and cultural globalization or internet penetration), and situation of women (female labor force participation and sex ratio) for the seven countries. The religious environment varies across the seven countries. Lebanon scored highest on religious liberty (7), followed by Turkey (6), Tunisia (5.5), and Saudi Arabia (4.5), Egypt and Pakistan (4 each), and Iraq (1.5). Lebanon is the most fractionalized country (0.76 where the maximum is 1), followed by Iraq (0.50), Turkey (0.20), Pakistan (0.18), Saudi Arabia (0.15), Egypt (0.08), and Tunisia (0.02). Measures of state structures and interventions also vary considerably; political exclusion varies

TABLE 5.4 Characteristics of National Context

	Pakistan	Egypt	Saudi Arabia	Iraq	Tunisia	Turkey	Lebanon
1. Religious environment							
a. Religious liberty	4	4	4.50	1.5	5.5	6	7
b. Religious fractionalization	0.18	0.08	0.15	0.50	0.02	0.20	0.76
2. State structures and interventions							
a. Political exclusion	4.5	5.5	6.5	5.5	3.5	3	4
b. Government regulation of religion	8.8	8.3	9.8	6	6.2	5.2	4.9
c. Fragmentation ratio	0.34	0.26	0.21	0.28	0.35	0.47	0.37
3. Economic development							
a. GDP per capita ($)	4,197	9,163	44,502	12,460	10,596	20,640	15,952
4. Globalization							
a. Economic globalization (standardized)	−2.37	−1.56	1.22	−0.76	0.47	−1.23	2.67
i. International trade ($)	32.67	49.67	84.67	73.67	102.67	54.33	97
ii. Foreign capital penetration	1.43	4.23	22.56	4	5.32	5.93	34.38
b. Cultural globalization: Internet	8.17	22.4	42.17	2.87	39.1	42.67	41.93
5. Situation of women							
a. Female labor force participation	21%	24%	14%	17%	27%	29%	23%
b. Sex ratio	107	103	118	102	101	102	96

between 3.0 (Turkey) and 6.5 (Saudi Arabia), the fragmentation ratio between 0.21 (Saudi Arabia) and 0.47 (Turkey), and government regulation of religion between 4.9 (Lebanon) and 9.8 (Saudi Arabia).

GDP per capita is highest in Saudi Arabia (44,502) mostly due to its rentier economy, and lowest in Pakistan (4,197). The standardized measure[8] of economic globalization fluctuates between −2.37 for Pakistan and 2.67 for Lebanon, and cultural globalization or internet use varies between 42.17 for Saudi Arabia and 2.87 for Iraq. Female labor force participation is highest in Turkey (29 percent) and lowest in Saudi Arabia (14 percent). Finally, the sex ratio is lowest for Lebanon (0.96), indicating that there are more females in the country than males, and highest for Saudi Arabia (1.18). A sex ratio of 1.18 is quite high, indicating that there are many more men in Saudi society than there are women.

Relationship of the National Context to Religious Fundamentalism and Liberal Values

The correlation coefficients measuring the strength of the association of the ten indicators for the five different features of the national context with the indices of religious fundamentalism and liberal values are reported in table 5.5. Most of these coefficients are statistically significant and in the expected directions. That is, the features of the national context that have negative effects on religious fundamentalism are positively linked to the indices of liberal values and its components, and those features that have positive effects on religious fundamentalism are negatively linked to the indices of liberal values and its components. However, there are some notable exceptions to the significance of these linkages.

Structure of the Religious Environment
Two indicators measure the structure of the religious environment. One is the religious liberty index, and the other is religious fractionalization index. Religious liberty is significantly inversely linked to religious fundamentalism ($r = -.72$). That is, the higher the level of religious liberty in a country, the weaker the support for religious fundamentalism. Religious liberty thus weakens the concept of an authoritarian deity, literalism, exclusivity, and intolerance. Religious liberty, on the other hand, is directly connected to the indices of expressive individualism, gender equality, secular politics, and liberal values ($r = .75, .69, .49,$ and $.71$, respectively), although its link to secular politics is not statistically significant. These relationships thus indicate that the stronger the conditions of religious liberty (meaning higher levels of religious freedom and

TABLE 5.5 Correlation Coefficients for Indices of Religious Fundamentalism and Liberal Values and Macro- or Country-level Variables

	Religious Fundamentalism	Expressive Individualism	Gender Equality	Secular Politics	Liberal Values
1. Religious environment					
a. Religious liberty	−.72[b]	.75[b]	.69[b]	.49	.71[b]
b. Religious fractionalization	−.64[a]	.43	.30	.43	.44
2. State structures and interventions					
a. Political exclusion	.63[a]	−.38	−.92[e]	−.76[c]	−.74[c]
b. Government regulation of religion	.82[b]	−.55[a]	−.85[d]	−.97[e]	−.88[d]
c. Fragmentation ratio	−.67[b]	.41	.93[e]	.71[b]	.72[b]
3. Economic development					
a. GDP per capita	−.09	.50	−.16	−.31	−.01
4. Globalization					
a. Economic globalization	−.64[a]	.81[c]	.25	.36	.55 [a]
b. Cultural globalization: Internet	−.61[a]	.85[d]	.50	.37	.65[a]
5. Situation of women					
a. Female labor force participation	−.43	.24	.74[b]	.69[b]	.60[a]
b. Sex ratio	.59[a]	−.22	−.64[a]	−.86[d]	−.64[a]

[a] $p < 0.1$.
[b] $p < 0.05$.
[c] $p < 0.025$.
[d] $p < 0.01$.
[e] $p < 0.001$.

fewer cases of religious persecution), the stronger people's attitudes in support of expressive individualism and gender equality.

The religious fractionalization index, measuring the extent to which a country's religious profile is segmented and divided into different religions and religious sects, tends to weaken religious fundamentalism ($r = −.64$) but has no significant effect on liberal values (although these relationships are in the expected direction).

State Structures and Interventions

The three measures of state structures and interventions reflect different attributes of the state. The first two indicators, the state's political exclusion and regulation of religion, are positively linked to religious fundamentalism ($r = .63$ and .82, respectively). These linkages are thus consistent with the hypotheses that an exclusivist state tends to channel oppositional politics through religion and that government interventions in religious affairs politicize religion, contributing to the rise of religious fundamentalism. Political exclusion, as expected, is inversely linked to the indices of gender equality, secular politics, and liberal values. The correlation coefficients between political exclusion and these indices are significant and negative ($r = -.92$, $-.76$, and $-.74$, respectively). Government regulation of religion is negatively correlated with all the four indices of expressive individualism, gender equality, secular politics, and liberal values ($r = -.55$, $-.85$, $-.97$, and $-.88$, respectively). Judged by the size of the correlation coefficients, it appears that government regulation of religion, which is apparently specifically targets religion, is generally a better predictor of religious fundamentalism and liberal values than is political exclusion, which is a more general state attribute.

Finally, the third indicator, the fragmentation ratio measures the authoritarian state's ability to regulate and control the civil society. A high value for the fragmentation ratio means that, while the authoritarian state has the resources—the technology, finances, and manpower—to repress the opposition within the civil society (that is, it has the *capacity*), it may not have the *ability* to actually repress the opposition. It faces difficulties in identifying, locating, and repressing members of the opposition. These difficulties are the result of the opposition having a diffused presence. Opposition is a matter of degree, ranging from individuals who support the state somewhat to those who are totally against it. In other words, politically active individuals or currents in civil society partly oppose the state and partly support it. In fact, the fragmentation of the state structure corresponds to and encourages gradations of support and opposition within the society. The outcome is a diminished repressive capability of the state.

The findings support this proposition. The fragmentation ratio, as a measure of the state's fragmented power structure, is negatively linked to the index of religious fundamentalism ($r = -.67$). Therefore, it weakens fundamentalist beliefs and attitudes. It is, on the other hand, positively linked to the indices of gender equality, secular politics, and liberal values ($r = .93$, $.71$, and $.72$, respectively). It therefore constitutes a favorable political context where attitudes toward gender equality, secular politics, and liberal values are strengthened. The ratio, however, has no significant relationship with the index of expressive individualism. Judging by the size of its correlation coefficients with the indices of fundamentalism and liberal values, the fragmentation ratio has a stronger effect in promoting liberal values than in weakening fundamentalism.

In sum, the fragmentation of the state power structure provides a political context favorable to liberal values and unfavorable to religious fundamentalism, while political exclusion and government regulation of religion generate a context that has the opposite effects, weakening liberal values and strengthening religious fundamentalism.

Economic Development

GDP per capita as a measure of the level of economic development appears to have no significant link with religious fundamentalism or any of the components of liberal values. Closer scrutiny, however, shows that the reason GDP per capita has no effect is that Saudi Arabia is an outlier. The kingdom had by far the highest GDP per capita among the seven countries. At the same time, Saudis were least supportive of liberal values and strongly supportive of religious fundamentalism. These attributes, which are the opposite of what developmental theories of social change predict, significantly lower the value of the correlation coefficient, rendering it statistically insignificant.

However, GDP per capita is a crude measure of economic development and in some cases does not adequately capture the operational meaning of the concept of development. Economic development is a multifaceted, self-propelled, and autonomous process of change in various aspects of the national economy. The Saudi economy, although it has undergone remarkable transformation since the founding of the kingdom in 1932, does not quite conform to this conception of economic development. The country is the archetype of a rentier economy, where economic growth is a function of the amount of petroleum the kingdom sells on the international market. This growth hardly produces the types of change that the autonomous process of economic development tends to bring about in social structures—including the emergence of industrial workers who form a basis for the rise of labor unions, female labor force participation, and the rise of a professional class working in the research-and-development departments of different industries. These changes are expected to support changes in values. Without such changes, the basis for the development of modern values would be quite weak (Beblawi and Luciani 1987; Mahdavy 1970).

Therefore, if Saudi Arabia is excluded and the coefficients recalculated, the values of the correlation coefficients are significantly increased, showing that economic development is negatively linked to the religious fundamentalism index (r −.81, not shown in table 5.5) and positively linked to the indices of expressive individualism, gender equality, secular politics, and liberal values ($r = .84, .73, .87,$ and $.85$, respectively, not shown in table 5.5).

Globalization

The two measures of globalization—economic and cultural globalization—are variably linked to religious fundamentalism and liberal values. Economic globalization is negatively linked to religious fundamentalism ($r = -.64$), indicating economic globalization weakens religious fundamentalism. Economic globalization is positively linked only to expressive individualism ($r = .81$) and liberal values (r = .55), but has no significant link with the indices of gender equality and secular politics. Again, economic globalization's weak relationship with religious fundamentalism and its lack of a significant relationship with the indices of gender equality and secular politics may be the result of Saudi Arabia being the outlier. If Saudi Arabia is excluded from the equation, then the values of the correlation coefficients between economic globalization and religious fundamentalism, expressive individualism, secular politics, and liberal values significantly increase (r −.80, .78, and .75, respectively, not shown in table 5.5). Still, the relationship between globalization and gender equality remains insignificant.

Likewise, the use of the internet, as an indicator of cultural globalization, is linked negatively to religious fundamentalism (r = −.61) and positively to expressive individualism and liberal values (r = .85 and .65, respectively), although having no significant linkages with the indices of secular politics and gender equality. Again, if Saudi Arabia is excluded, the values of the correlation coefficients between internet use and religious fundamentalism, expressive individualism, gender equality, secular politics, and liberal values significantly increase (r −.76, .86, .81, .79, and .85, respectively, not shown in table 5.5). In sum, the enhanced international system of communication and information flow weakens religious fundamentalism and strengthens liberal values.

Alternatively, Saudi Arabia may lend credence to the view that globalization reflects a multidimensional or even contradictory process, indicating how globalization promotes conservatism and fundamentalist religious discourses. Saudi conservative religious institutions have in fact benefited by globalization as it enables them to engage in worldwide promotion of Wahhabi version of Islam, a distinctive style of mosques, and its own vestimentary form—Saudis as an exporter of its own Islamic culture.

Situation of Women

Contrary to our expectation, the first factor, female labor force participation, has no significant link to the index of religious fundamentalism. It is, however, positively linked to the indices of gender equality, secular politics, and liberal values (r = .74, .69, and .60, respectively). Thus, when the percentage of women who are active in the labor force is higher in a country, support for liberal values is stronger in that country.

However, the second factor, sex ratio, is positively correlated with the religious fundamentalism index and negatively correlated with the indices of gender equality, secular politics, and liberal values, as shown in table 5.5 (r = .59, −.64, −.86, and −.64, respectively). These findings thus support the argument that the more a society's sex ratio is unbalanced in favor of men (i.e., a higher sex ratio), the stronger the patriarchal institutions and religious fundamentalism are, and the weaker the social support for liberal values is. Neither of these structural variables is significantly linked to the index of expressive individualism.

Summary

This chapter focused on variation in Islamic fundamentalism and liberal values across the seven countries. It showed that, in the same way religious fundamentalism and liberal values were inversely related on the micro (individual) level, the aggregate indices of the two constructs were negatively linked on the macro (country) level; countries that scored higher on the aggregate fundamentalism index scored lower on the aggregate indices of expressive individualism, gender equality, secular politics, and liberal values.

The chapter also assessed (1) the extent to which cross-national variation in aggregate fundamentalism and liberal values was influenced by such variable features of the national context as the structure of the religious environment, state structures and interventions in religion, economic development, economic and cultural globalization, and the situation of women in terms of female labor force participation and the sex ratio and (2) the direction of the relationships of these varying features of the national context with religious fundamentalism and liberal values. The analysis showed that religious fundamentalism was weaker and liberal values were stronger in a national context characterized by greater religious liberty, a more fragmented state power structure, greater globalization, and higher female labor force participation. Conversely, religious fundamentalism was stronger and liberal values were weaker where there was a stronger exclusionary state, greater government regulation of religion, and a higher sex ratio. Fundamentalism was also negatively linked to religious fractionalization, and liberal values to greater female labor force participation.

The linkages between the macro variables and expressive individualism only partially conformed to this pattern. Expressive individualism was linked positively only to the measures of religious liberty as well as economic and cultural globalization, and negatively to government regulation of religion. Globalization, however, indicated a relationship with expressive individualism, thus providing a favorable context for overall aggregate individual self-expression. The economic components of the national context, however, bore no significant relationship to attitudes toward gender equality or secular politics. Religious liberty, attributes of the state, and the situation of women were significantly linked to the indices of both gender equality and secular politics, religious liberty, fragmentation ratio, and female labor force participation were positively linked to these indices, while political exclusion, government regulation of religion, and sex ration were negatively linked.

The contrast between the predictors of expressive individualism, on the one hand, and gender equality and secular politics, on the other hand, is instructive. Expressive individualism is more directly linked to globalization, because the latter contributes to economic and cultural diversity and, as a result, a more favorable context for individual self-expression. Gender equality and secular politics, by contrast, are affected by factors related to distribution of power and political and religious freedom. Government regulation of religion, however, is the only factor that is significantly linked to religious fundamentalism and the indices of liberal values and its components, supporting the view that government regulation of religion not only more than other macro indicators reinforces religious fundamentalism but weakens all the components of liberal values as well.

CHAPTER 6

WHAT MAKES A COUNTRY
MORE DEVELOPED

Liberal Values Versus Religious Beliefs

W hat makes a country more developed and what contributes to economic stagnation and underdevelopment have been the subjects of considerable intellectual debate and contestation among Middle Eastern and North African intellectual leaders and political activists in the modern period. During this period, which began with Napoleon's invasion of Egypt in 1798, these intellectuals and activists displayed a growing awareness of the impressive scientific and technological progress made by the West, on the one hand, and the relative underdevelopment, if not decadence, of their own countries, on the other. For many, if not all, development itself was not an issue; it was considered good and desirable. Rather, their debates revolved around what aspects of social life had to change in order to make their countries more developed and prosperous. Though their responses varied during different cultural episodes, they may be summarized in a historical succession of three key concepts: *politics, economics,* and *religion*. Development, in the first concept, may be realized by fixing the existing political institution through the democratic transformation of the state. The second concept pushed forward the idea of economic nationalism and the expansion of the state-controlled national economy, and the third concept brought to the fore the rejection of secular politics, the revitalization of religious beliefs, and the establishment of an Islamic government.

In the late nineteenth and early twentieth centuries, facing the sultan's despotic rule, the obstructionism of the orthodox *ulama* (theologians), and, in some countries, foreign domination, intellectuals and political reformers developed critical attitudes toward their own political and religious institutions, arguing that for development to occur, the sultan's discretionary power had to be dismantled, on the one hand, and a constitutional and representative government had to be constructed, on the other. Referring to the developmental significance of a constitutional regime, a leader of the 1906 Iranian Constitutional Revolution, Ayatollah Sayyid Muhammad Tabatabaie, justified the demand for the constitutional change on the grounds that "constitutionalism will bring security and prosperity to the country" (cited in Admiyat 1976, 193).

In the mid-twentieth century, there was a shift in political attitudes and priorities, and establishing the right politics became less important than having the right economics as the foundation of development. The significance of economic issues gave rise to economic nationalism, which later developed into state socialism in some of the countries in the region. This new priority prompted states not only to nationalize foreign companies that had controlled the most important source of revenues (for example, the Suez Canal in Egypt and the oil industry in Algeria, Iraq, and Iran) but also to take control of a substantial portion of the national economy. In the second half of the twentieth century, states extensively intervened in the economy, the dominant classes lost much of their property and their political power declined as a result, political parties were dissolved by the ruling regimes, and single-party authoritarian secular states appeared. This process in turn weakened the secular discourse that had dominated politics and culture since the early twentieth century. The increasing unpopularity of the secular state provided a favorable context for the rise of Islamic fundamentalism, political Islam, and the notion of religious modernity (Moaddel and Karabenick 2018). The last rests on the idea that religious beliefs contribute to development. As Iranian Muslim intellectual Ali Shariati (1969, 23; see also Hanson 1983) stated, "Europe abandoned religion and made progress; we abandoned religion and went backward."

This chapter traces liberal-religious debate on development through the perceptions of the members of the ordinary public, analyzing their beliefs concerning the relative importance of the liberal or religious values that are considered to be the causes and consequences of development. It also analyzes their perceptions of the similarities and differences in the cultural outcomes resulting from Westernization and from development, trying to identify the set of changes where the two processes converge and the set where they diverge. In the past cultural episodes, people's beliefs about what must be changed in order for their country to develop framed their collective political actions and goals. In the same way, the analysis in this chapter will shed light on the respondents' visions concerning the future of their country and the extent to which liberal or religious beliefs are going to shape this future. This assessment is important, for it provides clues on the subjective conditions of the respondents and their readiness to accept changes in their social conditions to achieve liberal nationalism.

The chapter proceeds by first evaluating, through the respondents' perceptions, the relative significance of the expansion of liberal values versus religious beliefs in bringing about development. Then the reverse of this relationship is considered by assessing whether the respondents believed that development would bring about the expansion of liberal values or religious beliefs. Next the chapter compares and contrasts the respondents' views on the type of change in culture that would occur if their country became more like the West versus the type of change that would occur if it became more developed. Finally, it assesses the value or set of values, including democracy, freedom of choice over one's own life, religiosity, gender equality, and integrity in government officials, that the respondents considered the most important in making their country more developed.

Development as an Outcome of Ideological Change

To capture people's perceptions of the cultural causes of development, several survey questions on the kinds of changes that would contribute to development were formulated. The respondents were asked (the coding below is reversed from the original questionnaire):

✳ ✳ ✳

Would it make your country (1) a lot less developed, (2) a little less developed, (3) a little more developed, and (4) a lot more developed, if

  a. More parents choose who their children marry?
  b. Restrictions on personal freedom increase?
  c. There is more equality between women and men?
  d. The freedom to mix with the opposite sex increases?
  e. The influence of religion on politics increases?
  f. The faith in Allah increases?
  g. Belief in the truth of the Quran [Bible (for Christian respondents)] increases?

Question a taps into the respondents' views concerning their country's developmental prospects if parental authority over their children increases. This question is a different way of measuring expressive individualism, discussed in chapter 1; there the construct was measured in terms of the preference for parental approval or love as the basis for marriage. Question b, which asks about restrictions on personal freedom, also relates to individualism. Questions c and d, on increases in gender equality and the mixing of the sexes, are self-explanatory. They are considered valid and reliable attitudinal measures of gender equality and the freedom of men and women to interact. Questions e through g are measures of religious modernity, probing respondents on how religious beliefs contribute to development.[1] Religious modernity is considered a predictor of religious fundamentalism (Moaddel and Karabenick 2018).

Answers to these questions may reflect whether the respondents would connect a more liberal or a more religious vision to development. A more liberal vision is associated with the belief that their country would become less developed if there was an increase in (1) the number of parents choosing their children's spouse, (2) restrictions on personal freedom, (3) the influence of religion on politics, (4) faith in Allah, and (5) belief in the truth of the scriptures and that their country would become more developed if there was an increase in (6) the equality between women and men and (7) the freedom to mix with members of the opposite sex. A more religious vision belongs to those who thought otherwise; that a country would become more developed if items 1 through 5 happened and less developed if items 6 and 7 happened.

Empirical data on these questions were available for six of the seven countries—Egypt, Iraq, Lebanon, Pakistan, Saudi Arabia, and Turkey. The correlation coefficients of these seven items with the indices of liberal values and religious fundamentalism across the six countries are reported in table 6.1. The findings show that the seven items were significantly correlated with these indices and in the expected directions. As shown for the pooled sample in the Total column, people who were more liberal were more likely to believe that their country would be less developed if more parents choose who their children marry ($r = -.35$), restrictions on personal freedom increase ($r = -.24$), the influence of religion on politics increases ($r = -.45$), and the faith in Allah and belief in the truth of the scriptures expand ($r = -.34$ and $-.37$, respectively). The more liberal respondents also tended to support the view that their country would become more developed if gender equality expands and the freedom to intermingle with the opposite sex increases ($r = .24$ and $.32$, respectively). The links between these items and the index of religious fundamentalism were just the reverse of these relationships ($r = .28, .22, .35, .41, .47, -.08$, and $-.23$, respectively). These relationships were also true across the six countries, with some minor deviations that are highlighted in boldface type for Iraq, Saudi Arabia, Egypt, and Turkey (the highlighted correlation coefficients either are not significant or are in the unexpected direction).

The data in table 6.2 show the respondents' views on whether a more liberal vision or a more religious vision fosters development. The majority of the respondents from five of the six countries said that their country would be a lot less or less developed if more parents selected their children's spouse. These responses ranged between 53 percent among Iraqis and Saudis and 82 percent among Lebanese. Only a minority of Pakistanis (22 percent), concurred. Larger majorities across the same five countries believed that restricting personal

TABLE 6.1 Correlation Coefficients of the Indices of Liberal Values and Religious Fundamentalism with Responses to Questions on Development

	Iraq		Lebanon		Pakistan		Saudi Arabia		Egypt		Turkey		Total	
	Lib[a]	Rel Fund[b]	Lib	Rel Fund	Lib	Rel Fund	Lib	Rel Fund	Lib	Rel Fund	Lib	Rel Fund	Lib	Rel Fund
Would it make your country (1) a lot less developed, (2) less developed, (3) more developed, and (4) a lot more developed if . . .														
More parents choose who their children marry?	-.19[c]	.37[c]	-.32[c]	.32[c]	-.53[c]	.34[c]	-.21[c]	.07[c]	-.04[d]	.04[d]	-.21[c]	.19[c]	-.35[c]	.28[c]
Restrictions on personal freedom increase?	-.03	.31[c]	-.23[c]	.34[c]	-.51[c]	.34[c]	.003	.08[c]	.06[c]	.01	-.16[c]	.13[c]	-.24[c]	.22[c]
There is more equality between men and women?	.08[c]	.11[c]	.21[c]	-.13[c]	.47[c]	-.27[c]	-.07[d,e]	.04[e]	.18[c]	.03	.19[c]	-.01	.24[c]	-.08[c]
Freedom to mix with the opposite sex increases?	.25[c]	-.14[c]	.26[c]	-.23[c]	.44[c]	-.34[c]	.20[c]	-.01	.11[c]	-.13[c]	.03	.03	.32[c]	-.23[c]
The influence of religion on politics increases?	-.21[c]	.15[c]	-.34[c]	.35[c]	-.52[c]	.42[c]	-.37[c]	.07[c]	-.15[c]	.09[c]	-.24[c]	.26[c]	-.45[c]	.35[c]
The faith in Allah increases?	-.15[c]	.24[c]	-.17[c]	.43[c]	-.15[c]	.14[c]	-.25[c]	.27[c]	-.05[d]	.13[c]	-.16[c]	.26[c]	-.34[c]	.41[c]
Belief in the truth of the Quran [Bible (for Christian respondents)]?	-.10[c]	.30[c]	-.18[c]	.44[c]	-.13[c]	.15[c]	-.15[c]	.36[c]	-.07[c]	.20[c]	-.22[c]	.31[c]	-.37[c]	.47[c]

Note: Listwise n = 14,028. The coding of the responses is reversed for a higher value to indicate more developed.

[a] Lib = Liberal values index.

[b] Rel fund = Religious fundamentalism index.

[c] $p < .001$.

[d] $p < .01$.

[e] Influence of religion on politics was used as one of the proxy measures of secular politics for Saudi Arabia.

TABLE 6.2 Ideological Causes of Development

	Iraq	Lebanon	Pakistan	Saudi Arabia	Egypt	Turkey	Total
Would it make your country a lot more or more developed or a lot less or less developed if . . .							
Expressive individualism							
More parents choose who their children marry?							
A lot more or more developed	47%	18%	78%	48%	27%	35%	42%
A lot less or less developed	53%	82%	22%	53%	73%	65%	58%
Restrictions on personal freedom increase?							
A lot more or more developed	31%	23%	58%	48%	18%	31%	34%
A lot less or less developed	69%	78%	42%	52%	82%	69%	66%
Gender equality & the mixing of the sexes							
There is more equality between women and men?							
A lot more or more developed	93%	93%	76%	75%	84%	93%	86%
A lot less or less developed	7%	7%	25%	25%	16%	7%	14%
Freedom to mix with the opposite sex increases?							
A lot more or more developed	54%	72%	14%	52%	36%	35%	42%
A lot less or less developed	46%	28%	86%	48%	64%	66%	58%
Political Islam							
The influence of religion on politics increases?							
A lot more or more developed	46%	26%	86%	68%	53%	35%	52%
A lot less or less developed	54%	74%	15%	33%	47%	65%	48%
Religious beliefs							
Faith in Allah increases?							
A lot more or more developed	96%	78%	98%	83%	96%	84%	90%
A lot less or less developed	4%	23%	2%	17%	4%	16%	10%
Belief in the truth of the Quran [Bible (for Christian respondents) increases?							
A lot more or more developed	96%	77%	99%	86%	96%	80%	90%
A lot less or less developed	4%	23%	1%	14%	4%	20%	10%
Liberal development index (mean; range 1–4)	2.36	2.78	1.83	2.28	2.35	2.55	2.35
Liberal development index (median)	2.33	2.71	1.85	2.29	2.29	2.57	2.33

freedom would make their country a lot less or less developed, with responses ranging between 52 percent among Saudis and 82 percent among Egyptians. A sizable minority among Pakistanis (42 percent) also thought so. Thus, the majority of respondents connected a decline in expressive individualism, signified by an increase in parental authority and restrictions on personal freedom, to a lower level of development.

Considering the linkage between increased gender equality and development, an overwhelming majority of the respondents across the six countries believed that their country would be a lot more or more developed if there was more equality between women and men; the responses ranged between 93 percent among Iraqi, Lebanese, and Turkish respondents and 75 percent among Saudis. Concerning the relationship between the mixing of the sexes and development, the respondents across the countries were split. A majority of Iraqis (54 percent), Lebanese (72 percent), and Saudis (52 percent) believed that their country would be a lot more or more developed if people's freedom to mix with members of the opposite sex increased, while only a minority of respondents from Pakistan (14 percent), Egypt (36 percent), and Turkey (35 percent) thought so.

The respondents were also split between those who believed an increase in the influence of religion on politics promoted development and those who thought otherwise. Fully 86 percent of Pakistanis, 68 percent of Saudis, and 53 of percent Egyptians believed that the more religion influenced politics, the more developed their countries would be. But the majority of Iraqi, Lebanese, and Turkish respondents—54 percent, 74 percent, and 65 percent, respectively—thought otherwise, associating a lower level of development with an increase in the influence of religion on politics. On the other hand, between 78 percent of Lebanese and 98 percent of Pakistanis related an increase in the faith in Allah to a higher level of development, and between 77 percent Lebanese and 99 percent Pakistanis believed an increase in belief in the truth of the scriptures would have a similar result.

A liberal development index was created by averaging the seven variables (for the questions on gender equality and the mixing of the sexes, increase a little and increase a lot were coded as 3 and 4, respectively, and for the other five questions, decrease a little and decrease a lot, were coded as 3 and 4, respectively). This index ranges between 1 and 4. A higher value on this index indicates a stronger belief that expansion of liberal values would bring about more development, and a smaller value indicates greater support for religious modernity as a means to increase development. As shown in table 6.2, only Lebanese and Turkish respondents, with index values of 2.71 and 2.57, respectively, were above the median value of 2.5. This means that the majority of the respondents believed that greater expansion of liberal values contributes to development, were more favorable toward liberal modernity, and were less favorable toward religious modernity. The other four countries, with median liberal develop-ment index values ranging between 1.85 for Pakistan and 2.33 for Iraq, were leaning toward religious modernity.[2]

Ideology as an Outcome of Developmental Change

Development is believed to have consequences for human values. To assess the respondents' perspectives on the ideological outcomes of development and whether they believed these outcomes took a more liberal or more religious direction, a similar set of questions was formulated. In contrast to the pre-vious set, this time the questions focused on the consequences of develop-ment. The respondents were asked (coding below is reversed from the original questionnaire):

* * *

What things would increase and what things would decrease if your coun-try became more developed? Over time, would it cause the following to (1) decrease a lot, (2) decrease a little, (3) increase a little, or (4) increase a lot:

a. Parents choosing who their children marry?
b. Restrictions on personal freedom?
c. Equality between women and men?
d. Freedom to mix with the opposite sex?
e. The influence of religion on politics?
f. Faith in Allah?
g. Following the teachings of the Quran [Bible (for Christian respondents)]?

The results are reported in table 6.3. Higher percentages of respondents from five of the six countries said that, as their country became more devel-oped, the number of parents who would choose their children's spouse would decrease a lot or decrease. These percentages ranged between 65 percent among Saudis and 90 percent among Lebanese. There was a 50/50 split among Pakistani respondents. Concerning restrictions on personal freedom, the majority of the respondents across the six countries believed that with more development, such restrictions would diminish. These percentages ranged between 56 percent among Pakistanis and 84 percent among Egyptians. On the other hand, an overwhelming majority of the respondents (76 percent of Saudis and at least 92 percent of the respondents from the other five countries) believed that more development would bring about more gender equality, and 61 percent of Saudis and at least 74 percent of the respondents from the other

TABLE 6.3 Ideological Outcomes of Development

	Iraq	Lebanon	Pakistan	Saudi Arabia	Egypt	Turkey	Total

If your country became more developed, which of the following are more likely to increase a lot or increase or decrease a lot or decrease?

Expressive individualism

Parents choosing who their children marry

	Iraq	Lebanon	Pakistan	Saudi Arabia	Egypt	Turkey	Total
Increase a lot or increase	21 %	10%	50%	35%	19%	29%	27%
Decrease a lot or decrease	79%	90%	50%	65%	81%	71%	73%

Restrictions on personal freedom

	Iraq	Lebanon	Pakistan	Saudi Arabia	Egypt	Turkey	Total
Increase a lot or increase	20%	19%	44%	31%	16%	36%	28%
Decrease a lot or decrease	80%	81%	56%	69%	84%	64%	73%

Gender equality & the mixing of the sexes

Equality between women and men

	Iraq	Lebanon	Pakistan	Saudi Arabia	Egypt	Turkey	Total
Increase a lot or increase	95%	97%	94%	76%	93%	92%	92%
Decrease a lot or decrease	6%	3%	7%	24%	8%	8%	8%

Freedom to mix with the opposite sex

	Iraq	Lebanon	Pakistan	Saudi Arabia	Egypt	Turkey	Total
Increase a lot or increase	87%	86%	84%	61%	74%	82%	80%
Decrease a lot or decrease	13%	14%	16%	39%	26%	18%	20%

Political Islam

The influence of religion on politics

	Iraq	Lebanon	Pakistan	Saudi Arabia	Egypt	Turkey	Total
Increase a lot or increase	29%	17%	72%	41%	39%	27%	38%
Decrease a lot or decrease	71%	83%	29%	59%	61%	73%	62%

Religious beliefs

Faith in Allah?

	Iraq	Lebanon	Pakistan	Saudi Arabia	Egypt	Turkey	Total
Increase a lot or increase	71%	33%	95%	49%	74%	58%	66%
Decrease a lot or decrease	30%	67%	5%	51%	26%	42%	34%

Following the teachings of the Quran [Bible (for Christian respondents)]

	Iraq	Lebanon	Pakistan	Saudi Arabia	Egypt	Turkey	Total
Increase a lot or increase	55%	24%	75%	47%	59%	46%	53%
Decrease a lot or decrease	45%	76%	25%	53%	41%	54%	47%
Development liberal index (mean; range 1–4)	2.86	3.17	2.46	2.74	2.80	2.80	2.81
Development liberal index (median)	2.86	3.17	2.43	2.71	2.71	2.83	2.83

five countries stated that development would result in an increase in the freedom to mix with the opposite sex.

Concerning the influence of religion on politics, except for Pakistanis, a majority of respondents said that such influence would decline as their country became more developed. These percentages ranged between 59 percent among Saudis and 83 percent among Lebanese. Among Pakistanis, only 29 percent thought the influence of religion on politics would decrease. Concerning faith in Allah, a majority of Lebanese (67 percent) and a slim majority of Saudis (51 percent) believed that development would bring about a decline in faith in Allah. The rest who thought so ranged between 5 percent of Pakistanis and 42 percent of Turkish respondents. Finally, the countries on average were split concerning the decline in people following the teachings of the scriptures if their country became more developed. While 76 percent of Lebanese, 53 percent of Saudi, and 54 percent of Turkish respondents believed that more development would cause a decline in people's following the teachings of the Quran or the Bible, 55 percent of Iraqis, 75 percent of Pakistanis, and 59 percent of Egyptians thought that development would bring about an increase in people's following the teachings of the Quran or the Bible.

A development liberal index was created by averaging the seven indicator variables in the same way that the liberal development index was created earlier, and the mean and median values for each country are reported in table 6.3. This index also ranges between 1 and 4, and a greater value on this index indicates that respondents were more likely to believe that development would bring about greater liberal change. As shown in this table, the values of this index are much higher than the values of the liberal development index reported across the countries in table 6.2, showing that the respondents have a much clearer idea about the ideological outcomes of development. As table 6.3 shows, the median values for this index are well above 2.5 for all the countries, except Pakistan, meaning that the majority of the respondents from the five countries believed that development would bring about liberal changes in values. The values of this index ranged between 2.43 for Pakistan (the only country below 2.5) and 3.17 for Lebanon.

Westernization Versus Development and Cultural Outcomes

Westernization has been one of the most controversial topics in the cultural exchange between the Western world and less developed countries. Furthermore, not only did the term mean different things to its various enthusiasts and detractors, but also its operational definitions varied under different cultural episodes. For the enthusiasts of the Eurocentric conception of historical progress during the heyday of the colonial powers in the nineteenth century,

Westernization meant transplanting European laws and customs into the col-onies (Mill 1826; Forbes 1951), and for evangelical Christians, it meant Chris-tianization (Clark 1885; Richter 1908). The followers of the romantic school of sympathetic understanding in the late eighteenth century and Muslim reformers in the nineteenth and early twentieth centuries rejected Western-ization, while pointing to the intellectual capacity of the indigenous people to develop rational laws and a system of administration that were compatible with Western modernity (Forbes 1951; Hourani 1983; Moaddel 2005). Marxists and postcolonial critics connected Westernization to imperialism and colo-nial domination in different ways. Finally, for Muslim fundamentalists and sympathizers, Westernization meant the decline of religion and the adoption of Western decadent culture (Motahhari 1969; Shari'ati 1980; Khomeini 1981; Ale-Ahmad 1982; Sivan 1985).

There has, however, been little systematic assessment of how the members of the ordinary public felt about Westernization and how they saw it as different from and similar to development. To make this assessment, the respondents were presented with the same set of seven questions and were asked:

* * *

Which of the following changes are more likely to (1) increase a lot, (2) increase a little, (3) decrease a little, or (4) decrease a lot, if your country (i) becomes more like Western countries or (ii) becomes more developed:

a. Parents choosing who their children marry?
b. Restrictions on personal freedom?
c. Equality between women and men?
d. Freedom to mix with the opposite sex?
e. The influence of religion on politics?
f. Faith in Allah?
g. Following the teachings of the Quran [Bible (for Christian respondents)]?

The results, reported in table 6.4, reveal several facts about the respondents' views of the changes produced by Westernization and those produced by devel-opment. First, the majority of the respondents believed that both Westerniza-tion and development would bring about liberal changes in five of the seven domains. Focusing on the Total column, the percentages of the respondents who said that Westernization and development would decrease a little or a lot the number of parents choosing their children's spouse were 83 percent and 73 percent; for restrictions on personal freedom, they were 77 percent and 73 percent; and for the influence of religion on politics, they were 77 percent and 62 percent, respectively. The percentages of the respondents who believed

TABLE 6.4 Westernization Versus Development (%)

	Iraq			Lebanon			Pakistan			Saudi Arabia			Egypt			Turkey			Total		
	W[a]	D[b]	Diff[c]	W	D	Diff	W	D	Diff	W	D	Diff	W	D	Diff	W	D	Diff	W	D	Diff
If your country becomes more like Western countries versus more developed, which of the following changes are more likely to (1) increase a lot, (2) increase a little, (3) decrease a little, or (4) decrease a lot?																				
Parents choosing who their children marry—Decrease a little or a lot																				
	84	79	5	91	90	1	88	50	38	72	65	7	86	81	5	73	71	2	83	73	10
Restrictions on personal freedom—Decrease a little or a lot																				
	76	80	−4	80	81	−1	87	56	31	68	69	−1	83	84	−1	64	64	0	77	73	4
Equality between men and women—Increase a little or a lot																				
	93	95	−2	96	97	−1	96	94	2	82	76	6	90	93	−3	89	92	−3	92	92	0
Freedom to mix with the opposite sex—Increase a little or a lot																				
	89	87	2	89	86	3	93	84	9	65	61	4	88	74	14	83	82	1	86	80	6
The influence of religion on politics—Decrease a little or a lot																				
	79	71	8	87	83	4	72	29	43	63	59	4	76	61	15	78	73	5	77	62	15
Faith in Allah—Decrease a little or a lot																				
	55	30	25	79	67	12	39	5	34	65	51	14	59	26	33	60	42	18	58	34	24
Following the teachings of the Quran [Bible]—Decrease a little or a lot																				
	62	45	17	82	76	6	75	25	50	65	53	12	65	41	24	67	54	13	69	47	22
Average percentage difference across the seven domains																				
	77	70	7	86	83	3	79	49	30	69	62	7	78	66	12	73	68	5	77	66	12

[a]W = More like Western countries.
[b]D = More developed.
[c]Diff = Difference between W and D.

that Westernization and development would increase a little or a lot gender equality and freedom to mix with the opposite sex were 92 percent and 86 percent, and 92 percent and 80 percent, respectively. On the other hand, while the percentages of those who believed that Westernization would decrease a little or a lot the faith in Allah and the following of the teachings of the Quran/Bible were 58 percent and 69 percent, respectively, only a minority (34 percent and 47 percent, respectively) thought that development would reduce such beliefs, and the majority thought otherwise.

Second, from the respondents' perspectives, there were differences in the amounts of liberal change that would occur if their country became more like the West and if it became more developed, and these differences vary by domain and across the countries. In the pooled sample, the difference in the amounts of increase in gender equality is 0 percent. The difference in the amounts of increase in the mixing of the sexes is 6 percent. The difference in the amounts of decrease in restrictions on personal freedom is 4 percent, and in parents choosing their children's spouse, the difference is 10 percent. The greatest difference between Westernization and development is in the amounts of decrease in religious beliefs. The difference in the amounts of decrease between Westernization and development is 24 percent for faith in Allah, 22 percent for following the teaching of the scriptures, and 15 percent for the influence of religion on politics. There is also considerable variation across the six countries concerning the changes the respondents associated with Westernization and development. For respondents from more liberal countries like Lebanon and Turkey, these differences are minimal, but they are much higher for respondents from more conservative countries like Pakistan. Among the respondents, the difference in the amounts of decrease in parents choosing their children's spouse between Westernization and development is 1 percent to 2 percent in Lebanon and Turkey; 5 percent to 7 percent in Iraq, Egypt, and Saudi Arabia; and 38 percent in Pakistan. In restrictions on personal freedom, the difference is −4 percent in Iraq and −1 percent to 0 percent in Lebanon, Egypt, Saudi Arabia, and Turkey. The difference between Westernization and development in the amounts of increase in gender equality is −3 percent to −1 percent in Iraq, Lebanon, Egypt, and Turkey; 2 percent in Pakistan; and 6 percent in Saudi Arabia. It is thus interesting to note that the respondents in most of these countries believed development would expand individual freedom and gender equality by the same amount as or more than Westernization would.

The difference in the amounts of increase in the freedom to mix with the opposite sex is between 1 percent and 4 percent in Iraq, Lebanon, Saudi Arabia, and Turkey; 9 percent in Pakistan; and 14 percent in Egypt. For the influence of religion in politics, the difference in the amounts of decrease is between 4 percent and 5 percent in Lebanon, Saudi Arabia, and Turkey; 8 percent in Iraq; 15 percent in Egypt; and 43 percent in Pakistan. For the decline in faith in Allah, the difference is 12 percent in Lebanon, 14 percent in Saudi Arabia, 18 percent in Turkey, 25 percent in Iraq, and 33 percent to 34 percent in Egypt and Pakistan. Finally, the difference in the amounts of decrease in following the teaching of in the scriptures between Westernization and development is 6 percent in Lebanon, 12 percent to 13 percent in Saudi Arabia and Turkey, 17 percent in Iraq, 24 percent in Egypt, and 50 percent in Pakistan. Overall, the average difference between the two processes across the seven domains was 3 percent to 5 percent in Lebanon and Turkey, 7 percent in Iraq and Saudi Arabia, 12 percent in Egypt, and 30 percent in Pakistan.

One important takeaway from this table is that the major differences between Westernization and development in the respondents' perspectives occurred on the changes brought about in religious beliefs. While Westernization would reduce the significance of such beliefs for the majority of the respondents, development would not. On other issues, the differences did not appear to be large enough to indicate a serious gap between the views of Westernization and development among the respondents.

Value Priority and Development

The analysis presented in the previous sections showed that, in the respondents' perspectives, both religious and liberal values would contribute to development. To assess the relative significance of these values in making a country more developed and to determine which value is more important than the rest, the respondents were presented with several possible changes in culture—more democracy, more freedom of choice over one's own life, more religiosity, more gender equality, and more integrity in government officials—and were asked, "Which one would help the most to make your country more developed?" The results, which are presented in table 6.5, are available for only Iraq, Lebanon, Pakistan, Egypt, and Turkey. This question was not allowed in Saudi Arabia. In the pooled sample under the Total column, the highest percentage of the respondents (35 percent) considered more integrity in government officials to be the factor that would make their country more developed, followed by 32 percent who mentioned more democracy. Only 21 percent of the respondents believed that more religiosity would make their country more developed.

TABLE 6.5 Value Priority in Developmental Change

	Iraq	Lebanon	Pakistan	Egypt	Turkey	Total
Which one of the following would help the most to make your country more developed?						
More democracy	25%	37%	15%	37%	47%	32%
More freedom of choice over one's own life	7%	13%	10%	6%	11%	9%
More religiosity	15%	9%	39%	26%	12%	21%
More gender equality	4%	6%	2%	2%	3%	3%
More integrity in government officials	49%	36%	34%	29%	28%	35%
n	2,931	2,970	3,520	3,439	2,898	15,758

Finally, more freedom of choice over one's life and more gender equality were mentioned by 9 percent and 3 percent of the total respondents, respectively.

This distribution varied across the five countries. For Iraqis, more integrity in government officials was the top factor, but for Lebanese, Egyptian, and Turkish respondents, it was more democracy. Pakistani respondents were the only group who mentioned more religiosity as the most important factor in making their country more developed. However, among Pakistanis, only 24 percent of the youth bulge mentioned religiosity, compared to 47 percent among the older age group who did so. As in other cases, the gap between the two age groups in Pakistan was much larger than it was in other countries. While this difference was 23 percent for Pakistan, it was −1 percent for Iraq, 0 percent for Egypt and Turkey, and 6 percent for Lebanon (not shown in the table). The data in table 6.5 thus support the conclusion that, in the respondents' perspectives, liberal values that related to democracy and governmental integrity were far more important in making a country more developed than was religiosity.

Summary

The analysis presented in this chapter focused on the respondents' perceptions of the ideological causes and consequences of development and the difference between Westernization and development. As it showed, the respondents considered expansions in both liberal values and religious beliefs as factors that would make their country more developed. Moreover, while an overwhelming majority of these respondents linked an increase in faith in Allah and the truth of the Quran/Bible to more development, which indicated their adherence to religious modernity, a much smaller percentage of these respondents, but still a majority, believed that development would bring about an increase in such beliefs. On the other hand, an overwhelming majority of the respondents considered an increase in gender equality to be both a cause and a consequence of development. Generally, the majority of respondents believed that development would contribute to the rise of liberal values, except among Pakistanis, where only a sizable minority thought this would be the case.

Concerning the difference between Westernization and development, the majority of the respondents believed that both processes would bring about liberal changes in five of the seven domains. They would reduce the number of parents choosing their children's spouse, decrease restrictions on personal freedom, and diminish the influence of religion on politics. They also believed that Westernization and development would increase gender equality and freedom to mix with the opposite sex. On the other hand, while a majority believed that Westernization would reduce belief in Allah and in the truth of the Quran/Bible, only a minority thought that development would cause this to diminish. Moreover, from the respondents' perspectives, there are differences in the amounts of liberal change that would occur if their country became more like the West and if it became more developed, and these differences vary by domain and across the countries. On the questions of individual freedom and gender equality, the respondents believed that development would expand these values by the same amount as or more than Westernization would. On decreasing parents choosing their children's spouse and increasing the mixing of the sexes, Westernization appeared to have a moderately greater impact than development. The greatest differences between Westernization and development occurred in the amounts of decrease in religious beliefs; faith in Allah, following the teaching of the scriptures, and the influence of religion on politics. Thus, the differences in the ideological outcomes between Westernization and development are not consistent across domain and are not in a single direction. These differences varied by domain and across countries. For respondents from more liberal countries like Lebanon and Turkey, the differences between Westernization and development were minimal, but they were much higher for respondents from more conservative countries like Pakistan.

Finally, on the question of how the respondents prioritized among a set of values in bringing about more development, the data indicated that the respondents considered liberal values of democracy and integrity of governmental officials to be far more important in making a country more developed than religiosity. Reflecting this political attitude as a priority, findings from longitudinal surveys across several countries, which are presented in chapter 7, will show a significant increase in support for secular politics and national identity.

To recap, belief in Allah and in the truth of the scriptures is certainly important for the great majority of the respondents, and such beliefs are thought to enhance development. Believing in Allah and the scriptures does not indicate a commitment to religious fundamentalism, but it does reinforce fundamentalism, particularly if and when the individuals supporting liberal values are oriented toward secular fundamentalism, the firm belief in the decline of religion as a condition for modernity that was shared by many during the heyday of secularism in the twentieth century. Taken as a whole, while empirical analysis of the cross-national data showed that the majority of the respondents considered liberal values as the causes and consequences of development, it can be speculated that these respondents would be quite receptive to liberal changes in the sociopolitical institutions of their country insofar as they do not perceive these changes to be undermining their basic religious beliefs.

CHAPTER 7

THE ARAB SPRING AND
TRENDS IN VALUES

Egypt, Iraq, Saudi Arabia, Tunisia, and Turkey

Thus far, empirical evidence has been brought to bear in support of the pivotal claim that the clash of values in the Middle East and North Africa is principally between Islamic fundamentalism and liberal nationalism. Findings from surveys conducted between 2011 and 2013 across the seven countries of Egypt, Iraq, Lebanon, Pakistan, Saudi Arabia, Tunisia, and Turkey showed that support for these two ideological orientations varied considerably and that the factors that reinforced religious fundamentalism also weakened liberal values at both the micro (individual) and the macro (country) levels. These findings also indicated that there was stronger support for religious fundamentalism than there was for liberal values, except in Lebanon, where the level of support was about the same for both value orientations. The comparison between the indices of religious fundamentalism and liberal values showed the relative standing of respondents vis-à-vis fundamentalism and liberal democracy.

For a more effective understanding of trends in values, chapter 4 compared the index of religious intolerance with the index of liberal values after it was recalculated by excluding the index of expressive individualism and then averaging the indices of gender equality and secular politics. This comparison showed that support for liberal values was much higher than support for religious intolerance in Lebanon, Tunisia, and Turkey but that the opposite was the case in the other four countries.

Finally, to obtain a better understanding of the respondents' subjective orientations toward change in a liberal direction, chapter 6 assessed the types of cultural values, whether liberal or religious, that the respondents believed were among the causes and consequences of development and the differences between Westernization and development from their perspectives. The analysis showed that, in the respondents' perspectives, both liberal and religious beliefs promoted development. However, the percentages of respondents who considered that an increase in faith in Allah and in the belief in the truth of the scriptures would make their country more developed were higher than the percentage who believed that an increase in liberal values would prompt development. A majority of these respondents, on the other hand, agreed that more development would bring about the expansion of liberal values. Furthermore, the differences in the cultural consequences between Westernization and development were not in a single direction and varied by social domains and across countries. Finally, respondents considered more democracy and greater integrity of governmental officials more important in contributing to development than religiosity.

This chapter assesses a shift in people's value orientations in Egypt, Iraq, Saudi Arabia, Tunisia, and Turkey in the twenty-first century—one that demonstrates Islamic fundamentalism is declining and liberal nationalism is on the rise. This assessment rests on the longitudinal and panel data that are available for these countries. These data are from two waves of a panel survey in Egypt, Tunisia, and Turkey and from cross-sectional surveys in Egypt and Turkey since 2001, in Iraq between 2004 and 2011, and in Saudi Arabia between 2003 and 2011. These data, however, have some limitations. All the data from Saudi Arabia and Tunisia, as well as the data for some of the variables in the surveys carried out in Egypt and Turkey, are available for only two points in time. At least three observations in time are necessary to establish a trend. Despite these limitations, it may still be possible to advance a reasonable estimate of a trend in values in each of these countries. Findings from these surveys may lend credence to the claim that the Arab Spring ushered in a new cultural episode in the Middle East and North Africa.

Episodes and Values Change

It is accepted wisdom in the social sciences that people's value orientations and long-term concerns are not static entities that are set once and for all. They are subject to change according to changes in social conditions. From a historical perspective, some values change very quickly, while others change very slowly, if ever. At one extreme are such fundamental beliefs as, for example, the beliefs in God, the existence of soul, and life after death and such basic values as the importance one attaches to family, religion, and country, all of which may change only in the long run or may not change at all.[1] In other words, such values or beliefs are hardly turned into issues to be debated by intellectual leaders, opinion makers, or the public at large. At the other extreme are people's views on the likeability of a politician, the worth of a particular political party, and the value they assign to certain interpersonal relationships with colleagues or neighbors, all of which may fluctuate or radically change in a relatively short span of time. In between are the values and beliefs that change in the medium run (a time span between several years and a generation). People's orientations toward indicators of expressive individualism, gender equality, secular politics, national identity, religious exclusivity, and religious intolerance may change in the medium run.

The speed of change is also a function of whether people live in a settled or unsettled social environment. In an unsettled environment, shifts in value orientations may occur more dramatically than in a settled environment. Value changes are likely to occur in an unsettled environment as a result of an event like a major societal upheaval, military coup, foreign invasion, sectarian conflict, war, or revolution. Such events interrupt continuities in sociopolitical life; rearrange the balance of social forces; open up a new venue and angle from which sociopolitical and cultural issues are viewed, debated, and resolved; and punctuate historical routines into different segments, thus turning history into a succession of different cultural episodes. Examples of such episodes in the Middle East and North Africa are Islamic modernism in the late nineteenth and early twentieth centuries, liberal nationalism in the first half of the twentieth century, pan-Arab nationalism in Arab countries and various forms of authoritarian nationalism in other countries around the middle of the twentieth century, and Islamic fundamentalism in the second half of the twentieth century. All these episodes started or ended with a major event (Moaddel 2005).

The Arab Spring as a New Cultural Episode

The revolutionary movements in the Arab world sparked by the self-immolation of a Tunisian street vendor on December 17, 2010, signify the start of a new cultural episode in the region.[2] These movements eventually overthrew the ruling dictators in Tunisia, Egypt, Yemen, and Libya, but their departures did not lead to democratization of the political system or even political stability in these countries. Tunisia appears to be the only country that is making a steady transition to democracy, even though this transition has been marred by political instability and violence perpetrated by Islamic extremism. In Egypt, the military-based autocracy of the prerevolutionary period has been revived. Yemen has been experiencing the rise of sectarian strife between the Shia Houthis in the north, backed by the Islamic Republic of Iran, and the forces connected to former president Ali Abdullah Saleh, on the one hand, and the Sunni groups loyal to the government of Abd Rabbuh Mansur Hadi, supported by a Saudi-led coalition of Persian Gulf Arab states, on the other. Similarly, following the capture and execution of Colonel Muammar Gaddafi, Libya was turned into an arena of conflict between armed militia, controlling different parts of the country, and Islamic terror groups. The situation in Syria is the most tragic, as the initial peaceful protests against the authoritarian regime turned deadly, causing a loss of more than 500,000 lives and resulting in millions of refugees and displaced people.

The picture portrayed as a result of this chain of events is that of a region immersed in chaos, on the course to societal decline, or dominated by recon-stituted authoritarian regimes. Findings from cross-national and longitudinal surveys, however, provide quite a different picture. It is true that cultural change is often chaotic and conflict ridden and carries elements of societal decline as a result of disruption in social exchange, economic uncertainty, and political instability. Nonetheless, while the dust settles and chaos gives way to a degree of social serenity, there are indicators that provide reasonable expectations about the type of social order that one would expect to emerge and the pattern of historical growth that is likely to come into relief. These indicators, drawn from the available data, are limited, but they show a shift in people's value orienta-tions in a liberal direction, indicating an increase in support for secular politics, religious tolerance, national identity, and, to a limited extent, gender equality. Determining to what extent this shift is the result of the Arab Spring and to what extent the Arab Spring was an outcome of the changes in values that pre-ceded it is difficult. However, the longitudinal data from Iraq show that the shift toward secular politics and national identity among Iraqis predated the Arab Spring and was seen following the American invasion and occupation of the country in 2003. In Egypt, on the other hand, this shift appears to have emerged pari passu with these movements.

Competing Narratives on the Arab Spring

The Arab Spring prompted debates among observers and investigators about its key features and characters, the causes and processes of the mobilization of mass discontent, the factors underpinning its success in some Arab countries and its failure in others, and the background and objectives of the participants in the revolutionary movements that toppled the ruling regimes in Egypt, Tuni-sia, and Yemen (Anderson 2011; Brownlee et al. 2015; Beissinger, Jamal, and Mazur 2015; Howard and Hussain 2013; Wolfsfeld, Segev, and Sheafer 2013; Bruns, Highfield and Brugess. 2017; Hoffman and Jamal 2014; Moaddel 2017b; Tessler 2017). An important aspect of these debates is the formulation of two alternative narratives concerning the identity and objectives of the Arab Spring.

One is a liberal democratic narrative, and the other is an Islamic awakening narrative—opposing narratives that parallel the characterization in this book of the current cultural context of the Middle East and North Africa as an arena of conflict between Islamic fundamentalism and liberal nationalism.

This chapter assesses these two narratives empirically by focusing on the goals and identity of the Arab Spring movements from the perspectives of nationally representative samples of respondents in Egypt, Lebanon, Pakistan, Tunisia, and Turkey; analyzing the backgrounds and value orientations of the participants in the revolutionary movements in Egypt and Tunisia; and evaluating the changes in values after the Arab Spring.

Liberal Democratic Narrative

The liberal democratic narrative portrays the Arab Spring as an uprising against the incumbent authoritarian regimes by the people (the youth, in particular), who demanded freedom and economic prosperity (Wright 2011; Knickmeyer 2011). For one author, it constituted the third wave in a series of Arab awakening movements that started in the first quarter of the twentieth century (Ajami 2012). For another, it had little to do with religion or nationalism, reflecting instead the "classic political demands of liberty, democracy and economic justice" (Zubaida 2011). It is further argued that "the Arab Spring was not an Islamic Spring. That initial surge in early 2011 was not about religion but was an expression of anger over elite corruption, economic inequalities, widespread injustice and geriatric leaders who were out of touch with reality" (Noueihed and Warren 2012, 304).

Islamic Awakening Narrative

Pointing to the success of the followers of political Islam in the post-2011 elections, Islamic activists, as well as the ideologues of the Islamic Republic of Iran, portrayed the movement as an Islamic awakening. The latter hailed the 2011 uprisings as the perpetuation of the Islamic movement that started with the Iranian Revolution of 1979. These events, for them, revealed yet another instance of the Islamization process, in which the people of the region were turning to Islam to challenge Western hegemony (Parchami 2012; Mohseni 2013). From a scholarly perspective, some have argued that the Islamic character of the Arab Spring, which might have appeared as a form of religious revivalism, was an outcome of Islam's contribution to the mass mobilization of the public against the state. For them, Islam played a role in the Arab Spring not because people became aware of the importance of their religious beliefs, but rather because religious symbols and rituals facilitated the movements; mobilization became possible as a result of people congregating on Fridays in mosques (Lynch 2012; Ardıç 2012). Hoffman and Jamal (2014), on the other hand, linked participation to individual piety—not communal practice, such as mosque attendance. Their analysis of survey data from Egypt and Tunisia indicated a link between Quran reading and the likelihood of participation in protest. They argued, however, that this relationship is not a function of support for political Islam. Rather, Quran readers displayed a higher sensitivity to inequalities and were more supportive of democracy than nonreaders.

The Characters of the Arab Spring and Changes in Values

Several pieces of empirical evidence are used to assess the relative significance of the liberal democratic and Islamic awakening narratives and changes in values: (1) people's perceptions of the goals and objectives of the Arab Spring; (2) the backgrounds and value orientations of the participants in the movements of the Arab Spring; (3) findings from two waves of a panel survey carried out in Egypt, Tunisia, and Turkey on the respondents' orientations toward secular politics, religious tolerance, gender equality, and national identity; and (4) findings from longitudinal surveys carried out in Egypt and Iraq and from two cross-sectional surveys carried out in Saudi Arabia. This evidence points to a shift in people's values toward secular politics, religious tolerance, national identity, and, to a limited extent, gender equality.

The Goals of the Arab Spring

To assess people's perception concerning the goals of the movements of the Arab Spring, nationally representative samples of respondents in Egypt, Tunisia, and Lebanon (Arab countries) and in Turkey and Pakistan (non-Arab countries) were asked:

✳ ✳ ✳

[Concerning] recent political upheavals in Egypt, Libya, Tunisia and other places in the Middle East, which of the following is the most important purpose of these movements:

1. National movements for freedom and democracy?
2. Religious movements for the establishment of an Islamic government?
3. Movements to counter Western influence?

4. Movements for economic equality and prosperity?
5. These movements are a part of a Western conspiracy?
6. Movements of the Arab people for the unity of all Arab countries?
7. Other_____?

The responses across the five countries are reported in table 7.1. For a majority of the respondents in the three Arab countries—59 percent of Egyptians, 55 percent of Tunisians, and 51 percent of Lebanese—and the largest percentages in the two non-Arab countries—36 percent of Turkish and 42 percent of Pakistani respondents—the most important goal was freedom and democracy. For the respondents from the three Arab countries, the second-highest percentages—25 percent of Egyptians, 20 percent of Tunisians, and 15 percent of Lebanese—consisted of those who mentioned economic equality and prosperity; 7 percent and 16 percent of Turkish and Pakistani respondents, respectively, concurred on economic equality and prosperity. Adding the two values (the first two rows in the table), a large majority of the respondents from the three Arab countries—84 percent of Egyptians, 75 percent of Tunisians, and 66 percent of Lebanese; a majority among Pakistanis, 58 percent; and a sizable

TABLE 7.1 The Most Important Goal of the Arab Spring

	Egypt	Tunisia	Lebanon	Turkey	Pakistan
National movements for freedom and democracy	59%	55%	51%	36%	42%
Movements for economic equality and prosperity	25%	20%	15%	7%	16%
Religious movements for the establishment of an Islamic government	9%	8%	9%	12%	26%
Movements to counter Western influence	2%	2%	10%	13%	6%
These movements are a part of a Western conspiracy	2%	9%	9%	29%	9%
Movements of Arab people for the unity of all Arabs	3%	5%	4%	3%	1%
Other	1%	2%	1%	1%	0%
n	3,496	3,070	3,039	3,019	3,523

minority among Turkish respondents, 43 percent, believed that democracy and economic prosperity were the most important goals of the Arab Spring. By contrast, only a minority (9 percent or less) of the respondents in the Arab countries and 12 percent of Turkish and 26 percent of Pakistani respondents considered the establishment of an Islamic government to be the goal of the Arab Spring. Only 2 percent of Egyptian and Tunisian respondents and 10 percent of Lebanese, 13 percent of Turkish, and 6 percent of Pakistani respondents considered countering Western influence to be the goal of the movement, and only 2 percent of Egyptians and 9 percent of Tunisians, Lebanese, and Pakistanis and 29 percent of Turkish respondents believed in the Arab Spring as Western conspiracy. Finally, less than 5 percent across the five countries believed that the most important goal of the movements was the unity of all Arab countries.

While the distribution of the data in this table shows that there was overwhelming support for the liberal democratic narrative and that only a small minority supported the Islamic awakening narrative, as one moves away from the countries that were at the center of the Arab Spring movements—Egypt and Tunisia—and toward non-Arab countries, the percentages of the respondents who mentioned democracy and economic prosperity as the goals decline, and the percentages who mentioned Islamic government increase. Finally, compared to the other countries, a much larger percentage of Turkish respondents (29 percent) believed the movements were part of a Western conspiracy, and a much larger percentage of Pakistanis (26 percent) believed their goal was the establishment of an Islamic government. These figures may reflect the relative success of the anti-Western currents in Turkey, led by President Receb Tayyip Erdoğan, and of the Islamic activists in Pakistan who have framed the Arab Spring according to their own political views.

The Predictors of Participation

The relative significance of the liberal democratic and Islamic awakening narratives was further assessed by considering the backgrounds and the value orientations of the participants in the movements that toppled the ruling regimes in Egypt and Tunisia in 2011. An analysis of whether fundamentalists or liberal nationalists were more likely participants and of the extent to which the predictors of religious fundamentalism and liberal values were linked to participation in a consistent manner may provide additional clues as to whether liberal values or Islamic fundamentalism was a driving force behind the political engagement in the two countries.

Respondents were asked to rate their participation in the revolutionary movement: "On the scale of 1 to 10, with 1 indicating minimum to no

TABLE 7.2 Self-Reported Participation in the Revolutionary Movements in Egypt and Tunisia in 2011

	Egypt		Tunisia	
	Frequency	Percentage	Frequency	Percentage
1 = No participation	1,866	59.5%	1,565	51%
2	199	6.3	361	11.8
3	178	5.7	265	8.6
4	179	5.7	219	7.1
5	158	5	231	7.5
6	130	4.1	128	4.2
7	172	5.5	88	2.9
8	145	4.6	68	2.2
9	55	1.8	24	0.8
10 = Maximum participation	56	1.8	89	2.9
n	3,138	100	3,070	100
Mean (standard deviation)	2.75 (2.55)		2.68 (2.36)	
DK/NA	5	0.2	32	3

participation and 10 indicating utmost participation, where do you put the extent of your participation on this scale?" The frequency distribution of the respondents' self-rated participation, reported in table 7.2, shows that a clear majority of respondents (59.5 percent) in Egypt, and slightly over half of the respondents (51 percent) in Tunisia reported no participation. The percentages of those who reported participating, however, declined somewhat consistently as the participation rating increased from 2 to 10. If a rating of 7 or more is defined as high participation, then about 14 percent of Egyptians and 9 percent of Tunisians reported having high participation in the revolutionary upheaval.

To better analyze the data and to make sure the results were not significantly affected by the way participation was measured, the participation rating was recoded in two ways: first, as a dummy variable, using 0 for those who reported no or minimal participation and 1 otherwise and, second, as a four-category variable: 1 (1 = no participation), 2 (2–4 = low participation), 3 (5–7 = medium participation), and 4 (8–10 = high participation). The correlation coefficients between these three different types of coding of the participation variable

(1 to 10, 1 to 4, and 0 to 1) and the indices of religious fundamentalism and liberal values, as well as the predictors of religious fundamentalism and liberal values that were reported in table 4.11, were computed. These predictors include factors related to religion, demographics, socioeconomic status, internet use, cultural attitudes on gender interactions, hostility toward outsiders, and fatalism. The hypothesis is that the index of liberal values is positively linked to participation and the index of religious fundamentalism is negatively linked to participation. Furthermore, it is hypothesized that the factors positively linked to liberal values and negatively linked to religious fundamentalism (see table 4.11) are also positively and negatively linked to participation, respectively—in other words, that the factors that strengthen liberalism and weaken religious fundamentalism tend to strengthen participation.

The correlation coefficients are reported in table 7.3. A robust relationship between predictors and participation is the one that is statistically significant across all three coding categories. Accordingly, the fundamentalism index is negatively linked to participation in Tunisia ($r = -.09$, $-.11$, and $-.13$) but has no significant relationship with participation in Egypt. The index of liberal values, on the other hand, is positively linked to participation in both countries, no matter how participation is coded. This relationship, however, is weaker in Tunisia ($r = .05$, $.06$, and $.08$) than it is in Egypt ($r = .12$, $.13$, $.16$). Consistent with the hypotheses, all the three religion-related variables—religiosity, religious modernity (available only for Egypt), and confidence in religious institutions—are significantly negatively linked to all the measures of participation (r is between $-.04$ and $-.15$). Likewise, the demographics—socioeconomic status, being male, and young (aged 18–29)—are positively connected to participation across all the measures (r is between .06 and .24). Residence in the rural area, on the other hand, is negatively linked to all the three measures of participation in Egypt and only two measures of participation in Tunisia (r is between $-.04$ and $-.13$), again in the expected direction. So is internet use as a source of information, which is positively linked to participation (r is between .20 and .24). Attitude against the mixing of the sexes has inconsistent relationships with participation across the two countries. It has a weak positive link to only the first measure of participation in Tunisia ($r = .04$, not in the expected direction), but in Egypt it is negatively linked to all the three measures (r is between $-.06$ and $-.07$). Likewise, the belief in the immorality of pre-marital sex while having negative relationship with all the measures of participation in Tunisia (r is between $-.04$ and $-.06$), it is only connected, negatively and significantly, to the first measure of participation in Egypt ($r = -.04$). Hostility toward the outgroups or xenophobia and belief in conspiracy has generally no relationship with participation among Tunisian respondents, although xenophobia is weakly linked to only one of the measures of participation ($r = -.04$). Among Egyptians, on the other hand, both variables were significantly inversely related

TABLE 7.3 Correlation Coefficients for Three Coding Formats for Self-reported Participation Rates and Predictors

	Tunisia			Egypt		
	Coded 1 to 10	Coded 1 to 4	Coded 0 to 1	Coded 1 to 10	Coded 1 to 4	Coded 0 to 1
Value orientations						
Religious fundamentalism index	−.09[b]	−.11[b]	−.13[b]	−0.01	−0.01	−0.02
Liberal values index	.05[b]	.06[b]	.07[b]	.12[b]	.13[b]	.16[b]
Religion						
Religiosity	−.08[b]	−.08[b]	−.08[b]	−.05[b]	−.06[b]	−.11[b]
Religious modernity	—	—	—	−.14[b]	−.15[b]	−.15[b]
Confidence in religious institutions	−.04[a]	−.05[a]	−.06[b]	−.07[b]	−.08[b]	−.08[b]
Demographics						
Socioeconomic status	.20[b]	.20[b]	.19[b]	.24[b]	.24[b]	.22[b]
Male	.21[b]	.21[b]	.17[b]	.16[b]	.17[b]	.17[b]
Youth bulge	.09[b]	.09[b]	.10[b]	.07[b]	.07[b]	.06[b]
Rural residence	−.03	−.04[a]	−.06[b]	−.11[b]	−.12[b]	−.13[b]
Internet use						
Internet use	.24[b]	.24[b]	.22[b]	.20[b]	.21[b]	.22[b]
Attitudes toward sex and morality						
Mixing of the sexes corrupts	.04[a]	.03	.01	−.06[b]	−.06[b]	−.07[b]
Premarital sex is immoral	−.06[b]	−.06[b]	−.04[a]	−.04[a]	−.03	−.03
In-group solidarity and out-group hostility						
Xenophobia	−.02	−.03	−.04[a]	−.14[b]	−.16[b]	−.16[b]
Conspiracy (1 to 4 = strongly agree)	−.01	−.01	.02	−.07[b]	−.08[b]	−.10[b]
Fatalism						
Fatalism	−.08[b]	−.09[b]	−.10[b]	−.21[b]	−.20[b]	−.20[b]

[a] $p < .05$.
[b] $p < .01$.

to all the measures of participation, which are in the expected direction (r is between −.07 and −.16). Finally, fatalism is negatively linked to participation in both countries (r is between −.08 and −.21).

These findings are thus consistent with the hypotheses that all the factors that were positively linked to religious fundamentalism (table 4.11) are negatively linked to participation. These are religiosity, religious modernity, confidence in religious institutions, residence in rural areas, the belief that mixing of the sexes leads to social corruption (only among Egyptians, with a minor contrary to expectation among Tunisia), belief that premarital sex is immoral (only among Tunisians, and partially among Egyptians), xenophobia and belief in conspiracy (only among Egyptians), and fatalism. On the other hand, factors that were positively linked to liberal values are also positively connected to participation. These are socioeconomic status, being male, being a member of the youth bulge, and reliance on the internet as a source of information.

The findings reported in this table thus show that supporters of liberal values were more likely to participate, while religious fundamentalists were less likely to participate in Tunisia and were indifferent to participation in Egypt. These findings also indicate that the factors that strengthen liberal values tend to increase the likelihood of participation, while those that strengthen religious fundamentalism tend to decrease the likelihood of participation.

A Shift Toward Liberal Values in Egypt, Tunisia, and Turkey

The analysis of the cross-sectional data presented in the previous sections indicated that liberal factors provided a significant role in the movements of the Arab Spring. These factors appeared to have shaped perceptions of its goals and participation. To further underscore the increasing significance of liberal nationalism in shaping people's view of politics, religion, and gender relations, this section assesses trends in values in several countries in the region. Two sets of empirical data provide a clear indication of a shift in people's value orientations in a liberal direction in Egypt, Tunisia, and Turkey. The first set is from two waves of a panel survey carried out in the three countries. In Egypt, the first wave was completed in 2011, producing 3,496 completed face-to-face interviews. The second wave, conducted in 2016, re-interviewed 2,430 of these respondents (about 70 percent of the 2011 respondents). To compensate for sample attrition, 1,428 additional interviews were conducted, bringing the total interviews to 3,858. In Tunisia, of a nationally representative sample of 3,070 respondents interviewed in 2013, 2,395 were reinterviewed in 2015 (a response rate of 78 percent). In Turkey, of a nationally representative sample of 3,019 respondents interviewed in 2013, 1,682 were reinterviewed in 2016 (a response rate of 56 percent). In addition, 1,077 additional interviews were conducted in Turkey to compensate for sample attrition, bringing the total to 2,759. The second set is the longitudinal survey data that was collected in Egypt before 2011, Iraq since 2004, and Saudi Arabia in 2003 and 2011. This section focuses on Egypt, Tunisia, and Turkey; the following section on Iraq and Saudi Arabia; and the final section assesses changes in values by age, gender, and education between the first and the last survey conducted in these five countries.

The analysis of the data from the two waves of the panel survey in Egypt, Tunisia, and Turkey showed changes in the values of the respondents toward secular politics, religious tolerance, gender equality, and national identity across the three countries. The same results are obtained whether one uses the panel data or the cross-sectional data for comparative analysis.

Secular Politics

The same four questions used in chapter 3 were employed to measure orientation toward secular political values, ranging from strong support for secular politics to strong support for Islamic government. Two questions asked about the respondents' preference for separation of religion and politics and for Western-type government: "Do you (1) strongly agree, (2) agree, (3) disagree, or (4) strongly disagree that [respondent's country] will be a better society (i) if religion and politics were separated" (**separation of religion and politics**), and (ii) "if its government was similar to Western [American or European] governments?" (**Western government**) The other two questions probed the respondents' attitudes toward Islamic government and sharia law: "(iii) Is it (1) very good, (2) fairly good, (3) fairly bad, or (4) very bad to have an Islamic government where religious authorities have absolute power" (**Islamic government**), and (iv) "is it (1) very important, (2) important, (3) somewhat important, (4) least important, or (5) not important for a good government to implement only the laws of the sharia?" (**Sharia**) This variable is changed to range between 1 and 4 from 1 to 5 by applying this formulae: Sharia (1–4) = Sharia (1–5)*.75 +.25. The coding for the responses to questions on **separation of religion and politics** and **Western government** were reversed so that higher values indicate stronger support for the separation of religion and politics and for Western type government. Altogether, these variables are expected to provide balanced indicators of attitudes toward secular politics.

To create a more stable measure of secular politics, a secular politics index was constructed by averaging these four indicators of the construct. The index ranges between 1 and 4, with higher values indicating stronger support for secular politics. The results are reported in table 7.4.

In terms of three of the four measures, Egyptian respondents changed their political values toward secular politics. The percentage of those who either strongly agreed or agreed that their country would be a better society if religion and politics were separated went up from 54 percent in 2011 to 83 percent in 2016. The percentage of those favoring Western-type government also went up from 35 percent to 55 percent between the two waves. Consistent with these changes is the decline in the popularity of Islamic government, as the percentage of those who thought that it was fairly bad or very bad to have an Islamic

TABLE 7.4 Indicators of Secular Politics and Secular Politics Index

	Egypt (2011)	Egypt (2016)	Tunisia (2013)	Tunisia (2015)	Turkey (2013)	Turkey (2016)
[COUNTRY] will be a better society if religion and politics are separated.						
Strongly disagree	18%	9%	12%	14%	8%	5%
Disagree	28%	9%	15%	14%	18%	21%
Agree	18%	31%	22%	22%	36%	35%
Strongly agree	36%	52%	50%	51%	39%	39%
Strongly agree/agree	54%	83%	72%	73%	75%	74%
[COUNTRY] will be a better society if its government was similar to Western governments.						
Strongly disagree	34%	21%	25%	23%	19%	16%
Disagree	32%	24%	28%	20%	39%	34%
Agree	19%	31%	24%	27%	32%	33%
Strongly agree	16%	24%	23%	30%	10%	17%
Strongly agree/agree	35%	55%	47%	57%	42%	50%
How good is it to have an Islamic government where religious authorities have absolute power?						
Very good	25%	11%	16%	11%	9%	7%
Fairly good	33%	19%	21%	19%	27%	20%
Fairly bad	23%	37%	19%	19%	35%	28%
Very bad	19%	34%	43%	52%	30%	45%
Fairly bad/very bad	42%	71%	62%	71%	65%	73%
A good government should implement only the laws of the sharia						
Very important	27%	22%	12%	8%	6%	8%
Important	26%	29%	14%	11%	14%	15%
Somewhat important	24%	30%	20%	16%	14%	17%
Least important	13%	9%	20%	22%	22%	18%
Not important	10%	10%	33%	43%	45%	42%
Least/not important	23%	19%	53%	65%	67%	60%
Secular politics index (Mean)	2.34	2.72	2.82	2.99	2.83	2.93
Median	2.31	2.81	2.88	3.06	3.00	3.00
Standard deviation	0.65	0.66	0.75	0.73	0.66	0.68
n	2,411	2,324	2,374	2,340	1,688	1,674
Wave 1 – wave 2	$2.72 - 2.34 = 0.38^a$		$2.99 - 2.81 = 0.17^a$		$2.94 - 2.83 = 0.11^a$	

[a] $p < .001.$

government where religious authorities have absolute power went up from 42 percent to 71 percent. On the other hand, the percentage of those who said that it was least important or not important for a good government to implement only sharia law went down from 23 percent to 19 percent, and the percentage of those who said that it was very important also declined from 27 percent to 22 percent.

In Tunisia, all four measures changed in support of secular politics. The percentages of those who strongly agreed or agreed with the separation of religion and politics and the desirability of a Western-type government increased from 72 percent and 47 percent in 2013 to 73 percent and 57 percent in 2015, respectively. Consistent with these changes were the increases in the percentages of those expressed that it was very bad or fairly bad to have an Islamic government where religious authorities have absolute power, and that it was least important or not important for a good government to implement only sharia law from 62 percent and 53 percent in 2013 to 71 percent and 65 percent in 2015, respectively.

The responses to these measures among Turkish respondents did not change as consistently as they did among Tunisians. Support for the separation of religion and politics was high in both waves, at 75 percent and 74 percent, but support for a Western-type government increased from 42 percent to 50 percent between 2013 and 2016. The percentage of respondents expressing that is was fairly bad or very bad to have an Islamic government where religious leaders have absolute power went up from 65 percent to 73 percent, but the percentage of those expressing that is was least important or not important for a government to implement the sharia went down from 67 percent to 60 percent between the two waves.

Given that the index of secular politics varies between 1 (strong support for political Islam) and 4 (strong support for secular politics), any median value close to 2.5 means that there are as many respondents who are orientated toward secular politics as there are who are oriented toward political Islam. As table 7.4 shows, the value of this index went up from 2.31 to 2.81 among Egyptians and from 2.88 to 3.06 among Tunisians. It stayed the same at 3.00 among Turkish respondents; all are statistically significant ($p < .001$), indicating that a significant majority of respondents supported secular politics.

The changes in the three countries are based on two observations in time and cannot be construed as a trend. Nonetheless, given that the reported changes are from the same panel of respondents across the three countries and that all change in the same direction, it would be hard to consider the directional similarity to be simply a coincidence or attribute these changes to sampling fluctuations. Moreover, comparable data from longitudinal surveys on some of these questions for other years are available for Egypt. Altogether, findings from these surveys support changes in values toward secular politics. Figure 7.1 displays changes in attitudes toward the separation of religion and politics in five surveys carried out in the country between 2007 and 2016.

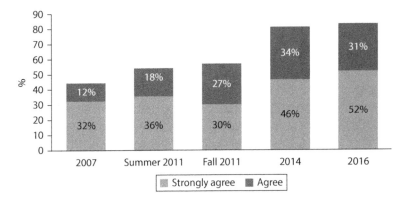

Figure 7.1 Egypt Would be a Better Place If Religion and Politics were Separated.

In 2007, 32 percent of respondents strongly agreed and 12 percent agreed that Egypt would be a better society if religion and politics were separated. These percentages increased to 36 percent and 18 percent in summer 2011, to 30 percent and 27 percent in fall 2011, to 46 percent and 34 percent in 2014, and to 52 percent and 31 percent in 2016, respectively.

Likewise, the percentage of Egyptians who preferred that their country have a Western-type government increased during the same survey period. According to figure 7.2, in 2007, 16 percent strongly agreed and 14 percent agreed that Egypt would be a better society if its government was similar to a Western-type government. These values increased to 16 percent and 19 percent in 2011 and to 24 percent and 31 percent in 2016, respectively.

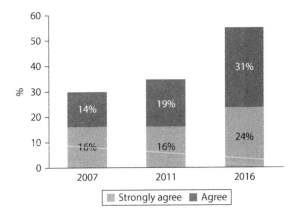

Figure 7.2 Egypt would be a Better Place If Its Government was Similar to a Western-Type Government.

National Identity

To measure identity, respondents were asked whether they defined themselves primarily in terms of their nationality (Egyptian, Tunisian, or Turkish),
religion (Muslim or Christian), or ethnicity (Arab, Turk, Berber, or other).
Because the great majority of respondents identified with either their territorial nationality or their religion, figure 7.3 contrasts those two responses. The
percentages of those who defined themselves above all as Egyptians were very
small, compared to the percentages of those who defined themselves above
all as Muslims or Christians in 2001 and 2007. Only 9 percent and 12 percent defined themselves as Egyptians in these years, respectively, compared to
78 percent and 84 percent who defined themselves as Muslims or Christians,
respectively. These percentages, however, changed dramatically following the
mass nationwide demonstrations that toppled President Hosni Mubarak in
January 2011. As shown, the percentage of those defining themselves as Egyptians jumped to 52 percent in summer 2011, to 56 percent in fall 2011, and to
61 percent in 2014, and then it dropped to 43 percent in 2016. The corresponding percentages over these years for those who defined themselves as Muslims
or Christians were 45 percent, 46 percent, 37 percent, and 54 percent. Among
Tunisians, adherence to national identity went up from 30 percent in 2013 to
37 percent in 2015, and adherence to religious identity went down from 59 percent to 52 percent, respectively. Among Turkish respondents, the percentage of
those who defined themselves as Turkish citizens went up from 34 percent in
2001 to 44 percent in 2013 and then to 53 percent in 2016, while the percentage of those who defined themselves as Muslims declined from 64 percent to
39 percent and then to 36 percent.

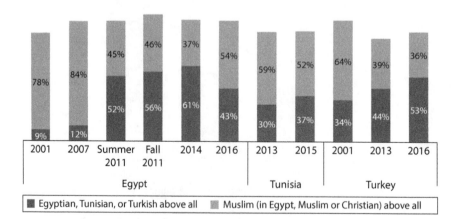

Figure 7.3 National Versus Religious Identity.

Figure 7.3 reveals an interesting fact about the cross-national difference in the shift in the basis of identity from religion to territorial nation. In Tunisia, this shift was not as dramatic as it was in Egypt and Turkey. The difference between Tunisia, on the one hand, and Egypt and Turkey, on the other, may result from the fact that religious fundamentalism in Tunisia has been much more moderate and the level of religious tolerance in the country much higher than in the other two countries, indicating a less contentious relationship between the sacred and secular in Tunisia. This may explain why Tunisians, while making a steady transition toward liberal democracy, were predominantly defining themselves above all as Muslims, rather than Tunisians. In Egypt, the Egyptian flag was ubiquitously and reverentially displayed by the demonstrators during their collective struggle against President Mubarak's authoritarian regime; this was intended to represent the collective reaffirmation of "we the people of Egypt" vis-à-vis the unrepresentative and unresponsive government and to confirm and mobilize patriotic attachments to the country of Egypt. The menace of the religious authoritarianism of the Muslim Brothers further reinforced the declaration of Egyptian identity. The 2013 military coup that overthrew the Muslim Brothers appeared to have weakened this process of change in identity. As a result, there was a significant drop in national identity and an increase in religious identity among Egyptians between 2014 and 2016. The dramatic shift in identity among Turkish respondents between 2001 and 2016 from 64 percent Muslim and 34 percent Turkish identity to almost the reverse of 36 percent Muslim and 53 percent Turkish identity also paralleled the contentious relationship between the secularists and fundamentalists in the country and the increasing Islamic authoritarianism of President Erdoğan.

As figure 7.4 shows, the respondents' attachment to the national community, in contradistinction to the religious community, was much higher than their identification with the nation, as shown in figure 7.3. Between the two waves, the respondents' attachment to the national community significantly increased in Egypt and Tunisia, while their attachment to religious community decreased. In Turkey, on the other hand, their attachment to the religious, national, and ethnic communities decreased, while their attachment to the world increased. The percentage of Egyptians who saw themselves as citizens of their country—rather than the world, religious community, or Arab nation—increased from 62 percent in 2011 to 77 percent in 2016, while those who saw themselves as citizens of the worldwide Islamic or Christian community and of the Arab nation decreased from 35 percent and 2 percent in 2011 to 19 percent and 1 percent, respectively, in 2016. Likewise, in Tunisia, between 2013 and 2015, the percentages of respondents who identified themselves as citizens of the Islamic community and of the Arab nation declined from 42 percent and 6 percent in 2013 to 39 percent and 5 percent, respectively, in 2015. On the other hand, those who considered themselves citizens of their county and of

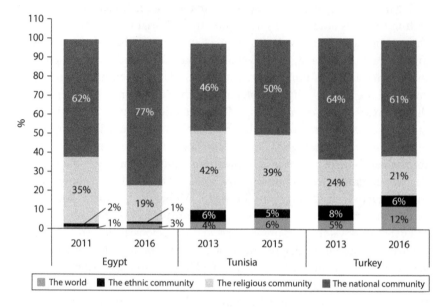

Figure 7.4 I See Myself as a Citizen of. . . .

the world increased from 46 percent and 4 percent to 50 percent and 6 percent, respectively, between the two surveys. Among Turkish respondents, between 2013 and 2016, those who considered themselves citizens of Turkey, the Islamic community, and the Turkish nation declined from 64 percent, 24 percent, and 8 percent to 61 percent, 21 percent, and 6 percent, respectively, while those who defined selves as citizens of the world jumped from 5 percent to 12 percent.

Turkish respondents and, to a small extent, Egyptians and Tunisians turned more globalist between the two surveys. However, identity with the nation is a component of liberal nationalism, and identity with the world relates to liberal internationalism. Combining the two categories, the change in identity in a liberal direction across the three countries was considerable between the two waves—from 63 percent to 80 percent in Egypt, from 50 percent to 56 percent in Tunisia, and from 69 percent to 73 percent in Turkey.

Western Culture

Hostility toward the West has been the hallmark of Islamic fundamentalism. The harbingers of the fundamentalist movements often warned their followers about the destructive influence of the "decadent Western culture" on their country. Findings from the surveys have shown, however, that smaller percentages of the respondents from Egypt and Turkey considered the menace

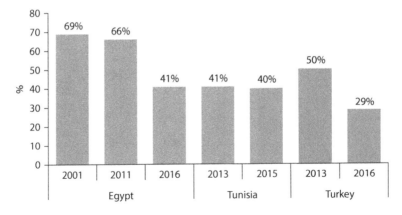

Figure 7.5 Percentages of Respondents Who Identify Western Cultural Invasion as a very Important Problem.

of Western culture to be an important issue. According to figure 7.5, the percentage of Egyptians who considered Western cultural invasion to be a very important problem declined steadily from 69 percent in 2001 to 66 percent in 2011 and then to 41 percent in 2016. Likewise, a smaller percentage of Turkish respondents expressed serious concerns with Western cultural invasion, as this percentage dropped from 50 percent in 2013 to 29 percent in 2016. Among Tunisian respondents, this perception did not significantly change; it decreased slightly from 41 percent to 40 percent between the two waves of the survey.

On average, citizens of these countries believed in varying degrees that Western cultural invasion was a problem. Yet the intensity of their concern with the West has significantly diminished among Egyptian and Turkish respondents and remained about the same among Tunisians between the two waves.

Religious Tolerance

Religious intolerance is one of the four components of Islamic fundamentalism discussed in chapter 4. Religious tolerance is based on the reverse coding of the indicators of religious intolerance. Four questions measure the construct, all in Likert-scale response format: "Do you (1) strongly agree, (2) agree, (3) disagree, or (4) strongly disagree that (i) our children should not be allowed to learn about other religions, (ii) the followers of other religions should not have the same rights as mine, (iii) criticism of religion should not be tolerated, and (iv) criticism of religious leaders should not be tolerated?" These four indicator variables are averaged in order to construct a religious tolerance index.

TABLE 7.5 Indicators of Religious Tolerance and Religious Tolerance Index

	Egypt (2011)	Egypt (2016)	Tunisia (2013)	Tunisia (2015)	Turkey (2013)	Turkey 2016
Our children should not be allowed to learn about other religions						
Strongly agree	25%	17%	20%	15%	17%	14%
Agree	20%	16%	14%	8%	26%	26%
Disagree	36%	30%	26%	22%	37%	33%
Strongly disagree	20%	38%	40%	55%	20%	27%
Strongly disagree/disagree	56%	68%	66%	77%	57%	60%
The followers of other religions should not have the same rights as mine						
Strongly agree	16%	5%	12%	10%	15%	8%
Agree	14%	9%	11%	6%	20%	8%
Disagree	42%	23%	29%	17%	39%	33%
Strongly disagree	28%	63%	48%	68%	26%	52%
Strongly disagree/disagree	70%	86%	77%	85%	65%	85%
Criticism of religion should not be tolerated						
Strongly agree	58%	46%	48%	44%	31%	32%
Agree	20%	29%	19%	17%	38%	37%
Disagree	16%	13%	19%	19%	22%	18%
Strongly disagree	7%	12%	15%	20%	8%	12%
Strongly disagree/disagree	23%	25%	34%	39%	20%	30%
Criticism of religious leaders should not be tolerated						
Strongly agree	43%	36%	16%	16%	23%	20%
Agree	24%	25%	15%	13%	37%	24%
Disagree	25%	22%	33%	29%	29%	30%
Strongly disagree	8%	18%	37%	42%	12%	26%
Strongly disagree/disagree	33%	40%	70%	71%	41%	56%
Religious tolerance index (Mean)	2.25	2.60	2.72	2.92	2.43	2.70
Median	2.25	2.50	2.75	3.00	2.50	2.75
Standard deviation	0.64	0.74	0.75	0.78	0.74	0.71
n	2,425	2,403	2,372	2,349	1,678	1,584
Wave 2 – wave 1	$2.60 - 2.25 = 0.35$		$2.92 - 2.72 = 0.20$		$2.70 - 2.43 = 0.27$[a]	

[a] $p < .001$.

This index varies between 1 (low tolerance) and 4 (high tolerance), and a median value for the religious tolerance index that is greater than 2.5 means that the majority of the respondents on average are more tolerant than intolerant. The results are presented in table 7.5.

Respondents grew more tolerant of other religions between the two waves of the panel survey across the three countries. Those who strongly disagreed or disagreed that children should not be allowed to learn about other religions increased from 56 percent to 68 percent in Egypt, from 66 percent to 77 percent in Tunisia, and from 57 percent to 60 percent in Turkey. Likewise, those who strongly disagreed or disagreed that the followers of other religions should not have the same rights increased from 70 percent to 86 percent in Egypt, from 77 percent to 85 percent in Tunisia, and from 65 percent to 85 percent in Turkey. Those who strongly disagreed or disagreed that criticism of religion should not be tolerated increased from 23 percent to 25 percent in Egypt, from 34 percent to 39 percent in Tunisia, and from 20 percent to 30 percent in Turkey. Finally, those who strongly disagreed or disagreed that criticism of religious leaders should not be tolerated increased from 33 percent to 40 percent in Egypt, from 70 percent to 71 percent in Tunisia, and from 41 percent to 56 percent in Turkey.

These changes reflect a significant increase in the overall measure of the religious tolerance index. The value of this index increased from 2.25 to 2.60 for Egypt, from 2.72 to 2.92 for Tunisia, and from 2.43 to 2.70 for Turkey—all significant at $p < .001$ (table 7.5). Also increased was the median value for religious tolerance among Egyptian respondents from 2.25 to 2.50, among Tunisian respondents from 2.75 to 3.00, and among Turkish respondents from 2.50 to 2.75 between the two waves. Except for Egypt where the population was divided fifty-fifty between religious tolerance and intolerance, the median value for Tunisia and Turkey was higher than the mean, indicting a great majority of the public displaying a much higher level of religious tolerance than they did in the first wave of the panel survey. Considering that religious tolerance is an important predictor of liberal democracy, an increase in the level of religious tolerance enhances support for liberal values.

Gender Equality

Changes in attitudes toward gender equality are measured using the same five indicators discussed in chapter 2. Respondents were asked whether they (1) strongly agree, (2) agree, (3) disagree, or (4) strongly disagree with the following: (i) "it is acceptable for a man to have more than one wife," (ii) "a wife must always obey her husband," (iii) "on the whole, men make better political leaders than women do," (iv) "a university education is more important for a boy than for a girl," and (v) "when jobs are scarce, men should have more right to a job than women." These measures are also averaged in order to construct a gender equality index. Table 7.6 reports the results.

Focusing on those who strongly disagreed or disagreed in order to explore the extent to which attitudes changed toward gender equality, changed toward

TABLE 7.6 Indicators of Attitudes Toward Gender Equality and Gender Equality Index

	Egypt (2011)	Egypt (2016)	Tunisia (2013)	Tunisia (2015)	Turkey (2013)	Turkey (2016)
Polygamy: It is acceptable for a man to have more than one wife						
Strongly agree	8%	22%	7%	10%	2%	2%
Agree	20%	25%	12%	9%	5%	5%
Disagree	29%	18%	17%	11%	25%	21%
Strongly disagree	43%	35%	65%	71%	69%	73%
Strongly disagree/disagree	72%	53%	82%	82%	94%	94%
Obedience: A wife must always obey her husband						
Strongly agree	70%	55%	45%	50%	19%	20%
Agree	25%	35%	34%	28%	53%	47%
Disagree	5%	8%	18%	17%	19%	20%
Strongly disagree	0.4%	3%	4%	5%	9%	13%
Strongly disagree/disagree	5.4%	11%	22%	22%	28%	33%
Political leadership: On the whole, men make better political leaders than women do						
Strongly agree	59%	52%	34%	44%	11%	12%
Agree	23%	25%	22%	18%	45%	38%
Disagree	11%	14%	27%	20%	32%	33%
Strongly disagree	7%	9%	16%	19%	12%	16%
Strongly disagree/disagree	18%	23%	43%	39%	44%	49%
Education: A university education is more important for a boy than for a girl						
Strongly agree	21%	12%	11%	8%	7%	7%
Agree	14%	11%	10%	6%	24%	21%
Disagree	33%	21%	35%	15%	44%	42%
Strongly disagree	33%	56%	45%	71%	25%	30%
Strongly disagree/disagree	66%	77%	80%	86%	69%	72%
Jobs: When jobs are scarce, men have more right to a job than women						
Strongly agree	64%	58%	53%	60%	16%	16%
Agree	22%	25%	22%	15%	41%	40%
Disagree	9%	11%	15%	10%	30%	29%
Strongly disagree	6%	7%	10%	15%	13%	15%
Strongly disagree/disagree	15%	18%	25%	25%	33%	44%
Gender equality index (Mean)	2.08	2.18	2.48	2.52	2.71	2.77
Median	2.00	2.20	2.40	2.50	2.60	2.80
Standard deviation	0.52	0.55	0.59	0.61	0.56	0.58
n	2,427	2,413	2,391	2,387	1,712	1,711
Wave 2 – wave 1	$2.18 - 2.08 = 0.10^b$		$2.52 - 2.48 = 0.04^a$		$2.77 - 2.71 = 0.06^a$	

[a] $p < .05$.
[b] $p < .001$.

inequality, and did not change, among Egyptian respondents, between 2011 and 2016, the percentage of those who strongly disagreed or disagreed with polygamy decreased from 72 percent to 53 percent, but the percentages of those who strongly disagreed or disagreed with wife obedience increased from 5.4 percent to 11 percent, with male superiority in political leadership from 18 percent to 23 percent, with boys having priority in university education from 66 percent to 77 percent, and with men having more right to a job from 15 percent to 18 percent. In other words, four out of five indicators show changes in favor of gender equality between the two waves.

While Tunisians were more favorable toward gender equality than Egyptians, the amount of change toward gender equality was smaller. On polygamy, wife obedience, and men having more right in the job market, those who strongly disagreed or disagreed remained unchanged at 82 percent, 22 percent, and 25 percent, respectively, between 2013 and 2015. Attitudes toward male superiority in political leadership changed in favor of men, as the percentage of those who strongly disagreed or disagreed dropped from 43 percent to 39 percent. However, the percentage of those who strongly disagreed or disagreed on boys having priority in university education increased from 80 percent to 86 percent between the two waves.

Turkish respondents were far more favorable toward gender equality than either Egyptian or Tunisian respondents, and their attitudes grew even more favorable between the two surveys. While they overwhelmingly rejected polygamy, with scores of 94 percent in both waves, their disapproval of wife obedience increased from 28 percent to 33 percent, of male supremacy in political leadership from 44 percent to 49 percent, of boys having priority in university education from 69 percent to 72 percent, and of men having more right to a job from 33 percent to 44 percent.

An overall picture of changes in attitudes toward gender equality across the three countries is provided by the gender equality index. The value for this index increased between the two waves across all three countries: from 2.08 to 2.18 among Egyptian respondents, from 2.48 to 2.52 among Tunisian respondents, and from 2.71 to 2.77 among Turkish respondents. The median values also increased from 2.00 to 2.20 among Egyptian respondents, 2.40 to 2.50 among Tunisian respondents, and 2.60 to 2.80 among Turkish respondents between the two waves. Although the amounts of change between the waves were small across the three countries, they are statistically significant (at $p < .001$ for Egypt and at $p < .05$ for Tunisia and Turkey). Moreover, given that the amount of increase in the median values was at least twice the amount of increase in the mean values across the countries between the two waves, more people appeared to have a more favorable attitude toward gender equality in the second wave than is indicated by the mean value.

Expressive Individualism and Liberal Values

Changes in attitudes toward expressive individualism represent an exception to the pattern of change seen across the three countries. As shown in table 7.7, between the two waves, the percentage of Egyptians who considered love, in contrast to parental approval, as the basis for marriage dropped significantly from 32 percent to 28 percent ($p < .01$); while the percentage who believed a woman should be free to dress as she wishes remained on average about the same, the percentage that supported the more liberal options on the child qualities index also significantly declined ($p < .01$), resulting in a significant decline in the value of the expressive individualism index between the two surveys from 1.78 to 1.67. Among Tunisians, there were no data on child qualities, but the percentages of those who considered love as the more important basis of marriage and who thought a woman should be able to dress as she wishes both significantly increased ($p < .01$), resulting in an increase in expressive individualism from 2.23 to 2.36. Finally, among Turkish respondents, changes in the

TABLE 7.7 Changes in the Measures of Expressive Individualism and Liberal Values Between the Two Waves of the Panel Survey

	Egypt		Tunisia		Turkey	
	Wave 1	Wave 2	Wave 1	Wave 2	Wave 1	Wave 2
Love as a basis for marriage	32%	28%	26%	29%	52%	36%
Woman dresses as she wishes						
Strongly agree	5%	6%	29%	38%	11%	16%
Agree	10%	13%	26%	26%	40%	39%
Disagree	36%	27%	26%	19%	37%	34%
Strongly Disagree	49%	55%	18%	17%	11%	12%
Mean (range 1–4)	1.71	1.70	2.67	2.84	2.52	2.58
Favorable qualities for children						
Independence (% selected)	38%	40%	—	—	35%	35%
Imagination (% selected)	9%	10%	—	—	24%	29%
Obedience (% not selected)	34%	13%	—	—	78%	81%
Religious (% not selected)	12%	15%	—	—	27%	28%
Child qualities index	1.69	1.49	—	—	2.21	2.28
Expressive individualism index	1.78	1.67	2.23	2.36	2.43	2.31
Liberal values index	2.06	2.23	2.52	2.65	2.65	2.70

measures of expressive individualism were not consistent. While the percentage who considered love as the basis for marriage significantly declined from 52 percent to 36 percent ($p < .001$), the percentages supporting a woman's freedom to dress as she wishes and the more liberal options on the child qualities index significantly increased between the two waves ($p < .01$). The significant decrease in support for love as the basis for marriage, however, resulted in a decline in the index of expressive individualism from 2.43 to 2.31.

To assess the overall changes in liberal values across the three countries, an index of liberal values was constructed in the same way that it was constructed in chapter 4: by averaging the measures of three of its indices—expressive individualism, gender equality, and secular politics. The index ranges between 1 and 4. The results show that between the two waves of the panel survey, the value of this index significantly increased from 2.06 to 2.23 for Egypt, from 2.52 to 2.65 for Tunisia, and from 2.65 to 2.70 for Turkey. The scores on the index of liberal values for the second wave of Tunisian and Turkish respondents are significantly larger than 2.5, so a majority of these respondents on average were predominantly liberal. Although in Egypt the value of this index also significantly increased between the two waves to 2.23, Egyptian respondents were still predominantly illiberal.

Changes in Values in Iraq and Saudi Arabia

Findings from cross-sectional surveys carried out in Iraq and Saudi Arabia display similar changes in values toward liberalism and national identity during the first decade of the twenty-first century. These findings are based on the analysis of the data from several surveys conducted in Iraq between 2004 and 2011 and from two surveys conducted in Saudi Arabia between 2003 and 2011.

American Occupation and Trends in Values Among Iraqis

Seven surveys of nationally representative samples of varied sizes (between 1,000 and 8,000 respondents) were carried out in Iraq in December 2004, April 2006, October 2006, March 2007, July 2007, December 2008, and January 2011. The December 2004, April 2006, and January 2011 surveys were full-scale national values surveys, using a large questionnaire with more than 250 items. The other four surveys included only a few questions on secular politics, gender relations, and the basis of identity. To make complete use of these datasets in assessing trends in values among Iraqis, two types of analysis are presented. One is based on the items that were common to all of these surveys. The other uses the measures of liberal values that were available only in the three complete datasets—December 2004, April 2006, and January 2011. These datasets were analyzed in order to assess changes in expressive individualism, gender equality, secular politics, and liberal values among Iraqis between 2004 and 2011.

Findings from the analysis of the responses to the common items across the seven surveys and the scores for the index of liberal values across the three surveys highlight an increase in support for expressive individualism, gender equality, secular politics, and national identity, all signifying a shift toward liberal values among Iraqis. As will be shown, among Iraqis, the amount of change toward secular politics and national identity was much greater than it was toward expressive individualism and gender equality, similar to the results in Egypt, Tunisia, and Turkey.

Secular Politics

Figure 7.6 illustrates the changes in support for the separation of religion and politics and for a Western political model in Iraq. The percentage of the respondents who strongly agreed or agreed that Iraq would be a better society if religion and politics were separated increased from 52 percent in December 2004 to 66 percent in January 2011. Likewise, the percentage of the respondents who strongly agreed or agreed about the desirability of Western-type government

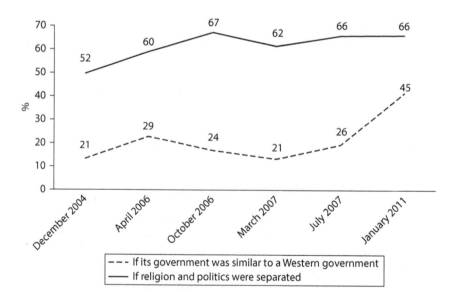

Figure 7.6 Percentages of Respondents Who Strongly Agree/Agree that Iraq would be a Better Place if Its Government was Similar to a Western Government and if Religious and Politics were Separated.

for Iraq increased from 21 percent in December 2004, with some fluctuations in the surveys between 2006 and 2007, to 26 percent in July 2007 and then to 45 percent in January 2011.

These changes are remarkable given the considerable amount of anti-Western propaganda generated by Sunni extremists and the extensive political influence the Islamic regime in Iran had on the Iraqi Shia political parties. These changes may be the result of the violence and suicide terrorism conducted by Sunni extremist groups, on the one hand, and the sectarian attitudes and behaviors of the dominant Shia political leaders, on the other, which may have prompted Iraqis to appreciate the utility of secular politics. In fact, the support for Western-style government among Iraqis (45 percent) in 2011 was more than it was among Egyptians (35 percent) in 2011, slightly less than it was among Tunisians (47 percent) in 2013, and more than it was among Turkish respondents (42 percent) in 2013, as reported in the first wave of the panel survey in these countries (see table 7.4).

Parallel to these changes is the decline in support for political Islam among Iraqis. Figure 7.7 highlights the trends in Iraqi attitudes toward Islamic government and sharia law between December 2004 and January 2011. The percentage of Iraqis who said that it was very important for a good government to implement only sharia laws declined steadily from 31 percent in December 2004 to 25 percent in April 2006, to 18 percent in October 2006, and then to 13 percent in January 2011. Likewise, those who mentioned that it was very important to have an Islamic government where the religious authorities had absolute power declined from 30 percent in December 2004 to 22 percent in April 2006, to

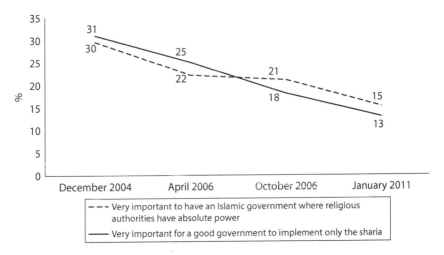

Figure 7.7 Percentages of Respondents who Mention that Islamic Government and the Sharia are very Important.

21 percent in October 2006, and then to 15 percent in January 2011. These figures indicate a systematic decline in support for the form of Islamic authoritarian regime that is currently in power in Iran.

National Identity

Between December 2004 and January 2011, there has been a remarkable increase
in the percentage of Iraqis who defined themselves above all as Iraqis, rather
than as Muslims, Arabs, or Kurds. According to figure 7.8, in January 2004,
only 24 percent of Iraqis defined themselves above all as Iraqis. This percentage
went up to 28 percent in April 2006, 55 percent and 60 percent in March and
July 2007, and 63 percent in December 2008, and then it fell to 57 percent in
January 2011. This rise in self-definition as Iraqis may in part reflect an increase
in favorable attitudes toward secular politics in this period. It may also indicate
the development of nationalist awareness in opposition to foreign occupation,
as it parallels the period of the U.S. occupation of the country. Such a steady
and notable increase in the percentage of Iraqis who clearly identified with the
national territorial community, in contrast to religion, gives further credence to
the proposition that foreign occupation provokes nationalist awareness, similar
to the historical rise of territorial nationalism among Egyptians and Algerians
under the British and the French occupations, respectively, between the late
nineteenth and early twentieth centuries.

There is, however, variation in the trend in Iraqi self-definition to identify by
ethnicity, as shown in table 7.8. Among Sunnis, Shias, and Muslims (those who
preferred not to be identified as members of any sect or reveal their sect identity
and who do not form a distinct ethnic group), there was an upward trend in the

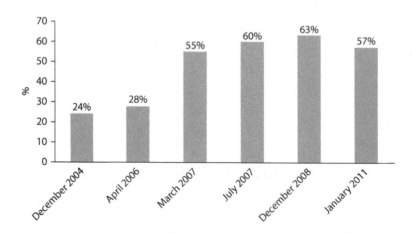

Figure 7.8 Percentages of Iraqi Respondents who Define Themselves above all as Iraqis.

TABLE 7.8 National Identity

Survey		Sunni	Shia	Kurd	Muslim	Total
Which of the following best describes you?						
December 2004	Above all, I am an Iraqi	21%	28%	9%	27%	23%
	Above all, I am a Muslim	76%	70%	26%	66%	64%
	Above all, I am an Arab	2%	2%	0%	4%	2%
	Above all, I am a Kurd	1%	0%	65%	1%	11%
	Other	0%	0%	0%	2%	0%
	Total	502	1,264	375	128	2,269
April 2006						
	Above all, I am an Iraqi	24%	32%	5%	44%	28%
	Above all, I am a Muslim	76%	67%	48%	55%	65%
	Above all, I am an Arab	0%	1%	0%	1%	1%
	Above all, I am a Kurd	0%	0%	47%	0%	6%
	Other	0%	0%	0%	0%	0%
	Total	510	1,376	345	347	2,578
March 2007						
	Above all, I am an Iraqi	53%	61%	20%	83%	53%
	Above all, I am a Muslim	46%	37%	22%	17%	36%
	Above all, I am an Arab	1%	0%	0%	0%	0%
	Above all, I am a Kurd	0%	0%	56%	0%	9%
	DK/NA	0	1%	2%	0%	1%
	Total	2,030	4,044	1,194	143	7,411
July 2007						
	Above all, I am an Iraqi	57%	71%	17%	64%	59%
	Above all, I am a Muslim	40%	27%	31%	32%	31%
	Above all, I am an Arab	2%	1%	1%	1%	1%
	Above all, I am a Kurd	0%	0%	49%	1%	8%
	Other	0%	0%	0%	0%	0%
	DK/NA	0%	1%	2%	2%	2%
	Total	2,012	4,132	1,199	389	7,732
January 2011						
	Above all, I am an Iraqi	68%	63%	13%	61%	56%
	Above all, I am a Muslim	28%	31%	57%	36%	35%
	Above all, I am an Arab	3%	4%	0%	1%	2.9%
	Above all, I am a Kurd	—		26%		4.2%
	DK	0%	1%	4%	1%	2%
	Total	829	1,234	485	403	2,951

recognition of nation as the primary basis of identity and a concomitant decline in considering religion as such during the survey period. In December 2004, 21 percent of Sunnis defined themselves above all as Iraqis versus 75 percent who defined themselves as Muslims. These percentages were 28 percent versus 70 percent of Shias and 27 percent versus 66 percent of Muslims, respectively. During the survey period, the percentage distribution between national and religious identity gradually reversed. In January 2011, in contrast to December 2004, 68 percent of Sunnis defined themselves above all as Iraqis versus 28 percent who defined themselves as Muslims. Among Shia respondents, these percentages also changed to 63 percent as Iraqis and 31 percent as Muslims, and among Muslims, they changed to 61 percent as Iraqis and 36 percent as Muslims, respectively. Only a negligible percentage of Arab respondents, 4 percent or less, defined themselves above all as Arabs. Considering that Iraq was the hotbed of pan-Arab nationalism in the interregnum between World War I and World War II, such a low percentage of Iraqi Arabs who identified primarily with their ethnicity indicates how little support there is for this once powerful ideological movement in the region and the extent of the changes in identity the country has experienced since the first half of the twentieth century.

The pattern of change in identity among Iraqi Kurds, on the other hand, is different from that of Iraqi Arabs during the survey period. As table 7.8 shows, among this group, Islamic nationalism appears to be competing with Kurdish nationalism, not Iraqi nationalism. In December 2004, 65 percent or the majority of Kurdish respondents defined themselves above all as Kurds and 26 percent defined themselves as Muslims. However, in the subsequent surveys, the percentages of those defining themselves as Kurds versus Muslims changed to 47 percent versus 48 percent in April 2006, 56 percent versus 22 percent in March 2007, 49 percent versus 31 percent in July 2007, and 26 percent versus 57 percent in January 2011. The last figure indicates a major reversal in identity among Kurds from Kurdish to Islamic. Given the predominance of secular tendencies among Kurdish political groups, however, this dramatic increase in religious identity among Kurds in 2011 was unexpected. Adherence to Iraqi identity was low among Kurdish respondents. It fluctuated between a minimum of 5 percent in April 2006 and a maximum of 20 percent in March 2007.

Western Culture

Parallel to changes in Iraqis' value orientations toward secular politics and national identity, there was a decline in unfavorable attitudes toward Western culture. As shown in figure 7.9, the percentage of Iraqis who considered Western cultural invasion to be a very important problem first increased from 79 percent in December 2004 to 85 percent in April 2006. It then dropped to 54 percent in 2011.

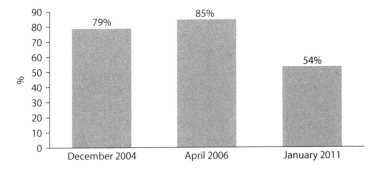

Figure 7.9 Percentages of Iraqi Respondents who Identify Western Cultural Invasion as a very Important Problem.

Expressive Individualism, Gender Equality, Secular Politics, and Liberal Values

Complete data on the measures of expressive individualism, gender equality, secular politics, and liberal values are available for the December 2004, April 2006, and January 2011 surveys in Iraq. The indices of these constructs are calculated in the same way that they were in chapters 1 through 3. They all vary between 1 and 4.

Table 7.9 shows the distributions of the values of these indices for the three surveys and the changes in these values between December 2004 and January 2011. The index of expressive individualism declined from 1.72 in 2004 to 1.65 in 2006; it then increased to 1.89 in 2011. The index of gender equality also declined slightly from 1.96 in 2004 to 1.94 in 2006; it then increased to 2.22 in 2011. The other two indices consistently increased between the surveys.

TABLE 7.9 Trends in Values among Iraqis, 2004–2011

	December 2004	April 2006	January 2011	January 2011 – December 2004 =
Expressive individualism	1.72	1.65	1.89	0.17[a]
Gender equality	1.96	1.94	2.22	0.26[a]
Secular politics	2.20	2.43	2.53	0.33[a]
Liberal values	1.95	1.99	2.21	0.26[a]
n	2,202	2,446	2,873	

[a] $p < 0.001$.

The secular politics index increased from 2.20 in 2004 to 2.43 in 2006 and then to 2.53 in 2011; the index of liberal values increased from 1.95 in 2004 to 1.99 in 2006 and then to 2.21 in 2011. The greater increase in the index of secular politics reflects the changes in the political views of Iraqis as a result of experiencing religious extremism and Sunni-Shia sectarian conflict in their country. Given the median value for the secular politics index among Iraqi respondents in 2011 was 2.56 (not shown in the table), which is significantly larger than 2.50 ($p < .001$), one may generalize that the majority of Iraqis favored this form of government rather than being against it at the time of the survey.

Changes in Values in Saudi Arabia

Findings from two national surveys carried out in Saudi Arabia in 2003 and 2011 reveal a similar pattern of change in expressive individualism, gender equality, secular politics, liberal values, and national of identity between the two surveys. These changes indicate an increase in support for gender equality, secular politics, and liberal values. While support for expressive individualism significantly declined, this decline was among respondents in the older age group (aged 30 and over). For those in the youth bulge (aged 18–29), there was an increase in favorable attitudes toward expressive individualism between 2003 and 2011. This increase, however, is not statistically significant.

Because of the limitations of the data, the construction of all the indices of liberal values had to be modified. Some of the items were not asked in either survey, and some were included in only one of the surveys; in some cases, their formats were different between the two surveys. As a result, first, expressive individualism was constructed by averaging only two of the three items that were used in chapter 1: (i) the child qualities index, which measured respondents' views of favorable qualities for children (i.e., the extent to which they mentioned independence and imagination but not obedience and religious faith), and (ii) the basis for marriage. The third indicator of the construct, the belief that it is up to a woman to dress as she wishes, was not included in the 2003 survey (see chapter 1).

Second, the gender equality index was constructed by averaging responses to only four items: "Do you (1) strongly agree, (2) agree, (3) disagree, or (4) strongly disagree that (i) men make better political leaders than women do, (ii) university education is more important for a boy than for a girl, (iii) a wife must always obey her husband, and (iv) it is acceptable for a man to have more than one wife?" The fifth item—"when jobs are scarce, men should have more right to a job than women"—had only three response categories in the 2003 survey: "Do you agree, disagree, does not matter?" The last item was thus excluded in constructing this index.

As was mentioned in chapter 3, because of the limitation of the data for Saudi Arabia, the concept of secular politics was measured as an average of three indicators: (i) attitudes toward the sharia (a good government implements only sharia law), (ii) confidence in religious institutions, and (iii) the question whether Saudi Arabia would be (1) a lot more, (2) more, (3) less, or (4) a lot less developed if the influence of religion on politics increases (used as a proxy for attitudes toward separation of religion and politics). This third item was not included in the 2003 Saudi survey. Therefore, a measure of the attitude toward democracy was substituted. To assess changes in attitude toward secular politics between 2003 and 2011, the following three measures were averaged to construct a secular politics index for Saudi Arabia:

1. Is it (1) very important, (2) important, (3) somewhat important, (4) least important, or (5) not important for a good government to implement only the laws of the sharia? [To make the construct vary between 1 and 4, these five response categories were adjusted by multiplying them by 0.75 and adding 0.25.]
2. Do you do you have (1) a great deal of confidence, (2) quite a lot of confidence, (3) not very much confidence, or (4) none at all in religious institution?
3. Do you (4) strongly agree, (3) agree, (2) disagree, or (1) strongly disagree that democracy may have problems, but it is the best form of government. [3]

An index of liberal values was also constructed by averaging the three indices of expressive individualism, gender equality, and secular politics. All these measures vary between 1 and 4. A higher value indicates stronger support for expressive individualism, gender equality, secular politics, and liberal values. The aggregate values of the four indices for 2003 and 2011 surveys are reported in table 7.10. The index of expressive individualism significantly declined from

TABLE 7.10 Changes in Values among Saudis, 2003–2011

	2003 Mean (Standard Deviation, n)	2011 Mean (Standard Deviation, n)	2011 – 2003 =
Expressive individualism	2.35 (0.85, 999)	2.25 (0.89, 1,535)	−0.10[a]
Gender equality	1.95 (0.60, 1,025)	2.11 (0.58, 1,635)	0.16[b]
Secular politics	1.73 (0.51, 997)	2.15 (0.53, 1,627)	0.42[b]
Liberal values	2.01 (0.43, 1,025)	2.17 (0.44, 1,634)	0.16[a]

[a] $p < .01$.
[b] $p < .001$.

2.35 to 2.25 between 2003 and 2011. This finding is consistent with a similar decline in Egypt and Turkey, but not in Iraq and Tunisia, during their respective survey periods. However, the indices of gender equality, secular politics, and liberal values significantly increased from 1.95 to 2.11, 1.73 to 2.15, and 2.01 to 2.17, respectively, between the two surveys. The values of all these indices are quite low, indicating Saudi Arabia is an illiberal society. Nonetheless, the data show noticeable changes toward liberal values.

National Identity

Consistent with changes in attitudes toward liberal values is a remarkable shift in Saudis' self-definition of the basis of identity from religion to nation between 2003 and 2011. As illustrated in figure 7.10, the percentage of Saudis who defined themselves above all as Saudis jumped from 17 percent in 2003 to 46 percent in 2011, that of those who defined themselves above all as Muslims dropped from 75 percent to 44 percent, and that of those who defined themselves above all as Arabs remained almost the same (9 percent and 8 percent) during the survey period. The decline in religion as the primary basis of identity is dramatic, particularly in one of the most religiously conservative countries in the Muslim world. In a country that is ostensibly ruled by an Islamic government, that the majority of the respondents (54 percent) defined their identity on a secular basis, by either nation or ethnicity, may be indicative of significance changes in values the people of Saudi Arabia are experiencing. Considering this change in conjunction with similar changes that transpired in Egypt, Iraq, Tunisia, and Turkey, it appears that the rise of national identity is one of the common changes in values in the region.

This shift toward national identity, in contradistinction to religion, parallels the decline in favorable attitudes toward the sharia and confidence in religious institutions between the 2003 and 2011 surveys. These changes may explain why

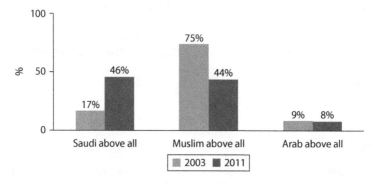

Figure 7.10 Changes in the Percentages of Saudi Respondents who Identify Themselves above all as Saudis, Muslims, or Arabs Between 2003 and 2011.

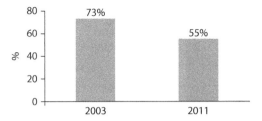

Figure 7.11 Percentages of Saudi Respondents who Identify Western Cultural Invasion as a very Important Problem.

the current Saudi rulers have decided to limit the power of the religious establishment in the country.

Western Culture

Parallel with changes in the Saudis' orientation toward liberal nationalism (with the exception of expressive individualism), there was a significant decline in their unfavorable attitudes toward Western culture. As illustrated in figure 7.11, the percentage of Saudi respondents who considered Western cultural invasion to be a very important problem declined from 73 percent in 2003 to 55 percent in 2011.

Value Changes by Gender, Age, and Education Across the Five Countries

To recap, significant changes in the respondents' value orientations toward secular politics, religious tolerance, gender equality, liberal values, and national identity have transpired in Egypt, Iraq, Saudi Arabia, Tunisia, and Turkey in recent years. The changes toward expressive individualism were inconsistent across these countries. Support for expressive individualism increased in Iraq and Tunisia but declined in Egypt, Saudi Arabia, and Turkey. This section assesses how age, gender, and university education affected these changes and whether these changes were uniform or different across age, gender, and education categories.

Age

Table 7.11 displays significant changes in values by age group between the two waves in terms of the indices of secular politics, religious tolerance, gender equality, expressive individualism, and liberal values. Accordingly, for both

TABLE 7.11 Changes in Values by Age Group (Range 1–4)

Age group	Secular Politics			Religious Tolerance			Gender Equality			Expressive Individualism			Liberal Values		
	W1[d]	W2[b]	Diff[c]	W1	W2	Diff	W1	W2	Diff	W1	W2	Diff	W1	W2	Diff
Egypt															
18–29	2.38	2.84	0.46[f]	2.30	2.64	0.34[f]	2.12	2.25	0.13[d]	1.91	1.83	−0.08[d]	2.13	2.32	0.19[e]
30+	2.33	2.69	0.36[f]	2.24	2.60	0.36[f]	2.07	2.17	0.10[d]	1.73	1.60	−0.13[d]	2.04	2.19	0.15[e]
Difference			0.10[d]			−0.02			0.03			0.05			0.04
Tunisia															
18–29	2.94	3.07	0.13[d]	2.89	3.03	0.14[e]	2.55	2.63	0.08[d]	2.36	2.44	0.08[d]	2.63	2.74	0.11[d]
30+	2.79	2.97	0.18[e]	2.68	2.90	0.21[e]	2.47	2.50	0.03	2.19	2.34	0.15[e]	2.49	2.62	0.13[d]
Difference			−0.05			−0.07[d]			0.05			−0.07[d]			−0.02
Turkey															
18–29	2.85	3.00	0.15[e]	2.45	2.73	0.28[f]	2.74	2.87	0.13[e]	2.65	2.63	−0.02	2.71	2.89	0.18[e]
30+	2.83	2.92	0.09[d]	2.42	2.69	0.27[f]	2.70	2.75	0.04	2.35	2.21	−0.14[d]	2.63	2.64	0.01
Difference			0.06			0.01			0.09[d]			0.12[d]			0.17[e]
Iraq															
18–29	2.20	2.54	0.34[f]				2.00	2.29	0.29[f]	1.78	2.01	0.23[f]	1.99	2.28	0.29[f]
30+	2.19	2.46	0.27[f]				1.94	2.18	0.24[f]	1.69	1.81	0.12[d]	1.94	2.15	0.21[f]
Difference			0.07[d]						0.05			0.11[d]			0.08[d]
Saudi Arabia															
18–29	1.75	2.17	0.42[f]				1.99	2.16	0.17[e]	2.44	2.49	0.05	2.06	2.27	0.21[f]
30+	1.72	2.09	0.37[f]				1.91	2.05	0.14[d]	2.26	2.05	−0.21[f]	1.96	2.07	0.11[d]
Difference			0.05						0.03			0.26[f]			0.10[d]

[a] W1 = wave 1.
[b] W2 = wave 2.
[c] Diff = W2−W1.
[d] $p < .05$.
[e] $p < .01$.
[f] $p < .001$.

age groups there were significance increases in the indices of secular politics, religious tolerance, gender equality (except for the older age group [aged 30+] in Tunisia and Turkey for which there was no significant change), and liberal values (except for the older age group [aged 30+] in Turkey for which there was no significant change). The change in the index of expressive individualism, however, was inconsistent by age group and across the countries. For Egypt, this index declined significantly for both age groups, for Turkey and Saudi Arabia, it declined only among the older age group (aged 30+) but no significant change for the youth bulge (aged 18-29). For Tunisia and Iraq, on the other hand, the index of expressive individualism increased significantly for both groups between the waves.

In terms of which of the age groups experienced a greater amount of change in values between the two waves than the other age group, table 7.11 shows that in a few cases respondents in the youth bulge (aged 18–29) either exhibited a significantly greater amount of change than did those in the older age group (aged 30+) or were the only group showing a significant change. These differences, as underlined, were for the index of (1) secular politics for Egypt and Iraq (where the amount of increase for youth bulge was 0.10 and 0.07, more than the amount of increase for the older age group, respectively), (2) gender equality in Tunisia and Turkey (where it increased significantly only for the youth bulge by 0.08 and 0.13, respectively), (3) expressive individualism in Iraq (where the amount of increase for the youth bulge was 0.11 more than the amount of increase for the older age group), and (4) liberal values in Turkey, Iraq, and Saudi Arabia (where the amount of increase for the youth bulge was 0.17, 0.08, and 0.10 more than the amount of increase for the older age group, respectively). On the other hand, respondents in the older age group exhibited a significantly greater amount of change on religious tolerance and expressive individualism in Tunisia (the amount of increase for the youth bulge was 0.07 less than the amount of increase for the older age group for both indices). Finally, respondents in the older age group in Turkey and Saudi Arabia exhibited a significant amount of decline in the index of expressive individualism between the two waves (the amount of decline was 0.14 and 0.21, respectively).

Gender

Table 7.12 displays changes in values by gender in terms of the indices of secular politics, religious tolerance, gender equality, expressive individualism, and liberal values across the five countries between the two waves. For both male and female respondents, there were significance increases in the indices of secular politics, religious tolerance, gender equality (except for male in Tunisia and female in Saudi Arabia), and liberal values (except for male in Turkey). The change in the index of expressive individualism, however, was inconsistent by gender and across the countries. For Egypt and Turkey, the value of this index declined significantly for both male and female. For Saudi Arabia, it declined only for male. For Tunisia and Iraq, it increased for both male and female.

In terms of which gender experienced a greater amount of change in values between the two waves, table 7.12 shows inconsistencies. Male respondents exhibited a lesser amount of increase than female respondents on (1) gender equality index in Egypt and Iraq (where the amount of increase for female respondents was 0.14 and 0.09 more than the amount of increase for male respondents between the two waves, respectively), (2) liberal values in Egypt and

TABLE 7.12 Changes in Values by Gender (Range 1–4)

Gender	Secular Politics W1[a]	W2[b]	Diff[c]	Religious Tolerance W1	W2	Diff	Gender Equality W1	W2	Diff	Expressive Individualism W1	W2	Diff	Liberal Values W1	W2	Diff
Egypt															
Male	2.42	2.81	0.39[f]	2.27	2.64	0.37[f]	2.00	2.04	0.04[d]	1.81	1.66	−0.15[e]	2.09	2.21	0.12[e]
Female	2.25	2.63	0.38[f]	2.23	2.57	0.34[f]	2.16	2.33	0.18[f]	1.76	1.68	−0.08[d]	2.05	2.26	0.21[f]
Difference			0.01			0.03			−0.14[f]			−0.07[d]			−0.09[d]
Tunisia															
Male	2.85	3.01	0.16[f]	2.76	2.97	0.21[f]	2.33	2.36	0.03	2.16	2.28	0.12[d]	2.46	2.58	0.12[e]
Female	2.79	2.97	0.18[f]	2.69	2.88	0.19[f]	2.60	2.64	0.04[d]	2.28	2.43	0.15[e]	2.57	2.69	0.12[e]
Difference			−0.02			0.02			−0.01			−0.03			0.00
Turkey															
Male	2.85	2.92	0.07[d]	2.45	2.70	0.27[f]	2.59	2.64	0.05[d]	2.42	2.29	−0.13[d]	2.62	2.65	0.03
Female	2.81	2.94	0.12[e]	2.41	2.70	0.30[f]	2.80	2.86	0.07[e]	2.43	2.33	−0.10[d]	2.68	2.74	0.06[d]
Difference			−0.05			−0.04			−0.02			−0.03			−0.03
Iraq															
Male	2.25	2.53	0.28[f]				1.87	2.09	0.22[f]	1.74	1.89	0.15[e]	1.95	2.17	0.22[f]
Female	2.14	2.45	0.31[f]				2.04	2.37	0.33[f]	1.70	1.89	0.19[e]	1.95	2.23	0.28[f]
Difference			−0.03						−.09[d]			−0.04			−0.06[d]
Saudi Arabia															
Male	1.72	2.13	0.41[f]				1.71	1.98	0.27[f]	2.46	2.31	−0.15[e]	1.96	2.14	0.18[e]
Female	1.75	2.17	0.42[f]				2.19	2.23	0.04	2.24	2.19	−0.05	2.06	2.20	0.14[e]
Difference			−0.01						0.23[f]			−0.10[d]			0.04

[a] W1 = wave 1.
[b] W2 = wave 2.
[c] Diff = W2−W1.
[d] $p < .05$.
[e] $p < .01$.
[f] $p < .001$.

Iraq (where the amount of increase for female respondents was 0.09 and 0.06 more than the amount of increase for male respondents between the two waves, respectively) and in Turkey, where only female respondents exhibited increase between the two waves (the amount of increase was 0.06); or male respondents displayed greater amount of decrease than female respondents on expressive individualism in Egypt and Saudi Arabia (where the amount of decrease for male respondents was 0.07 and 0.10 more than the amount of decrease for female respondents between the two waves, respectively). Finally, in one case, Saudi Arabia, only male respondents displayed a significant increase in the index of gender equality between the two waves (with the increase of 0.27).

Education

Table 7.13 shows the differential effects of university education versus no university education on changes in values across the five countries. Although respondents with university education scored higher than those without university education in their orientations toward liberal values, they were not always ahead of the latter in exhibiting such changes. Nor was the amount of change between the two waves of the survey greater among respondents with university education than it was among those without. As shown in table 7.13,

TABLE 7.13 Changes in Values by Level of Education (Range 1–4)

Education	Secular Politics			Religious Tolerance			Gender Equality			Expressive Individualism			Liberal Values		
	W1[a]	W2[b]	Diff[c]	W1	W2	Diff	W1	W2	Diff	W1	W2	Diff	W1	W2	Diff
Egypt															
No university	2.32	2.71	0.39[f]	2.22	2.59	0.37[f]	2.06	2.17	0.11[d]	1.76	1.63	−0.13[e]	2.04	2.21	0.17[f]
University	2.47	2.79	0.32[f]	2.45	2.71	0.26[f]	2.18	2.28	0.10[d]	1.93	1.86	−0.07[d]	2.20	2.36	0.16[f]
Difference			−0.06			−0.11[d]			−0.01			0.06			−0.01
Tunisia															
No university	2.80	2.97	0.17[f]	2.67	2.87	0.19[f]	2.45	2.49	0.04[d]	2.17	2.32	0.15[e]	2.46	2.59	0.13[e]
University	2.89	3.08	0.19[f]	3.00	3.27	0.26[f]	2.71	2.72	0.01	2.47	2.57	0.10[e]	2.78	2.89	0.11[e]
Difference			0.02			0.07			−0.03			−0.05			−0.02
Turkey															
No university	2.80	2.91	0.10[f]	2.38	2.68	0.31[f]	2.68	2.74	0.05[e]	2.37	2.26	−0.11[e]	2.61	2.66	0.05[e]
University	3.07	3.15	0.08[e]	2.77	2.90	0.15[d]	2.89	2.99	0.10[d]	2.83	2.66	−0.17[f]	2.94	3.00	0.06
Difference			−0.02			−0.16[d]			0.04			−0.06			0.01
Iraq															
No university	2.14	2.45	0.31[f]				1.93	2.20	0.27[f]	1.68	1.86	0.18[f]	1.91	2.17	0.26[f]
University	2.42	2.63	0.21[f]				2.09	2.30	0.21[f]	1.89	2.00	0.11[e]	2.13	2.31	0.18[f]
Difference			−0.10[d]						−0.06			−0.07			−0.08[d]
Saudi Arabia															
No university	1.74	2.15	0.41[f]				1.96	2.09	0.13[e]	2.31	2.22	−0.09[d]	2.01	2.15	0.14[e]
University	1.72	2.14	0.42[f]				1.89	2.15	0.26[f]	2.49	2.32	−0.17[e]	2.03	2.20	0.17[e]
Difference			0.01						0.13[e]			−0.08			0.03

[a] W1 = wave 1.
[b] W2 = wave 2.
[c] Diff = W2−W1.
[d] $p < .05$.
[e] $p < .01$.
[f] $p < .001$.

between the two waves both educational groups displayed significant changes toward secular politics, religious tolerance, and gender equality (except for respondents with university education in Tunisia where this change was not significant), and liberal values (except for respondent with university education in Turkey where this increase was not significant).

In a few cases, the amount of increase between the two waves was larger for respondents without university education than it was for respondents with university education on (1) secular politics index for Iraq (where the amount of increase for respondents without university education was 0.10 more than the amount of increase for those with university education), (2) religious tolerance index for Egypt and Turkey (where the amount of increases for respondents without university education were 0.11 and 0.16 more than the amount of increase for those with university education, respectively), (3) gender equality index for Tunisia and Saudi Arabia (where the amount of increase for respondents without university education was 0.04 for Tunisia, and 0.13 more than the amount of increase for those with university education for Saudi Arabia), and (4) liberal values for Turkey and Iraq (where the amount of increase for respondents without university education was 0.05 for Turkey, and 0.08 more than the amount of increase for those with university education for Iraq). On expressive individualism, both education groups significantly declined in Egypt, Turkey, and Saudi Arabia, while both significantly increased in Tunisia and Iraq.

Inconsistencies in the Process of Values Change

Changes in values are not uniform and consistent across different domains of social life. As the data showed, the indices of expressive individualism, gender equality, secular politics, and national identity did not change by the same amount. This was also the case with the indices of the different components of fundamentalism: a disciplinarian deity, literalism, religious exclusivity, and religious intolerance. Table 7.14 summarizes the changes in values by showing the differences in the indices of the components of liberal values and fundamentalism between the first and the last observations. Across the five countries, the amount of change was greater for the index of secular politics than it was for the indices of gender equality and expressive individualism. For Egypt, the index of secular politics increased by 0.38, the gender equality index increased by 0.10, and the expressive individualism index decreased by 0.11. For Tunisia, these values were 0.17, 0.04 and 0.13; for Turkey, 0.11, 0.06, and −0.12; for Iraq, 0.33, 0.26 and 0.17; and for Saudi Arabia, 0.42, 0.16, and −0.10, respectively. Likewise, the amount of increase in the percentage of the respondents who defined themselves in terms of national identity, rather than religious identity,

TABLE 7.14 Changes in Indices of Liberal Values and Religious Fundamentalism and their Components

	Egypt	Tunisia	Turkey	Iraq	Saudi Arabia
Expressive individualism	−0.11	0.13	−0.12	0.17	−0.10
Gender equality	0.10	0.04	0.06	0.26	0.16
Secular politics	0.38	0.17	0.11	0.33	0.42
Liberal values	0.17	0.13	0.05	0.26	0.16
National identity	40%	7%	29%	45%	29%
Disciplinarian deity	−0.08	0.05	−0.09	—	—
Literalism	−0.01[a]	0.03	−0.10	—	—
Religious exclusivity	0.09	−0.02[a]	−0.12	—	—
Religious intolerance	−0.35	−0.20	−0.29	—	—
Religious fundamentalism	−0.09	−0.04	−0.16	—	—

Note: All changes are statistically significant at $p < .05$ unless noted otherwise.
[a] Not significant.

was remarkable. This increase was 40 percent for Egypt, 7 percent for Tunisia, 29 percent for Turkey, 45 percent for Iraq, and 29 percent for Saudi Arabia.

Moreover, the amount of change toward liberal values was much greater for more conservative countries like Egypt, Iraq, and Saudi Arabia, where the fundamentalists were relatively successful in launching attacks on the secular order (e.g., in Egypt and Iraq) or in maintaining religious rule (e.g., in Saudi Arabia) than in countries where political Islam was relatively weaker (e.g., in Tunisia and Turkey). Reflecting changes in the three measures of expressive individualism, gender equality, and secular politics, the index of liberal values increased by 0.17 for Egypt, 0.26 for Iraq, and 0.16 for Saudi Arabia, while the increases for Tunisia and Turkey were 0.13 and 0.05, respectively.

Likewise, changes in religious fundamentalism and its four components were inconsistent between the two waves of the panel survey and across the three countries. The decline in the index of religious intolerance was consistent across the three countries and was significantly greater than the declines in the indices of the other components of fundamentalism. While the index of religious fundamentalism declined by 0.09 for Egypt, 0.04 for Tunisia, and 0.16 for Turkey, the value of the religious intolerance index dropped dramatically between the two waves by 0.35, 0.20, and 0.29 for the three countries, respectively. The changes in the other three measures between the waves were inconsistent. For Egypt, the decline in the literalism index was not significant, while the index of religious exclusivity increased. For Tunisia, the indices of the disciplinarian deity and literalism increased, but the change in religious exclusivity was not significant. Turkey was the only country where all the indices significantly declined between the two waves,

This cross-country comparison is certainly crude, as the beginnings and ends of the observations are not the same. There were also differences in the length of time between the two observations for different countries. Finally, the possibility cannot be ruled out that the greater amount of change toward liberal values among the more conservative countries of Egypt, Iraq, and Saudi Arabia, compared to what it was for the more liberal countries of Tunisia and Turkey, simply reflected regression toward the mean—that is, the countries that are extremely conservative are more likely to turn less conservative in the future than are those that are moderately conservative. At the same time, these figures may indicate a stronger desire among the Egyptian, Iraqi, and Saudi respondents for secular change because they had experienced a stronger presence of Islamic extremism and terrorism in their societies than had the respondents from Tunisia and Turkey. Finally, it may be speculated that the greater amount of change toward liberal values among Egyptian, Iraqi, and Saudi respondents was indicative of a greater convergence of values toward secularism and national territorial identity across the region.

Summary

The central claim of this chapter was that the conflict between Islamic fundamentalism and liberal nationalism appears to have been resolved toward the latter and the Arab Spring therefore signifies the dawn of a new cultural episode in the Middle East and North Africa. Three different empirical facts support this claim. One is that, for the majority of the respondents in Egypt, Tunisia, Lebanon, and Pakistan and the largest percentage of the respondents from Turkey, the goals of the Arab Spring were freedom, democracy, and economic prosperity. Less than 12 percent of the respondents from Egypt, Tunisia, Lebanon, and Turkey and about 26 percent of those from Pakistan thought that goal was the formation of an Islamic government. Second, the analysis of the self-reported participation in the movements of the Arab Spring showed that the index of fundamentalism was negatively linked to participation among Tunisians but had no significant connection with participation among Egyptians. The index of liberal values, on the other hand, was positively linked to participation across both countries. Moreover, the factors that were positively linked to religious fundamentalism were negatively linked to participation. These are religiosity, religious modernity, confidence in religious institutions, residence in rural areas, the belief that mixing of the sexes leads to social corruption (only among Egyptians, with a minor contrary to expectation among Tunisia), belief that premarital sex is immoral (only among Tunisians, and partially among Egyptians), xenophobia and belief in conspiracy (only among Egyptians), and fatalism. On the other hand, factors that were positively linked to liberal values were also positively connected to participation. These are socioeconomic status, being male, being a member of the youth bulge, and reliance on the internet as a source of information.

Finally, the third was based on findings from the analysis of changes in values across Egypt, Iraq, Saudi Arabia, Tunisia, and Turkey. This analysis rested on two sets of data. One set was from two waves of a comparative panel survey in Egypt, Tunisia, and Turkey. The other set was from cross-sectional surveys carried out in Egypt, Iraq, Saudi Arabia, and Turkey. Data for at least three points in time were available on measures of identity for Egypt, Iraq, and Turkey; secular politics for Egypt and Iraq; and attitudes toward Western culture for Egypt. On other measures or on similar measures for other countries, data for only two points in time were available.

Strictly speaking, data on a variable must be available for at least three points in time in order to establish a trend for that variable. Nonetheless, because virtually all the changes reported in this chapter are in the same direction—indicating the rise of liberal values, religious tolerance, and national identity—it is reasonable to claim that these changes represent a major shift in values in the Middle East and North Africa.

Changes toward secular politics: Among the components of liberal values, changes toward secular politics have been the most remarkable shift in values across Egypt, Iraq, Saudi Arabia, Tunisia, and Turkey. The findings from the panel survey in Egypt, Tunisia, and Turkey showed a significant increase in the value of the composite index of secular politics. A most interesting aspect of this change has been a significant increase in the percentage of the respondents who expressed favorable attitudes toward Western-type government. The latest surveys in Egypt, Tunisia, and Turkey reported in this book showed that the percentage of the respondents who expressed a favorable attitude toward this type of government was significantly higher that the percentage expressing an unfavorable attitude. These surveys and the latest survey in Iraq showed that the majority of respondents in Egypt, Iraq, Tunisia, and Turkey favored secular politics.

Increase in support for religious tolerance: Across Egypt, Tunisia, and Turkey, there was a significant increase in religious tolerance between the two waves of the panel survey. The latest surveys showed that the majority of the respondents from Tunisia and Turkey were religiously tolerant and Egyptians were fifty-fifty divided between being tolerant and intolerant.

Changes toward gender equality: Although the amounts of change were small, the increases in the value of the gender equality index across the five countries were statistically significant. The support for gender equality varied considerably across the five countries. Tunisian and Turkish respondents were more egalitarian than inegalitarian, but the majority of respondents from Egypt, Iraq, and Saudi Arabia still supported gender inequality.

Inconsistent changes in expressive individualism: The change in expressive individualism was inconsistent across the five countries. The values of the index of expressive individualism for Egypt, Saudi Arabia, and Turkey declined, but they significantly increased for Iraq and Tunisia.

Changes in liberal values: All five countries showed a significant increase in the index of liberal values. The amount of change appears to be larger among the less liberal countries. For Egypt, this index rose from 2.06 in 2011 to 2.23 in 2016; for Iraq, from 1.95 in 2004 to 1.99 in 2006 and then to 2.20 in 2011; for Saudi Arabia, from 2.01 in 2003 to 2.17 in 2011; for Tunisia, from 2.52 in 2013 to 2.65 in 2015; and for Turkey, from 2.65 in 2013 to 2.70 in 2016. Based on these figures, the values of the index of liberal values for Tunisia and Turkey are significantly above the 2.5 threshold, so these two countries may be classified as predominantly liberal. Egypt, Iraq, and Saudi Arabia, having indices of liberal values significantly below 2.5, are predominantly illiberal countries.

The rise of national identity: The percentages of the respondents who defined themselves primarily in terms of their nationality rather than their religion significantly increased across the five countries. These increases were accompanied by concomitant declines in the percentages of those who defined themselves above all as Muslims across the countries.

Changes by Age, Gender, and Education: There were significant changes in values by age group between the two waves in terms of the indices of secular politics, religious tolerance, gender equality (except for the older age group in Tunisia and Turkey), and liberal values (except for the older age group in Turkey for which there was no significant change). The change in the index of expressive individualism was inconsistent by age group and across the countries. For Egypt, this index declined significantly for both age groups, for Turkey and Saudi Arabia, it declined only among the older age group but no significant change for the youth bulge. For Tunisia and Iraq, on the other hand, the index of expressive individualism increased significantly for both groups between the waves. In terms of which of the age groups experienced a greater amount of change in values between the two waves, in a few cases respondents in the youth bulge either exhibited a significantly greater amount of change than did those in the older age group or were the only group showing a significant change.

There were also significant changes in values by gender. For both male and female respondents, there were significance increases in the indices of secular politics, religious tolerance, gender equality (except for male in Tunisia and female in Saudi Arabia), and liberal values (except for male in Turkey).

The change in the index of expressive individualism, however, was inconsistent by gender and across the countries. For Egypt and Turkey, the value of this index declined significantly for both male and female. For Saudi Arabia, it declined only for male. For Tunisia and Iraq, it increased for both male and female. Both genders experienced about the same amount of change in values, except in few cases where male respondents either exhibited a lesser amount of increase in values than female respondents or greater decrease in values than female respondents.

Finally, although respondents with university education scored higher than those without university education in their orientations toward different components of liberal values, they were not always ahead of the latter in exhibiting such changes. Nor was the amount of change between the two waves of the survey greater among respondents with university education than it was among those without. Between the two waves both educational groups displayed significant changes toward secular politics, religious tolerance, and gender equality (except for respondents with university education in Tunisia where this change was not significant), and liberal values (except for respondent with university education in Turkey where this increase was not significant). In a few cases, the amount of increase between the two waves was larger for respondents without university education than it was for respondents with university education.

It thus appeared that younger age group, women, and those without university education are more likely to experience a greater amount of change in values than their counterparts.

CONCLUSION

The Viability of Liberal Nationalism

T he foregoing empirical analysis showed the depth and breadth of the clash of values between Islamic fundamentalism and liberal nationalism within and between Egypt, Iraq, Lebanon, Pakistan, Saudi Arabia, Tunisia, and Turkey. This analysis showed that not only the indices of Islamic fundamentalism and liberal nationalism were inversely related, but also the factors that strengthened fundamentalism tended to weaken liberal nationalism on both the micro (individual) and macro (country) levels. Moreover, although the analysis of the cross-sectional data showed that more people on average tended to support fundamentalism than they did liberal nationalism, two sets of empirical evidence highlighted the significance of liberal values in shaping the prospect for political change in these countries and probably beyond. One set indicated the importance of such values, chiefly gender equality, in people's perspectives concerning the causes and consequences of development. The respondents in fact associated liberal changes with development. The second set, and more significantly, revolved on the respondents' understanding of the goals of the Arab Spring and the trends in their values. Accordingly, they predominantly viewed freedom, democracy, and economic prosperity as the most important goals of the movements of the Arab Spring, and that those who participated in these movements were more likely to adhere to liberal values and less likely to spouse fundamentalist beliefs and attitudes. Furthermore, the analysis of the longitudinal and panel data showed the rise of liberal values and the decline of political Islam. The trends in values thus warrant the conclusion that the Arab Spring signified the ushering in of a new cultural episode in the Middle East and North Africa.

These empirical data also support the argument that Islamic fundamentalism is the key factor underpinning the multitude of overlapping conflicts occurring in the region in the form of the violence of the state against the subjugated populations, political violence and suicide terrorism, Shia-Sunni sectarian warfare, maltreatment of women, and discriminations against ethnic and religious minorities. Liberal nationalism has emerged as an alternative oppositional discourse to fundamentalism and religious extremism. Therefore viewing the region's contemporary problems from the liberal nationalist perspective keeps one from being distracted by the multitudes of unforeseen (and often horrific) events; the ill-thought-out political actions of powerful actors beyond the borders of one's country, which tend to provoke the feeling of national pride, in-group (i.e., nationalist or sectarian) solidarity, and hostility toward out-groups (i.e., members of other religious sects, ethnicities, or nations); and the propagandistic behavior of the nationalist demagogues in one's own country, whose sole objective has habitually been to demonize the ethnic or religious minorities and people from other nations. It also expands the intellectual attention span and enhances one's ability to stay focused on the issues that matter most in the construction of a new political order: the recognition and institutionalization of individual rights, support for gender equality, tolerance of other religions and ethnic groups, and demand for a transparent, responsive, and nonideological regime. Furthermore, liberal nationalism is significant not simply because it is a better way of organizing one's political community. Rather, the pattern of empirical relationships established by the extensive cross-national data demonstrated that liberal nationalism is a real political alternative. In fact, staying focused on realizing and institutionalizing the value of individual equality in all the domains of social life as the governing principle of political action is the key to restoring the status of the Middle East and North Africa as a historical cradle of human civilization.

The theoretical framework that informed the empirical analysis and illuminated the rise of liberal nationalist discourse as the single-most important development among the numerous emergent processes in the region rests on the premises that (1) ideological discourses on how to resolve historically significant sociopolitical and cultural issues are terribly important in bringing into relief a new pattern of historical development and (2) the formulation of the specific content and character of such discourses has its own autonomy. Therefore, incipient or emergent discourses may not be viewed as being a reflection of or having a determinate relationship with economic development and other objective aspects of social life, although resources are undeniably necessary for the production and dissemination of ideas. Delinking the presumed connection between economic development and changes in values and belief systems, this theory implies that there is little utility in categorizing societies using a stage theory of evolutionary change (e.g., primitive versus advanced, traditional versus modern). As an alternative, it argues that social change occurs when intellectual leaders and the public at large engage in various forms of back-and-forth discussions and ideological contentions as they address and try to resolve the issues they encounter in their daily lives. The manner in which they resolve issues, however, occurs in opposition to the discourse of the groups and institutions that are dominant, or perceived to be dominant, in their society.

The dominant discourse, or what is expressly imposed on the subject population, provokes the thought process in order to develop responses to it, driving the intellectual desire to search for an alternative perspective and unleashing cognitive rebellion. Cognitive rebellion, however, does not necessarily lead to cognitive liberation and evolutionary change. Only one type of resolution of issues indicates such liberation. Generally, the back-and-forth discussions, ideological debates, religious disputations, and the warring of positions over issues produce alternative discourses that in turn shape the agenda of the opposition movement, structure the attention span of the oppositional leaders, and turn a given historical period into a distinct cultural episode. History from this perspective is viewed as a succession of diverse cultural episodes. In the modern period, the Middle East and North Africa have experienced a succession of such episodes as Islamic modernism, liberal nationalism or authoritarian secular nationalism, and Islamic fundamentalism. The movements of the Arab Spring, as the analysis of the data presented here has demonstrated, have ushered in a new liberal nationalist episode in the region.

Islamic Fundamentalism Versus Liberal Nationalism

Survey research methodology was employed to understand the value orientations of the adult populations in Egypt, Iraq, Lebanon, Pakistan, Saudi Arabia, Tunisia, and Turkey. A nationally representative sample of respondents in each of these countries was drawn in order to collect the necessary data on the extent to which the values and perceptions of these respondents conformed to religious fundamentalism and the extent to which they displayed affinity with liberal values. To establish cross-nationally comparable patterns of the empirical relationship between liberal values and religious fundamentalism, both terms were first conceptualized as multidimensional constructs and then carefully measured by multiple sets of indicators. The components of liberal values included expressive individualism, gender equality, secular politics, and national identity. Six questionnaire items measured the index of expressive individualism, five the index of gender equality, and four the index of secular politics. A composite index of liberal values was constructed by averaging these three indices. Two questions measuring the basis of identity were analyzed separately and were not included in the construction of the index of liberal values. Religious fundamentalism was conceptualized as a set of beliefs about and attitudes toward one's and others' religions. Included among its components were (1) a disciplinarian conception of the deity, (2) the belief in the literal truth or the inerrancy of the scriptures, (3) the belief in religious exclusivity or in the superiority of one's faith and religious community over other religions and religious communities, and (4) intolerance of other religions. Four survey questions measured each of these components, and a religious fundamentalism index was constructed by averaging the responses to all sixteen questions. This measure was applicable to fundamentalism in Christianity and both sects of Islam (Shia and Sunni). All the indices varied between 1 and 4.

The analysis of the data showed the following: (1) The indices of liberal values and religious fundamentalism displayed considerable variation among individuals. (2) The national aggregates of these measures also varied considerably across the seven countries. (3) The measures of the two constructs were negatively correlated (inversely linked) on both the micro (individual) and the macro (country) levels; this indicated conflicts of values between those who were oriented toward religious fundamentalism and those leaning toward liberal values. (4) The micro and macro factors that were positively linked to religious fundamentalism were negatively connected to liberal values. (5) Both liberal values and religious beliefs were important in shaping the respondents' views on what makes their country more developed, but the respondents predominantly considered that development would bring about liberal changes; this meant that religious beliefs and liberal values, from the respondents' perspectives, were consequential for developmental change and that the latter was also believed to shape the perceptions of how changes in religious beliefs and liberal values would occur. (6) A shift in values occurred toward liberal democracy and national identity across Egypt, Iraq, Saudi Arabia, Tunisia, and Turkey. Although longitudinal surveys were not carried out in Pakistan, analysis of the 2011 data showed a considerable gap in values between the youth bulge (aged 18–29) and the older age group (aged 30 and older): members of the Pakistani youth bulge exhibited much stronger support for liberal values and a weaker orientation toward religious fundamentalism than did members of the older age group. The percentage of the youth bulge that adhered to national identity was also higher than that of the older age group. The gap in value orientations between the young and the old was much wider among the respondents in Pakistan than it was among the respondents in the other six countries. This finding plausibly signified a generational shift in values toward liberalism and religious tolerance in Pakistan.

Variation in Values at the Micro (Individual) Level

The analysis of the data at the micro level showed variation in support for different components of liberal values and religious fundamentalism, including variation by age, gender, and education. This analysis also showed the link between the attitudes and attributes of the respondents, on the one hand, and their fundamentalist and liberal orientations in each of the seven countries, on the other.

Expressive individualism: Members of the youth bulge were more strongly supportive of individualistic values than were those in the older age group. Respondents with university education were also more individualistic than were those without university education, except in Saudi Arabia, where there was no difference in expressive individualism between the two educational groups. There was, however, no significant difference between men and women on expressive individualism across the countries, except among Tunisian and Pakistani respondents, where women appeared to be more supportive of expressive individualism than men.

Cross-tabulation of age and education showed that among respondents in the youth bulge, those with university education were more individualistic than those without university education only in Lebanon, Tunisia, and Turkey; this was less the case in Saudi Arabia (the Saudi youth with university education were *less* individualistic than their peers with no university education), and there was no difference in expressive individualism between the two educational groups in the other three countries. Among the older are group, those with university education were consistently more individualistic across the countries, except in Saudi Arabia, where university education had no effect on expressive individualism.

The difference in expressive individualism between age groups was greatest among Pakistanis and second-greatest among Saudis, compared to the other countries. These significant differences between the age groups probably signified a generational change.

Gender equality: Respondents in the youth bulge were significantly more favorable toward gender equality than were those in the older age group, with the difference between the two groups being the greatest among Pakistani respondents. Young Turkish respondents were the most egalitarian in their attitudes toward women, and older Saudis were the least egalitarian. In all seven countries, women reported greater support for gender equality than men, with the greatest gender difference among Lebanese and the smallest among Egyptians. Furthermore, among women, age differences in favor of gender equality were significant, and those in the youth bulge scored higher on the gender equality index than did those in the older age group across all seven countries.

Among men, there were inconsistent but significant age differences across the seven countries: in some countries, respondents in the youth bulge were more supportive of gender equality, while in others it was just the opposite. Finally, respondents with university education were consistently more favorable toward gender equality, with the exception of Saudis, whose attitudes on gender equality were not differentiated by education. Among those in the youth bulge, respondents with university education were more supportive of gender equality than were those without university education only in Lebanon, Pakistan, Tunisia, Egypt, and Turkey. For Iraq and Saudi Arabia, this difference was not statistically significant. Among those in the older age group, those with university education scored significantly higher on the gender equality index across six of the seven countries. In Saudi Arabia, there was no difference in the gender equality index between the two educational groups. In sum, university education made the greatest difference in attitudes toward gender equality among Pakistanis in both age groups, the least difference among Iraqis, and no difference among Saudis. Again, as was the case with expressive individualism, university education appeared to have little effect on attitudes toward gender equality among Saudis.

On veiling preference, members of the youth bulge and people with university education opted for a more liberal veiling style than did the older age group and those without university education. There was no consistent pattern of gender difference in veiling preference. Finally, the analysis of the data showed that people who favored a more conservative veiling style for women were also less supportive of gender equality and expressive individualism.

Secular politics: Respondents in the youth bulge were more favorable toward secular politics than were those in the older age group in Lebanon, Pakistan, Saudi Arabia, and Tunisia, with this difference again greater in Pakistan than it was in the other countries. In Egypt, Iraq, and Turkey, there was no significant difference in support for secular politics between the two age groups. Nor was there a consistent pattern concerning the effect of gender on secular politics across the seven countries. There was, however, a significant link between university education and support for secular politics among the respondents from all seven countries except Saudi Arabia; those with university education were more supportive of secular politics than were those without university education. In Saudi Arabia, there was no difference in support for secular politics between the two educational groups.

Liberal values: The analysis showed that respondents in the youth bulge were consistently more liberal than were respondents in the older age group across the seven countries. Female respondents were also more liberal across the seven countries than were male respondents, except for Egyptian females and males, who were similar in liberal values. Those with university education were more supportive of liberal values than were those without university education in all the countries, except Saudi Arabia, where there was no significant difference in liberal values between those with and without university education. The distribution of gender and age showed that among females, those in the youth bulge were more liberal than those in the older age group across the seven countries. This relationship was also true among males, except in Tunisia, where there was no significant difference between the age groups. The distribution of the liberal values index by age and education showed that people with university education were more liberal across both age groups and all countries, except Saudi Arabia, where the respondents did not differ on liberal values by education.

As was the case for the indices of expressive individualism, gender equality, and secular politics, the difference between the two age groups on the index of liberal values was greatest among Pakistani respondents, compared to the other six countries.

National versus religious identity: Respondents varied considerably on identity; some defined themselves in terms of religion, while others considered their nation or their ethnicity as the basis of their identity. In Pakistan and Tunisia, the majority of respondents considered religion rather than nation to be the primary basis of identity, while respondents in the other five countries primarily identified with their nation. At the communal level, a much higher percentage of respondents identified with the national community than with the supranational religious community. On ethnicity, among Kurds in both Iraq and Turkey, a majority defined themselves above all as Muslims, followed by those who defined themselves as Kurds and those who saw themselves as Iraqis or Turkish citizens, respectively. Turks, on the other hand, predominantly defined themselves as Turkish citizens, followed by those who adhered to religious identity and then those who identified as ethnic Turks. Adherence to Arab identity was quite weak in Egypt and Iraq, with less than 4 percent of respondents defining themselves above all as Arabs. In Lebanon, Saudi Arabia, and Tunisia, this percentage was significantly higher, but they were still small minorities (between 7 and 10 percent of respondents) who considered themselves above all as Arabs. Ethnic identity was even weaker among Pakistani respondents.

Religious fundamentalism: Respondents in the youth bulge were less fundamentalist than were those in the older age group, except among Egyptians, who did not differ on fundamentalism by age group. This finding is consistent with the youth bulge having a stronger orientation toward liberal values than the older age group. Gender had an inconsistent relationship with fundamentalism across the seven countries. But respondents with university education had significantly weaker fundamentalist beliefs and attitudes than did those without university education across all the countries, except Saudi Arabia, where there was no significant difference between the two educational groups. In terms of age and education, respondents with university education had weaker fundamentalist orientations than did those without university education across both age groups in Lebanon, Pakistan, Tunisia, Egypt, and Turkey, but only the older age group with university education had a weaker fundamentalist orientation in Iraq. There was no difference in fundamentalism between the two educational groups within either age group in Saudi Arabia.

Liberal values and religious fundamentalism by religion and sect: Christians were significantly more liberal and were also more likely to define themselves in nationalist terms (in contradistinction to religion terms) than were their Muslim counterparts in Egypt and Lebanon, where there were substantial Christian populations. Likewise, a higher percentage of Shias than Sunnis defined themselves in nationalist terms in Iraq, Lebanon, Pakistan, and Turkey. However, there was no significant difference between Shias and Sunnis in terms of identifying themselves in national rather than religious terms in Saudi Arabia. Shias were less liberal in Iraq but more liberal in Lebanon, Pakistan, Saudi Arabia, and Turkey.

Christians in Egypt and Lebanon scored lower on each of the four indices of the components of religious fundamentalism, and Shias scored lower than Sunnis on these indices in Lebanon, Iraq, Pakistan, Saudi Arabia, and Turkey, with the exception that Iraqi Shias and Sunnis scored almost the same on the index of literalism. Lebanese Christians and Turkish Shias (mainly Alavis) were the least intolerant (or the most tolerant) of other religions, and Saudi Sunnis were the most intolerant (or the least tolerant) group in the samples. Considering the religious fundamentalism index, Christians were less fundamentalist than either Sunnis or Shias in Lebanon or Sunnis in Egypt. Lebanese Christians were considerably less fundamentalist than Egyptian Christians, showing the effect of a more pluralistic context in Lebanon, compared to Egypt, on fundamentalism. Shias were significantly less fundamentalist than Sunnis across the samples from Iraq, Lebanon, Pakistan, Saudi Arabia, and Turkey. Finally, Saudi Shias scored the lowest on the index of fundamentalism, compared to Shias from other countries, Sunnis, and even Christians.

The weaker fundamentalism of the members of the minority religions and religious sects is attributed to their desire to be accommodating to the religious majority and reduce religious tension, and the stronger fundamentalism among members of the majority religion or sect is attributed to their claim of a greater ownership or stewardship of religion and their perception that the religious minorities have deviated from the true path and are therefore posing a threat to their religion.

Religious fundamentalism versus liberal values: Religious fundamentalism and its four components were negatively linked to the components of liberal values—expressive individualism, gender equality, and secular politics—across the seven countries. Much higher percentages of the respondents favored fundamentalism over liberal values across the seven countries, except among Lebanese, where support was about the same for the two opposing movements. While this analysis indicated the relative stand of the respondents on religious fundamentalism vis-à-vis liberal values, it also showed that there was significantly more support for liberal values in Lebanon, Tunisia, and Turkey than there was in Egypt, Iraq, Pakistan, and Saudi Arabia, where the proportion of the respondents who favored liberal values varied between 10 percent among Pakistanis and 30 percent among Iraqis. Although support for religious fundamentalism was relatively high across the seven countries, support for religious intolerance was comparatively much lower than support for the other three components of fundamentalism—a disciplinarian deity, literalism, and religious exclusivity.

Finally, the analysis of the data uncovered a set of individual characteristics that were linked to the indices of religious fundamentalism and liberal values, and these linkages remained invariant across the seven countries. The characteristics that were positively linked to religious fundamentalism were negatively connected to liberal values. Religious fundamentalism was weaker and liberal values stronger among individuals who (1) had a higher socioeconomic status, (2) were younger, (3) resided in an urban area, (4) were less religious, (5) had lower trust in religious institutions, (6) were less likely to believe in religious modernity (i.e., the belief that religious beliefs would make one's country more developed), (7) were less likely to consider premarital sex immoral, (8) were less likely to believe that the mixing of the sexes in the workplace causes social corruption, (9) believed less strongly in conspiracy theory, (10) were less xenophobic, (11) had weaker sectarian solidarity, (12) were less fatalistic, and (13) relied more strongly on the internet as a source of information.

Although the survey conducted in Iran in 2005 measured these characteristics differently, the data also showed that religious fundamentalism among Iranians followed a similar pattern. It was weaker among individuals who (1) had a higher socioeconomic status, (2) resided in an urban area, (3) were less religious, (4) were less hostile to Western culture, (5) exhibited more tolerance, (6) displayed a stronger liberal outlook, and (7) relied more on the internet as a source of information and less on the government-controlled TV as a source of entertainment (Moaddel 2017c).

Cross-National Variation in Liberal Values and Religious Fundamentalism

The seven countries varied considerably in terms of their national aggregate scores for religious fundamentalism and liberal values. In Lebanon, Tunisia, and Turkey, the national aggregate indices of religious fundamentalism were lower and liberal values higher than they were in the other four countries. In Egypt and Pakistan, on the other hand, the national aggregate idices of religious fundamentalism were higher and liberal values lower than they were in the other five countries. In between were Iraq and Saudi Arabia. Moreover, in the same way that the indices of religious fundamentalism and liberal values were inversely related at the micro (individual) level, they were inversely related at the macro (country) level; countries that scored higher on the aggregate index of religious fundamentalism also scored lower on the aggregate indices of expressive individualism, gender equality, secular politics, and liberal values. The correlation coefficients between religious fundamentalism and liberal values were negative and significant across the seven countries.

The data also showed that (1) variation in religious fundamentalism and liberal values on the macro (country) level was influenced by such variable features of the national context as the structure of the religious environment (that is, whether this environment was pluralistic and free or monolithic and unfree), state structures and interventions in religion, economic development, economic and cultural globalization, and the situation of women in terms of female labor force participation and the sex ratio; and (2) the features of the national context that strengthened religious fundamentalism tended to weaken liberal values. The results of the analysis showed that religious fundamentalism was weaker and liberal values stronger in countries where there was greater religious liberty, higher fractionalization (diversification) of religion, more fragmentation in the structure of the state power, more globalization of the national context, and higher female labor force participation. Conversely, fundamentalism was stronger in countries where the state was more exclusionary, government regulation of religion was greater, and the sex ratio was higher. Finally, the youthfulness of a country's population, as indicated by the size of the youth bulge, was linked positively to religious fundamentalism and negatively to liberal values.

What Makes a Country More Developed: Liberal Values Versus Religious Beliefs

Development is presumed to be something desirable for the members of the ordinary public, perhaps anywhere in the world, including the Middle East and North Africa. Understanding how these people view the cultural causes and consequences of development would provide empirical knowledge on the extent of their receptivity to liberal ideas. Findings from the comparative cross-national surveys on the perceptions of the cultural causes and consequences of development across Egypt, Iraq, Lebanon, Pakistan, Saudi Arabia, and Turkey showed that respondents believed that the expansion of both liberal values and religious beliefs would make their country more developed. However, the percentage of the respondents who related religious beliefs to development was higher than that of those who linked liberal values to development. Concerning the cultural outcomes of development, respondents predominantly believed that development would bring about the rise of liberal values. A most remarkable finding from the surveys was that, for well over 80 percent of respondents, more egalitarian gender relations would make a country more developed and that, for more than 90 percent of respondents, a higher level of development would bring about greater gender equality.

Moreover, although respondents differentiated development from Westernization in terms of the cultural outcomes, these outcomes varied by social domains and countries. In the respondents' perspectives, the effect of development in expanding gender equality and individual liberty was either greater than or the same as the effect of Westernization in these domains. On the other hand, they saw Westernization as having greater impact than development in promoting the intermingling of members of the opposite sex and in enhancing individualistic values. The widest gap in the cultural outcomes between development and Westernization was found in their effects on religious beliefs. Westernization was thought to have much greater impact in causing a decline in religious beliefs than was development. Finally, the majority of the respondents believed that more democracy and governmental integrity would contribute more to development than would more religiosity.

In sum, the analysis of the cross-national data on the respondents' visions concerning what would make their country more developed indicated their favorable subjective orientations toward the reception of liberal values. Moreover, except for their differential effects on religious beliefs, the differences between Westernization and development were not as marked as one might have thought.

Trends in Values: Egypt, Iraq, Saudi Arabia, Tunisia, and Turkey

Three empirical facts were presented to support the view that the Arab Spring marked the dawn of a new cultural episode in the Middle East and North Africa. The first was based on the respondents' perceptions of the Arab Spring's objectives: a great majority mentioned freedom, democracy, and economic prosperity as the goals of the movements of the Arab Spring, while a small minority considered the goal to be the formation of an Islamic government. The second rested on the empirical assessment of fundamentalism and liberalism as the driving ideology of the movements: the index of religious fundamentalism either was negatively linked to or had no relationship with participation in the movements of the Arab Spring among Tunisian and Egyptian respondents, while the index of liberal values was positively linked to participation across both countries. This empirical assessment also showed that the factors that had positive links with liberal values were also positively connected to participation, while those that had positive connections with fundamentalism were negatively connected to participation. That is, socioeconomic status, being male, being a member of the youth bulge, and reliance on the internet as a source of information are linked positively to both liberal values and participation. On the other hand, religiosity, religious modernity, confidence in religious institutions, residence in rural areas, the belief that mixing of the sexes leads to social corruption or belief that premarital sex is immoral, xenophobia, belief in conspiracy (only among Egyptians), and fatalism were all positively linked to fundamentalism but negatively to participation.

Finally, the third consisted of the longitudinal data that showed trends in values. These trends were established by analyzing changes in values across Egypt, Iraq, Saudi Arabia, Tunisia, and Turkey using two sets of data. One set was from two waves of a comparative panel survey carried out in Egypt, Tunisia, and Turkey. The other set was from cross-sectional surveys conducted in Egypt, Iraq, Saudi Arabia, and Turkey. Findings from both sets showed a remarkable shift in some of the key values toward the rise of liberal nationalism and the decline of fundamentalism across the five countries.

Expressive individualism: Among the components of liberal values, the change in the index of expressive individualism was inconsistent. The value of this index significantly declined for Egypt, Saudi Arabia, and Turkey but increased for Iraq and Tunisia.

Gender equality: The trend showed a statistically significant increase in the value of the gender equality index across the five countries. The amount of increase in this index, however, was modest for some of these countries. Tunisian and Turkish majorities expressed egalitarian attitudes toward women, but majorities from Egypt, Iraq, and Saudi Arabia still supported gender inequality.

Secular politics: The shift toward secular politics was remarkable in Egypt, Iraq, Saudi Arabia, Tunisia, and Turkey. A most striking aspect of this change was a significant increase in the percentages of the respondents who expressed favorable attitudes toward Western-type government in Egypt, Iraq, Tunisia, and Turkey. The latest surveys in Egypt, Tunisia, and Turkey reported here showed that the percentages of the respondents who expressed favorable attitudes toward Western-type government were significantly higher than those who expressed unfavorable attitudes.

Liberal values: The index of liberal values, constructed by averaging the indices of expressive individualism, gender equality, and secular politics, also significantly increased across the five countries. The amount of change, however, was higher for illiberal countries—Egypt, Iraq, and Saudi Arabia— than it was for liberal countries—Tunisia and Turkey.

Religious tolerance versus religious fundamentalism: Data on religious tolerance were available for Egypt, Tunisia, and Turkey. Across these three countries, the religious tolerance index significantly increased (or the religious intolerance index significantly decreased) between the two waves of the panel survey. The index of religious fundamentalism significantly declined for the three countries between the two waves. Among the four components of religious fundamentalism, the decline in the index of religious intolerance was the greatest. The changes in other components did not follow a consistent pattern across the three countries.

National identity: There was a significant increase in support for national identity, as the percentages of the respondents who defined themselves primarily in terms of their nationality rather than their religion increased considerably in all five countries. This increase was accompanied by a concomitant decline in the percentages of those who defined themselves above all as Muslims across the countries.

Amount of change by age: The cross-tabulation showed there were twenty-three instances of change in values by age, coded as the youth bulge and the older age group. In eleven instances, or 48 percent of the total of twenty-three, age had a significant effect on the changes in values. In nine instances, or 39 percent, respondents in the youth bulge either exhibited a significantly greater amount of positive change than those in the older age group or were the only group that exhibited change. In two instances (both among Tunisians), or 9 percent, respondents in the older age group displayed a significantly greater amount of change. These findings suggest that respondents in the youth bulge are more likely to change their values than are those in the older age group— but not in all types of values or in all instances.

Although the requisite longitudinal survey data to construct trends in values for Pakistan were not available, the 2011 cross-sectional survey showed that respondents in the youth bulge were consistently and significantly more favorable toward expressive individualism, gender equality, secular politics, and liberal values than were respondents in the older age group and that the difference between the two age groups for each of these measures was consistently greater among Pakistani respondents than it was among respondents from the other countries. This finding may indicate a significant intergenerational change toward liberalism in Pakistan.

Amount of change by gender: The cross-tabulation of the changes in values by gender showed there were again twenty-three instances of changes in values. In nine instances, or 39 percent of the total of twenty-three, gender affected the changes in values. In eight instances, or 35 percent, women either displayed a greater amount of change toward liberal values or were the only group that exhibited such changes. In one instance (in Saudi Arabia), or 4 percent, men showed a greater amount of change than women. Comparatively, the changes in values are more likely to occur among women than men, although this relationship is not always the case across all instances.

Amount of change by education: The cross-tabulation of changes in values by education, coded as respondents with and without university education, also showed twenty-three instances of changes in values. In seven instances, or 30 percent of the total of twenty-three, education made a difference in the amount of change exhibited or in whether any change was exhibited between the two waves. In six instances, or 26 percent, those without university education either exhibited a significantly greater amount of change than those with university education or were the only group that exhibited a change in values. In only one instance (in Saudi Arabia), or 4 percent, respondents with university education exhibited a greater amount of change. These findings thus indicate that, while university-educated respondents had stronger liberal orientations, they did not necessarily experience a greater amount of change or a higher frequency of change than those without university education.

The Shift in Values and the National Context

The shift in values across the five countries may represent the activation of secular, liberal, and nationalist awareness among the citizens of these countries. This awareness, one may argue, amounts to cognitive liberation, which has opened up a new vista for individual emancipation from the yoke of the totalitarian ideologies (pan-Arab and other forms of ethnic nationalism, various types of state socialism, and Islamic fundamentalism) that invaded the region's cultural landscape in the twentieth and early twenty-first centuries. Although linked to the attributes of the respondents and the characteristics of the national context, this awareness does not appear to reflect the changes in these attributes or the national characteristics. Rather, it signifies, as it were, an oppositional response to the havoc wreaked across the region's sociopolitical environment by the followers of political Islam; to the religious despotism of the Islamic regimes and religious parties in Iran, Saudi Arabia, Afghanistan, and Iraq; to the violence of al-Qaeda, Boko Haram, Hezbollah, ISIS, and the Taliban, as well as the prevalence of torture, rape, and en masse executions of political prisoners by these terror groups; to the extremists' involvement in drug trafficking; and to the intensification of Shia-Sunni sectarian conflict.

Paralleling this shift in values have been the religious reformist movements among Iranians underpinning the landslide victory of reformist candidate Mohammad Khatami in the presidential elections in 1977 and the rise of the Green Movement in 2009; the movements of the Arab Spring in 2011, followed by a wave of protest demonstrations and unrest in Turkey in 2013; and, finally, the outbreak of spontaneous nationwide protests in Iran in 2018. These upheavals showed that the Arab Spring was not confined to the Arab countries but rather reflected the desire for democratic change in the entire region, indicated a significant decline in public perception of the utility of mixing religion with politics, and pointed to the people's interest in assigning less importance to religious values in shaping the behavior and conduct of the government.

The seven countries in the region, however, may follow their own nationally specific paths toward liberal democracy. The intensity and the type of values change, on the one hand, and the form of transition, on the other, may be a function of the intensity of the cultural warfare and the arrangement of the existing sociopolitical forces at the national level. Despite their diversity, for each of these countries the available evidence appears to point to liberal democracy as a most viable option under the current conditions. To begin with, Egypt, Tunisia, and Turkey provide varying political contexts that shaped the manner in which this warfare was waged. The victory of the Justice and Development Party in the 2002 parliamentary elections in Turkey and the upheavals of the Arab Spring that ousted the Egyptian and Tunisian authoritarian regimes in 2011 marked the transition of power from secular politicians to the advocates of political Islam. This change, however, was followed by a tripartite conflict among the military, secular parties, and Islamic fundamentalist groups, bringing into relief diverse patterns of power relations across the countries. In Tunisia, the Islamization policies of the ruling Ennahda (Islamic Revival) Party and the assassination of secular politicians by Muslim extremists resulted in the formation of the Nidaa Tounes (Voice of Tunisia)—a front that united secularists, trade unionists, liberals, and others. The conflict was resolved at the ballot box, where Nidaa Tounes won a plurality of seats in the parliamentary elections in 2014, paving the way for a peaceful transition to democracy (Honwana 2013; Zoubir 2015).

Tunisia's transition to democracy pacified the Islamic fundamentalist movement in the country, and the Ennahda, in the words of its founder, Rached Ghannouchi, "embraced a new identity as a party of Muslim democrats. . . . Under the new constitution, the rights of Tunisians to worship freely, express their convictions and beliefs, and embrace an Arab Muslim identity are guaranteed, and so Ennahda no longer needs to focus its energies on fighting for such protections" (Ghannouchi 2016, 58). Pointing to the new democratic stage in the country's history, he further stated, "The question is no longer one of secularism versus religion: the state no longer imposes secularism through repression, and so there is no longer a need for Ennahda or any other actor to defend or protect religion as a core part of its political activity" (59). It thus appears that the transition to democracy resulted in religion serving less as a contested domain between warring political parties and more as a purveyor of sacred spirituality for the individual faithful than was the case under the regime before the Arab Spring and that identification with Islam was not a mark of distinction between fundamentalism and liberal democracy, as was the case in the other countries.

In Egypt also, the Islamization efforts of President Mohamed Morsi of the Muslim Brothers prompted secular political parties to form the National Salvation Front, which launched mass protests against what they perceived to be an impending religious dictatorship. Unlike in Tunisia, this conflict was not resolved at the ballot box. The military decided to intervene, overthrew Morsi, outlawed the Muslim Brothers, and reconstituted the pre-2011 authoritarian rule (Dunne and Hamzawy 2017). Evidently, the coup leaders appeared to have benefited from the interaction among the same three forces—the military, the Muslim Brothers, and the liberal nationalists—that also brought about the 1952 coup. There were, however, some key differences in the social context that ensured the political stability of the military rule in the post-1952 period but that have provided an uncertain future for the current regime. First, in 1952, the military was backed by the Muslim Brothers, while in 2013 the two political forces confronted each other. Second, in 1952, the military successfully came to power under the banner of the popular ideology of pan-Arab nationalism; there was little support for this ideology or for military rule in 2013, short of the desire to end the incipient religious dictatorship in the country. Third, in 1952, the Muslim Brothers was a powerful religious and political organization whose backing of the military ensured its success in the coup, and the ideology of liberal nationalism was discredited for its identification with the country's dominant classes (Moaddel 2005). In 2013, on the other hand, the Muslim Brothers was considerably weakened, and liberal nationalism had been gaining popularity among Egyptians. Although the outcome was the same and the country once again came under the domination of a military-backed authoritarian regime, history is far from repeating itself. Given the shift in values of the Egyptian public toward secular politics, religious tolerance, gender equality, and national identity, one may expect the rise of liberal nationalist oppositional movement in the country.

Finally, in Turkey, interactions among similar political forces—Islamic fundamentalism, secular and liberal parties, and the military—were also at work but produced a different outcome: the consolidation of Recep Tayyip Erdoğan's Islamic fundamentalist-cum-nationalist regime. Political Islam expanded in Turkey in the 1990s against the backdrop of the ineffectiveness of center-right parties, which were considered responsible for the country's economic malaise. On the international level, the AKP, Erdoğan's Justice and Development Party, was supported by such diverse actors as Saudi Arabia, the Muslim Brothers, the European Union, and the United States, and its electoral victory in 2002 was hailed as the triumph of market capitalism and democracy. After consolidating power, President Erdoğan, however, dashed the prospect for Islamic democracy and turned toward authoritarianism. He expanded control over the parliament and the judiciary, restricted the freedom of the press, and promoted Islamic-Turkish nationalism, a process that was reinforced by the failed military coup in 2016. As a result, economic growth stalled, and polarization of the country's politics between fundamentalists and the followers of liberal democracy was aggravated (Özkan 2017; Romano 2018; Kirişci and Sloat 2019). Given the relative strength of liberal values among Turkish citizens—particularly in terms of the increase in support for gender equality, religious tolerance, secular politics, and national identity—it is likely that the pattern of political development in Turkey will approach that of Tunisia rather than Egypt. The outcome of the mayoral elections for the city of Istanbul held on June 23, 2019, which resulted in the victory of the liberal opposition candidate, Ekrem İmamoğlu from Republican People's Party, and the defeat of the Erdoğan's candidate of Justice and Development Party confirms this prospect.

Saudi Arabia, by contrast, displays a different trajectory of historical experience. Although as early as 1929 (that is, three years before the establishment of the kingdom in 1932) the Saudi leadership defeated the Ikhwan, a Muslim extremist group, and pursued a policy of pro-Western pragmatism, the challenges it faced prompted it to promote the proselytization of Islam in the region and beyond from the 1960s. This new religious policy benefited the Wahhabi establishment and contributed to the rise of Islamic extremism. The first challenge came from pan-Arab nationalism in the sixties, a movement led by Egyptian President Gamal Abdel Nasser, which had already threatened or overthrown the monarchies in the Arab world. To fend off this challenge and project power globally, the Saudis established the Muslim World League in 1962, the Organization of the Islamic Conference in 1969, and the World Association of Muslim Youth in 1972. They also began building mosques and Islamic centers around the world. This process was reinforced following the outbreak of the Iranian Revolution in 1979 and the Mecca incident several months later when Muslim militants led by Juhaiman al-Utaibi forcibly took control of the Great Mosque (Okruhlik 2002, 23). To respond and to further strengthen its Islamic credentials, the Saudi regime allocated large sums to religious institutions, increased mosque construction, reinforced the Islamic content of the schools' curricula, and further empowered the religious police. By 1986, more than 16,000 of the kingdom's 100,000 students were enrolled in Islamic studies, and by the early 1990s, one-quarter of all university students were studying in religious institutions (Okruhlik 2002, 23; Prokop 2003, 78). While these policies further restricted the freedom of the youth and women, one unintended result was the rise of a new generation of sheikhs and preachers who expressed anger at the subservience of the official clerics and denounced the state's failure to live up to Islamic values (International Crisis Group 2004, 7; Dekmejian 1994, 638; Moaddel 2006). These religious policies thus turned into an important political liability for the monarchy, and extremism expanded to form a powerful force that challenged the state's legitimacy.

The launching of cultural and economic reforms by Crown Prince Muhammad Ben Salman was a welcome development for the country's youth and women, whose interests and freedom were particularly undermined by the proselytization policies of the earlier decades. These reforms limited the power and prerogatives of the Wahhabi clerics, stripped the religious police of much of their legal authority, lifted the ban on women driving, and allowed women to work and participate in recreational activities outside the home. For these segments of the Saudi population, these reforms were in fact life-changing measures (Grand 2017). These changes, which accompanied a more assertive foreign policy, may explain the shift in the basis of identity from religion to nation and the rise of Saudi nationalism. Given the large gap in support for expressive individualism between the younger and older generations, these policies appear to have resonated with the interests of the youth. The liberalization of religion, the decline in the Wahhabi religious monopoly, the expansion of religious liberty and tolerance, and the integration of the Shias into the political and cultural life of the kingdom appear to be have formed a plausible path toward liberal democracy in Saudi Arabia. The attack on liberal activists in the country and the harassment and murder of regime critics abroad threaten to erode the kingdom's legitimacy among the very people who were the staunch supporters of the reforms.

The prospect for liberal democracy in Iraq and Lebanon, by contrast, is a function of interethnic or interfaith relations and the decline of sectarianism. Both countries are divided into three major religious and ethnic groups; Christians, Sunnis, and Shias in Lebanon and Sunni Arabs, Shia Arabs, and Sunni Kurds in Iraq. Their national contexts are thus among the most vulnerable to the political instability, interethnic violence, and civil war that are cited in the literature (Ellingsen 2000; Collier 2001; Fearon 2003; Campos and Kuzeyev 2007; Collier, Hoefflery, and Rohner 2009; Wimmer, Cederman, and Min 2014). In Iraq, the policy of Shia sectarianism promoted by Prime Minister Nouri al-Maliki (in office from 2006 to 2014) proved disastrous, contributing to the alienation of Sunni Arabs and the rise of ISIS. The only option for the dominant political parties in this country and in Lebanon is to depart from sectarian solidarity and enhance intergroup relations and religious tolerance. Finally, in Pakistan, the youth may be a major agent for democratic change. To be sure, for some, there is the prospect for the radicalization of the youth. This prospect is said to be a consequence of the poor quality of public education, disparities in economic opportunities across different segments of society, the presence of extremist infrastructure as well as the organizational discipline and networks of Islamic militants in the country, and the failure of moderate forces (Yusuf 2008). Analysis of the data, however, painted quite a different picture of Pakistani youth. As discussed throughout this book, a much larger percentage of the youth adhered to liberal values and national identity, and a much smaller percentage displayed fundamentalist orientations than was the case for the older generation. Given that the gap between young and old on such values was much wider among Pakistani respondents than it was among respondents in the other six countries and given that, according to a 2003 report (Sathar et al. 2003), Pakistan had the largest cohort of young people in its history and subsequent cohorts were projected to be even larger, then a major shift in values toward liberal nationalism may be expected in the future.

For liberal nationalism to be fully articulated within the social environment of the Middle East and North Africa, the liberal democratic discourse must be grounded in organizations with resources and networks of dedicated activists, objectified in the symbols of individual liberty and gender equality, embodied in leaders and exemplary personalities with strong liberal attitudes and commitments, enacted in daily rituals that reaffirm commitments to liberal values, and employed as a part of daily conversation. To make the transition to liberal democracy, conscious planning and action by intellectual leaders and political activists is certainly necessary. This transition may be triggered by an event that brings together diverse groups and social forces in harmony against the ruling religious fundamentalist or authoritarian exclusivist regimes. Organization and resources are thus important for the rise of liberal democracy. What this book has demonstrated is that people's value orientations have been changing in a liberal democratic direction and that the notion relating democratic deficiency to people's desire to follow the dictates of a strongman is decidedly wrong. What is important for political activists is to stay focused on issues that matter most: individual liberty, gender equality, and secular politics.

APPENDIX

THE QUESTIONNAIRE

(Note: For the complete data set in SPSS, SAS, and STATA format and a copy of the codebook, see https://mevs.org/data/survey-summary/1004.)

Cross-National Analysis of Values and Values Change
Production Questionnaire
December 2010

Questionnaire ID, four digit _____
Country _____

Instruction to Interviewer: This Introduction Must Be Read to Each Respondent Before Beginning the Interview:

Hello. I am from the [NAME OF ORGANIZATION]. We are carrying out research in many different countries on what people value in life. This research will interview a nationally representative sample of the adult population in your country. Your home address has been selected randomly as part of a representative sample of the people living in [STUDY SITE COUNTRY].

We are seeking your permission to ask your opinion on topics such as development, beliefs about families, media use, and various other attributes of individual and family life. Please be assured that there is no right or wrong answer to any of these questions. Your help is extremely important because it will contribute to a better understanding of what people around the world believe and want out of life.

Your answers will be kept completely confidential. We will not ask you for your name, and we believe there is no risk to you for taking part in this study. Any answers you give will be combined with the responses of all other participants. This means that no one will be able to trace the identities of any of our individual participants. The results of this research will be used for academic purposes only and will be disseminated in scholarly journals and presentations. This research may be beneficial to you because it contributes to the development of the social sciences and to public policy.

This interview will take about an hour or so and I want to assure you that it is completely voluntary and confidential. If we should come to any question that you do not want to answer, please let me know and we will go on to the next question. There is no penalty for not participating or for refusing to answer any question. You may stop the interview at any time.

If you have any questions, you may ask me, contact my organization at [the phone number of the organization], Human Subject Review (the name and contact information of the chairperson of the Human Subject Review Committee) or Mansoor Moaddel (the principal investigator).

Section A

v1. EXACT TIME NOW:_____

v2. I would like begin the interview by asking a few questions about you. Taking all things together, would you say you are very happy, happy, not very happy, or not at all happy?

1. Very happy
2. Happy
3. Not very happy
4. Not at all happy
8. DK [DO NOT READ OUT]
9. NR [DO NOT READ OUT]

v3. All things considered, how satisfied are you with your life as a whole these days? Please use this card to help with your answer. [**Respondent Show Card 1**]

Completely Dissatisfied		Completely Satisfied	DK	NR
1	2 3 4 5 6 7 8 9	10	98	99

v4. How important is family in your life?

    1. Very important
    2. Rather important
    3. Not very important
    4. Not important at all
    8. DK [DO NOT READ OUT]
    9. NR [DO NOT READ OUT]

v5. How important is religion in your life?

    1. Very important
    2. Rather important
    3. Not very important
    4. Not important at all
    8. DK [DO NOT READ OUT]
    9. NR [DO NOT READ OUT]

v6. Are you currently [READ OUT AND CODE ONE ONLY]

    1. Never been married? ————›Skip to v8
    2. Married?
    3. Divorced?
    4. Separated?
    5. Widowed?
    8. DK [DO NOT READ OUT]
    9. NR [DO NOT READ OUT]

v7. Altogether, how many children have you had?

    0. No child
    1. 1 child
    2. 2 children
    3. 3 children
    4. 4 children
    5. 5 children
    6. 6 children
    7. 7 children
    8. 8 or more children
    96. Inappropriate [DO NOT READ OUT]
    98. DK [DO NOT READ OUT]
    99. NR [DO NOT READ OUT]

v8. Can you tell me your year of birth, please? 19————————
    [ENTER ONLY THE LAST TWO DIGITS OF THE YEAR: "19" IS ASSUMED]
    998. DK   999. NR

v9. This means you are _____ years old. Is that correct? [RESOLVE ANY DIFFERENCES BETWEEN BIRTH YEAR AND AGE]

v10. People in different countries sometimes give different answers when they are asked about their religion. If I asked you about your religion, what do you prefer your answer to be?

Egypt:

101. Muslim-Shia

102. Muslim-Sunni

103. Christian

196. None

197. Other (Specify)

Iraq:

301. Muslim-Shia

302. Muslim-Sunni

303. Christian

304. Catholic

305. Orthodox

396. None

397. Other (Specify)

Lebanon:

401. Muslim-Shia

402. Muslim-Sunni

403. Roman Catholic

404. Druze

405. Maronite

406. Greek Orthodox

496. None

497. Other (Specify)

Pakistan:

501. Muslim-Shia

502. Muslim-Sunni

503. Christian

504. Hindu

596. None

597. Other (Specify)

Saudi Arabia:

601. Muslim-Shia

602. Muslim-Sunni

603. Christian

604. Hindu

696. Not a member of a religious denomination

697. Other (Specify)

Turkey:

801. Muslim-Shia

802. Muslim-Sunni

803. Muslim-Alevi

804. Christian

896. None

897. Other (Specify)

Tunisia:

901. Muslim-Shia

902. Muslim-Sunni

903. Jewish

904. Atheist

905. Muslim (sect not specified)

906. Maliki

996. None

997. Other (Specify)

ALL COUNTRIES

998. DK

999. NR

	Parental Approval	Love	DK	NR
v11. Next I will ask your opinions about marriage and family life. In your view, which of the following is the more important basis for marriage:	1	2	8	9

	Agree	Disagree	DK	NR
v12. Please tell me whether you agree or disagree with the following statement: Marriage is an out-dated institution.	1	2	8	9

[CODE FIVE ONLY]
Here is a list of qualities that children can be encouraged to learn at home. Which, if any, do you consider to be especially important? **Please choose up to five. [Respondent Show Card 2]**

	Selected	Not Selected	DK	NR
v13. Independence?	1	2	8	9
v14. Hard work?	1	2	8	9
v15. Feeling of responsibility?	1	2	8	9
v16. Imagination?	1	2	8	9
v17. Tolerance and respect for other people?	1	2	8	9
v18. Thrift?	1	2	8	9
v19. Determination, perseverance?	1	2	8	9
v20. Religious faith?	1	2	8	9
v21. Unselfishness?	1	2	8	9
v22. Obedience?	1	2	8	9

Among religious teachers, parents/ guardians, and school teachers, who do you think should be most responsible for the following:	Religious Teachers	Parents/ Guardians	School Teachers	DK	NR
v23. Teaching children about religion?	1	2	3	8	9
v24. Teaching children about politics?	1	2	3	8	9
v25. Teaching children about history?	1	2	3	8	9
v26. Teaching children about science?	1	2	3	8	9

Next, please tell me if you strongly agree, agree, disagree, or strongly disagree:	Strongly Agree	Agree	Disagree	Strongly Disagree	DK	NR
v27. It is acceptable for a man to have more than one wife.	1	2	3	4	8	9
v28. A wife must always obey her husband.	1	2	3	4	8	9
v29. On the whole, men make better political leaders than women do.	1	2	3	4	8	9
v30. A university education is more important for a boy than for a girl.	1	2	3	4	8	9
v31. It is up to a woman to dress whichever way she wants.	1	2	3	4	8	9
v32. When jobs are scarce, men should have more right to a job than women.	1	2	3	4	8	9
v33. Which one of these women is dressed most appropriately for public places? Just tell me the number on the card. [**Respondent Show Card 3**]		1 2 3 4 5 6			8 DK	9 NR

Next, I will read you a list of traits that women can have. For each one, please tell me whether you think it is very important, important, somewhat important, not very important, or not at all important for women to have that trait.

	Very Important	Important	Somewhat Important	Not Very Important	Not at All Important	DK	NR
v34. Being religious?	1	2	3	4	5	8	9
v35. Being educated?	1	2	3	4	5	8	9
v36. Having a job outside the home?	1	2	3	4	5	8	9

Section B

v37. Now think about customs and habits in your society. Which of the following statements comes closer to your sentiment:

1. I feel constrained by the number of customs and habits that exist in my society.
2. There are not enough customs and habits in my society to guide me.
3. There are just about the right amount of customs and habits in my society.
8. DK [DO NOT READ OUT]
9. NR [DO NOT READ OUT]

v38. Now think about governmental laws and regulations. Which of the following statements comes closer to your sentiment:

1. I feel constrained by the number of governmental laws and regulations.
2. There are not enough governmental laws and regulations to guide me.
3. There are just about the right amount of governmental laws and regulations.
8. DK [DO NOT READ OUT]
9. NR [DO NOT READ OUT]

Thinking about what should change to make your country a better place to live, please tell us if you agree strongly, agree, disagree, or disagree strongly with the following:

[STUDY SITE COUNTRY] will be a better society	Agree Strongly	Agree	Disagree	Disagree Strongly	DK	NR
v39. If religion and politics are separated.	1	2	3	4	8	9
v40. If its government was similar to Western governments.	1	2	3	4	8	9
v41. If it had the technology of the West.	1	2	3	4	8	9

I am going to name a number of groups and organizations. For each one, please tell me whether you have a great deal of confidence in it, quite a lot of confidence, not very much confidence, or none at all.

	A Great Deal	Quite a Lot	Not Very Much	None at All	DK	NR
v42. Religious institutions?	1	2	3	4	8	9
v43. The public sector/? [COUNTRY-SPECIFIC QUESTION]	1	2	3	4	8	9
v44. The United Nations?	1	2	3	4	8	9

Among the following, which problems **for your country** do you consider very important (very serious), important, somewhat important, least important, or not important?

	Very Important	Important	Somewhat Important	Least Important	Not Important	DK	NR
v45. Aggression from a neighboring country	1	2	3	4	5	8	9
v46. The exploitation of this country's natural resources by more powerful countries	1	2	3	4	5	8	9
v47. Cultural invasion by the West	1	2	3	4	5	8	9

Section C

Next, I'm going to describe various types of political systems and ask what you think about each as a way of governing this country. For each one, would you say it is a very good, fairly good, fairly bad, or very bad way of governing this country?

	Very Good	Fairly Good	Fairly Bad	Very Bad	DK	NR
v48. Having a democratic political system	1	2	3	4	8	9
v49. Having an Islamic government [a government inspired by Christian values (for Christian respondents)] where religious authorities have absolute power	1	2	3	4	8	9
v50. Having a strong head of government who does not have to bother with parliament and elections	1	2	3	4	8	9
v51. Having the army rule	1	2	3	4	8	9

v52. People have different views about the ideal way of governing this country. Here is a scale for rating how well the government is doing: 1 means "very bad"; 10 means "very good." [COUNTRY-SPECIFIC QUESTION] **[Respondent Show Card 4]**

What point on this scale would you choose to describe how well the government is doing?

1	2 3 4 5 6 7 8 9	10	98	99
Very bad		Very good	DK	NR

v53. How important is it for you to live in a country that is governed democratically? On this scale where 1 means it is "not at all important" and 10 means "absolutely important," what position would you choose? **[Respondent Show Card 5]**

Not at all important		Absolutely important	DK	NR
1	2 3 4 5 6 7 8 9	10	98	99

v54. And how democratically is [STUDY SITE COUNTRY] being governed today? Again using a scale from 1 to 10, where 1 means that it is "not at all democratic" and 10 means that it is "completely democratic," what position would you choose? [COUNTRY-SPECIFIC QUESTION] [**Respondent Show Card 6**]

Not at all democratic		Completely democratic	DK	NR
1	2 3 4 5 6 7 8 9	10	98	99

v55. Do you believe the politicians of [STUDY SITE COUNTRY] agree on political and social issues always, most of the time, occasionally, or never?

1. Always
2. Most of the time
3. Occasionally
4. Never
8. DK [DO NOT READ OUT]
9. NR [DO NOT READ OUT]

v56. How often are diverse views represented in your country's political system—all of the time, most of the time, occasionally, or never?

1. All of the time
2. Most of the time
3. Occasionally
4. Never
8. DK [DO NOT READ OUT]
9. NR [DO NOT READ OUT]

v57. How proud are you to be [STUDY SITE COUNTRY NATIONALITY]?

1. Very proud
2. Quite proud
3. Not very proud
4. Not at all proud
8. DK [DO NOT READ OUT]
9. NR [DO NOT READ OUT]

v58. Which of the following best describes you?

1. Above all, I am an Egyptian/Iranian/Iraqi/Lebanese/Pakistani/Saudi/ Turkish citizen.
2. Above all, I am a -Muslim [Christian (for Christian respondents)/Hindu (for Hindu respondents)].
3. Above all, I am an Arab.
4. Above all, I am a Kurd [for Iran, Iraq, and Turkey].
5. Above all, I am a Punjabi [for Pakistan].
6. Above all, I am a Sindhi [for Pakistan].
7. Above all, I am a Mohajar [for Pakistan].

8. Above all, I am a Pathan [for Pakistan].

9. Above all, I am a Baluchi [for Pakistan and Iran].

10. Above all, I am a Turkman [for Iran and Iraq].

11. Above all, I am an Azeri Turk [for Iran].

98. DK [DO NOT READ OUT]

99. NR [DO NOT READ OUT]

How much do you agree or disagree with each of the following statements?

		Strongly Agree	Agree	Disagree	Strongly Disagree	DK	NR
v59.	Religious leaders should not interfere in politics.	1	2	3	4	8	9
v60.	It would be better for [STUDY SITE COUNTRY] if more people with strong religious beliefs held public office.	1	2	3	4	8	9
v61.	There are conspiracies against Muslims.	1	2	3	4	8	9
v62.	Democracy may have problems but it's better than any other form of government.	1	2	3	4	8	9

Now, I would like to know your views about a good government. How important is each of the following traits for a good government?

		Very Important	Important	Somewhat Important	Least Important	Not Important	DK	NR
v63.	It should make laws according to the people's wishes.	1	2	3	4	5	8	9
v64.	It should implement only the laws of the shari'a.	1	2	3	4	5	8	9

Let's talk about what things would *increase* and what things would *decrease* if [STUDY SITE COUNTRY] became more like Western countries. [**Respondent Show Card 7**]

	Increase a Lot	Increase a Little	Decrease a Little	Decrease a Lot	DK	NR
v65. Equality between women and men? (If [STUDY SITE COUNTRY] became more like western countries, would equality between women and men increase a lot, increase a little, decrease a little, or decrease a lot?)	1	2	3	4	8	9
v66. Faith in Allah?	1	2	3	4	8	9
v67. Restrictions on personal freedom?	1	2	3	4	8	9
v68. Parents choosing who their children marry?	1	2	3	4	8	9
v69. The influence of religion on politics?	1	2	3	4	8	9
v70. Freedom to mix with the opposite sex?	1	2	3	4	8	9
v71. The number of children couples have?	1	2	3	4	8	9
v72. Following the teachings of the Quran [Bible (for Christian respondents)]?	1	2	3	4	8	9
v73. Age at marriage?	1	2	3	4	8	9
v74. Selfish people?	1	2	3	4	8	9
v75. Democracy?	1	2	3	4	8	9
v76. Immodest dress?	1	2	3	4	8	9

v77. Respect for elders?	1	2	3	4	8	9
v78. Emphasis on material possessions?	1	2	3	4	8	9
v79. The number of educated individuals running the national economy?	1	2	3	4	8	9
v80. The overall standard of living?	1	2	3	4	8	9
v81. The role of science and technology in people's lives?	1	2	3	4	8	9
v82. Respect for human rights?	1	2	3	4	8	9

Section D

The next set of questions is about religion. Please be assured they are in no way intended to reveal doubts about anyone's faith in their religion. These questions are being asked to people of different religions all over the world including Muslims, Christians, Hindus, Buddhists, and so on. We compare people's responses in different countries in order to understand the similarities and differences in their religious faiths. We appreciate everyone's generous contributions to our research.

Please tell me if you strongly agree, agree, disagree, or strongly disagree with the following statements. [Respondent Show Card 8]

	Strongly Agree	Agree	Disagree	Strongly Disagree	DK	NR
v83. Any infraction of religious instruction will bring about Allah's severe punishment.	1	2	3	4	8	9
v84. Only Islam [Christianity (for Christian respondents)] provides comprehensive truth about Allah.	1	2	3	4	8	9

v85. Non-Muslims [Non-Christians (for Christian respondents)] should be prohibited from practicing their religion in [STUDY SITE COUNTRY].	1	2	3	4	8	9
v86. Only the fear of Allah keeps people on the right path.	1	2	3	4	8	9
v87. The Quran [Bible (for Christian respondents)] is true from beginning to end.	1	2	3	4	8	9
v88. Only Islam [Christianity (for Christian respondents)] gives a complete and unfailing guide to human salvation.	1	2	3	4	8	9
v89. The followers of all religions should have equal rights to practice their religion in [STUDY SITE COUNTRY].	1	2	3	4	8	9
v90. Non-Muslims [Non-Christians (for Christian respondents)] should be free to build their places of worship in [STUDY SITE COUNTRY].	1	2	3	4	8	9
v91. Allah requires his slaves to repent (tobbah).	1	2	3	4	8	9
v92. The Quran's [Bible's (for Christian respondents)] description of past historical events is not always accurate.	1	2	3	4	8	9

		1	2	3	4	8	9
v93.	Only Muslims [Christians (for Christian respondents)] will go to heaven.	1	2	3	4	8	9
v94.	Our children should not be allowed to learn about other religions.	1	2	3	4	8	9
v95.	Allah is the source of everything good.	1	2	3	4	8	9
v96.	The Quran [the Bible (for Christian respondents)] has correctly predicted all the major events that have occurred in human history.	1	2	3	4	8	9
v97.	All religions are equally acceptable to Allah.	1	2	3	4	8	9
v98.	The followers of other religions should not have the same rights as mine.	1	2	3	4	8	9
v99.	Satan is behind any attempt to undermine belief in Allah.	1	2	3	4	8	9
v100.	The Quran [the Bible (for Christian respondents)] contains general facts, but some of its stories need to be interpreted.	1	2	3	4	8	9
v101.	Criticism of Islam [Christianity (for Christian respondents)] should not be tolerated.	1	2	3	4	8	9
v102.	People stay on the right path only because they expect to be rewarded in heaven.	1	2	3	4	8	9

v103. In the presence of the Quran [the Bible (for Christian respondents)], there is no need for man-made laws.	1	2	3	4	8	9
v104. Criticism of Muslim [Christian (for Christian respondents)] religious leaders should not be tolerated.	1	2	3	4	8	9
v105. Different interpretations of the Quran [the Bible (for Christian respondents)] are equally valid.	1	2	3	4	8	9
v106. Islam [Christianity (for Christian respondents)] is the only true religion.	1	2	3	4	8	9
v107. Whenever there is a conflict between religion and science, religion is always right.	1	2	3	4	8	9

Let's talk about a bit about the people you trust in giving you information about the role of religion in politics.

	A Great Deal	Some	Not Very Much	Not at All	DK	NR
v108. Family members? (Do you trust what they tell you about the role of religion in politics a great deal, some, not very much, or not at all?)	1	2	3	4	98	99
v109. Friends?	1	2	3	4	98	99
v110. Local religious leaders?	1	2	3	4	98	99
v111. Tele-evangelists (da'ya)?	1	2	3	4	98	99
v112. Political leaders?	1	2	3	4	98	99
v113. Tribal leaders? [COUNTRY-/REGION-SPECIFIC QUESTION]	1	2	3	4	98	99

v114. Which of the following is the most important attribute of God?

    1. Any infraction of Allah's law will bring about Allah's severe punishments.

    2. Allah is forgiving and kind.

    8. DK [DO NOT READ OUT]

    9. NR [DO NOT READ OUT]

v115. Which of the following statements is closer to your view of religious laws?

    1. It is OK to change the religious laws according to changes in social conditions.

    2. The religious laws practiced during the time of the Prophet must still be practiced in our society today.

    8. DK [DO NOT READ OUT]

    9. NR [DO NOT READ OUT]

Now, the next set of questions talks about many different aspects of the Muslim [Christian (for Christian respondents)] religion. Generally speaking, do you think that the religious authorities in this country are giving adequate answers to the following:

	Yes	No	DK	NR
v116. The moral problems and needs of the individual?	1	2	8	9
v117. The problems of family life?	1	2	8	9
v118. People's spiritual needs?	1	2	8	9
v119. The social problems facing [STUDY SITE COUNTRY] today?	1	2	8	9

v120. Apart from funerals, about how often do you go to a mosque [church (for Christian respondents)] these days?

    1. More than once a week

    2. Once a week

    3. Once a month

    4. Only on the religious events

    5. Once a year

    6. Rarely

    7. I do not go to mosque [church (for Christian respondents)]

    8. DK [DO NOT READ OUT]

    9. NR [DO NOT READ OUT]

v121. How often do you pray?

    1. Five times a day

    2. Two to four times a day

3. Once a day

4. Once or twice a week

5. Once or twice a month

6. Never

8. DK [DO NOT READ OUT]

9. NR [DO NOT READ OUT]

v122. To what extent do you consider yourself a religious person, on a scale from 1 to 10? [**Respondent Show Card 9**]

1	2 3 4 5 6 7 8 9	10	98	99
Not at all religious		Very religious	DK	NR

Again, please keep in mind that we ask the next set of questions because we will compare the results from [STUDY SITE COUNTRY] with many other countries. Which, if any, of the following do you believe in?

	Yes	No	DK	NR
v123. First, do you believe in God?	1	2	8	9
v124. Do you believe in life after death?	1	2	8	9
v125. Do you believe people have a soul?	1	2	8	9
v126. Do you believe in hell?	1	2	8	9
v127. Do you believe in heaven?	1	2	8	9

v128. How important is the presence of God in your life? Please use this scale to indicate: 10 means "very important" and 1 means "not at all important." [**Respondent Show Card 10**]

Not at all important		Very important	DK	NR
1	2 3 4 5 6 7 8 9	10	98	99

Section E

v129. How much time do you usually spend watching television on an average per day?

0. I do not watch TV

1. Less than 1 hour per day

2. 1–2 hours per day

3. 2–3 hours per day

4. More than 3 hours per day

8. DK [DO NOT READ OUT]

9. NR [DO NOT READ OUT]

v130. How much do you rely on domestic television as a source of information?

1. A great deal

2. Some

3. Not very much

4. Not at all————› Skip to v132

8. DK [DO NOT READ OUT]————› Skip to v132

9. NR [DO NOT READ OUT]————› Skip to v132

v131. Which domestic channel is the most reliable source of information for you? [PRE-CODED OPEN-ENDED QUESTION]

———————————

v132. How much do you rely on satellite television (foreign) as a source of information?

1. A great deal

2. Some

3. Not very much

4. Not at all————› Skip to v134

8. DK [DO NOT READ OUT]————› Skip to v134

9. NR [DO NOT READ OUT]————› Skip to v134

v133. Which satellite television channel (foreign) is the most reliable source of information for you? [PRE-CODED OPEN-ENDED QUESTION]

———————————

v134. How much do you rely on radio as a source of information?

1. A great deal

2. Some

3. Not very much

4. Not at all————› Skip to v136

8. DK [DO NOT READ OUT]————› Skip to v136

9. NR [DO NOT READ OUT]————› Skip to v136

v135. Which radio channel is the most reliable source of information for you? [PRE-CODED OPEN-ENDED QUESTION]

———————————

v136. How much do you rely on newspapers as a source of information?

1. A great deal

2. Some

3. Not very much

4. Not at all————› Skip to v138

8. DK [DO NOT READ OUT]————› Skip to v138

9. NR [DO NOT READ OUT]————› Skip to v138

v137. Which newspaper is the most reliable source of information for you?
[PRE-CODED OPEN-ENDED QUESTION]

———————————

v138. How much do you rely on the internet as a source of information?

1. A great deal

2. Some

3. Not very much

4. Not at all

8. DK [DO NOT READ OUT]

9. NR [DO NOT READ OUT]

v139. How much do you rely on mobile, that is, SMS or MMS, as a source of information?

1. A great deal

2. Some

3. Not very much

4. Not at all

8. DK [DO NOT READ OUT]

9. NR [DO NOT READ OUT]

Section F

Next, we are interested in your views concerning business and the economy here in [STUDY SITE COUNTRY]).

v140. How would you place your views on this scale? 1 means you agree completely with the statement on the left; 10 means you agree completely with the statement on the right; and if your views fall somewhere in between, you can choose any number in between. [**Respondent Show Card 11**]

Incomes should be made more equal.		We need larger income differences as incentives for individuals.	
1	2 3 4 5 6 7 8 9	10	DK = 98 NR = 99

v141.   [Respondent Show Card 12]

Private ownership   Government
of business and   ownership of
industry should be   business and
increased.   industry should
                                     be increased.

1	2 3 4 5 6 7 8 9	10	DK = 98 NR = 99

v142.   [Respondent Show Card 13]

People can   People can become
only get rich at   rich without it being
the expense of   at the expense of
others.   others.

1	2 3 4 5 6 7 8 9	10	DK = 98 NR = 99

v143.   [Respondent Show Card 14]

Competition   Competition
is good.   is bad.

1	2 3 4 5 6 7 8 9	10	DK = 98 NR = 99

v144.   [Respondent Show Card 15]

The government   People should
should take more   take more
responsibility to   responsibility
ensure that everyone   to provide for
is provided for.   themselves.

1	2 3 4 5 6 7 8 9	10	DK = 98 NR = 9 9

v145. Generally speaking, would you say that this country's economy is run by a few big influential people and organizations who are looking out for themselves only or that it is run for the benefit of all the people?

1. Run by a few big interests
2. Run for all the people
8 DK [DO NOT READ OUT]
9. NR [DO NOT READ OUT]

v146. Let's talk about people from other countries coming here to work. Which one of the following do you think the government should do?

1. Let anyone come who wants to
2. Let people come as long as there are jobs available
3. Place strict limits on the number of foreigners who can come here
4. Prohibit people coming here from other countries
8. DK [DO NOT READ OUT]
9. NR [DO NOT READ OUT]

Section G

Some people think that [STUDY SITE COUNTRY] will become more developed in the future. Let's talk about what things would increase and what things would decrease if [STUDY SITE COUNTRY] became more developed. **[Respondent Show Card 7]**

	Increase a Lot	Increase a Little	Decrease a Little	Decrease a Lot	DK	NR
v147. Equality between women and men? (If [STUDY SITE COUNTRY] became more developed, over time would equality between women and men increase a lot, increase a little, decrease a little, or decrease a lot?	1	2	3	4	8	9
v148. Faith in Allah?	1	2	3	4	8	9
v149. Restrictions on personal freedom?	1	2	3	4	8	9
v150. Parents choosing who their children marry?	1	2	3	4	8	9

v151. The influence of religion on politics?	1	2	3	4	8	9
v152. Freedom to mix with the opposite sex?	1	2	3	4	8	9
v153. The number of children couples have?	1	2	3	4	8	9
v154. Following the teachings of the Quran [Bible (for Christian respondents)]?	1	2	3	4	8	9
v155. Age at marriage?	1	2	3	4	8	9
v156. Selfish people?	1	2	3	4	8	9
v157. Democracy?	1	2	3	4	8	9
v158. Immodest dress?	1	2	3	4	8	9
v159. Respect for elders?	1	2	3	4	8	9
v160. Emphasis on material possessions?	1	2	3	4	8	9
v161. Respect for human rights?	1	2	3	4	8	9

Now we are going to talk about something different—what might happen to [STUDY SITE COUNTRY] if some things about [STUDY SITE COUNTRY'S]) everyday life changed. For each of the following things, please tell me whether you think it would help make [STUDY SITE COUNTRY] more developed or help make [STUDY SITE COUNTRY] less developed. [**Respondent Show Card 16**]

	A Lot More Developed	A Little More Developed	A Little Less Developed	A Lot Less Developed	DK	NR
v162. If there is more equality between women and men? (If there is more equality between women and men, would that help make [STUDY SITE COUNTRY] a lot more developed, a little more developed, a little less developed, or a lot less developed?)	1	2	3	4	8	9

v163. If faith in Allah increases?	1	2	3	4	8	9
v164. If restrictions on personal freedom increase?	1	2	3	4	8	9
v165. If more parents choose who their children marry?	1	2	3	4	8	9
v166. If the influence of religion on politics increases?	1	2	3	4	8	9
v167. If the freedom to mix with the opposite sex increases?	1	2	3	4	8	9
v168. If couples have fewer children?	1	2	3	4	8	9
v169. If belief in the truth of the Quran [Bible (for Christian respondents)] increases?	1	2	3	4	8	9

v170. We have been talking about making [STUDY SITE COUNTRY] more developed. Which one of these five things would help the *most* to make [STUDY SITE COUNTRY] more developed? [**Respondent Show Card 17**]

1. More democracy
2. More freedom of choice over one's own life
3. More religiosity
4. More gender equality
5. More integrity in government officials
8. DK [DO NOT READ OUT]
9. NR [DO NOT READ OUT]

v171. Which one would help *second most* to make [STUDY SITE COUNTRY] more developed? [**Respondent Show Card 17**]

1. More democracy
2. More freedom of choice over one's own life

3. More religiosity

4. More gender equality

5. More integrity in government officials

8. DK [DO NOT READ OUT]

9. NR [DO NOT READ OUT]

In this next part of the interview we will ask your opinions about development around the world and life in your society today.

We would like you to think about development in different countries around the world today. **We will be talking about countries as different as Japan and Bangladesh.** Think of a development scale that rates countries from 1 to 10. The *least* developed places in the world are rated 1 and the *most* developed places in the world are rated 10. You can use both of those numbers for rating countries plus all of the numbers in between. Now, using this development scale, where would you put the following: [**Respondent Show Card 18**]

	Country	Low Development			High Development	DK	NR
v172.	France? [IF R ASKS YOU MAY INFORM: "1 is least developed, 10 is most developed"])	1	2	3 4 5 6 7 8	9 10	98	99
v173.	Yemen? [IF R ASKS YOU MAY INFORM: "1 is least developed, 10 is most developed"]	1	2	3 4 5 6 7 8	9 10	98	99
v174.	Egypt? [IF R ASKS YOU MAY INFORM: "1 is least developed, 10 is most developed"]	1	2	3 4 5 6 7 8	9 10	98	99
v175.	The UAE? [IF R ASKS YOU MAY INFORM: "1 is least developed, 10 is most developed"]	1	2	3 4 5 6 7 8	9 10	98	99

v176. Sudan? [IF R ASKS YOU MAY INFORM: "1 is least developed, 10 is most developed"]	1	2	3 4 5 6 7 8	9	10	98 99
v177. Iran? [IF R ASKS YOU MAY INFORM: "1 is least developed, 10 is most developed"]	1	2	3 4 5 6 7 8	9	10	98 99
v178. Saudi Arabia? [IF R ASKS YOU MAY INFORM: "1 is least developed, 10 is most developed"]	1	2	3 4 5 6 7 8	9	10	98 99
v179. The U.S.? [IF R ASKS YOU MAY INFORM: "1 is least developed, 10 is most developed"]	1	2	3 4 5 6 7 8	9	10	98 99
v180. China? [**FOR EGYPT, IRAN, AND SAUDI ARABIA**] **OR** [STUDY SITE COUNTRY]? [**FOR LEBANON, IRAQ, PAKISTAN, TURKEY**] [IF R ASKS YOU MAY INFORM: "1 is least developed, 10 is most developed"]	1	2	3 4 5 6 7 8	9	10	98 99

Section H

We would like you to think about morality levels in countries around the world. **We will be talking about countries as different as Japan and Bangladesh.** Countries where people have the *lowest* morality levels are rated 1 and countries where people have the *highest* morality levels are rated 10. You can use both of

those numbers for rating morality levels plus all of the numbers in between.
[Respondent Show Card 19]

Country	Low Morality		High Morality	DK	NR
v181. France? [IF R ASKS YOU MAY INFORM: "1 is least moral, 10 is most moral"]	1	2 3 4 5 6 7 8	9 10	98	99
v182. Yemen? [IF R ASKS YOU MAY INFORM: "1 is least moral, 10 is most moral"]	1	2 3 4 5 6 7 8	9 10	98	99
v183. Egypt? [IF R ASKS YOU MAY INFORM: "1 is least moral, 10 is most moral"]	1	2 3 4 5 6 7 8	9 10	98	99
v184. The UAE? [IF R ASKS YOU MAY INFORM: "1 is least moral, 10 is most moral"]	1	2 3 4 5 6 7 8	9 10	98	99
v185. Sudan? [IF R ASKS YOU MAY INFORM: "1 is least moral, 10 is most moral"]	1	2 3 4 5 6 7 8	9 10	98	99
v186. Iran? [IF R ASKS YOU MAY INFORM: "1 is least moral, 10 is most moral"]	1	2 3 4 5 6 7 8	9 10	98	99
v187. Saudi Arabia? [IF R ASKS YOU MAY INFORM: "1 is least moral, 10 is most moral"]	1	2 3 4 5 6 7 8	9 10	98	99
v188. The U.S.? [IF R ASKS YOU MAY INFORM: "1 is least moral, 10 is most moral"]	1	2 3 4 5 6 7 8	9 10	98	99
v189. China? [FOR EGYPT, IRAN, AND SAUDI ARABIA] OR [STUDY SITE COUNTRY]? [FOR LEBANON, IRAQ, PAKISTAN, TURKEY] [IF R ASKS YOU MAY INFORM: "1 is least moral, 10 is most moral"]	1	2 3 4 5 6 7 8	9 10	98	99

v190. Now I will ask your opinion about certain kinds of behaviors. Which one of the following four actions is most immoral?

1. Stealing other people's property
2. Violence against other people
3. Premarital sex
4. Telling lies to other people to protect one's own interests
8. DK [DO NOT READ OUT]
9. NR [DO NOT READ OUT]

	Always	Most of the Time	Occasionally	Never	DK	NR
v191. How often does allowing men and women to work together in public places lead to moral decay?	1	2	3	4	8	9

I will read you a list of behaviors. Behaviors that are immoral are rated 1 and behaviors that are moral are rated 10. You can use both of those numbers for rating behaviors plus all of the numbers in between. Using this scale where 1 is immoral and 10 is moral, where would you put the following: [**Respondent Show Card 20**]

	Immoral Moral	DK	NR
v192. Stealing other people's property?	1 2 3 4 5 6 7 8 9 10	98	99
v193. Violence against other people?	1 2 3 4 5 6 7 8 9 10	98	99
v194. Premarital sex?	1 2 3 4 5 6 7 8 9 10	98	99
v195. Telling lies to other people to protect one's own interests?	1 2 3 4 5 6 7 8 9 10	98	99

Section I

v196. What language do you normally speak at home?

Egypt:	Iraq:	Saudi Arabia:
101. Arabic	301. Arabic	601. Arabic
102. English	302. Kurdish/Esid	602. English
197. Other (Specify)____	397. Other (Specify)____	603. Filipino
		604. Urdu
		697. Other (Specify)____

Iran:	Lebanon:	Syria:
201. Azari	401. Arabic	701. Arabic
202. Farsi	402. English	702. Kurdish
203. Baluchi	403. French	703. Armenian
204. Kurdish/Esid	497. Other (Specify)____	704. Circassian
205. Lori	**Pakistan:**	797. Other (Specify)____
206. Gilaki	501. Baluchi	**Turkey:**
207. Armenian	502. Barahvi	801. Turkish
208. Turkman	503. Hindko	802. Kurdish
209. Assyrian (Ashouri)	504. Punjabi	897. Other (Specify)____
210. Zoroastrian	505. Pushto	**USE FOR ALL**
297. Other (Specify)____	506. Seriaki	**COUNTRIES**
	507. Sindhi	998. DK
	508. Urdu	999. NR
	597. Other (Specify)____	

v197. What is your ethnic origin? [CHOOSE ONE ETHNICITY ONLY]

Egypt:	Iraq:	Saudi Arabia:
101. Egyptian—From Nile Delta	301. Arabic	601. Saudi
102. Egyptian—From Upper Egypt	302. Ashuri	602. Arabs—Other
	303. Kildani	603. Bangladeshi/Pakistani
	304. Kurdish	604. Egyptian/Sudanese
103. Egyptian—Noba	305. Turk	605. European/American
104. Egyptian—Other	397. Other (Specify)____	606. Filipino
197. Other (Specify)____		607. Indian/Sri Lankan
		608. Jordanian/ Palestinian
		609. Yemini
		697. Other (Specify)____

	Lebanon:	Tunisia:
	401. Arabic	901. Arabic
	402. Armenian	902. Berber
	497. Other (Specify)_____	903. Turkish
	Pakistan:	997. Other (Specify)_____
	501. Baluchi	**Turkish:**
	502. Punjabi	801. Turkish
	503. Sindhi	802. Kurdish
	504. Urdu-speaking	897. Other (Specify) _____
	597. Other (Specify)_____	**FOR ALL COUNTRIES:**
		998. DK
		999. NR

Now I am going to read off a list of voluntary organizations (associations, communities, networks). For each one, could you tell me whether you are an active member, an inactive member, or not a member of that type of organization? [READ OUT AND CODE ONE ANSWER FOR EACH ORGANIZATION]

		Active Member	Inactive Member	Don't Belong	DK	NR
v198.	Religious organization	2	1	0	8	9
v199.	Political party [none for Iran]	2	1	0	8	9
v200.	Humanitarian or charitable organization	2	1	0	8	9

Section J

v201. Some people feel they have completely free choice and control over their lives, while other people feel that what they do has no real effect on what happens to them. Please use this scale where 1 means "none at all" and 10 means "a great deal" to indicate how much freedom of choice and control you feel you have over the way your life turns out. [**Respondent Show Card 21**]

None at All									A Great Deal	DK	NR
1	2	3	4	5	6	7	8	9	10	98	99

v202. To what extent are you optimistic/pessimistic about your future? Please use this scale where 1 means "highly pessimistic" and 10 means "highly optimistic" to indicate how you feel about your future. [**Respondent Show Card 22**]

Highly Pessimistic									Highly Optimistic	DK	NR
1	2	3	4	5	6	7	8	9	10	98	99

Please tell us if you strongly agree, agree, disagree, or strongly disagree with the following statements:

	Strongly Agree	Agree	Disagree	Strongly Disagree	DK	NR
v203. In [STUDY SITE COUNTRY] these days, life is unpredictable and dangerous.	1	2	3	4	8	9
v204. It is not possible to live happily in this world.	1	2	3	4	8	9

v205. Some people believe that individuals can decide their own destiny, while others think that it is impossible to escape a predetermined fate. Please tell me which comes closest to your view on this scale on which 1 means "everything is determined by fate" and 10 means "people shape their fate themselves." [CODE ONE NUMBER] [**Respondent Show Card 23**]

Everything is Determined by Fate.									People Shape their Fate Themselves.	DK	NR
1	2	3	4	5	6	7	8	9	10	98	99

Section K

Next let's talk about neighbors. On this list are various groups of people. Could you please sort out any that you would not like to have as neighbors? [CODE AN ANSWER FOR EACH]

	Don't Like	Like	DK	NR
v206. People with criminal record	1	2	8	9
v207. Sunnis	1	2	8	9
v208. Kurds	1	2	8	9
v209. Shia	1	2	8	9
v210. Americans	1	2	8	9
v211. French	1	2	8	9
v212. British	1	2	8	9
v213. Jews	1	2	8	9
v214. Christians	1	2	8	9
v215. Iranians [Pakistanis for Iran]	1	2	8	9
v216. [Kuwaitis for Iraq/Indian for Pakistan/Iraqis for all other countries]	1	2	8	9
v217. [Turkish for Iraq, Saudi Arabia, and Iran/Saudis for all other countries]	1	2	8	9
v218. [Jordanians for Iraq/Saudis for Iran/Afghanis for Pakistan/Pakistanis for Saudi Arabia/Syrians for all other countries]	1	2	8	9

I am going to name a number of groups. For each one, could you tell me how much trust, in general, you have in them: is it a great deal of trust, some trust, not very much trust, or none at all?

	A Great Deal	Some	Not Very Much	None at All	DK	NR
v219. Shia	1	2	3	4	8	9
v220. Sunni	1	2	3	4	8	9

| v221. | [**Kurd** for Iraq/**Christian** for Lebanon/**Copt** for Egypt/**Followers of other religions** for all other countries] | 1 | 2 | 3 | 4 | 8 | 9 |

Section L

Now I would like to ask a few more questions about you and your family.

v222. What is the highest educational level that you have attained? [IF STUDENT, CODE HIGHEST LEVEL HE/SHE EXPECTS TO COMPLETE] [Please revise the list in conformity with the educational categories in [STUDY SITE COUNTRY].]

1. No formal education
2. Incomplete primary school
3. Complete primary school
4. Incomplete secondary school: technical/vocational type
5. Complete secondary school: technical/vocational type
6. Incomplete secondary: university-preparatory type
7. Complete secondary: university-preparatory type
8. Some university-level education, without degree
9. University-level education, with degree (include post-graduate education)
98. DK [DO NOT READ OUT]
99. NR [DO NOT READ OUT]

v223. Are you employed now including self-employment?

1. Yes → Skip to v224

2. No → Skip to v225

v224. About how many hours do you work per week on your main job?

_____Hours Per Week → Skip to v227

v225. Why aren't you employed at the present time?

1. Lost job/laid off → Skip to v227

2. Retired
3. Housewife
4. Student
5. Permanently disabled
7. OTHER (SPECIFY):_____

v226.	Have you ever done any work for pay including self-employment?	1. Yes → Skip to v227
		2. No → Skip to v230
v227.	What is/was your main profession? What type of work do/did you do?	1. Employer/manager of establishment with 10 or more employees
		2. Employer/manager of establishment with less than 10 employees
		3. Professional worker lawyer, accountant, teacher, etc
		4. Supervisory—office worker: supervises others
		5. Non-manual—office worker: non-supervisory
		6. Foreman and supervisor
		7. Skilled manual worker
		8. Semi-skilled manual worker
		9. Unskilled manual worker
		10. Farmer: has own farm
		11. Agricultural worker
		12. Member of armed forces, security personnel
		13. Never had a job
v228.	Are/Were you self-employed?	1. Yes
		2. No
v229.	Are/Were you working for the government or public organization, a private business or industry, or what?	1. Government or public organization
		2. Private business or industry
		3. Private non-profit organization [IF VOLUNTEERED]
		7. OTHER(SPECIFY):_____
v230.	Are you the chief wage earner in your household?	1. Yes →Skip to v233
		2. No →Skip to v231
v231.	Is the chief wage earner in your household employed now?	1. Yes
		2. No

v232. What is/was the main profession of the chief wage earner in your household? What type of work does/did the chief wage earner do?

1. Employer/manager of establishment with 10 or more employees
2. Employer/manager of establishment with less than 10 employees
3. Professional worker lawyer, accountant, teacher, etc
4. Supervisory—office worker: supervises others.
5. Non-manual—office worker: non-supervisory
6. Foreman and supervisor
7. Skilled manual worker
8. Semi-skilled manual worker
9. Unskilled manual worker
10. Farmer: has own farm
11. Agricultural worker
12. Member of armed forces, security personnel
13. Never had a job

v233. Sex of respondent:

1. Male → Skip to v234
2. Female →Skip to v239

v234. Please remind me, are you currently married?

1. Yes → Skip to v235
2. No → Skip to v239

v235. Is your wife employed now including self-employment?

1. Yes → Skip to v236

2. No → Skip to v237

v236. About how many hours does she work per week on her main job?

_____Hours Per Week → Skip to v238

v237. Has she ever done any work for pay **including self-employment?**

1. Yes → Skip to v238

2. No → Skip to v239

v238. What is/was her main profession?   1. Employer/manager of
       What type of work does/did she do?   establishment with 10 or more
                                        employees

2. Employer/manager of establishment with less than 10 employees
3. Professional worker lawyer, accountant, teacher, etc
4. Supervisory—office worker: supervises others.
5. Non-manual—office worker: non-supervisory
6. Foreman and supervisor
7. Skilled manual worker
8. Semi-skilled manual worker
9. Unskilled manual worker
10. Farmer: has own farm
11. Agricultural worker
12. Member of armed forces, security personnel
13. Never had a job

v239. How satisfied are you with the financial situation of your household? If 1 means you are completely dissatisfied on this scale and 10 means you are completely satisfied, where would you put your satisfaction with your household's financial situation? [**Respondent Show Card 1**]

Completely Dissatisfied		Completely Satisfied	DK	NR
1	2 3 4 5 6 7 8 9	10	98	99

v240. During the past year, did your family

1. Save money?
2. Just get by?
3. Spend some savings?
4. Spend savings and borrow money?
8. DK [DO NOT READ OUT]
9. NR [DO NOT READ OUT]

v241. People sometimes describe themselves as belonging to the working class, the middle class, or the upper or lower class. Would you describe yourself as belonging to

1. The upper class?
2. The upper middle class?

3. The lower middle class?

4. The working class?

5. The lower class?

8. DK [DO NOT READ OUT]

9. NR [DO NOT READ OUT]

v242. On this card is a scale of household incomes **per year**. We would like to know in what group your household is, counting all wages, salaries, pensions, and other incomes that come in **per year**. Just give the number of the group your household falls into, before taxes and other deductions. [**Respondent Show Card 24**]

10	Country-specific highest income range decile
9	Country-specific income range 9th decile
8	Country-specific income range 8th decile
7	Country-specific income range 7th decile
6	Country-specific income range 6th decile
5	Country-specific income range 5th decile
4	Country-specific income range 4th decile
3	Country-specific income range 3rd decile
2	Country-specific income range 2nd decile
1	Country-specific lowest income range decile

98. DK [DO NOT READ OUT]

99. NR [DO NOT READ OUT]

[COUNTRY-SPECIFIC INCOME RANGE AMOUNTS: LIST ACTUAL CURRENCY AMOUNT IN DECILE RANGES ON EACH CORRESPONDING LINE OF SHOW CARD AND HAVE THE RESPONDENT CHOOSE INCOME RANGE (1–10) THAT HOUSEHOLD FALLS INTO]

v243. Next we will talk about the characteristics of a good government. Which of the following two statements comes closest to the way you feel?

1. A good government implements only the law of the shari'a [laws inspired by Christian values (for Christian respondents)/laws inspired by Hindu values (for Hindu respondents)].

2. A good government makes laws according to the people's wishes.

8. DK [DO NOT READ OUT]

9. NR [DO NOT READ OUT]

v244. Which of these two statements comes closest to the way you feel?

1. It would be better for [STUDY SITE COUNTRY] if more people with strong religious views held public office.
2. It would be better for [STUDY SITE COUNTRY] if more people with strong commitment to national interests held public office.
8. DK [DO NOT READ OUT]
9. NR [DO NOT READ OUT]

v245. People have different views about themselves and how they relate to the world. Pease tell me which of these four statements comes closest to the way you feel.

1. I see myself as a citizen of the world.
2. I see myself as a citizen of [STUDY SITE COUNTRY].
3. I see myself as a citizen of the Islamic umma [worldwide Christian community (for Christian Respondents)/worldwide Hindu community (for Hindu respondents)].
4. I see myself as a citizen of the Arab community.
5. I see myself as a citizen of the Kurdish community [for Iran, Iraq, and Turkey].
6. I see myself as a citizen of the Turkish community [for Turkey].
7. I see myself as a citizen of the Punjabi community [for Pakistan].
8. I see myself as a citizen of the Sindhi community [for Pakistan].
9. I see myself as a citizen of the Mohajar community [for Pakistan].
10. I see myself as a citizen of the Pathan community [for Pakistan].
11. I see myself as a citizen of the Baluchi community [for Pakistan and Iran].
12. I see myself as a citizen of the Torkman community [for Iran].
13. I see myself as a citizen of the Azeri Turk community [for Iran].
98. DK [DO NOT READ OUT]
99. NR [DO NOT READ OUT]

This very last set of questions asks about all kinds of attacks on different groups of people. I will read you a list and ask you if you strongly approve of the attacks, somewhat approve of them, somewhat disapprove of them, or strongly disapprove of them. [**Respondent Show Card 25**]

	Strongly Approve	Somewhat Approve	Somewhat Disapprove	Strongly Disapprove	DK	NR
v246. Attacks on [STUDY SITE COUNTRY] security forces?	1	2	3	4	8	9

		1	2	3	4	8	9
v247.	**Suicide bomb attacks against civilians in [STUDY SITE COUNTRY]?**	1	2	3	4	8	9
v248.	**Attacks on civilian foreigners working in [STUDY SITE COUNTRY]?**	1	2	3	4	8	9
v249.	Attacks on U.S. military troops in Iraq **or Afghanistan?**	1	2	3	4	8	9
v250.	Attacks on U.S. civilians working for U.S. companies in Europe?	1	2	3	4	8	9
v251.	Attacks on U.S. civilians working for U.S. companies in Islamic countries?	1	2	3	4	8	9
v252.	Attacks on Iraqis or Afghanis working for U.S. companies in Iraq **or Afghanistan?**	1	2	3	4	8	9

v253. EXACT TIME NOW: _____

Those are all of the questions I have for you today. Thank you very much for your kind help with our research.

v254. Total length of interview: _____ Minutes

v255. During the interview the respondent was

1. Very interested.
2. Somewhat interested.
3. Not very interested.

v256. Size of town:

1. Under 2,000
2. 2,000–5,000
3. 5,000–10,000
4. 10,000–20,000
5. 20,000–50,000
6. 50,000–100,000
7. 100,000–500,000
8. 500,000 and more

v257. Region where the interview was conducted: [use 2-digit regional code or 9-digit regional/province/district code appropriate to your own society]

_____

v258. Language in which interview was conducted: _____

1. Arabic
2. Persian
3. Kurdish
4. Lori
5. Gilaki
6. Azari (Iranian Turk)
7. Punjabi
8. Pushto
9. Sindhi
10. Urdu/Hindi
11. **Turkish**
97. Other (Specify):_____

v259. Interviewer ID: _____

v260. Sex of interviewer:

1. Male
2. Female

v262. Interviewer year of birth: 19_____

v263. Education of interviewer:

(Please revise the list in conformity with the educational categories in [STUDY SITE COUNTRY].)

1. No formal education
2. Incomplete primary school
3. Complete primary school
4. Incomplete secondary school: technical/vocational type
5. Complete secondary school: technical/vocational type
6. Incomplete secondary: university-preparatory type
7. Complete secondary: university-preparatory type
8. Some university-level education, without degree
9. University-level education, with degree (include post-graduate education)

v264. Female interviewers: Type of head covering you wore during this interview. (Use Respondent Show Card 3.)

1	2	3	4	5	6

NOTES

Introduction: People and Their Issues

1. For example, such different historical formations as democracy, communism, and fascism are made possible by varying combinations of class coalition, state structure, and the sequence of commercialization of agriculture and industrial development (Moore 1966); the outbreak of revolution is an outcome of the varied structural relations between social classes, between social classes and the state, and between states in the international context (Skocpol 1979) or of the variations in the relations of cultivators and noncultivators to the means of production (Paige 1975).
2. An example of structural reductionism of human agency is Bourdieu's conception of the subjectivity of the working class: "the working class internalizes that its life chances are limited; that is, the objective probabilities at the systems level are subjectively internalized" (Calhoun, LiPuma, and Postone 1993, 24).
3. Gelfand's classification parallels Durkheim's typology of anomie versus fatalism. The former is the pathological consequence of a loose social structure and societal normlessness, while the latter is the consequence of a tight structure characterized by "excessive regulations," such that, as Durkheim noted, "futures [are] pitilessly blocked and passions violently choked by oppressive discipline" (cited in Dohrenwend 1959, 467).
4. See "Iranian Women Removing Hijab Charged with 'Inciting Prostitution,'" *World Tribune*, February 28, 2018, http://www.worldtribune.com/iranian-women-removing -hijab-charged-with-inciting-prostitution/.
5. In one of her later works, Ahmed acknowledges that the veil is in effect "a statement of a commitment to a belief in men as the natural and God-ordained authorities" (Ahmed 2005, 165).
6. Muhammad Ali was an ambitious officer who had come to Egypt in 1801 with an Albanian detachment in a Turkish expeditionary force to repel the French (Vatikiotis 1980).

7. The *Description de l'Egypte* is the subject of "Napoleon and the Scientific Expedition to Egypt," an online exhibition presented by the Linda Hall Library, Kansas City, MO. https://napoleon.lindahall.org/learn.shtml. Retrieved June 11, 2018.

8. Abdullah Assam, *Join the Caravan*, Internet Archive, https://archive.org/stream /JoinTheCaravan/JoinTheCaravan_djvu.txt, retrieved May 3, 2017.

9. Abu Bakr Naji, *The Management of Savagery*, https://archive.org/details/TheManagement OfBarbarismAbuBakrNaji/page/n1, retrieved July 25, 2019.

10. Abu Musab al-Suri, *The Global Islamic Resistance Call*, Internet Archive, https://archive .org/details/TheGlobalIslamicResistanceCall, retrieved May 3, 2017.

11. For a concise discussion of the problems and issues related to the comparative survey project that produced the data used in this book and the broader problem of conducting surveys in the Middle East, see de Jong and Young-Demarco (2017).

1. Expressive Individualism

1. A single measure of expressive individualism was constructed by, first, recoding the variable on the basis of marriage into 1 and 4, where love is coded as 4 and parental approval as 1. Then the child qualities index was transformed so that the range was from 1 to 4 rather than 0 to 4, using the following formula: ((childquality + 1)*(0.75)) + (0.25). Then the three indicators were averaged. To reduce the size of the questionnaire for Tunisia, the question about child qualities was excluded from that questionnaire, so the expressive individualism index that was created includes only variables related to the basis for marriage and a woman's freedom to dress as she wishes.

2. Using the pooled data, a single factor for expressive individualism had an eigenvalue of 1.47, explaining 49 percent of variance, and a Cronbach's alpha of 0.44.

3. Because there is no data on child qualities for Tunisia—and thus no child qualities index—Tunisia's overall measure of expressive individualism is not comparable with those of the other six countries.

2. The Social Status of Women and Gender Equality

1. "The Quranic Arabic Corpus," Sahih International translation, University of Leeds, http://corpus.quran.com/translation.jsp?chapter=4&verse=34, retrieved February 2, 2017. Unless indicated otherwise, subsequent references to the Quran are to this resource.

2. Sarah Sirgany and Laura Smith-Spark, "Landmark Day for Saudi Women as Kingdom's Controversial Driving Ban Ends," CNN, updated June 24, 2018, https://www.cnn .com/2018/06/23/middleeast/saudi-women-driving-ban-lifts-intl/index.html.

3. Secular Politics, Liberal Values, and National Identity

1. Discursive space is defined as an interstitial capacity or opening in a belief system that allows its practitioners to detect, recognize, discuss, and sometime reconcile inconsistencies in that belief system (Moaddel and Karabenick 2013).

2. Attitude toward democracy was not used as an indicator of secular politics because this measure, while important, has different meanings for different secular and religious

groups in the Middle East and North Africa. For religious groups, in particular, democracy basically means participation in elections without necessarily believing in freedom of expression (which includes the freedom to criticize religion) and separation of religion and politics. While attitude toward democracy is positively linked to the secular politics index, the measure has inconsistent and weak relationships with the indices of expressive individualism and gender equality across the seven countries.

3. To maintain consistency, the range of the last variable was converted from 1 to 5 points to 1 to 4 points by multiplying this variable by 0.75 and then adding 0.25 (i.e., $1 \times 0.75 + 0.25 = 1$ and $5 \times 0.75 + 0.25 = 4$).

4. Religious Fundamentalism as Disciplinarian Deity, Literalism, Religious Exclusivity, and Religious Intolerance

1. Some of the key ideas and empirical analysis presented in this chapter were also discussed in Moaddel and Karabenick (2018).
2. Allama Muhammad Umar Icharwi claims that Shah Waliullah was radicalized after he came under the influence of the Wahhabi teachings. See Allama Muhammad Umar Icharwi, "Shah Waliullah's Links with Muhammad ibn Abd al-Wahhab," Let Us Build Pakistan, https://lubpak.com/archives/313032, retrieved June 22, 2017.

5. Macro-Contextual (Country) Variation in Religious Fundamentalism and Liberal Values

1. Information on religious freedom and religious prosecution was collected by Director Roger Finke and Associate Director Christopher Bader of the Association of Religious Data Archives, www.thearda.com. Retrieved August 2, 2019.
2. This measure was calculated using the ethnic-linguistic fractionalization index formula, which in turn was based on the Herfindahl ethnic concentration formula (cited in Posner 2004, 849).
3. The measures of political rights and civil liberties are from "Freedom in the World, 2018," Freedom House, https://www.freedomhouse.org/report-types/freedom-world#.vi6jtcvf9u1. Retrieved August 2, 2019.
4. See Association of Religious Data Archives, http://www.thearda.com/QL2010/QuickList_198.asp. Retrieved August 2, 2019.
5. "Fragile States Index, https://fragilestatesindex.org/indicators/. Retrieved August 2, 2019.
6. "Freedom in the World, 2018," Freedom House, https://www.freedomhouse.org/report-types/freedom-world#.vi6jtcvf9u1.
7. For GDP per capital, see "Preview: GDP per Capita," https://databank.worldbank.org/indicator/NY.GDP.PCAP.CD/1ff4a498/Popular-Indicators; for different measures to construct FCP, see the following World Bank webpages: "Foreign Direct Investment, Net Inflows (% of GDP)," http://data.worldbank.org/indicator/bx.klt.dinv.wd.gd.zs; "Foreign Direct Investment, Net Inflows (Balance of Payments), http://data.worldbank.org/indicator/bx.klt.dinv.cd.wd; "Labor Force, Total," http://data.worldbank.org/indicator/sl.tlf.totl.in; and "Gross Capital Formation," http://data.worldbank.org/indicator/ne.gdi.totl.cd; and for the internet, see the following World Bank webpage: https://data.worldbank.org/indicator/it.net.user.zs. Retrieved August 2, 2019.

8. The standardized measure of international trade and foreign capital penetration was necessary in order to linearly combine these two variables and create a single measure of globalization.

6. What Makes a Country More Developed: Liberal Values Versus Religious Beliefs

1. Question e, which taps into attitudes toward the relationship between religion and politics, is worded to measure the extent of support for political Islam. This question is a reversal of the survey item concerning the separation of religion and politics that was used as one of the indicators of secular politics, which was discussed in chapter 3. It was also used as a proxy measure of secular politics for Saudi Arabia.
2. This comparison measures the relative significance of liberal modernity versus religious modernity, not religious fundamentalism, in contributing to development. Although religious modernity and fundamentalism are significantly linked (Moaddel and Karabenick 2018), the beliefs in Allah and in the truth of the scriptures are among the most basic religious beliefs and are quite different from religious fundamentalism. Moreover, given that such religious beliefs are strong among the respondents and development is considered something desirable, the respondents on the face of it are therefore more likely to connect higher religiosity to more development than otherwise. Thus, our liberal modernity index carries a conservative bias toward religious modernity.

7. The Arab Spring and Trend in Values: Egypt, Iraq, Saudi Arabia, Tunisia, and Turkey

1. This does not rule out the effect of a dramatic event like the Holocaust experienced by the Jews or the sudden death of a loved one that might provoke the feeling of being abandoned or even betrayed by God, shattering that person's belief in the almighty and causing them to abandon religion altogether and turn secular.
2. The Arab Spring has been widely covered, generating an extensive list of articles, books, and commentaries on the subject. Using Google's search engine to locate materials that include the expression "Arab Spring" yielded over 58,000 references on July 5, 2017.
3. Attitude toward democracy was not used as an indicator of secular politics because this measure, while important, has different meanings for different secular and religious groups in the Middle East and North Africa. For religious groups, in particular, democracy basically means participation in elections, without necessarily believing in freedom of expression (which includes freedom to criticize religion) and the separation of religion and politics. While attitude toward democracy is positively linked to the secular politics index, the measure has inconsistent and weak relationships with the indices of expressive individualism and gender equality across the seven countries.

REFERENCES

Abrahamian, Ervand. 1982. *Iran between Two Revolutions*. Princeton: Princeton University Press.

Abu-Lughod, Janet L. 1971. *Cairo: 1001 Years of the City Victorious*. Princeton, NJ: Princeton University Press.

Adamiyat, Fereydoun. 1976 (1355 AH). *Idi'olozhi-ye Nahzat-i Mashrutiyat-i Iran* [The ideology of the constitutional movement in Iran]. Tehran: Payam Publications.

Afary, Janet. 1996. *The Iranian Constitutional Revolution, 1906–1911: Grassroots Democracy, Social Democracy, and the Origin of Feminism*. New York: Columbia University Press.

Ajami, Fouad. 2012. "The Arab Spring at One: A Year of Living Dangerously." *Foreign Affairs* 91 (2): 56–65.

Ahmad, Aziz. 1964. *Studies in Islamic Culture in the Indian Environment*. Oxford: Clarendon Press.

Ahmad, Aziz. 1967. *Islamic Modernism in India and Pakistan: 1857–1964*. London: Oxford University Press.

Ahmad, Qeyamuddin. 1966. *The Wahabi Movement in India*. Calcutta: Firma K. L. Mukhopadhyay.

Ahmed, Leila. 1992. *Women and Gender in Islam: Historical Roots of a Modern Debate*. New Haven, CT: Yale University Press.

Ahmed, Leila. 2005. "The Veil Debate—Again." In *On Shifting Ground: Muslim Women in the Global Era*, ed. F. Nouraie-Simone, 53–171. New York: Feminist Press at the City University of New York.

Alavi, Hamza. 2009. "The Rise of Religious Fundamentalism in Pakistan." Secular Pakistan, March 10, 2009. https://secularpakistan.wordpress.com/2009/03/10/the-rise-of-religious-fundamentalism-in-pakistan-hamza-alavi/.

Ale-Ahmad, Jalal. 1982. *Plagued by the West (Ghrabzadegi or Westoxication)*. Trans. Paul Sprachman. New York: Columbia University Press.

Alexander, Jeffrey C., and Philip Smith. 1993. "The Discourse of American Civil Society: A New Proposal for Cultural Studies." *Theory and Society* 22 (2):151–207.

Algar, Hamid. 1960. *Religion and State in Modern Iran*. Berkeley: University of California Press.

Almond, Gabriel A., R. Scott Appleby, and Emanuel Sivan. 2002. *Strong Religion: The Rise of Fundamentalisms Around the World*. Chicago: University of Chicago Press.

Altemeyer, Bob R. 2003. "What Happens When Authoritarians Inherit the Earth? A Simulation." *Analyses of Social Issues and Public Policy* 3 (1): 161–69.

Altemeyer, Bob R., and Bruce Hunsberger. 2004. "A Revised Religious Fundamentalism Scale: The Short and Sweet of It." *International Journal for the Psychology of Religion* 14 (1): 47–54.

Anderson, Lisa. 2011. "Demystifying the Arab Spring: Parsing the Differences Between Tunisia, Egypt, and Libya." *Foreign Affairs* 90 (3): 2–7.

Amin, Qasim. (1899) 1992. *The Liberation of Women*. Trans. Samiha Sidhom. Cairo: American University in Cairo Press.

Antonius, George. 1961. *The Arab Awakening: The Story of the Arab National Movement*. London: Hamish Hamilton.

Apter, David. 1964. *Ideology and Discontent*. New York: Free Press.

Apter, David E. 1965. *The Politics of Modernization*. Chicago: University of Chicago.

Ardıç, Nurullah. 2012. *Islam and the Politics of Secularism: The Caliphate and Middle Eastern Modernization in the Early 20th Century*. SOAS/Routledge Studies on the Middle East. New York: Routledge.

Arjomand, Said Amir. 1984. *The Shadow of God and the Hidden Imam*. Chicago: University of Chicago Press.

Ayubi, Nazih Nassif M. 1980. *Bureaucracy and Politics in Contemporary Egypt*. London: Ithaca Press.

Bahktin, Mikhail. 1983. *The Dialogic Imagination: Four Essays*. Trans. Michael Holquist and Caryl Emerson, ed. Michael Holquist. Austin: University of Texas Press.

Baki, Roula. 2004. "Gender-Segregated Education in Saudi Arabia: Its Impact on Social Norms and the Saudi Labor Market." *Education Policy Analysis Archives* 12 (28): 1–12.

Ball, Terence. 2014. "James Mill." In *The Stanford Encyclopedia of Philosophy*, ed. Edward N. Zalta. https://plato.stanford.edu/archives/sum2014/entries/james-mill/%3E. Retrieved February 1, 2017. Retrieved August 2, 2019.

Banna, Hasan al-. 1978. *Five Tracts of Hasan al-Banna (1906–1949)*. Trans. Charles Wendell. Berkeley: University of California Press.

Bayat, Mongol. 1991. *Iran's First Revolution: Shi'ism and the Constitutional Revolution of 1905–1909*. New York: Oxford University Press.

Beblawi, Hazem, and Giacomo Luciani, eds. 1987. *The Rentier State*. Kent, UK: Croom Helm.

Beissinger, Mark, Amaney A Jamal, and Kevin Mazur. 2015. "Explaining Divergent Revolutionary Coalitions: Regime Strategies and the Structuing of Participation in the Tunisian and Egyptian Revolutions." *Comparitive Politics* 48 (1): 1–24.

Bellah, Robert N., Steven M. Tipton, William M. Sullivan, Richard Madsen, and Ann Swinder. 1985. *Habits of the Heart: Individualism and Commitment in American Life*. Berkeley: University of California Press.

Berger, Peter L., and Thomas Luckmann. 1969. "Sociology of Religion and Sociology of Knowledge." In *Sociology of Religion*, ed. Roland Robertson, 61–73. New York: Penguin.

Bhadra, Gautam. 1988. "Four Rebels of Eighteen-Fifty-Seven." In *Selected Subaltern Studies*, ed. Ranajit Guha and Gayatri Chakravorty Spivak, 129–75. Oxford: Oxford University Press.

Blau, Judith R., Kenneth C. Land, and Kenneth Redding. 1992. "The Expansion of Religious Affiliation: An Explanation of the Growth of Church Participation in the United States 1850–1930." *Social Science Research* 21 (4): 329–52.

Blau, Judith R., Kenneth Redding, and Kenneth C. Land. 1993. "Ethnocultural Cleavages and the Growth of Church Membership in the United States, 1860–1930." *Sociological Forum* 8 (4): 609–37.

Booth, Leo 1991. *When God Becomes an Addiction*. New York: Penguin.

Boudon, R. 2001. *The Origins of Values: Essays in the Sociology and Philosophy of Beliefs*. New York: Transaction.

Breault, Kevin D. 1989. "New Evidence on Religious Pluralism, Urbanism and Religious Participation." *American Sociological Review* 54 (6): 1048–53.

Brink, David. 2014. "Mill's Moral and Political Philosophy." In *Stanford Encyclopedia of Philosophy*, ed. Edward N. Zalta. https://plato.stanford.edu/entries/mill-moral-political/#LibDem. Retrieved August 2, 2019.

Brink, Judy and Joan Mencher. 2014. *Mixed Blessing: Gender and Religious Fundamentalism Cross-Culturally*. New York: Routledge.

Brownlee, Jason, Tarek Masoud, and Andrew Reynolds. 2015. *The Arab Spring: Pathways of Repression and Reform*. New York: Oxford University Press.

Bruns, Axel, Tim Highfield, and Jean Brugess. 2017. "The Arab Spring and Social Media Audiences: English and Arabic Twitter Users and Their Networks." *American Behavioral Scientist* 57 (7): 871–98.

Calhoun, Craig, Edward LiPuma, and Moishe Postone, eds. 1993. *Bourdieu: Critical Perspectives*. Chicago: University of Chicago Press.

Campos, Nauro, and Vitaliy Kuzeyev. 2007. "On the Dynamics of Ethnic Fractionalization." *American Journal of Political Science* 51 (3): 620–39.

Campante, Filipe R., and Davin Chor. 2012. "Why Was the Arab World Poised for Revolution? Schooling, Economic Opportunities, and the Arab Spring." *Journal of Economic Perspectives* 26 (2): 167–87.

Caudill, Harry M. 1963. *Night Comes to the Cumberlands*. Boston: Little, Brown.

Cavatorta, Franceso, and Rikke H. Haugbølle. 2012. "The End of Authoritarian Rule and the Mythology of Tunisia Under Ben Ali." *Mediterranean Politics* 17 (2): 179–95.

Chaaban, Jad. 2009. "Youth and Development in the Arab Countries: The Need for a Different Approach." *Middle Eastern Studies* 45 (1): 33–55.

Champion, Daryl. 2003. *The Paradoxical Kingdom: Saudi Arabia and the Momentum of Reform*. New York: Columbia University Press, 2003.

Charrad, Mounira. 2001. *States and Women's Rights: The Making of Postcolonial Tunisia, Algeria, and Morocco*. Berkeley: University of California Press.

Chase-Dunn, Christopher, and Richard Rubinson. 1977. "Toward a Structural Perspective on the World-System." *Politics and Society* 7:453–76.

Charrad, Mounira. 2011. "Gender in the Middle East: Islam, State, Agency." *Annual Review of Sociology* 37: 417–37.

Cheragh [Chiragh] Ali, Moulvi. 1883. *The Proposed Political, Legal, and Social Reforms in the Ottoman Empire and Other Mohammadan States*. Bombay: Education Society Press.

Choueiri, Youssef M. 2010. *Islamic Fundamentalism: The Story of Islamist Movements*. New York: Continuum International.

CIA [Central Intelligence Agency]. 2011. *The World Factbook*. Washington, DC: United States Government Printing Office.

CIA [Central Intelligence Agency]. 2013. *The World Factbook*. Washington, DC: United States Government Printing Office.

Clark, Robert. 1885. *The Punjab and Sindh Missions of the Church Missionary Society*. 2nd ed. London: Church Missionary Society.

Cleveland, William L. 1971. *The Making of an Arab Nationalist: Ottomanism and Arabism in the Life and Thought of Sati' al-Husri*. Princeton, NJ: Princeton University Press.

Cohen-Mor, Dalya 2001. *A Matter of Fate: The Concept of Fate in the Arab World as Reflected in Modern Arabic Literature*. Oxford: Oxford University Press.

Collier, Paul. 2001. "Ethnic Diversity: An Economic Analysis." *Economic Policy* 32 (16): 128–66.

Collier, Paul, Anke Hoefflery, and Dominic Rohner. 2009. "Beyond Greed and Grievance: Feasibility and Civil War." *Oxford Economic Papers* 61 (1): 1–27.

Collins, Randall. 1998. *The Sociology of Philosophies: A Global Theory of Intellectual Change*. Cambridge, MA: Harvard University Press.

Cooper, Fredrick. 1994. "Conflict and Connection: Rethinking Colonial African History." *American Historical Review* 99 (5): 1516–45.

Coreno, Thaddeus. 2002. "Fundamentalism as a Class Culture." *Sociology of Religion* 63 (3): 335–60.

Cordesman, Anthony H. 2003. *Saudi Arabia Enters the Twenty-First Century*. Westport, CT: Praeger.

Cragg, Kenneth. 1957. "The Tests of 'Islamicity.'" *Middle East Forum* 32 (November): 15–17, 33.

Dawn, C. Ernest. 1973. *From Ottomanism to Arabism: Essay on the Origins of Arab Nationalism*. Urbana: University of Illinois Press.

Dawn, C. Ernest. 1988. "The Formation of Pan-Arab Ideology in the Interwar Years." *International Journal of Middle East Studies* 20: 67–91.

Davis, Nancy. J. and Robert V. Robinson. 2006. "The Egalitarian Face of Islamic Orthodoxy: Support for Islamic Law and Economic Justice in Seven Muslim-majority Nations." *American Sociological Review* 71 (2): 167–90.

De Figueiredo, Rui J. P. Jr., and Zachary Elkins. 2003. "Are Patriots Bigots? An Inquiry Into the Vices of In-Group Pride." *American Journal of Political Science* 47 (1): 171–88.

De Jong, Julie, and Linda Young-Demarco. 2017. "Best Practices: Lessons from a Middle East Survey Research Program." In *Values, Political Action, and Change in the Middle East and the Arab Spring*, ed. Mansoor Moaddel and Michele Gelfand, 295–323. Oxford: Oxford University Press.

Dekmejian, Hrair R. 1994. "The Rise of Political Islamism in Saudi Arabia." *Middle East Journal* 48 (4): 627–43.

Deutsch, Karl W. 1961. "Social Mobilization and Political Development." *American Political Science Review* 55 (3): 493–514.

Deutsch, Karl W. 1981. "On Nationalism, World Religion, and the Nature of the West." In *Mobilization, Center-Periphery Structures and National Building*, ed. Per Torsvik. Bergen, Norway: Universitestsvorlaget.

Dohrenwend, Bruce P. 1959. "Egoism, Altruism, Anomie, and Fatalism: A Conceptual Analysis of Durkheim's Types." *American Sociological Review* 24 (4): 466–73.

Dunne, Michele, and Amr Hamzawy. 2017. "Egypt's Secular Political Parties: A Struggle for Identity and Independence." New York: Carnegie Endowment for International Peace. https://carnegieendowment.org/2017/03/31/egypt-s-secular-political-parties-struggle -for-identity-and-independence-pub-68482.

Durkheim, Emile. 1893. *The Division of Labor in Society*. Glencoe, IL: Free Press.

El-Ashker, Ahmed, and Rodney Wilson. 2006. *Islamic Economics: A Short History*. Themes in Islamic Studies 3. Leiden, Netherlands: Brill.

Ellerbe, Helen 1995. *The Dark Side of Christian History*. San Rafael, CA: Morning Star.

Ellingsen, Tanja. 2000. "Colorful Community or Ethnic Witches' Brew? Multiethnicity and Domestic Conflict During and After the Cold War." *Journal of Conflict Resolution* 44 (2): 228–49.

Ellison, Christopher G., and Darren E. Sherkat. 1995. "Is Sociology the Core Discipline for the Scientific Study of Religion?" *Social Forces* 73 (4): 1255–66.

el-Sanabary, Nagat. 1994. "Female Education in Saudi Arabia and the Reproduction of Gender Division." *Gender and Education* 6 (2), 141–50.

Emerson, Michael O., and David Hartman. 2006. "The Rise of Religious Fundamentalism." *Annual Review of Sociology* 32: 127–44.

Euben, Roxanne. 1999. *Enemy in the Mirror: Islamic Fundamentalism and the Limits of Modern Nationalism.* Princeton, NJ: Princeton University Press.

Fearon, James D. 2003. "Ethnic and Cultural Diversity by Country." *Journal of Economic Growth* 8 (2): 195–222.

Forbes, Duncan. 1951. "James Mill and India." *Cambridge Journal* 5 (1): 19–33.

Ford, Thomas R. 1962. "The Passing of Provincialism." In *The Southern Appalachian Region: A Survey,* ed. T. R. Ford, 9–34. Lexington: University of Kentucky Press.

Frankel, Jeffery A. 2000. "Globalization of the Economy." NBER Working Paper 7858. National Bureau of Economic Research, Cambridge, MA, August 2000.

Fullbrook, Mary. 1983. *Piety and Politics: Religion and the Rise of Absolutism in England, Wurttemberg and Prussia.* Cambridge: Cambridge University Press.

Fuller, Gary. 1995. "The Demographic Backdrop to Ethnic Conflict: A Geographic Overview." In *The Challenge of Ethnic Conflict to National and International Order in the 1990s,* 151–54. Langley, VA: Central Intelligence Agency.

Gelfand, Michele J., Jana L. Raver, Lisa Nishii, Lisa M. Leslie, Janetta Lun, Beng Chong Lim, Lili Duan et al. 2011. "Differences Between Tight and Loose Cultures: A 33-Nation Study." *Science* 332 (6033): 1100–1104.

Gershoni, Israel, and James P. Jankowski. 1986. *Egypt, Islam, and the Arabs: The Search for Egyptian Nationhood, 1900–1930.* Oxford: Oxford University Press.

Gershoni, Israel, and James P. Jankowski. 1995. *Redefining the Egyptian Nation, 1930–1945.* Cambridge: Cambridge University Press.

Ghannouchi, Rached. 2016. "From Political Islam to Muslim Democracy: The Ennahda Party and the Future of Tunisia." *Foreign Affairs* 95: 58–75.

Gibb, Hamilton A. R. 1947. *Modern Trends in Islam.* Chicago: University of Chicago Press.

Giddens, Anthony. 1990. *The Consequences of Modernity.* Stanford, CA: Stanford University Press.

Giddens, Anthony. 1991. *Modernity and Self-Identity: Self and Society in the Late Modern Age.* Stanford, CA: Stanford University Press.

Goldstone, Jack. 1991. *Revolution and Rebellion in the Early Modern World.* Berkeley: University of California Press.

Goodwin, Laura D., and Nancy L. Leech. 2006. "Understanding Correlation: Factors That Affect the Size of r." *Journal of Experimental Education* 74 (3): 249–66.

Grand, Stephen. 2019. "The Khashoggi Killing Through Saudi Eyes." *MENASource* (blog), Atlantic Council, March 21. https://www.atlanticcouncil.org/blogs/menasource/the-khashoggi-killing-through-saudi-eyes.

Guha, Ranajit. 1999. *Elementary Aspects of Insurgency in Colonial India.* Durham, NC: Duke University Press.

Guha, Ranajit, and Gayatri C Spivak. 1988. *Selected Subaltern Studies.* New York: Oxford University Press.

Guizot, Francois Pierre Guillaime. 1890. *The History of Civilization in Europe*. Trans. William Hazlitt. 3 vols. New York: Appleton.

Guttentag, Marcia, and Paul F. Secord. 1983. *Too Many Women? The Sex Ratio Question*. Beverly Hills, CA: Sage.

Haim, Sylvia G. 1962. *Arab Nationalism: An Anthology*. Berkeley: University of California Press.

Hairi, Hadi. 1977. *Shi'ism and Constitutionalism in Iran*. Leiden: Brill.

Handy, Charles. 1991. *The Age of Unreason*. Boston: Harvard Business Review Press.

Hanson, Brad. 1983. "The 'Westoxication' of Iran: Depictions and Reactions of Behrangi, al-e Ahmad, and Shariati." *International Journal of Middle East Studies* 15 (1): 1–23.

Hardy, Peter. 1972. *The Muslims of British India*. Cambridge: Cambridge University Press.

Harrison, L. E., and S. P. Huntington, eds. 2000. *Cultures and Matters: How Values Shape Human Progress*. New York: Basic Books.

Haugbølle, Rikke Hostrup, and Francesco Cavatorta. 2012. "Beyond Ghannouchi. Islamism and Social Change in Tunisia." *Middle East Report* 262: 20–25.

Hinnebusch, Raymond A. 1982. "The Islamic Movement in Syria: Sectarian Conflict and Urban Rebellion in an Authoritarian Populist Regime." In *Islamic Resurgence in the Arab World*, ed. Ali E. Hillal Dessouki, 138–69. New York: Praeger.

Hinnebusch, Raymond A. 1990. *Authoritarian Power and State Formation in Ba'thist Syria: Army, Party, and Peasant*. Boulder, CO: Westview.

Hoffman, Michael, and Amaney Jamal. 2012. "The Youth and the Arab Spring: Cohort Differences and Similarities." *Middle East Law and Governance* 4 (1): 168–88.

Hoffman, Michael and Amaney Jamal. 2014. "Religion in the Arab Spring: Between Two Competing Narratives." *The Journal of Politics* 76 (3): 593–606.

Holmström, David. 1973. "Syria: Unity, Liberty, and Socialism." *Middle East International* 22 (April): 11–13.

Honwana, Alcinda. 2013. *Youth and Revolution in Tunisia*. London: Zed Books.

Hourani, Albert. 1983. *Arabic Thought in the Liberal Age: 1798–1939*. Cambridge: Cambridge University Press.

Howard, Philip N. and Muzammil M. Hussain. 2013. *Democracy's Fourth Wave? Digital Media and the Arab Spring*. Oxford: Oxford University Press.

Huisman, Kimberly, and Pierrette Hondagneu-Sotelo. 2005. "Dress Matters: Change and Continuity in the Dress Practices of Bosnian Muslim Refugee Women." *Gender and Society* 19 (1): 44–65.

Huntington, Samuel P. 1968. *Political Order in Changing Societies*. New Haven, CT: Yale University Press.

Huntington, Samuel P. 1996a. *The Clash of Civilizations and the Remaking of World Order*. New York: Simon and Schuster.

Huntington, Samuel P. 1996b. "The West Unique, Not Universal." *Foreign Affairs* 75 (6): 28–46.

Hvistendahl, Mara. 2011. "Young and Restless Can Be a Volatile Mix." *Science* 333: 552–54.

Ibn Khaldun, Abd al-Rahman. 1967. *The Muqaddhimah: An Introduction to History*. Trans. Franz Rosenthal. Princeton: Princeton University Press.

Inglehart, Ronald. 1971. "The Silent Revolution in Europe: Intergenerational Change in Post-Industrial Societies." *American Political Science Review* 65 (4): 991–1017.

Inglehart, Ronald. 1977. *The Silent Revolution: Changing Values and Political Styles Among Western Publics*. Princeton, NJ: Princeton University Press.

Inglehart, Ronald. 1997. *Modernization and Postmodernization: Cultural, Economic, and Political Change in 43 Societies*. Princeton, NJ: Princeton University Press.

Inglehart, Ronald. 2017. "Changing Values in the Islamic World and the West: Social Tolerance and the Arab Spring." In *Values, Political Action, and Change in the Middle East and the Arab Spring*, ed. Mansoor Moaddel and Michele Gelfand, 3–24. Oxford: Oxford University Press.

Inglehart, Ronald, Mansoor Moaddel, and Mark Tessler. 2006. "Xenophobia and In-Group Solidarity in Iraq: A Natural Experiment on the Impact of Insecurity." *Perspectives on Politics* 4 (3): 495–505.

Inglehart, Ronald, and Pippa Norris. 2003. "The True Clash of Civilizations." *Foreign Policy* 135 (March–April): 62–70.

Inglehart, Ronald, and Christian Welzel. 2005. *Modernization, Cultural Change, and Democracy: The Human Development Sequence*. Cambridge: Cambridge University Press.

International Crisis Group (ICG). 2004. *Can Saudi Arabia Reform Itself?* ICG Middle East Report No. 28. Cairo: ICG.

Kamrava, Mehran. 2008. *Iran's Intellectual Revolution*. Cambridge: Cambridge University Press.

Karamustafa, Ahmet T. 2012. "Individualism." In *The Encyclopedia of Islamic Political Thought*, ed. Gerhard Böwering and Patricia Crone, 253–54. Princeton, NJ: Princeton University Press.

Kazemi, Farhad. 2012. Fedāʾiān-e Eslām. *Encyclopedia Iranica* IX(5): 470–74.

Keohane, Robert O., and Joseph S. Nye. 2000. "Globalization: What's New? What's Not? (And So What?)." *Foreign Policy* 118: 104–19.

Kepel, Gilles. 1985. *Muslim Extremism in Egypt: The Prophet and Pharaoh*. Trans. Jon Rothschild. Berkeley: University of California Press.

Kerr, Malcolm. 1966. *Islamic Reform: The Political and Legal Theories of Muhammad ʿAbduh and Rashid Rida*. Berkeley: University of California Press.

Kerrou, Mohamed. 2010. *Hijab: New Veils and Public Spheres [Hijab: Nouveaux Voiles et Espaces Publics]*. Tunis: Ceres Editions.

Khomeini, R. 1981. *Islam and Revolution: Writings and Declarations of Imam Khomeini*. Trans. H. Algar. Berkeley, CA: Mizan Press.

Kinnvall, Catarina. 2004. "Globalization and Religious Nationalism: Self, Identity, and the Search for Ontological Security." *Political Psychology* 25 (4): 741–67.

Kirişci, Kemal, and Amanda Sloat, 2019. *The Rise and Fall of Liberal Democracy in Turkey: Implications for the West*. Washington, DC: Brookings Institution. https://www.brookings.edu/research/the-rise-and-fall-of-liberal-democracy-in-turkey-implications-for-the-west/.

Knickmeyer, Ellen. 2011. "The Arab World's Youth Army." *Foreign Policy*. January.

Koopmans, Ruud. 2014. "Religious Fundamentalism and Hostility against Out-groups: A Comparison of Muslims and Christians in Western Europe." *Journal of Ethnic and Migration Studies* 41 (1): 33–57.

Krueger, Alan B., and Jitka Malečková. 2003. "Education, Poverty and Terrorism: Is There a Causal Connection?" *Journal of Economic Perspectives* 17 (4): 119–44.

LaGraffe, Daniel. 2012. "The Youth Bulge in Egypt: An Intersection of Demographics, Security, and the Arab Spring." *Journal of Strategic Security* 5 (2): 65–80.

Lapidus, Ira M. 1988. *A History of Islamic Societies*. Cambridge: Cambridge University Press.

Lapidus, Ira M. 1992. "The Golden Age: The Political Concepts of Islam." *The Annals of the American Academy of Political and Social Science* 524 (1): 13–25.

Larson, Pier M. 1997. " 'Capacities and Modes of Thinking': Intellectual Engagements and Subaltern Hegemony in the Early History of Malagasy Christianity." *American Historical Review* 102 (4): 969–1002.

Lazreg, Marina. 1994. *The Eloquence of Silence: Algerian Women in Question.* New York: Routledge.

Levy, Marion J. Jr. 1966. *Modernization and the Structure of Society.* Princeton, NJ: Princeton University Press.

Lewis, Bernard. 1993. "Islam and Liberal Democracy." *Atlantic Monthly*, February.

Lewis, Bernard. 1988. *The Political Language of Islam.* Chicago: University of Chicago Press.

Lia, Brynjar. 1998. *The Society of the Muslim Brothers in Egypt: The Rise of an Islamic Mass Movement, 1928–42.* Reading, UK: Ithaca Press.

Lukes, Steven. 1971. "The Meaning of 'Individualism.'" *Journal of the History of Ideas* 32 (1): 45–66.

Lukes, Steven. 2006. *Individualism.* Wivenhoe Park, UK: ECPR Press.

Lynch, Gordon. 2012. *The Sacred in the Modern World: A Cultural Sociological Approach.* New York: Oxford University Press.

Macpherson, C. B. 1965. "Post-Liberal-Democracy?" *New Left Review* 1 (33): 1–16.

Madeley, John T. S., and Zsolt Enyedi, eds. 2003. *Church and State in Contemporary Europe: The Chimera of Neutrality.* London: Frank Cass.

Maehr, Martin L., and S. A. Karabenick. Editors. 2005. *Advances in Motivation and Achievement.* Amsterdam: Elsevier.

Mahdavy, Hussein. 1970. "Patterns and Problems of Economic Developments in Rentier States: The Case of Iran." In *Studies in the Economic History of the Middle East*, ed. Michael A. Cook, 428–67. London: Oxford University Press.

Mahdavi, Mojtaba. 2011. "Post-Islamist Trends in Post-Revolutionary Iran." *Comparative Studies of South Asia, Africa, and the Middle East* 31 (1): 94–109.

Mallon, Florencia E. 1994. "The Promise and Dilemma of Subaltern Studies: Perspectives from Latin American History." *American Historical Review* 99 (5): 1491–1515.

Mani, Lata. 1987. "Contentious Traditions: The Debate on Sati in Colonial India." *Cultural Critique: The Nature and Context of Minority Discourse II* no. 7 (Autumn): 119–56.

Marsot, Afaf Lutfi. 1977. *Egypt's Liberal Experiment: 1922–1936.* Los Angeles: University of California Press.

Marx, Karl, 1976. "The German Ideology." In *Karl Marx and Frederick Engels: Collected Works.* 5, 17–539. New York: International Publishers.

Marx, Karl. 1977. "Civil War in France." In *Karl Marx and Frederick Engels: Selected Works.* New York: International Publishers.

Mercier, Jean L. 1995. "Truth of Orthodoxy." *Cross Currents* 45 (1): 68–79.

Metcalf, Barbara Daly. 1995. "Presidential Address: Too Little and Too Much: Reflections on Muslims in the History of India." *Journal of Asian Studies* 54 (4): 951–67.

Mill, James. 1826. *The History of British India.* London: Baldwin, Cradock, and Joy. http://oll .libertyfund.org/titles/mill-the-history-of-british-india-vol-1.

Millar, John. 1781. *The Origin of the Distinction of Ranks; Or, An Inquiry Into the Circumstances Which Give Rise to Influence and Authority in the Different Members of Society.* 3rd ed. London: Murray.

Minault, Gail. 1990. "Sayyid Mumtaz Ali and 'Huquq Un-Niswan': An Advocate of Women's Rights in Islam in the Late Nineteenth Century." *Modern Asian Studies* 24 (1): 147–72.

Mitchell, Richard P. 1969. *The Society of the Muslim Brothers.* London: Oxford University Press.

Moaddel, Mansoor. 1993. *Class, Politics, and Ideology in the Iranian Revolution.* New York: Columbia University Press.

Moaddel, Mansoor. 2002. "The Study of Islamic Culture and Politics: An Overview and Assessment." *Annual Review of Sociology* 28: 359–86.

Moaddel, Mansoor. 2005. *Islamic Modernism, Nationalism, and Fundamentalism: Episode and Discourse*. Chicago: University of Chicago Press.

Moaddel, Mansoor. 2006. "The Saudi Public Speaks: Religion, Gender, and Politics." *International Journal of Middle East Studies* 38 (1): 79–108.

Moaddel, Mansoor. 2009. "The Iranian Revolution and Its Nemesis: The Rise of Liberal Values Among Iranians." *Comparative Studies of South Asia, Africa, and the Middle East* 29 (1): 126–36.

Moaddel, Mansoor. 2016. "El Dilema Religioso." *Vanguardia Dossier* 41 (July–September): 46–51.

Moaddel, Mansoor. 2017a. "National Identity Versus National Pride in the Modalities of Liberal-Territorial Nationalism and Islamic Nationalism in Muslim-Majority Countries." In *Values, Political Action, and Change in the Middle East and the Arab Spring*, ed. Mansoor Moaddel and Michele Gelfand, 61–100. Oxford: Oxford University Press.

Moaddel, Mansoor. 2017b. "The Arab Spring and Egyptian Revolution Makers: Predictors of Participation." In *Values, Political Action, and Change in the Middle East and the Arab Spring*, ed. Mansoor Moaddel and Michele J Gelfand, 205–49. New York: Oxford University Press.

Moaddel, Mansoor. 2017c. "Monolithic Religious Markets, Fragmented State Structures, and Islamic Fundamentalism among Iranian and in the Middle East and North Africa." *Revue Internationale des Etudes du Développement* 229 (June): 33–62.

Moaddel, Mansoor, and Julie De Jong. 2013. "Trends in Values Among Saudi Youth: Findings from Values Surveys." *Journal of the History of Childhood and Youth* 6 (1): 153–64.

Moaddel, Mansoor, and Michele Gelfand, eds. 2017. *Values, Political Action, and Change in the Middle East and the Arab Spring*. Oxford: Oxford University Press.

Moaddel, Mansoor, and Stuart Karabenick. 2008. "Religious Fundamentalism Among Young Muslims in Egypt and Saudi Arabia." *Social Forces* 86 (4): 1675–1710.

Moaddel, Mansoor, and Stuart Karabenick. 2013. *Religious Fundamentalism in the Middle East: A Cross-National, Inter-Faith and Inter-Ethnic Analysis*. Leiden, Netherlands: Brill.

Moaddel, Mansoor, and Stuart Karabenick. 2018. "Religious Fundamentalism in Eight Muslim-Majority Countries: Reconceptualization and Assessment." *Journal for Scientific Study of Religion* 57 (4): 676–706.

Mohseni, Payam. "The Islamic Awakening: Iran's Grand Narrative of the Arab Uprisings." *Middle East Brief* 71, CCMES, April 2013. Accessed July 5, 2017. http://www.brandeis.edu/crown/publications/meb/meb71.html.

Montgomery, James D. 2003. "A Formalization and Test of the Religious Economies Model." *American Sociological Review* 68 (5): 782–809.

Moore, Barrington Jr. 1966. *Social Origins of Dictatorship and Democracy: Lord and Peasant in the Making of the Modern World*. Boston: Beacon Press.

Motahhari, M. 1969. *Mas'aleh-ye Hijab* [The problem of veiling]. Tehran: Islamic Society of Physicians.

Nashat, Guity, and Judith E. Tucker. 1999. *Women in the Middle East and North Africa: Restoring Women to History*. Bloomington: Indiana University Press.

Neuburger, Mary C. 1997. "Difference Unveiled: Bulgarian National Imperatives and the Re-dressing of Muslim Women in the Communist Period 1945–89." *Nationalities Papers* 25 (1): 169–81.

Noueihed, Lin and Alex Warren. 2012. *The Battle for the Arab Spring: Revolution, Counter-Revolution, and the Making of a New Era*. New Haven, CT: Yale University Press.

Okruhlik, Gwenn. 2002. "Networks of Dissent: Islamism and Reform in Saudi Arabia." *Current History*, January 2002, 22–28.

Olson, Robert W. 1982. *The Ba'th and Syria, 1947–1982: The Evolution of Ideology, Party, and State.* Princeton, NJ: Princeton University Press.

Osborne, Samuel. 2018. "Iranian Women Protest Hijab as Defiant Headscarf Demonstrations Spread." *Independent,* January 30, 2018. https://www.independent.co.uk/news/world/asia/iran-women-hijab-protests-arrests-no-headscarf-take-off-girl-of-enghelab-street-vida-movahed-a8185611.html.

Özkan, Behlül. 2017. "The Cold War-Era Origins of Islamism in Turkey and Its Rise to Power." Hudson Institute, November 5, 2017. https://www.hudson.org/research/13807-the-cold-war-era-origins-of-islamism-in-turkey-and-its-rise-to-power.

Paige, Jeffery M. 1975. *Agrarian Revolution: Social Movements and Export Agriculture in the Underdeveloped World.* New York: Free Press.

Parchami, Ali. 2012. "The 'Arab Spring': the View from Tehran." *Contemporary Politics* 18 (1): 35–52.

Parsa, Misagh. 2000. *States, Ideologies, and Social Revolutions: A Comparative Analysis of Iran, Nicaragua, and the Philippines.* Cambridge: Cambridge University Press.

Parsons, Talcott. 1949. *The Structure of Social Action: A Study in Social Theory with Special Reference to a Group of Recent European Writers.* Glencoe, IL: Free Press.

Parsons, Talcott. 1951. *The Social System.* Toronto: Collier-Macmillan.

Parsons, Talcott. 1964. "Evolutionary Universal." *American Sociological Review* 29 (3): 339–57.

Parsons, Talcott. 1966. *Societies: Evolutionary and Comparative Perspective.* Englewood Cliffs, NJ: Prentice-Hall.

Pipes, Daniel. 1996. *The Hidden Hand: The Middle East Fears of Conspiracy.* New York: Palgrave.

Posner, Daniel N. 2004. "Measuring ethnic fractionalization in Africa." *American Journal of Political Science* 48 (4): 849–63.

Prakash, Gyan. 1992. "Postcolonial Criticism and Indian Historiography." *Social Text* 31/32: 8–19.

Prakash, Gyan. 1994. "Subaltern Studies as Postcolonial Criticism." *American Historical Review* 99 (4): 1475–90.

Prokop, Michael. 2003. "Saudi Arabia: The Politics of Education." *International Affairs* 79 (1): 77–89.

Quinney, Richard. 1964. "Political Conservatism, Alienation, and Fatalism: Contingencies of Social Status and Religious Fundamentalism." *Sociometry* 27 (3): 372–81.

Rabinovich, Itamar. 1972. *Syria Under the Ba'th, 1963–66.* Jerusalem: Israel University Press.

Rajaee, Farhang. 2007. *Islamism and Modernism: The Changing Discourse in Iran.* Austin: University of Texas Press.

Reid, Donald Malcolm. 1975. *The Odyssey of Farah Antun: A Syrian Christian's Quest for Secularism.* Chicago: Bibliotheca Islamica.

Richards, David L., and Ronald Gelleny. 2007. "Women's Status and Economic Globalization." *International Studies Quarterly* 51 (4): 855–76.

Richter, Julius. 1908. *A History of Missions in India.* Trans. Sydney H. Moore. London: Oliphant Anderson & Ferrier.

Riesebrodt, Martin. 1993. *Pious Passion: The Emergence of Modern Fundamentalism in the United States and Iran.* Trans. D. Reneau. Chicago: University of Chicago Press.

Ritzer, George. 1993. *The McDonaldization of Society.* Thousand Oaks, CA: Pine Forge Press.

Roberts, David. 1987. *The Ba'th and the Creation of Modern Syria.* London: Croom Helm.

Rodinson, Maxime. 2007. *Islam and Capitalism.* London: Saqi.

Rokeach, Milton. 1968. "A Theory of Organization and Change Within Value-Attitude Systems." *Journal of Social Issues* 24 (1): 13–33.

Rokeach, Milton. 1971. "Long-Range Experimental Modification of Values, Attitudes, and Behavior." *American Psychologist* 26 (5): 453–59.

Rokeach, Milton. 1973. *The Nature of Human Values*. New York: Free Press.

Romano, David. 2018. "Erdogan, Ottomanism and Turkish Nationalism a Century After WWI." Rudaw, November 14, 2018. http://www.rudaw.net/english/opinion/14112018.

Rosenthal, Erwin I. J. 1958. *Political Thought in Medieval Islam: An Introductory Outline*. Cambridge: Cambridge University Press.

Rostow, W. W. 1960. *The Stages of Economic Growth: A Non-communist Manifesto*. Cambridge: Cambridge University Press.

Roy, Oliver. 1994. *The Failure of Political Islam*. Trans. Carol Volk. Cambridge, MA: Harvard University Press.

Ruedy, John. 1992. *Modern Algeria: The Origins and Development of a Nation*. Bloomington: Indiana University Press.

Sadri, Mahmoud. [2004] 2012. Hojjatiya. *Encyclopedia Iranica* XII (4): 426–28.

Safran, Nadav. 1961. *Egypt in Search of Political Community*. Cambridge, MA: Harvard University Press.

Sahlins, M. D., and E. R. Service. 1960. *Evolution and Culture*. Ann Arbor: University of Michigan Press.

Sassen, Saskia. 2001. *The Global City: New York, London, Tokyo*. 2nd ed. Princeton, NJ: Princeton University Press.

Sathar, Zeba, Minhaj ul Haque, Azeema Faizunnissa, Munawar Sultana, and Cynthia B. Lloyd. 2003. *Adolescents and Youth in Pakistan 2001–2002: A Nationally Representative Survey*. New York: Population Council. https://knowledgecommons.popcouncil.org/cgi/viewcontent.cgi?article=1028&context=departments_sbsr-pgy.

Schussman, Alan, and Sarah A. Soule. 2005. "Process and Protest: Accounting for Individual Protest Participation." *Social Forces* 84 (2): 1083–1108.

Schwartz, Jonathan P., and Lori D. Lindley. 2005. "Religious Fundamentalism and Attachment: Prediction of Homophobia." *International Journal for the Psychology of Religion* 15 (2): 145–57.

Schwartz, S. H. 2006. "A Theory of Cultural Value Orientations: Explication and Applications." *Comparative Sociology* 5: 136–82.

Schwartz, S. H. 2012. "An Overview of the Schwartz Theory of Basic Values." *Online Readings in Psychology and Culture* 2 (1). http://dx.doi.org/10.9707/2307-0919.1116.

Secor, Anna. 2002. "The Veil and Urban Space in Istanbul: Women's Dress, Mobility and Islamic Knowledge." *Gender, Place & Culture* 9 (1): 5–22.

Service, E. R. 1971. *Cultural Evolutionism: Theory in Practice*. New York: Holt, Rinehart & Winston.

Shaarāwī, Huda. 1987. *Harem Years: The Memoirs of an Egyptian Feminist (1879–1924)*. Trans. Margot Badran. New York: Feminist Press at CUNY.

Shapiro, Henry D. 1978. *Appalachia On Our Mind*. Chapel Hill: University of North Carolina Press.

Sharabi, Hisham. 1963. "Power and Leadership in the Arab World." *Orbis* 7 (3): 583–95.

Shariati, Ali. 1969. *Islamshenasi* [Islamology]. Mashhad, Iran: Tous.

Shariati, Ali. 1980. *Marxism and Other Western Fallacies: An Islamic Critique*. Trans. R. Campbell. Berkeley, CA: Mizan Press.

Shavitt, Sharon, Carlos J. Torelli, and Hila Riemer. 2010. "Horizontal and Vertical Individualism and Collectivism: Implications for Understanding Psychological Processes." In *Advances in Culture and Psychology*, ed. Michele J. Gelfand, Chi-yue Chiu, and Ying-yi Hong, 1:309–50. New York: Oxford University Press.

Singelis, Thedore M., Harry C. Triandis, Dharm P. S. Bhawuk, and Michele J. Gelfand. 1995. "Horizontal and Vertical Dimensions of Individualism and Collectivism: A Theoretical and Measurement Refinement." *Cross-Cultural Research* 29 (3): 240–75.

Sivan, Emmanuel. 1985. *Radical Islam: Medieval Theology and Modern Politics*. New Haven, CT: Yale University Press.

Skocpol, Theda. 1979. *States and Social Revolutions: A Comparative Analysis of France, Russia, and China*. Cambridge: Cambridge University Press.

Smith, Christian. 1998. *American Evangelicalism: Embattled and Thriving*. Chicago: University of Chicago Press.

Smith, Edward E., and Douglas L Medin. 1981. *Categories and Concepts*. Cambridge, MA: Harvard University Press.

Sniderman, Paul M., Philip E. Tetlock, and Edward G. Carmines, eds. 1993. *Prejudice, Politics and the American Dilemma*. Stanford, CA: Stanford University Press.

South, Scott J., and Katherine Trent. 1988. "Sex Ratios and Women's Roles: A Cross-National Analysis." *American Journal of Sociology* 93 (5): 1096–1115.

Stepan, Alfred. 1985. "State Power and the Strength of Civil Society in the Southern Cone of Latin America." In *Bringing the State Back In*, ed. Peter Evans, Dietrich Rueschemeyer, and Theda Skocpol, 317–43. New York: Cambridge University Press.

Stohl, Cynthia. 2005. "Globalization Theory." In *Engaging Organizational Communication Theory and Research: Multiple Perspectives*, ed. Steve May and Dennis K. Mumby, 223–62. Thousand Oaks, CA: Sage.

Summers, Frank. 2006. "Fundamentalism, Psychoanalysis, and Psychoanalytic Theories." *Psychoanalytic Review* 93 (2): 329–53.

Swanson, Guy E. 1967. *Religion and Regime: A Sociological Account of the Reformation*. Ann Arbor: University of Michigan Press.

Talattof, Kamran. 2000. "Nizami's Unlikely Heroines: A Study of the Characterizations of Women in Classical Persian Literature." In *The Poetry of Nizami Ganjavi: Knowledge, Love, and Rhetoric*, ed. Kamran Talattof and Jerome Clinton, 51–81. New York: Palgrave.

Taraki, Lisa. 1996. "Jordanian Islamists and the Agenda for Women: Between Discourse and Practice." *Middle Eastern Studies* 32 (1): 140–58.

Tessler, Mark. 2017. "Change and Continuity in Arab Attitudes toward Political Islam: The Impact of Political Transitions in Tunisia and Egypt in 2011–2013." In *Values, Political Action, and Change in the Middle East and the Arab Spring*, ed. Mansoor Moaddel and Michele J Gelfand, 249–70. New York: Oxford University Press.

Therborn, Goran. 1977. "The Rule of Capital and the Rise of Democracy." *New Left Review* 103: 3–41.

Thornton, A. 2005. *Reading History Sideways: The Fallacy and Enduring Impact of the Developmental Paradigm on Family Life*. Chicago: University of Chicago Press.

Tilly, Charles. 1984. *Big Structures, Large Processes, Huge Comparisons*. New York: Russell Sage Foundation.

Torrey, Charles. 1892. *The Commercial-Theological Terms in the Koran* (Ph.D. diss., University of Strasbourg). Leiden, Netherlands: Brill.

UNDP [United Nations Development Program]. 2015. Human Development Report. Retrieved from http://hdr.undp.org/sites/default/files/2015_human_development_report.pdf.

Urdal, Henrik. 2006. "A Clash of Generations? Youth Bulge and Political Violence." *International Studies Quarterly* 50 (30): 607–29.

Vatikiotis, Panayiotis J. 1973. "Tradition and Political Leadership: The Example of Algeria." In *Man, State, and Society in the Contemporary Maghrib*, ed. I. William Zartman, 50–64. New York: Praeger.

Vatikiotis, Panayiotis J. 1980. *The History of Egypt*. Baltimore, MD: Johns Hopkins University Press.

Viroli, Maurizio. 1995. *For Love of Country: An Essay on Patriotism and Nationalism*. Oxford: Clarendon Press.

Wallerstein, Immanuel. 1979. *The Capitalist World-Economy*. New York: Cambridge University Press.

Wallerstein, Immanuel. 1984. *The Politics of the World-Economy: The States, the Movements, and the Civilizations*. Cambridge: Cambridge University Press.

Wallerstein, Immanuel. 2000. *The Essential Wallerstein*. New York: New Press.

Walls, Stephanie M. 2015. *Individualism in the United States: A Transformation in American Political Thought*. New York: Bloomsbury.

Waters, Malcolm. 1995. *Globalization*. New York: Routledge.

Watt, W. Montgomery. 1960. "Shi'ism under the Umayyads." *Journal of the Royal Asiatic Society* nos. 1–2: 158–72.

Weber, Max. 1964. *The Sociology of Religion*. Boston: Beacon.

Weber, Max. 1992. *The Protestant Ethic and the Spirit of Capitalism*. New York: Routledge.

Weller, Jack E. 1965. *Yesterday's People*. Lexington: University of Kentucky Press.

Wimmer, Andreas, Lars-Erik Cederman, and Brian Min. 2009. "Ethnic Politics and Armed Conflict: A Configurational Analysis of a New Global Data Set." *American Sociological Review* 74 (2): 316–37.

Wolf, Erik. 1969. *Peasants War of the Twentieth Century*. New York: Harper and Row.

Wolfsfeld, Gadi, Elad Segev, and Tamir Sheafer. 2013. "Social Media and the Arab Spring: Politics Comes First." *The International Journal of Press/Politics* 18 (2): 115–37.

Wright, Robin. 2011. *Rock the Casbah: Rage and Rebellion Across the Islamic World*. New York: Simon and Schuster.

Wuthnow, Robert. 1985. "State Structures and Ideological Outcomes." *American Sociological Review* 50 (6): 799–821.

Wuthnow, Robert. 1989. *Communities of Discourse: Ideology and Social Structure in the Reformation, the Enlightenment, and European Socialism*. Cambridge, MA: Harvard University Press.

Wuthnow, Robert. 2005. *America and the Challenges of Religious Diversity*. Princeton, NJ: Princeton University Press.

Yusuf, Moeed. 2008. *Prospects of Youth Radicalization in Pakistan: Implications for U.S. Policy*. Washington, DC: Brookings Institution. https://www.brookings.edu/wp-content/uploads/2016/06/10_pakistan_yusuf.pdf.

Zaret, David. 1985. *The Heavenly Contract: Ideology and Organization in Pre-revolutionary Puritanism*. Chicago: University of Chicago Press.

Zeidan, David. 2001. "The Islamic Fundamentalist View of Life as a Perennial Battle." *Middle East Review of International Affairs* 5(4):26–53.

Zeine, Zeine N. 1973. *The Emergence of Arab Nationalism*. Delmar, NY: Caravan.

Zoubir, Yahia. 2015. "The Democratic Transition in Tunisia: A Success Story in the Making." *Conflict Trends* (January): 1–17.

INDEX

Page numbers in *italics* indicate figures or tables.